Concrete Invention

Colección Patricia Phelps de Cisneros

Reflections on Geometric Abstraction from Latin America and Its Legacy

Concrete Invention

Colección Patricia Phelps de Cisneros

Reflections on Geometric Abstraction from Latin America and Its Legacy

Geometry
Illusion
Dialogue
Vibration
Universalism

Concrete Invention

Colección Patricia Phelps de Cisneros

Reflections on Geometric Abstraction from Latin America and Its Legacy

Geometry
Illusion
Dialogue
Vibration
Universalism

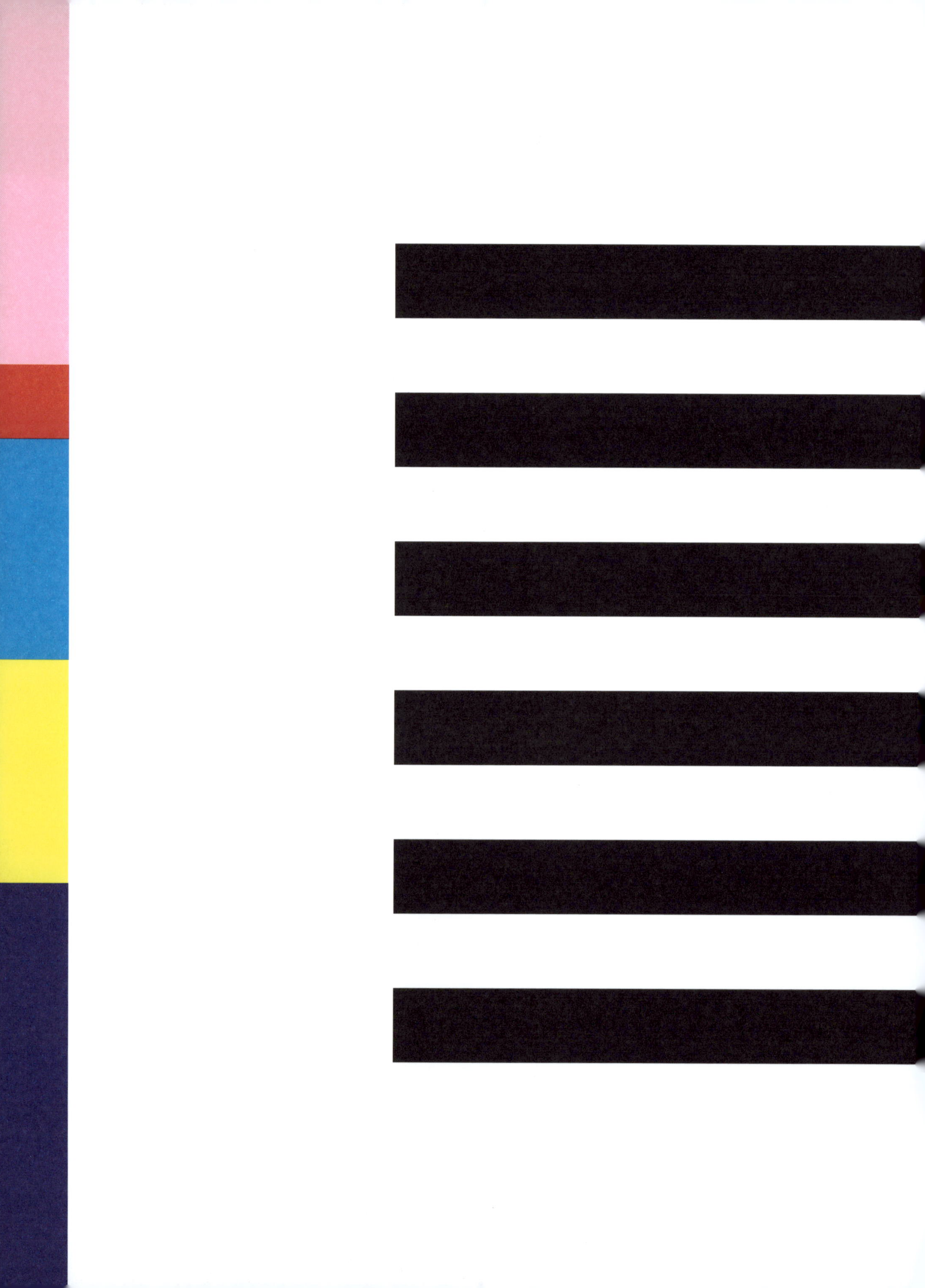

Concrete Invention

Colección Patricia Phelps de Cisneros

Reflections on Geometric Abstraction from Latin America and Its Legacy

Geometry
Illusion
Dialogue
Vibration
Universalism

te
on

Phelps de Cisneros
rom Latin America and Its Legacy

etry

ue

on

salism

José León Cerrillo, 2013

The important partnership agreement reached in the early months of 2012 between the Museo Nacional Centro de Arte Reina Sofía and the Fundación Cisneros-Colección Patricia Phelps de Cisneros marked the start of a productive working relationship. This relationship bore fruit later that year with the seminar "Rethinking Latin American Modernisms: Flows and Overflows." Having generated a great deal of interest, this event laid the foundations for the development of new interpretations within a key chapter of what we now feel is a shared history.

The exhibition we present here represents a fundamental step forward for the Museo Reina Sofía, in whose institutional discourse Latin America has taken on particular relevance. In addition, this exhibition capacitates the museum, as a space of meeting and dialogue, to function as a platform that expands and supports the work of the Fundación Cisneros toward generating thought and culture through its art collection.

The principal contribution of the Colección Patricia Phelps de Cisneros is undoubtedly its ability to convey a better understanding of the development of abstraction within a social and creative reality as plural and multifaceted as that of Latin America. The works of Mira Schendel, Lygia Clark, Joaquín Torres-García, or Jesús Soto unleash new poetics that contest Eurocentric or essentialist visions of twentieth-century art and force us to revise our own modernity in a dialogue with that *other* to which we are bound by a fundamental historical link.

In this exhibition there resonates many of the activities realized at the Museo Reina Sofía that both impulse the "rethinking" of history as an open and fluid discourse and move further away from closed and exclusive visions.

We would like to express our very special gratitude for the collaboration of Patricia Phelps de Cisneros, whose work has received unanimous recognition on numerous occasions in the form of different awards and honors. These distinctions have accentuated both the historic value of the collection that bears her name and her unconditional support for education and the diffusion of contemporary art.

We also extend our thanks to the contributors to the present catalogue who have managed to broaden the scientific horizon of the exhibition beyond its chronological and conceptual limits, drawing up new navigational charts for the publics of an increasingly plural museum.

Ministry of Education, Culture, and Sport

In all those endeavors that enrich our lives, each the result of a history of its own and a long process of rumination, there are people without whose support that history would be different. For me, that privileged place has been occupied by my family. Their love and solidarity has accompanied me through all the enterprises that have marked my life.

I share with them the vision that has guided my work with the foundation: the desire to learn about Latin American art and to educate others through it—ideas that illuminate my continuing formation as a collector and that were decisive in the creation of the Colección Patricia Phelps de Cisneros; a strong calling to bring people together, to create links and forge alliances with people and institutions pursuing similar interests; and the goal of transforming the lives of others through my actions, of making a positive difference in the world. These ideas, the leitmotifs of my existence, come together most strikingly in the newly formed alliance between our collection and the Museo Nacional Centro de Arte Reina Sofía. The creativity resulting from this contact has led to *Concrete Invention*, a sample of our collection of geometric abstraction, the organization of which is a notable example of the kind of collaboration possible between two institutions with common aims.

Throughout its existence, the Colección Patricia Phelps de Cisneros has actively labored toward facilitating the integration of Latin American modernity into the history of modern art. We have worked in order to urge others to share the vision we have created in our collection, which allows a rereading of modernity with Latin America in mind. In particular, the Latin American artists who devoted themselves to geometric abstraction undertook radical inquiries that profoundly transformed artistic practices in their respective countries. By breaking with traditions of the past, they created magnificent, inimitable works of art expressive of a singular vision, original and uplifting, of another modernity developed through a dialogue that was quite different from the European and North American canon.

During my early years as a collector, I felt a deep affinity with nonobjective abstraction, that fragment of modernity with its fascinating taste for geometry, light, and immateriality. I was attracted by the spatial drama of certain pieces, and by the formal purity of others. I was interested in the utopian nature of those works and their creators' desire to change the world and construct a society inhabited by a new man. Stirred by all this, I progressively collected works that captivated my gaze and constructed a different and unexplored history, far removed from figuration and exoticism. These works represented to me the highest standard of modernity, and this added an element of adventure and intellectual passion to the course I took as a collector. Every piece was thus born of a particular history, of a dialogue between taste and reason that contributed a density of meaning to the nuances and complexities already embodied in the collection. And to see this, the essence of our collection, now represented in all its creative intention in *Concrete Invention* at the Museo Reina Sofía is more than a gift.

It is a votive offering, and I receive it with joy and pride at the recognition it entails. It is above all a symbol of hope that highlights the synergy between institutions from different latitudes that share a view of cultural space as a tool for social inclusion.

The Museo Reina Sofía is a place where, through art, the community can find spaces of reflection and knowledge on themes that concern us all, and are part of our history. Producing *Concrete Invention* within the framework of our collaborative alliance has not only proved an enriching professional experience for both institutions, but it has meant above all sharing and celebrating our conviction in the power of art and education to activate emotional and intellectual fibers that awaken our consciousness and drive us to alter our perception.

My aspiration is for *Concrete Invention* to stimulate profound reflection on the four decades—from the 1940s to the 1970s—on which its exploration is centered, and that the connections stimulated by the works, whether with one another or with other realities not represented in the exhibition, inspire their further investigation, conceding to them a more profound meaning within the framework of the artistic and human manifestations of the twentieth century. My dream is that these pieces of iconic value and great visual strength, which form part of our family history, should become part of the collective imagery of the West. My hope is that the interactive digital experience specially designed for the show will not only connect those interested but also transform their perception of these artists, who have made a gift to the world of their dreams forged in lucidity and beauty.

I am profoundly grateful to Manuel Borja-Villel and Gabriel Pérez-Barreiro, the curators of the exhibition, for their innovative work in constructing diverse significations based on the intention of the artist, thus grouping these talented creators in a more universal and accessible manner that transcends geographical limits without ever losing sight of them.

It has been a pleasure and a privilege to work with them.

I also wish to make special mention of Paulo Herkenhoff, Luis Pérez-Oramas, Rafael Romero, and Ariel Jiménez, who share my appreciation for these works and offered me advice when various important decisions had to be taken.

My thanks go to them, to the teams at the Museo Reina Sofía and the Colección Patricia Phelps de Cisneros, and to Andrea Giunta, Reinaldo Laddaga, Olga Fernández López, Steve Roden, Jorge Pedro Núñez, Txomin Badiola, Sofía Hernandez Chong Cuy, Ana Longoni, Luis Camnitzer, and Jesús Carrillo, whose contributions are to be enjoyed in this catalogue. I thank them for their work, their texts, and above all for sharing the passion that has made this project possible. In leaving behind the intellectual legacy generated by this exhibition, we will help many others to enjoy and learn about our passion for the subject, and to appreciate the creative strength of this period in Latin America.

In addition to this catalogue, we have created an app and a website which will provide a novel way of interacting with the show's contents and disseminating them via social networks. I must express my thanks here to the Bluecadet company and to Sara Meadows of the Colección Patricia Phelps de Cisneros for their impeccable and highly motivated work on these educational components.

Collecting seems to be a basic human instinct that occasionally leads to something sublime and marvelous. For me, it has been an exhilarating intellectual adventure, a passion, and a privilege I have had the fortune to share with my husband Gustavo and my children Guillermo, Carolina, and Adriana, for whose support and complicity I am also most grateful. *Concrete Invention* gives us a chance to share that passion with others and, above all, to look to the future, as these artists did in their own day.

Patricia Phelps de Cisneros

The presentation of the Colección Patricia Phelps de Cisneros at the Museo Nacional Centro de Arte Reina Sofía assumes its full meaning in the context of the new narratives of modernity, and the incorporation into those narratives of chapters that were once considered, in a reductionist fashion, peripheral. In this regard, the *disembarkation* of an art collection from Latin America inverts the logic that has for decades inspired the presentation in Europe of artistic or productive phenomena hailing from the other side of the Atlantic; namely their consideration as exotic and laden with magical components. Such an interpretive approach lies closer to a cloistered world, such as that which gave birth to the colonial exhibitions, than to the definitive rupture of the center-periphery dynamics that define today's world. From William Shakespeare's *The Tempest* to recent exhibitions on pre-Hispanic cultures, the cultures of Latin America have remained chained to that marginalized vision of the Other.

And yet, the space occupied by art from Latin America in those museums and institutions that recognize the South as an active entity with a growing presence is today a dialectical and fluid one. An early example of this was the replacement of the hot "tópico del trópico," the stereotype of the tropics, an expression used by Miguel de Unamuno in his *Epistolario americano*, with the powerful new image of a "cold America." This alternative vision of an entire continent has it roots in the great explosion of abstract, Neoconcrete, and Kinetic art that served in some sense as a passport allowing Latin America entry to the debates of modernity, both early (with Joaquín Torres-García) and late (with Lygia Pape or Lygia Clark, to cite two examples). Nevertheless, this other vision is also problematic. It is worth asking—and this is the reason for the exciting complexity of the project at hand—whether there is not also a kind of *trademark* attached to it that excessively delimits the true historical scope of these artists and their context. A rereading of the Colección Patricia Phelps de Cisneros greatly facilitates the understanding of the ways in which both readings construct a rigid and reductionist canon that ultimately dilutes the validity and poetic strength of what is shown. And there lies the deeper meaning of this project, a curatorial exercise that has its origins in a question we now extend to the public: How do we undo the canon? That is, how to make of an exhibition a space for the necessary dissension from these reductionist views?

To answer that basic question, the curators and institutions involved in the exhibition have established two parallel paths for reflection. The first is a more abstract examination of the phenomenon of art collecting, in which the figure of Patricia Cisneros allows us to take up the theoretical legacy of Walter Benjamin. The German thinker spoke of the collection as a complex entity born of the impulse and mentality of a *marginal*—in the most refined and least suggestive sense of the term—figure, meaning one situated on the margins of the space defined by (as we interpret it) the fluctuations of the market or the vagaries of taste. The accumulating act of the collector is philosophical in that it is an exercise of memory and anticipation. For the collector, ownership is not an instrument of financial speculation but a mechanism for an intimate relationship with the world and the process of history. In the extraction of one element (in this case a work of art) from its context to situate it in another, there is no alienation, only an enrichment through contact with others and, above all, with *Others*, unknowns with which it is impelled to enter into dialogue.

Like Benjamin's collector, Latin American art has also been *marginal*. Although such marginality was waved as a banner for a time by Hélio Oiticica (to cite one well-known case), today it demands a reinterpretation. If we take the particular sociopolitical situation of many parts of Latin America in the last century as a paradigmatic example of the South's marginality, we reach the conclusion that it was really at the *margins* of the world map where the fate of us all was in great part decided. Directly related to this observation, the second reflection that offers itself as a tentative reply has to do with the opportunity presented by the collection to analyze in greater depth a concrete case study (insofar as it is limited historically and geographically): the links between Latin American geometric abstraction and its parallel and succeeding contexts. This includes both the conceptualisms that began in the seventies as well as contemporaneous phenomena in other parts of the world.

Filling in the historiographical gaps between chapters is one of the objectives of a project that now takes concrete shape in a museum, a space that forges narratives and history, drawing up new diagrams of art history in which there must always be fissures to allow us to explore more deeply and move toward the completion of a complex and exciting cartography. For the Museo Reina Sofía, a rereading of the Colección Patricia Phelps de Cisneros cannot therefore be separated from a whole line of work that also includes other activities, ranging from the inclusion of Neoconcretism or Tropicalist art in the museum's reorganization of its collections to exhibitions like "Drifts and Derivations" or the recent *Losing the Human Form*, as well as other collaborative projects with the Conceptualismos del Sur network. Only from this diagrammatic concept that challenges times, spaces, and imaginary frontiers can we perceive history as a complex phenomenon. In Latin America, as in the complex layers of the human mind, the cold therefore lives on alongside the tropical, the political with the abstract, the kinetic with the seismic.

Far from the colonial idea of a "presentation," as we said before, the Museo Reina Sofía presents itself not as a container of objects but as a node of encounters and a space for dialogue. In this regard and connected to the aforementioned events, it was an international seminar on Latin American modernisms, organized in conjunction with the Fundación Cisneros and held in March 2012, whose significant findings fed the theoretical core sustained today by this exhibition. Such a collaboration responds to a model of networking that is proving itself more efficient by the day, allowing work to progress horizontally through long-term transitional projects brought to fruition in various phases. This working method and the results thereof have an impact on the

Museo Reina Sofía's position as a museum of the South, a fact that explains why it has established such a rich dialogue with the Fundación Cisneros, recognized for its support for education and its policy of collaborating with and assisting universities and centers of thought. Its mission, like the museum's, has been the search for the other as a guarantee for the future, and as a support for new narratives with open endings.

In this way, the echo of Walter Benjamin is heard once more in the notion of the collection as something dynamic and in transit: "It must be kept in mind that, for the collector, the world is present, and indeed ordered, in each of his objects. Ordered, however, according to a surprising and, for the profane understanding, simply incomprehensible connection.… All of these—the 'objective' data together with the other—come together, for the true collector, in every single one of his possessions, to form a whole magic encyclopedia, a world order, whose outline is the *fate* of his object. Here, therefore, within this circumscribed field, we can understand how great physiognomists (and collectors are physiognomists of the world of things) become interpreters of fate."[1]

Manuel Borja-Villel
Director of the Museo Nacional Centro de Arte Reina Sofía

1. Walter Benjamin, "The Collector," in *The Arcades Project*, trans. Howard Eiland and Kevin McLaughlin (Cambridge, Mass.: Harvard University Press, 1999), 207 [H2,7; H2a,1].

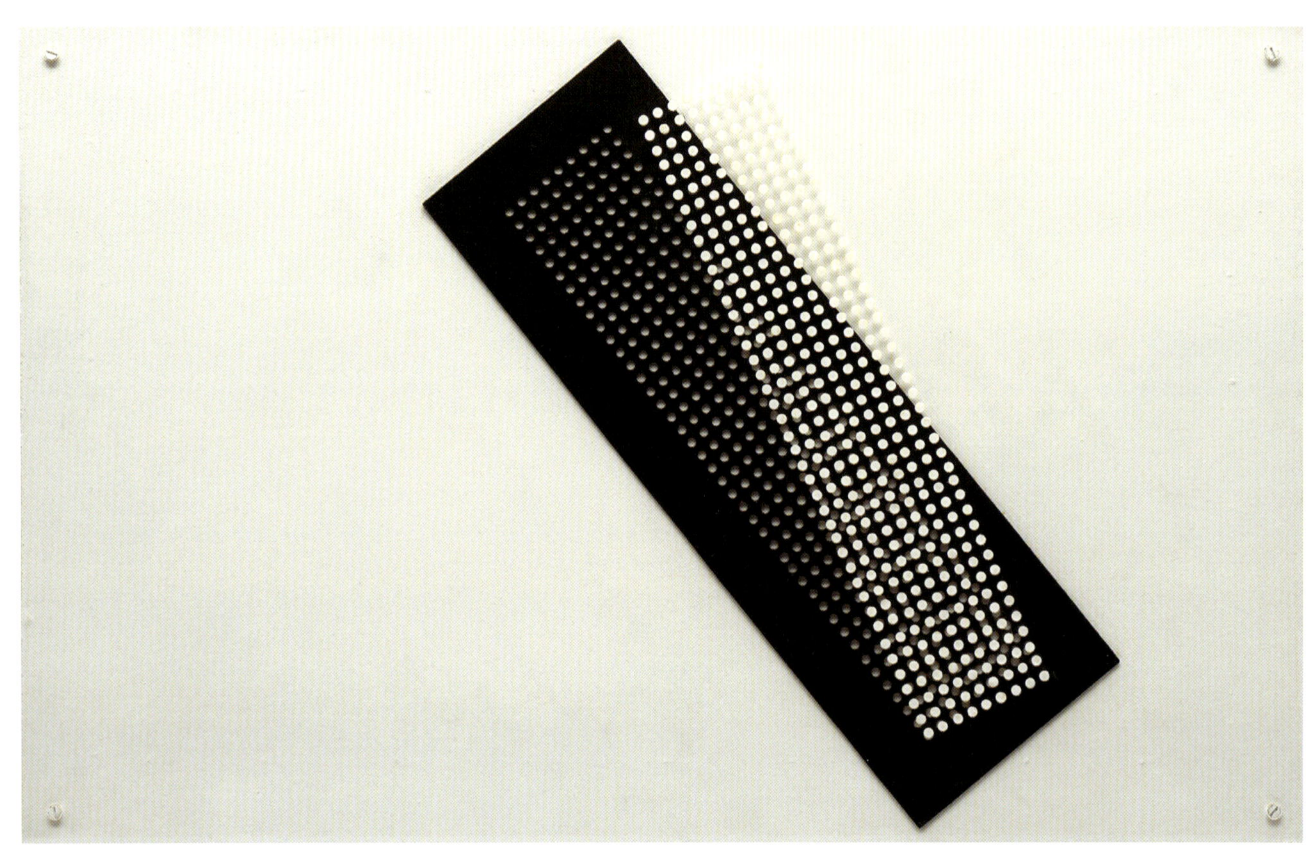

Jesús Soto
Desplazamiento de un elemento luminoso,
[Displacement of a Luminous Element], 1954

Concrete Invention
Gabriel Pérez-Barreiro

Declarative Images

In June 1946, a group of young men and women in Buenos Aires signed the "Inventionist Manifesto," launching a movement with the name Asociación de Arte Concreto-Invención that was to become one of the major players in the development of abstraction in South America. In this manifesto they declared, "The battle unleashed by so-called abstract art is, in fact, the battle for concrete invention" (La batalla librada por el arte llamado abstracto es, en el fondo, la batalla por la invención concreta). It is interesting to note the grammatical difference between abstract *art* (noun) and concrete *invention* (the result of a verb) in this sentence. The implication is that invention is somehow different from art, an active rather than a passive function. Part of this is the natural effervescence of youth, but another part speaks to an important sense that what these artists were doing was somehow beyond art as we understood it before: the result of an *action* rather than the creation of a *thing*.

The idea of self-contained art, an art that requires nothing other than its intentions to communicate, is simultaneously one of the great contributions and myths of modernity. We are familiar with the narrative: at the end of the nineteenth century art is finally freed of its bonds to the Church, to patronage, and to narrative, and starts to develop "its own" inherent language through the reduction of the elements of art to primary forms and colors. So far so good, but this seductive and tidy story posits that we can start from zero, clean our eyes and minds of all former habits of art, and create a shortcut between visual forms and direct experience. French philosopher Bruno Latour refers to this tension between the modern desire to overcome mediation and the creation of some of the most mediated forms of communication to date.[1] For many artists of mid-century Latin America —as in Europe and the United States— abstraction represented this opportunity to start again, to leave behind the past and embark on a democratic and positivist future (although of course positivism itself was already two hundred years old at this point). Once we accept the impossibility of an art that seamlessly communicates its telepathic qualities, the question becomes what exactly is this content that wishes to be communicated? We can find two paths to answer this question: one relating to the construction of meaning through the interaction of viewer and object, and the other relating to the artist's declared intentions. The first of these follows a constructivist model, one of whose pioneers was John Dewey with his concept that an artwork, any artwork, is *an* experience as opposed to the general experience of everyday life.[2] In this model, each viewer brings their own interests, background, and psychology to the encounter, and meaning is built through a dynamic interaction between the viewer and the object. To engage the artist's intent requires quite a different model: declarative rather than dialogic, based on imposition rather than negotiation.[3] By stating intentions, the artist, perhaps

1. Bruno Latour, *We Have Never Been Modern* (Cambridge, Mass.: Harvard University Press, 1993).

2. John Dewey, *Art as Experience* (New York: Minton, Balch & Co., 1934; repr. New York: Perigee Books, 2005).

3. For a good overview of the debates about intention and interpretation, see Hans Maes, "Intention, Interpretation and Contemporary Visual Art," *British Journal of Aesthetics* 50, no. 2 (April 2010): 121–38.

somewhat unconsciously, declares his or her fundamental principles and beliefs about art in general and his/her art in particular. The evidence of that declaration reinforces the contradiction between an abstraction that is supposedly universal, and the need to explain its origins and effects. The history of modern art is in many ways the history of the manifesto, the declaration, the magazine, and the broadsheet. This is perhaps ironic considering that it is the first time that visuality was considered a pure value *per se*, independent of, and often in opposition to, the written word. As abstraction in particular tried to free itself from narrative and description, two of the inherent values of the written word, it also created a rich body of writing in its wake. This tension between the proposition of an autonomous non-literary and self-evident artwork and the declarations of the artists who made them is the fault line along which this exhibition is built.

All that Glitters is not Gold

Not all geometric abstraction is the same. Even works created in the same context, time, and place, even by artists who joined the same movements and signed the same manifestos, often show irreconcilable differences in intent. One of the challenges in the history and exhibition-making of geometric abstraction is precisely that many of the works *look* the same, implying that they perhaps *mean* the same. For the last two decades or so we have finally come to understand that geometric abstraction existed in Latin America, and that it posited a worldview that was positive, optimistic, and constructive in the broadest sense of the word. This was perhaps especially important as an antidote to the predominant and stereotypical view of Latin America from Europe and the United States as the natural home of magical and tragic figuration. This broad division of Latin American art history into the abstract and the figurative has created two large blocks of content, and now the task is perhaps to start to unravel the particular characteristics of abstraction: To what extent were those artists aligned and how many different approaches can we find?

Let us take one of many examples: Gyula Kosice and Rhod Rothfuss were two of the cofounders of the Madí movement in Buenos Aires in the 1940s, close friends and allies, united in their cause to revolutionize the art world, and by extension the world in general. However, while Rothfuss constructed his works using the golden mean, Kosice avidly rejected any prescriptive form of geometry.[4] Why does this matter? Rather than a being a minor issue of technique or preference, signing up to a universal geometric principle like the golden mean or the Fibonacci series is tantamount to entering a society in which the members agree that geometry is something absolute, no less than a fundamental building block of the universe; the fact that the construction of a snail shell or the arrangement of the seeds in a sunflower follow this same proportion is proof that nature itself is built on these principles. For Kosice, however, this was reason enough to reject it, art being in his eyes a form of human invention that had to overcome the limitations of the natural to create new and unexpected forms and relations. Kosice's need to break free of all former constructs led him to the radical proposition of a sculpture made purely of hinged bronze strips, in which the very notion of stable form is undermined every time it is picked up and reconfigured. Similar contradictions exist between Franz Weissmann and Lygia Clark, two signatories of the "Neoconcrete Manifesto" in 1959, but whose artistic careers point to radically opposed ideas of the artwork and its place in the world. So what we can conclude is that just because two artists say they are

4. *Gyula Kosice in Conversation with Gabriel Pérez-Barreiro* (New York: Fundación Cisneros, 2012), 115–16.

En este momento, cuando más lejos parece que está el artista de la naturaleza, Vicente Huidobro dirá: "Nunca el hombre ha estado más cerca de la naturaleza, que ahora que no trata de imitarla en sus apariencias, sino haciendo como ella, imitándola en lo profundo de sus leyes constructivas, en la realización de un todo dentro del mecanismo de la producción de formas nuevas."

Pero, mientras se solucionaba el problema de la creación plástica, pura, la misma solución (por un principio dialéctico inquebrantable) creaba otro, que se siente menos en el neoplasticismo y en el constructivismo, por su composición ortogonal, que en el cubismo o en el no-objetivismo, y fué: *el marco*.

El cubismo y el no objetivismo, por sus composiciones basadas, ya en ritmos de líneas oblícuas, ya en figuras triangulares o poligonales, se crearon a sí mismos el problema de que un marco rectangular, cortaba el desarrollo plástico del tema. El cuadro, inevitablemente, quedaba reducido a un fragmento.

Pronto se intuye ésto. Y los cuadros muestran las soluciones buscadas. Por ejemplo MAN RAY, LÉGER, BRAQUE y más cerca nuestro, el cubista de otoño Pettoruti, entre otros, componen algunas de sus obras en círculos, elipses o polígonos, que inscriben en el cuadrilongo del marco. Pero esto no es tampoco una solución. Porque, precisamente es lo regular de esas figuras, el contorno ininterrumpido, simétrico, lo que domina la composición, cortándola.

Es por esto que la generalidad de esos cuadros siguieron en aquel concepto de *ventana* de los cuadros naturalistas, dándonos una parte del tema pero no la totalidad de él. Una pintura con un marco regular hace presentir una continuidad del tema, que sólo desaparece, cuando el marco está rigurosamente estructurado de acuerdo a la composición de la pintura.

Vale decir, cuando se hace jugar al borde de la tela, un papel activo en la creación plástica. Papel que debe tenerlo siempre. Una pintura debe ser algo que empiece y termine en ella misma. Sin solución de continuidad.

R H O D   R O T H F U S S

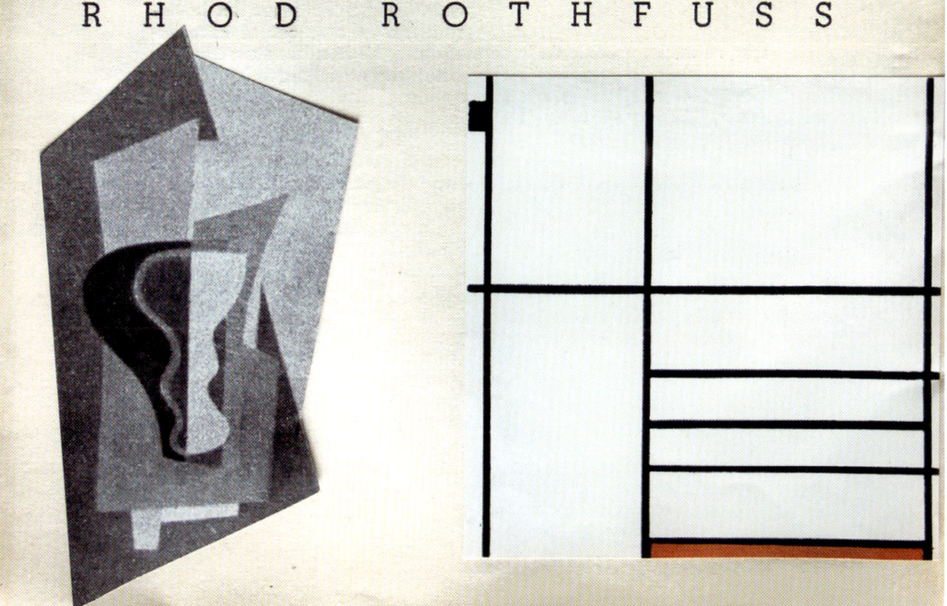

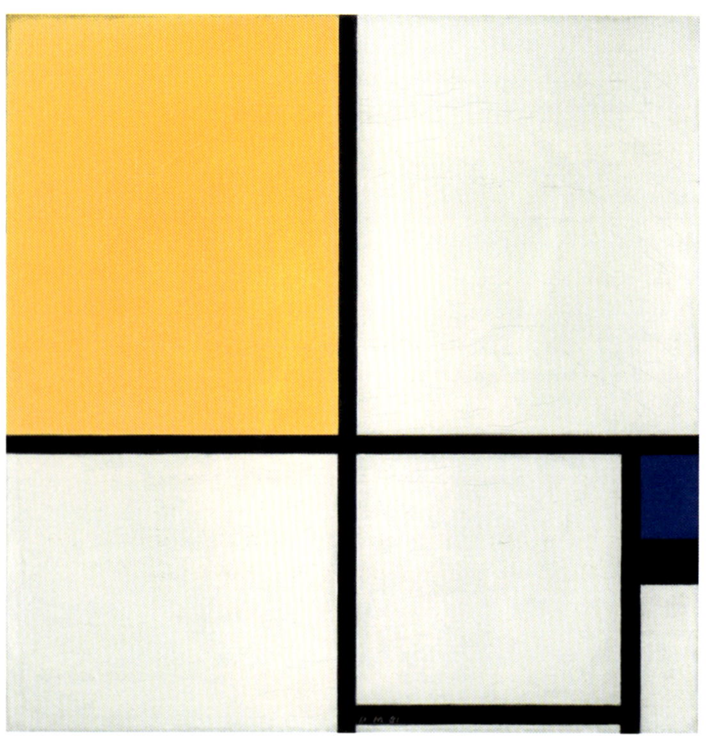

Piet Mondrian
Composition No. II with Yellow and Blue, 1931

aligned, the evidence of the work may prove otherwise. The exercise of judging an abstract work that declares its principles is twofold, implicating the written text and then the work itself. Intention, therefore, is something both said and done, declared in principle and then realized in practice.

Content and Context

One of the founding principles of geometric abstraction is that it is universal, not local, cosmopolitan not contextual. This is presented as a self-evident truth: the elements of art are pure and absolute and therefore independent of their specific circumstances. When, as in the case of most of the artists in this exhibition, the politics were of the internationalist Left, this desire was reinforced politically. When an artist from Latin America joined Abstraction-Creation or had a work reproduced in *Art d'aujourd'hui*, or a European artist had his or her work reproduced in *Nueva Visión*, this was confirmation that they were part of a community of equals, a United Nations of Form, open to all regardless of their national origin. Half a century later we can only look back at this situation with a certain sense of melancholy. Once the center of power in writing art history moved to the United States, the interpretation of Latin America became part of a broader Cold War agenda. Latin America became a political imperative, and it still largely is in terms of academic and museum practice. Where it was once feared it is now sought after, but as its own specialized domain, its own flavor, isolated from the broader history of ideas. The particular circumstances of the United States since the 1960s also make it inevitably part of an institutional attempt to represent or reach a "community" (an abstraction that is usually a synonym for people of darker skin as defined by museum trustees and staff). In this calcification of what was originally a more fluid relationship, we lose the international context for abstraction, or it is simplified into a discourse of "influence" or justification.

El caso **Mondrian**

In Latin America, as in so many other places, Mondrian was an icon, and like all icons, open to different interpretations.[5] His contact with Latin America was limited (he worked alongside Joaquín Torres-García in Paris in the 1930s, but we have to remember that Torres-García had left Uruguay at the age of seventeen). However, through the circulation of images of his work, Mondrian was a central protagonist of abstraction in Latin America. A comparative study of the different readings and impacts of Mondrian in Latin America can be instructive not only to trace the multiple and varied readings of the work of one artist, but also in terms of what it implies as a model in which "influence" (passive) can be replaced by "interpretation" (active). We can start with Torres-García, the only artist in this exhibition to have ever met Mondrian. Torres-García and Mondrian were engaged in a direct debate about the nature of abstraction, with the Dutch artist (who was only two years older) rejecting the Uruguayan's use of icons and symbols in his work. The dispute was intense, but also warm, and Torres-García dedicated his 1935 book *Estructura* to Mondrian. Both artists, despite their differences, shared an interest in spirituality and mystical ideas of the meaning of form. Mondrian's theosophy would not have been a stretch for Torres-García, while it would have been anathema to almost all of the Latin American artists who followed him and fiercely defended him.

5. I am grateful to Ariel Jiménez for his discussions on this topic. See Ariel Jiménez's title essay in *Desenhar no Espaço: Artistas Abstratos do Brasil e da Venezuela na Coleção Patricia Phelps de Cisneros*, exh. cat. Fundação Iberê Camargo, Porto Alegre and Pinacoteca do Estado de São Paulo, 2010 (Porto Alegre: Fundação Iberê Camargo, 2010), 11–35, and the presentations at the Seminario Fundación Cisneros, "Piet Mondrian: Lecturas paralelas," 2011; see http://www.ustream.tv/recorded /15365076 (beginning at 00:35:13) (accesed January 16, 2013).

A PIET MONDRIAN

1) ESTAMOS EN EL CAOS. Nada sabemos de nada, nada de arte, nada de nosotros mismos. Caos no significa confusión, mezcla de todo, sino más bien embrión. El desorden es solo aparente. Epoca geológica, época de formación, período no imaginable que precede a la aparición de la vida organizada; millones de años. Enfriamiento progresivo de la tierra, que se resquebraja por todas partes, se arruga como la piel de un fruto maduro, se forman las cadenas de las montañas, los hondos valles. Fuerzas volcánicas provocan horrendos cataclismos. Nuevos elementos intervienen, lluvia, viento, temblores de tierra que todo lo transforman, desequilibrios atmosféricos, nieve y fuego a la vez. Poco a poco todo se aquieta, los ríos arrastran enormes cantidades de piedras, tierras, limo; solo los restos volcánicos, las lavas, el esqueleto resiste. Aún hoy podemos ver esos testimonios por todo el globo. El cielo se despeja, la regularidad del movimiento de los astros da las alternativas de hoy.

Apesar de todo esto, podemos decir que aún nuestra tierra está como en gestación, por que no está formada completamente. Es cierto que la vida ha comenzado: el minúsculo pez, primero; las plantas; después los enormes animales; pero falta el hombre. Y, nacido éste, estará por tiempo, como en la inconsciencia.

Estamos en el caos, colores y formas nada expresan, no sabemos nada de nada, vemos sin comprender; como artistas plásticos estamos en un momento de balbuceo.

2) LA TIERRA HA LLEGADO AL TERMINO DE SU FORMACION — EL HOMBRE YA EXISTE. Se inicia un leve fulgor de razón, el hombre va como despertando, y entonces conoce a aquel otro hombre que está antes que la misma Creación, pues es el arquetipo de todo. El ser humano que acaba de nacer descubre a ese hombre en su interior. Entonces vemos la aparición de algo que difiere absolutamente de la naturaleza: la geometría, el orden, las leyes que él manifestará en sus obras. Un mundo completo, infinito, que nos revela otra existencia; lo abstracto. Por esto vemos como el arte abstracto corresponde a un grado muy superior de evolución en cualquier período.

3) ENTRE LO ABSTRACTO Y LA NATURALEZA tenemos ahora que hacer una separación. En esta nueva vía que se abre ante nosotros vemos la posibilidad de una gigantesca construcción, que será la obra humana. Ordenamos, clasificamos, generalizamos. Lo que propiamente

Dedication to Piet Mondrian by Joaquín Torres-García in *Estructura*, Montevideo: Ed. Alfar, 1935

Once Mondrian's images were detached from a firsthand experience with the artist and his theories they began to re-signify in important ways. For the young artists involved with *Arturo* magazine in 1944 Buenos Aires, Mondrian's work (or rather reproductions of his work that traveled without text) represented the maximum extreme point of abstraction, and they overlaid this with their own interests in Communism and extreme formalism. When Rothfuss juxtaposed a work by Mondrian with his own early shaped canvas in *Arturo* (see p. 19), the point he was making is that Mondrian's formalism was constrained by his use of the regular rectangular frame, implying that had Mondrian known better he would have structured the frame itself. Anyone familiar with Mondrian's ideas and writings would know that the regular frame was not itself an issue for the artist. As Mondrian's images began to circulate through magazines and publications, they became detached from the artist's own intentions and interpretations, becoming   on the one hand less faithful to the original motivation and on the other more productive as actors in a discussion they themselves did not start. So we have the apparently paradoxical situation that as the images become less dependent on or connected to the artist's intention, they also become more likely to be catalysts for something else, gaining in importance and richness as they are reinterpreted. Had Mondrian's texts traveled to Argentina along with the (poor) illustrations, he would likely have been dismissed as a romantic idealist—as was Torres-García— and he would have been far less important to the next generation.

"Mondrian: You believed in Man. You did more: In a stupendous, Utopian dream you thought of times to come in which 'constructed' life itself would be a plastic reality. " Lygia Clark wrote these words in a letter to Mondrian (who had been dead for over a decade) in 1959.[6] Her statement shows eloquently how Mondrian's legacy was an inspiration for the next generation of artists in Brazil who identified in him a utopian potential for transcending the limits of art. Both Clark and Hélio Oiticica saw the seeds of a radical project in Mondrian, and developed their work in a direction that they felt preserved the spirit if not the letter of his intentions. Unlike the Argentine artists a decade earlier, the issue was less about composition and more about the transformational potential of form and color in space. However, in both cases the artists believed that they were realizing an intention that Mondrian himself had been unable to achieve.

A similar re-signification occurred in Venezuela when Jesús Soto identified Mondrian, particularly the works of the 1930s and the transatlantic paintings, as a proto-kinetic artist. Once again, Soto's own interests allowed his eye to pick up on an implicit unrealized potential in Mondrian's work, that *had he lived longer* he would surely have developed. In this case, Soto's attention was drawn to the vibration between colors, or the little gray points that appear optically at the intersections of the dense black lines in Mondrian's compositions. For Soto, as for Carlos Cruz-Diez, the realization that a strict and rigorous geometry could simultaneously dematerialize through optical effects was fundamental to his own artistic development, and this again was one of Mondrian's unintended contributions to the development of Latin American abstraction. In all of the cases cited here there was never a process of emulation or copying, instead the artist's original intentions were replaced by a projection of what others thought he was trying to do. As a result, the more interesting impact of Mondrian's work in Latin America is not necessarily through the artists whose work looks similar (of which there are numerous examples), but those who consciously tried to "complete" his work through a conversation at the level of underlying intention and not of formal results.

6. Lygia Clark, "Letter to Mondrian," in *Lygia Clark*, exh. cat. Fundació Antoni Tàpies, Barcelona et al. (Barcelona: Fundació Antoni Tàpies, 1997), 114.

The Exhibition: *Concrete Invention*

After many successful exhibitions of geometric abstraction for Latin America, what does *Concrete Invention* propose as a curatorial model? Most previous exhibitions dedicated to the subject have oscillated between a generalizing approach in which all abstraction is grouped together within a broader regional framework dealing with Latin America,[7] or a looser, more suggestive and essay model largely developed within Latin America in which abstraction itself is a given.[8] *The Geometry of Hope* in 2007 posited a model in which context and chronology worked together to trace a linear history of the development of geometric abstraction, using the city as the unit of context.[9] For this project at the Museo Reina Sofía the challenge was how to create a different organizing principle that would be less linear and less tied to specific contexts, while avoiding the generalization of "Latin America." The path we followed was to use intention as the structural backbone.

When looking at a broad and representative group of works such as those in the Colección Patricia Phelps de Cisneros, one starts to see that certain works produced in different times and places nonetheless share a certain *Weltanschauung*. We propose that this is not just at the level of a formal or romantic affinity, but that there are a number of different approaches and beliefs at play during the four decades covered by the exhibition that create their own groupings and tendencies. In our linear version of history, we tend to present these in sequence: Torres-García is superseded by Madí/Concreto-Invención, which is superseded by São Paulo Concretism, which is superseded by Rio Concretism, which all leads to a culmination in Neoconcretism. This evolutionary, even Darwinist, model ignores the fact that these ideas coexist in time and space. Also, when one looks closely at each context or movement it becomes clear that even when artists have signed up to the same group, their works can have quite different intentions. We cited the case of Gyula Kosice and Rhod Rothfuss above, but we can see it again in Alejandro Otero and Soto, or Hélio Oiticica and Ivan Serpa. So what are these core ideas that allow us to group works in a nonlinear way?

Following the sequence of the exhibition, the first of these is the interest in the dialogical artwork, the idea of art as mediation between the artist and the spectator. Some of the protagonists here are Kosice with his articulated bronze sculpture, Lygia Pape's *Livro da criação* (Book of Creation, p. 92), and Lygia Clark's *bichos*. In all of these works, the object is transitional and contingent on its relationship with another person. In terms of movements, these works are usually association with Neoconcretism and Madí, but there were many members of these groups (in fact the majority) who did not produce works of this type.

Another grouping brings together those artists who believed in a stable and absolute form of geometry. The ethos here is Neoplatonic, in the belief that the universe is structured according to archetypal geometric forms and the task of the artist is to somehow reveal or reflect this in his or her work. For some artists this implies a quasi-religious activity, while for the majority it was quite the opposite: a declaration of an absolute materialism, often in line with their political beliefs. This section includes works by Tomás Maldonado, Alfredo Hlito, and Alberto Molenberg, who as members of the Asociación de Arte Concreto-Invención proposed an uncompromising collectivist geometry, equating illusion in art to classism. Also

7. See, for example, *Art in Latin America* curated by Dawn Ades for the Hayward Gallery in 1989, or *Heterotopias* curated by Mari Carmen Ramírez for the Museo Nacional Centro de Arte Reina Sofía in 2000.

8. Examples include Ariel Jiménez (curator), *Desenhar no Espaço: Artistas Abstratos do Brasil e da Venezuela na Coleção Patricia Phelps de Cisneros*, Fundação Iberê Camargo, Porto Alegre, 2010; Ariel Jiménez (curator), *Cruce de Miradas: Visiones de America Latina; Colección Patricia Phelps de Cisneros*, Museo del Palacio de Bellas Artes, Mexico City, 2006; and Luis Pérez-Oramas (curator), *León Ferrari and Mira Schendel: Tangled Alphabets*, The Museum of Modern Art, New York, 2009.

9. Note that *América Fría: Abstración Geometrica en América Latina, 1934–1973*, Fundación Juan March, Madrid, 2011, applied this same model, expanding it to include Cuba and Mexico. A more nuanced reading of work and context can be found in Mary Kate O'Hare's exhibition *Constructive Spirit: Abstract Art in South and North America, 1920s–50s*, Newark Museum, New Jersey, 2010, that posited a dialogue between artists of North and South America.

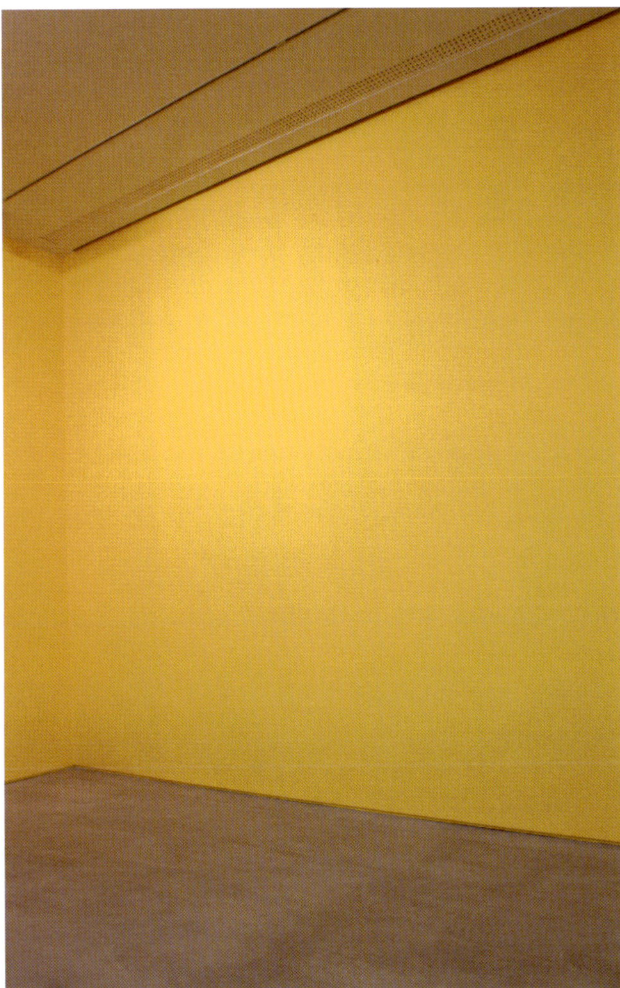

Carlos Cruz-Diez
Chromosaturation: 1970–1979, 1970
Venezuela Pavilion at the 35th Venice Biennale
(Not in exhibition)

Héctor Fuenmayor
Citrus 6906 (originally *Amarillo Sol K7YV68* [*Sun Yellow K7YV68*]), 1973/2013
Installation view at the Museo Nacional Centro de Arte Reina Sofía, 2013

in this section are artists from the Grupo Frente like Aluísio Carvão, or the Madí movement like Martín Blaszko. Works by Josef Albers and Max Bill are also included as important foreign referents for this type of work.

Works like Geraldo de Barros's *Função Diagonal* (Diagonal Function, p. 65), while absolutely pure in their construction, nonetheless embrace illusionism, creating a constant back-and-forth effect. Similar effects can be found in the paintings of Judith Lauand, the *metaesquemas* of Oiticica, the early sculptures of Gego and Weissmann, or the shimmering compositions of Hermelindo Fiaminghi. The idea that pure form could generate a virtual effect in the eye of the viewer was compounded by an interest in phenomenology and particularly in Gestalt theory. As opposed to the artists in the previous section, the interest here is in the fictional or narrative possibilities of a form that declares itself to be absolute yet is perceived as something else. While those artists were interested in the contradiction between geometry and motion, a different group aspired to the dematerialization of form itself through vibration and juxtaposition. Of all of the groupings, this is the one that is most limited to a time and place (Caracas and Paris in the 1960s and 1970s) through the works of Soto and Cruz-Diez, whose life project was to project color and light into space, from geometry but not of geometry. The works of Torres-García and Mira Schendel, while distant in time and space, share some fundamental beliefs. Both artists were interested in spirituality, non-reductive geometry, and a work that uses pre-existing language rather than the "new" language of pure form. Schendel for many years would be grouped with the Neoconcrete artists, but aside from a few (very few) formal similarities, her work was concerned with sign and symbol in a way that corresponds with Torres-García's lifelong exploration of symbol and sign. In the exhibition these five thematic (or intentional) sections are punctuated with solo artist galleries presenting the work of Alejandro Otero, Willys de Castro, and Gego, all artists who in some way intersect and escape these categories. They are there also as reminders that any grouping is fluid and suggestive, rather than absolute.

Citrus

The exhibition closes with a single work: Hector Fuenmayor's *Citrus* (pp. 168–73), which consists of an empty room in which the walls have been painted with a commercially available yellow paint (from where the name *Citrus* is taken). Made in 1973 for an exhibition at the Sala Mendoza in Caracas, the work serves as an indication of what was to come next. Despite the wealth of ideas and the intensity of the debate of the heroic first generations of geometric abstraction, the question of their legacy after 1970 is still unresolved. In conventional accounts, abstraction is followed by conceptualism, but the nature of conceptualism and its relationship to the previous generation is only now being studied systematically. What is clear is that by the 1970s the question of what pure form could mean was no longer a burning question, replaced by the political, institutional, and existential concerns of a generation more marked by the Cuban Revolution than by World War II. Fuenmayor's chromatic dematerialized readymade opens the door to a radically different type of experience in which color is no longer a symbol of a pure absolute but a domestic product, in which art is no longer contained within a discrete object in a space but literally becomes the space. It is interesting to contrast Fuenmayor's yellow room with Cruz-Diez's *cromosaturaciones* of the early 1970s in which white rooms are delicately tinted by racks of colored light. Where Cruz-Diez's work is delicate, suggestive, and retinal, Fuenmayor's matter-of-factness speaks to a new relationship to the real and to consumer culture, and a critical reflection on the role of the institution in that culture. This simple and yet evocative work seems to declare the end of an era, and a virtual sunrise of the decades to come.

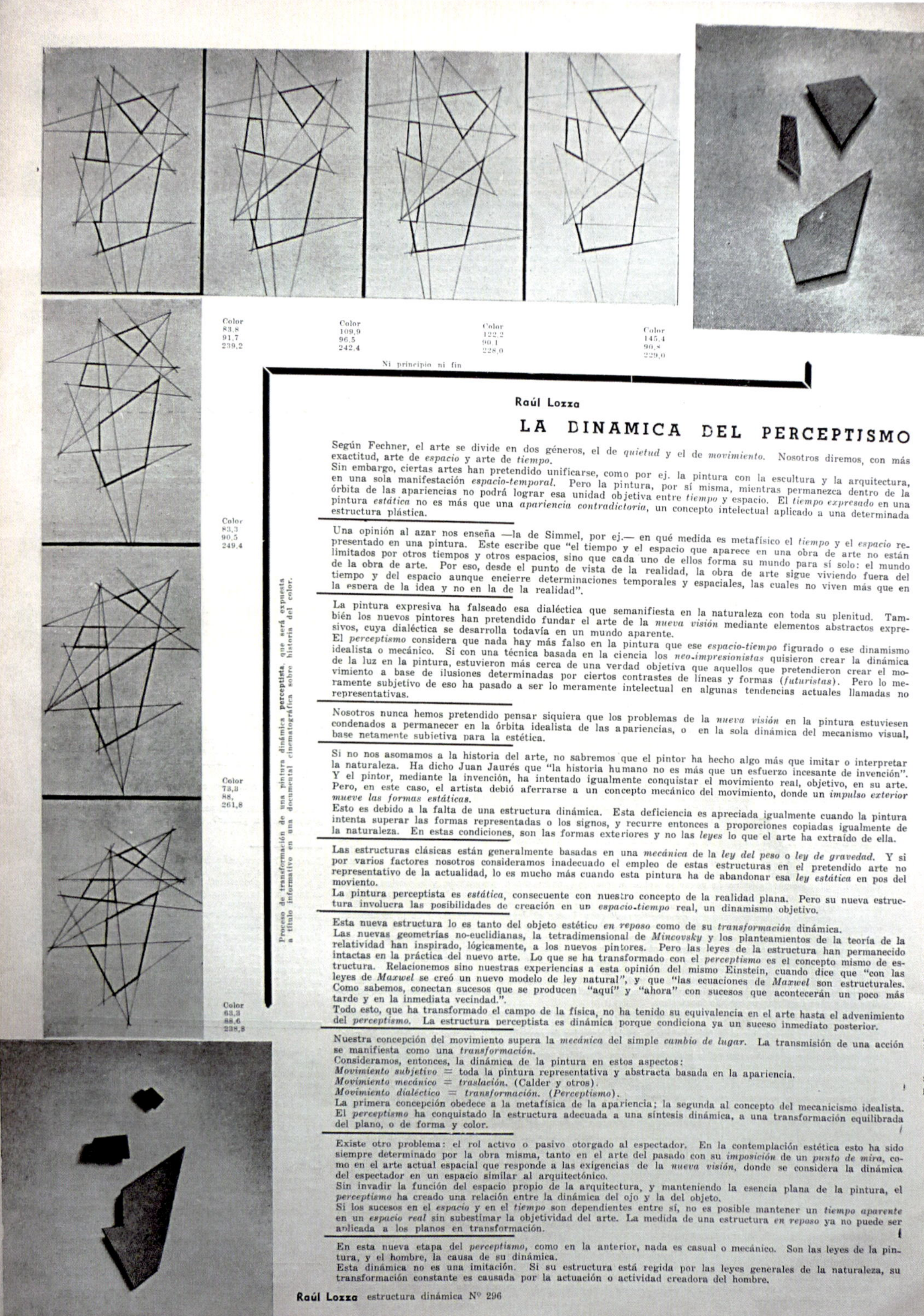

Raúl Lozza

LA DINAMICA DEL PERCEPTISMO

Según Fechner, el arte se divide en dos géneros, el de *quietud* y el de *movimiento*. Nosotros diremos, con más exactitud, arte de *espacio* y arte de *tiempo*.

Sin embargo, ciertas artes han pretendido unificarse, como por ej. la pintura con la escultura y la arquitectura, en una sola manifestación *espacio-temporal*. Pero la pintura, por sí misma, mientras permanezca dentro de la órbita de las apariencias no podrá lograr esa unidad objetiva entre *tiempo* y espacio. El *tiempo expresado* en una pintura *estática* no es más que una *apariencia contradictoria*, un concepto intelectual aplicado a una determinada estructura plástica.

Una opinión al azar nos enseña —la de Simmel, por ej.— en qué medida es metafísico el *tiempo* y el *espacio* representado en una pintura. Este escribe que "el tiempo y el espacio que aparece en una obra de arte no están limitados por otros tiempos y otros espacios, sino que cada uno de ellos forma su mundo para sí solo: el mundo de la obra de arte. Por eso, desde el punto de vista de la realidad, la obra de arte sigue viviendo fuera del tiempo y del espacio aunque encierre determinaciones temporales y espaciales, las cuales no viven más que en la esfera de la idea y no en la de la realidad".

La pintura expresiva ha falseado esa dialéctica que semanifiesta en la naturaleza con toda su plenitud. También los nuevos pintores han pretendido fundar el arte de la *nueva visión* mediante elementos abstractos expresivos, cuya dialéctica se desarrolla todavía en un mundo aparente.

El *perceptismo* considera que nada hay más falso en la pintura que ese *espacio-tiempo* figurado o ese dinamismo idealista o mecánico. Si con una técnica basada en la ciencia los *neo-impresionistas* quisieron crear la dinámica de la luz en la pintura, estuvieron más cerca de una verdad objetiva que aquellos que pretendieron crear el movimiento a base de ilusiones determinadas por ciertos contrastes de líneas y formas (*futuristas*). Pero lo meramente subjetivo de eso ha pasado a ser lo meramente intelectual en algunas tendencias actuales llamadas no representativas.

Nosotros nunca hemos pretendido pensar siquiera que los problemas de la *nueva visión* en la pintura estuviesen condenados a permanecer en la órbita idealista de las apariencias, o en la sola dinámica del mecanismo visual, base netamente subjetiva para la estética.

Si no nos asomamos a la historia del arte, no sabremos que el pintor ha hecho algo más que imitar o interpretar la naturaleza. Ha dicho Juan Jaurés que "la historia humano no es más que un esfuerzo incesante de invención". Y el pintor, mediante la invención, ha intentado igualmente conquistar el movimiento real, objetivo, en su arte. Pero, en este caso, el artista debió aferrarse a un concepto mecánico del movimiento, donde un *impulso exterior mueve las formas estáticas*.

Esto es debido a la falta de una estructura dinámica. Esta deficiencia es apreciada igualmente cuando la pintura intenta superar las formas representadas o los signos, y recurre entonces a proporciones copiadas igualmente de la naturaleza. En estas condiciones, son las formas exteriores y no las *leyes* lo que el arte ha extraído de ella.

Las estructuras clásicas están generalmente basadas en una *mecánica* de la *ley del peso* o *ley de gravedad*. Y si por varios factores nosotros consideramos inadecuado el empleo de estas estructuras en el pretendido arte no representativo de la actualidad, lo es mucho más cuando esta pintura ha de abandonar esa *ley estática* en pos del moviento.

La pintura perceptista es *estática*, consecuente con nuestro concepto de la realidad plana. Pero su nueva estructura involucra las posibilidades de creación en un *espacio-tiempo* real, un dinamismo objetivo.

Esta nueva estructura lo es tanto del objeto estético *en reposo* como de su *transformación* dinámica.

Las nuevas geometrías no-euclidianas, la tetradimensional de *Mincovsky* y los planteamientos de la teoría de la relatividad han inspirado, lógicamente, a los nuevos pintores. Pero las leyes de la estructura han permanecido intactas en la práctica del nuevo arte. Lo que se ha transformado con el *perceptismo* es el concepto mismo de estructura. Relacionemos sino nuestras experiencias a esta opinión del mismo Einstein, cuando dice que "con las leyes de *Maxwel* se creó un nuevo modelo de ley natural", y que "las ecuaciones de *Maxwel* son estructurales. Como sabemos, conectan sucesos que se producen "aquí" y "ahora" con sucesos que acontecerán un poco más tarde y en la inmediata vecindad.".

Todo esto, que ha transformado el campo de la física, no ha tenido su equivalencia en el arte hasta el advenimiento del *perceptismo*. La estructura perceptista es dinámica porque condiciona ya un suceso inmediato posterior.

Nuestra concepción del movimiento supera la *mecánica* del simple *cambio de lugar*. La transmisión de una acción se manifiesta como una *transformación*.

Consideramos, entonces, la dinámica de la pintura en estos aspectos:

Movimiento subjetivo = toda la pintura representativa y abstracta basada en la apariencia.
Movimiento mecánico = *traslación*. (Calder y otros).
Movimiento dialéctico = *transformación*. (Perceptismo).

La primera concepción obedece a la metafísica de la apariencia; la segunda al concepto del mecanicismo idealista. El *perceptismo* ha conquistado la estructura adecuada a una síntesis dinámica, a una transformación equilibrada del plano, o de forma y color.

Existe otro problema: el rol activo o pasivo otorgado al espectador. En la contemplación estética esto ha sido siempre determinado por la obra misma, tanto en el arte del pasado con su *imposición* de un *punto de mira*, como en el arte actual espacial que responde a las exigencias de la *nueva visión*, donde se considera la dinámica del espectador en un espacio similar al arquitectónico.

Sin invadir la función del espacio propio de la arquitectura, y manteniendo la esencia plana de la pintura, el *perceptismo* ha creado una relación entre la dinámica del ojo y la del objeto.

Si los sucesos en el *espacio* y en el *tiempo* son dependientes entre sí, no es posible mantener un *tiempo aparente* en un *espacio real* sin subestimar la objetividad del arte. La medida de una estructura *en reposo* ya no puede ser aplicada a los planos en transformación.

En esta nueva etapa del *perceptismo*, como en la anterior, nada es casual o mecánico. Son las leyes de la pintura, y el hombre, la causa de su dinámica.

Esta dinámica no es una imitación. Si su estructura está regida por las leyes generales de la naturaleza, su transformación constante es causada por la actuación o actividad creadora del hombre.

Raúl Lozza estructura dinámica Nº 296

Raúl Lozza, "La dinámica del perceptismo" [Perceptivist Dynamics] in *Perceptismo: Teórico y polémico*, no. 2, Buenos Aires, 1951

"Painting, like any other form of art, must abide by the structure, which can no longer be reduced to the superficial conditioning of images or signs, but must constitute the product itself of a process, that of the visible matter, known in practice as reality."

Raúl Lozza

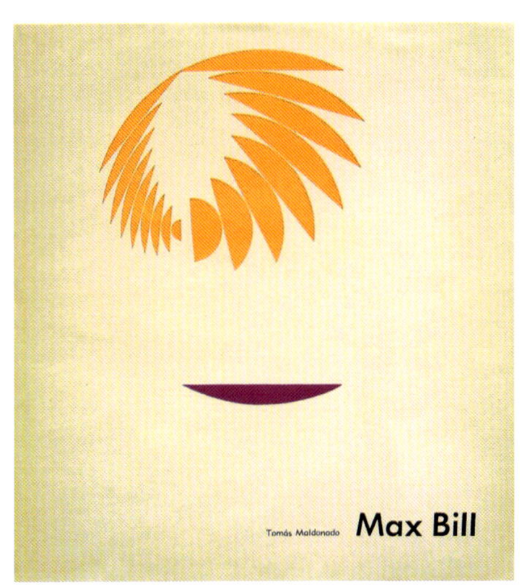

Tomás Maldonado, *Max Bill*, Buenos Aires: Ed. Nueva Visión, 1953

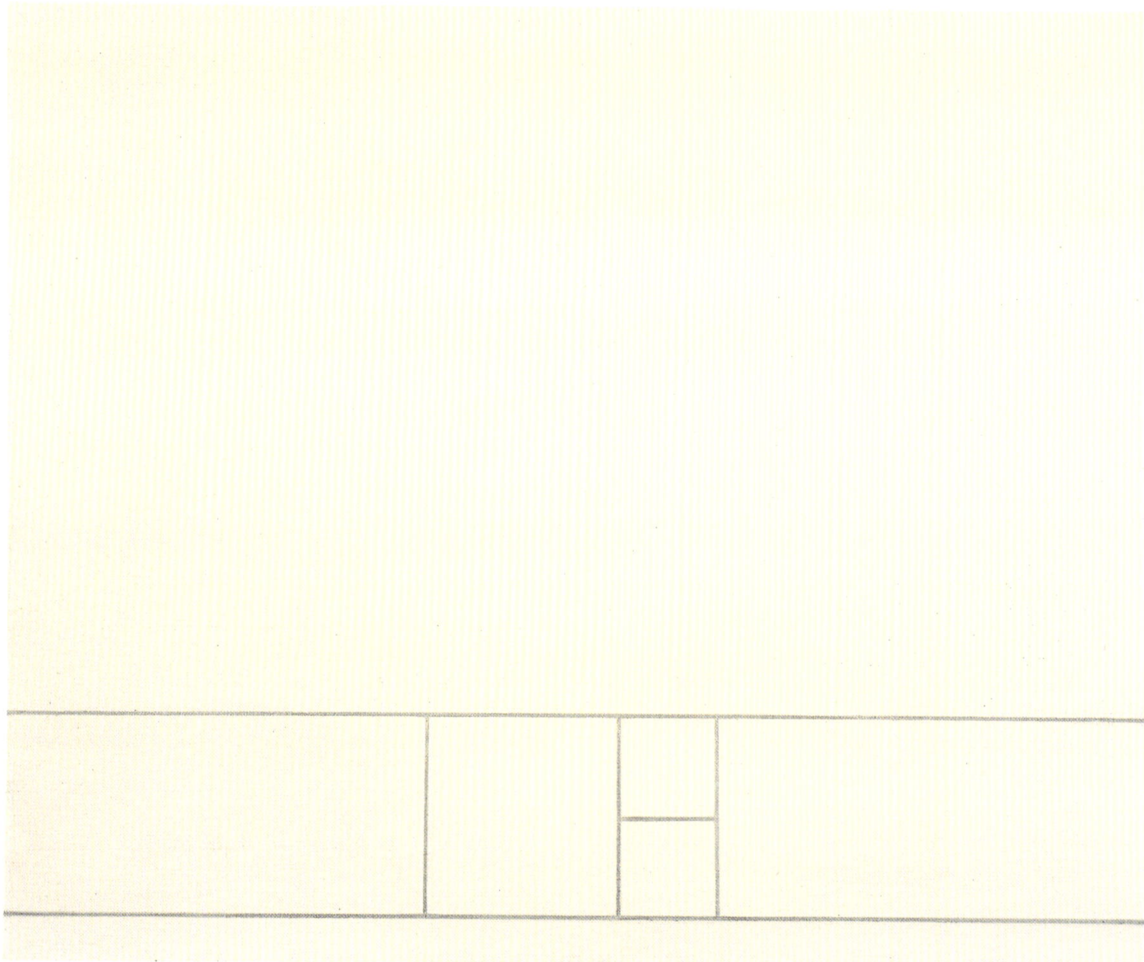

Milton Dacosta
Em branco [In White], 1958–59

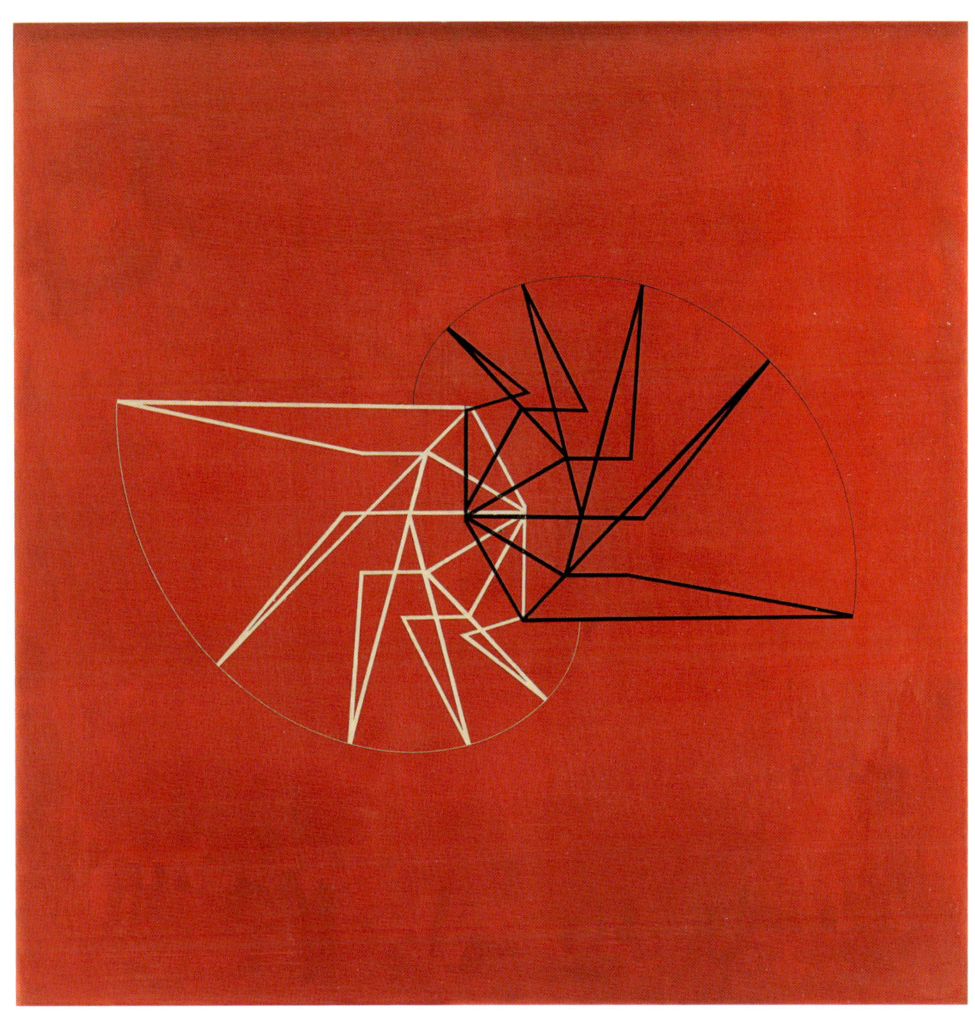

Waldemar Cordeiro
Idéia visível [Visible Idea], 1956

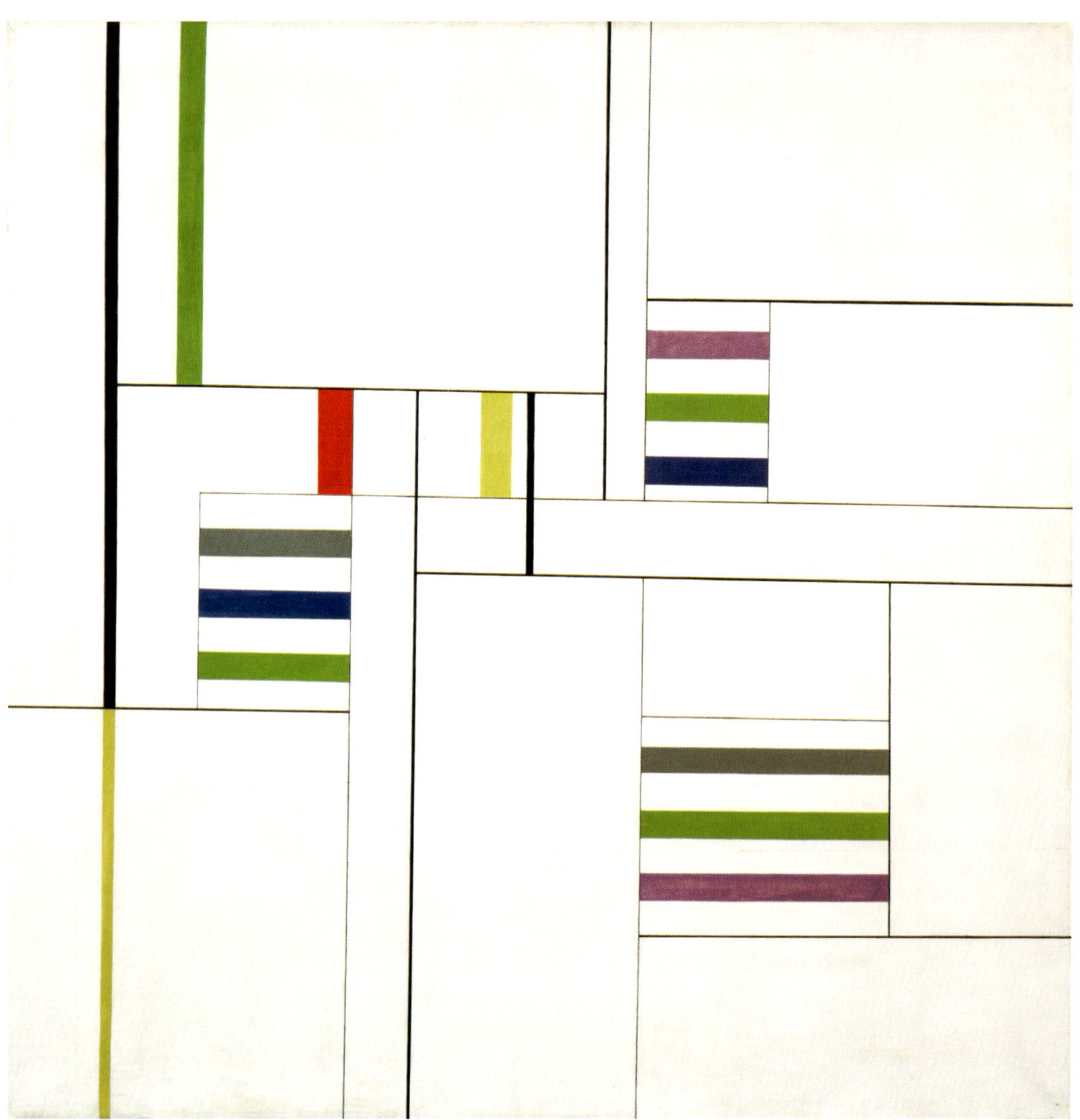

Alfredo Hlito
Ritmos cromáticos III [Chromatic Rhythms III], 1949

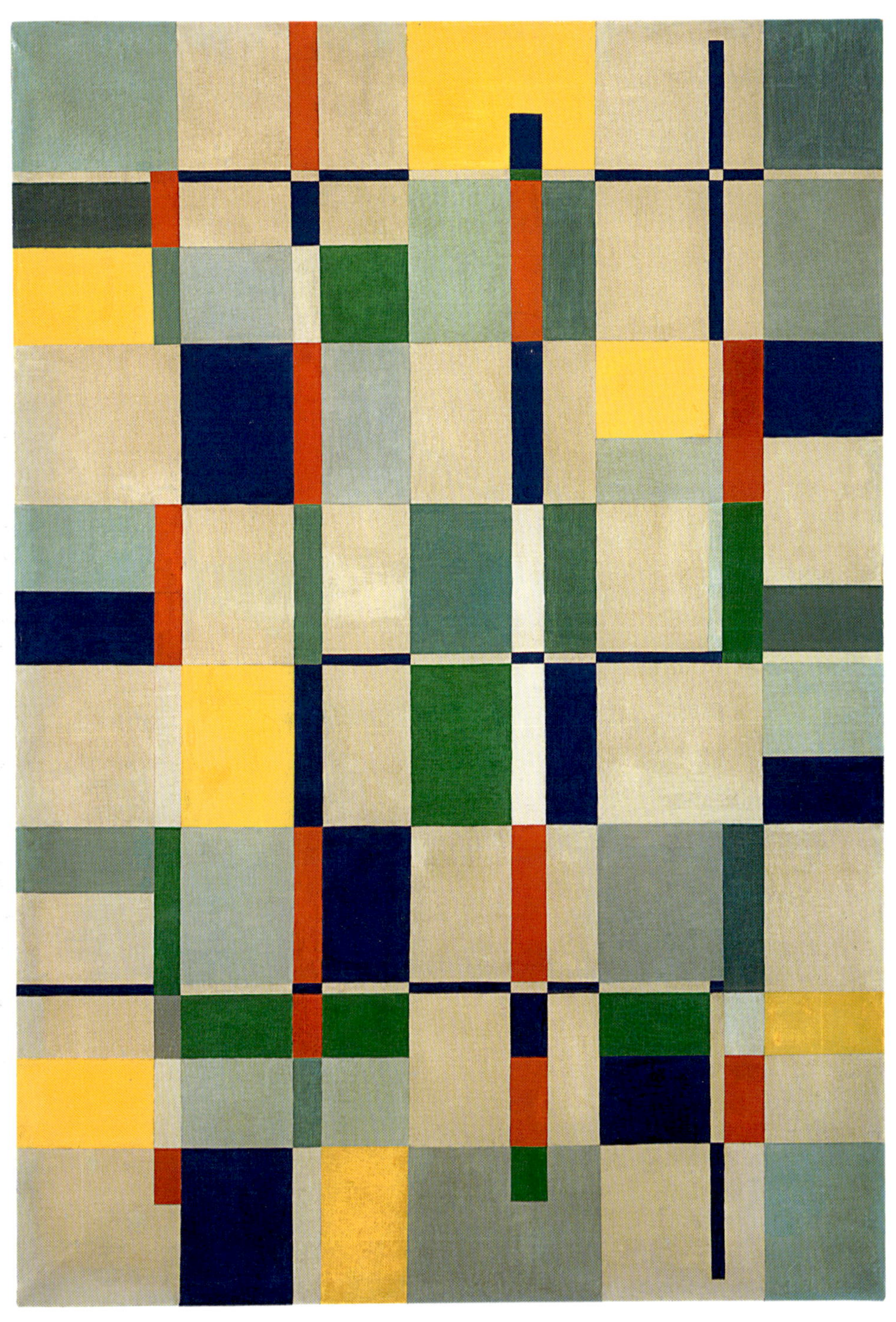

Lygia Clark
Composição [Composition], 1953

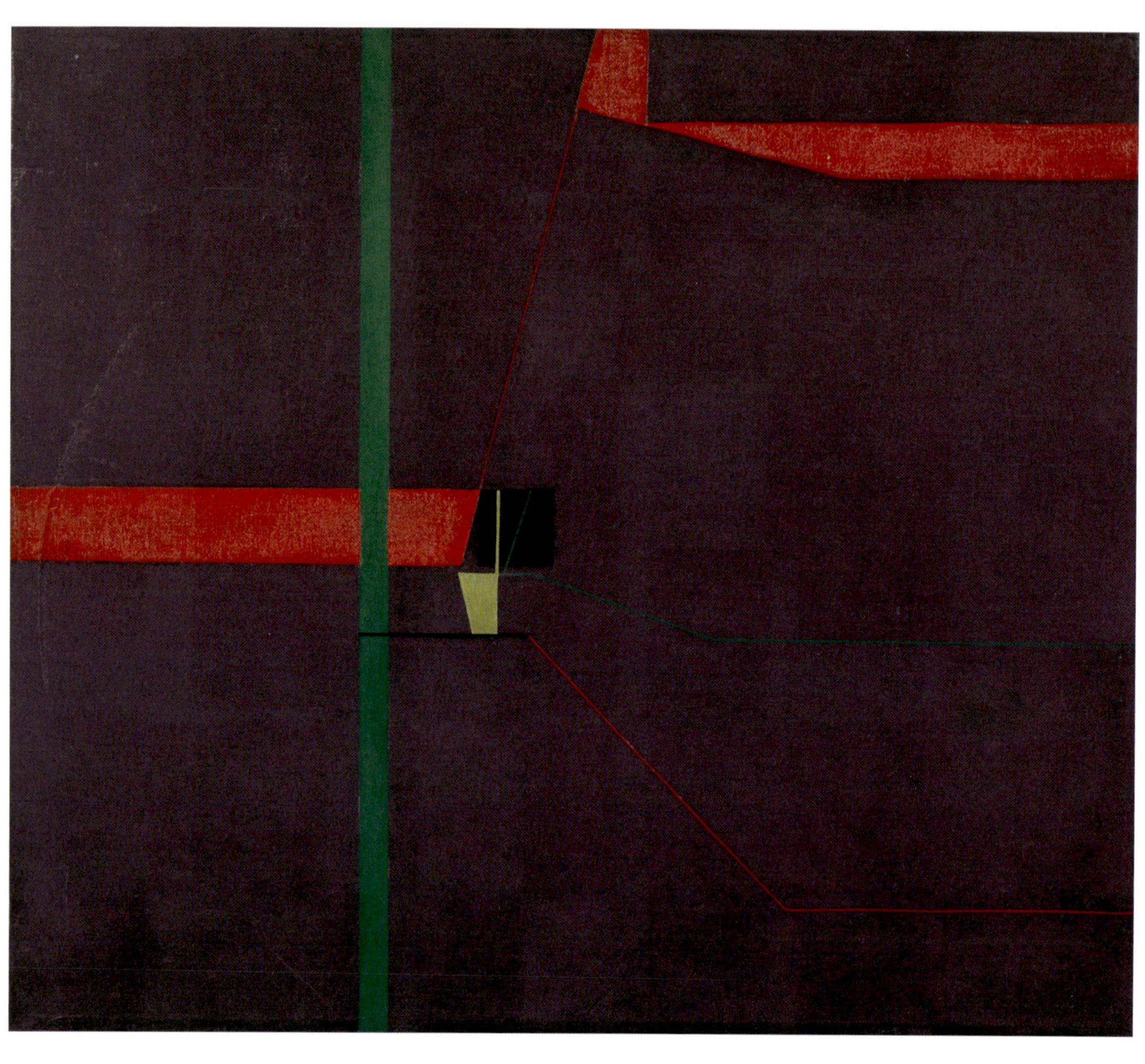

Alfredo Hlito
Desarrollo de un tema [Development of a Theme], 1952

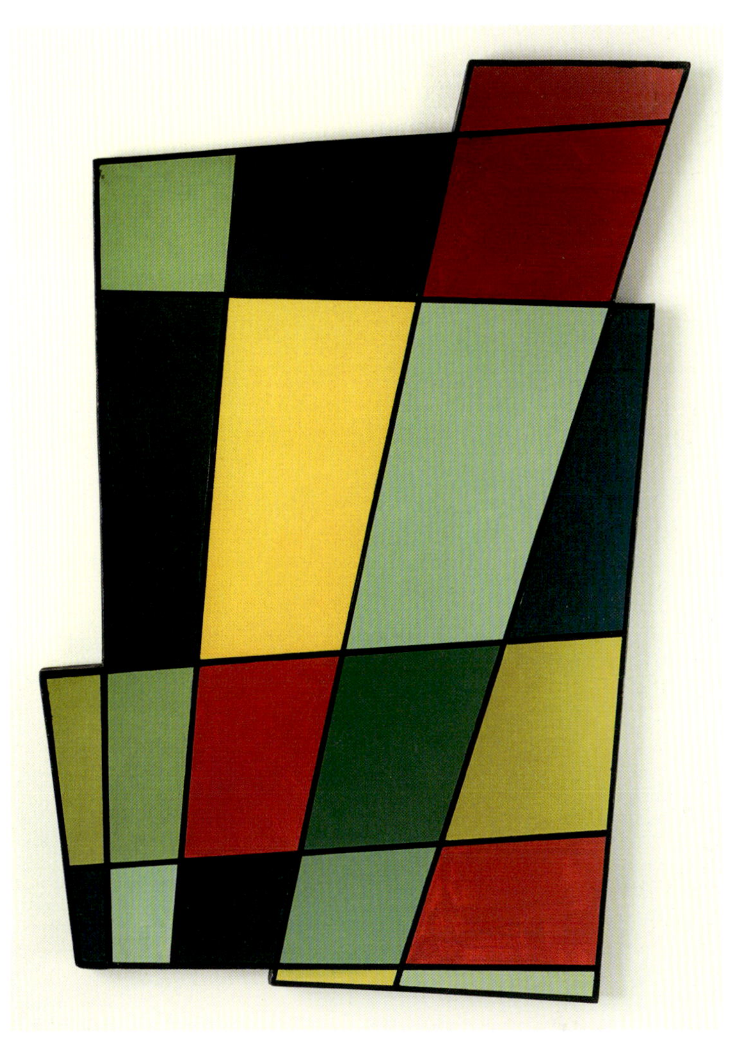

Juan Melé
Marco recortado n.º 2 [Irregular Frame No. 2], 1946

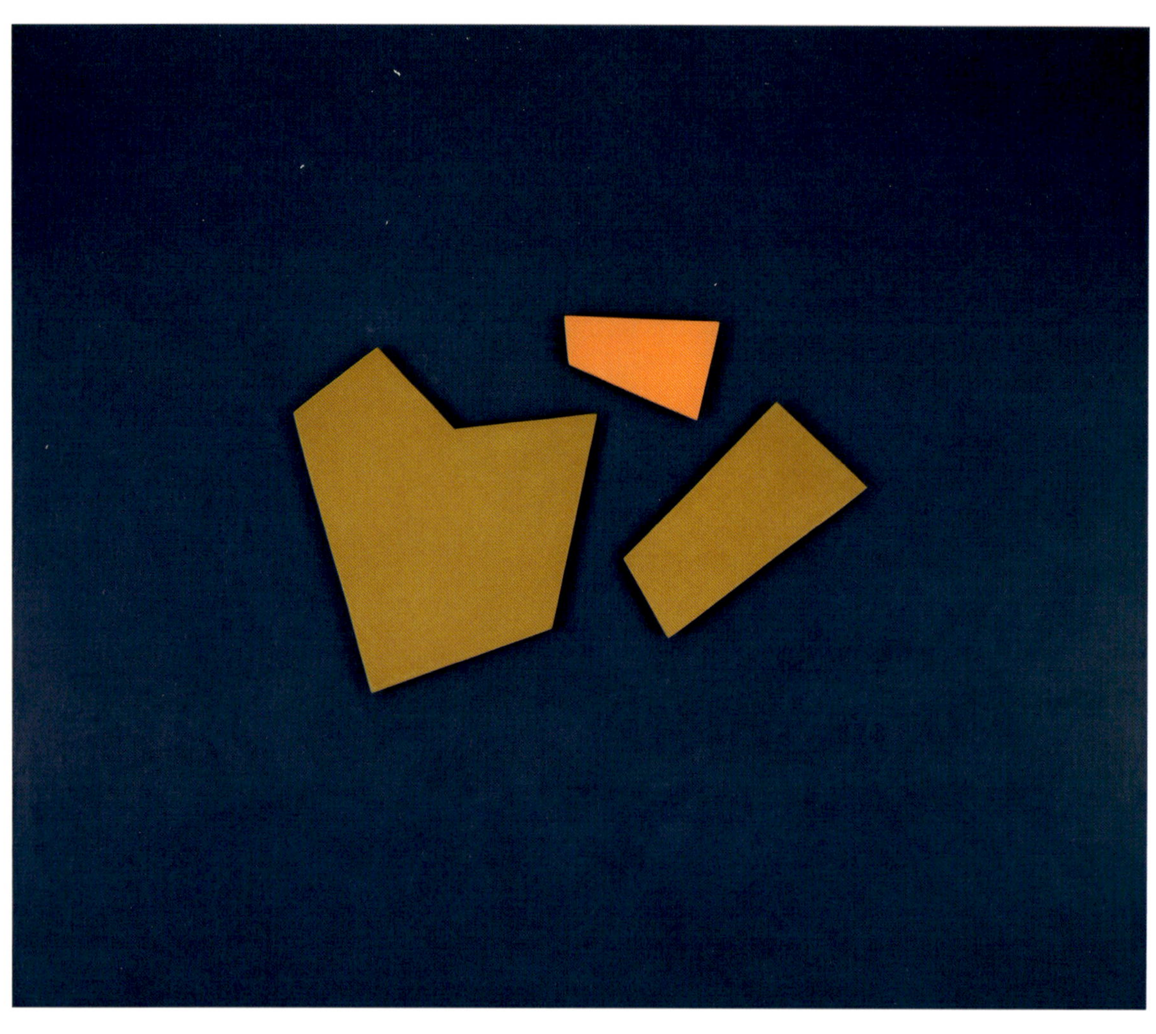

Raúl Lozza
Invención n.º 150 [Invention No. 150], 1948

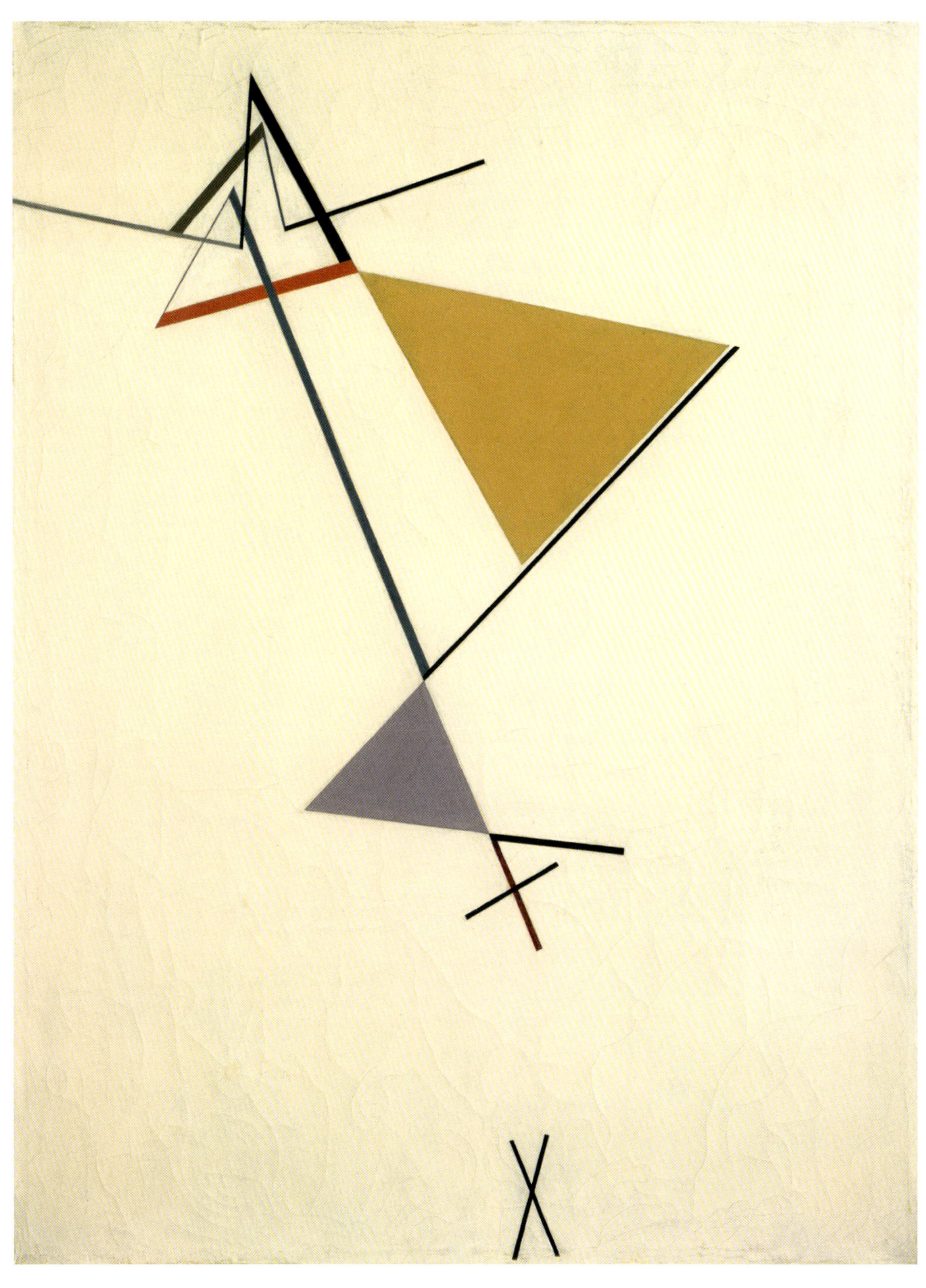

Tomás Maldonado
Desarrollo de un triángulo [Development of a Triangle], 1949

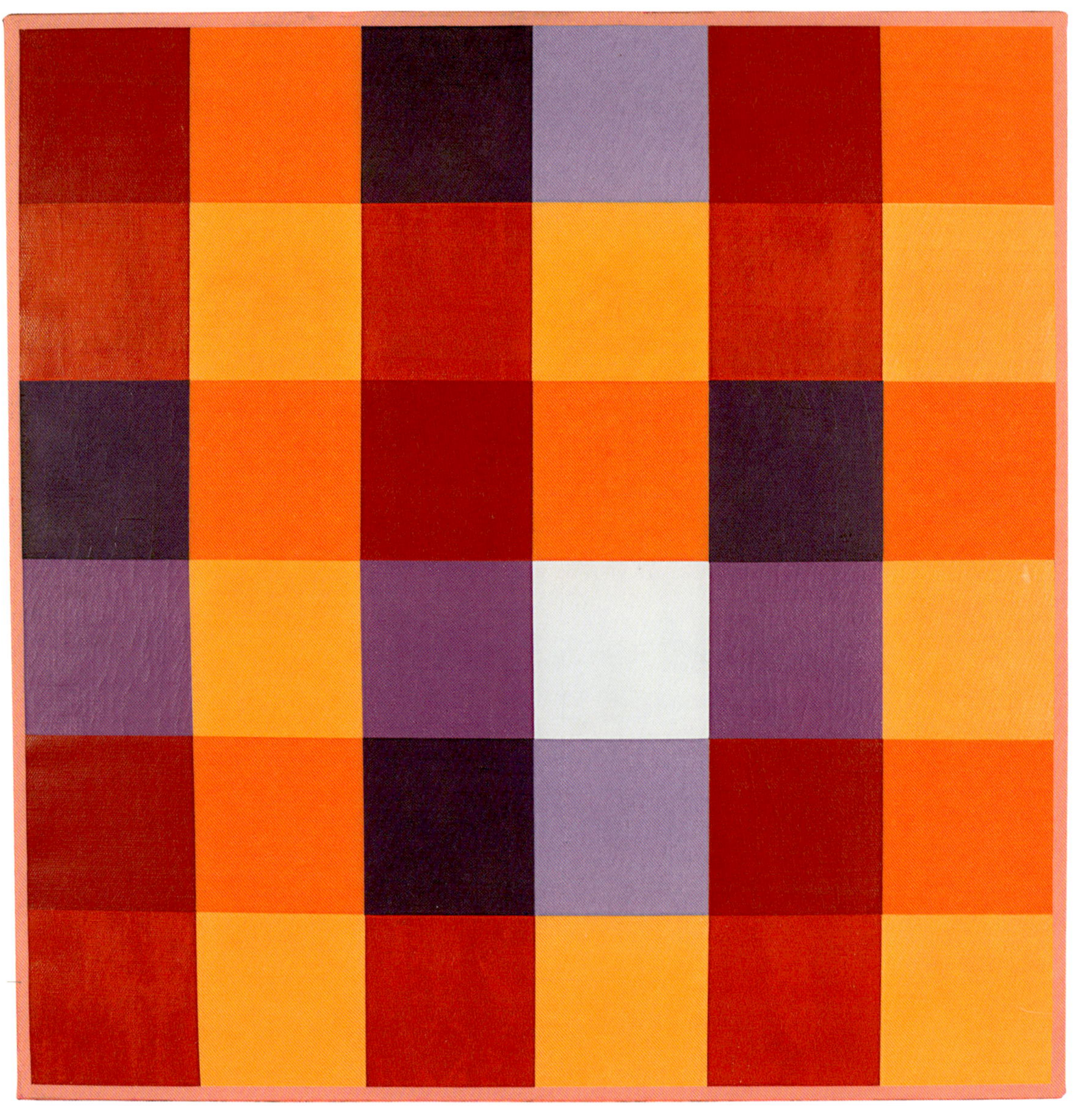

Max Bill
1–8 in vier Gruppen [1–8 in Four Groups], 1955–63

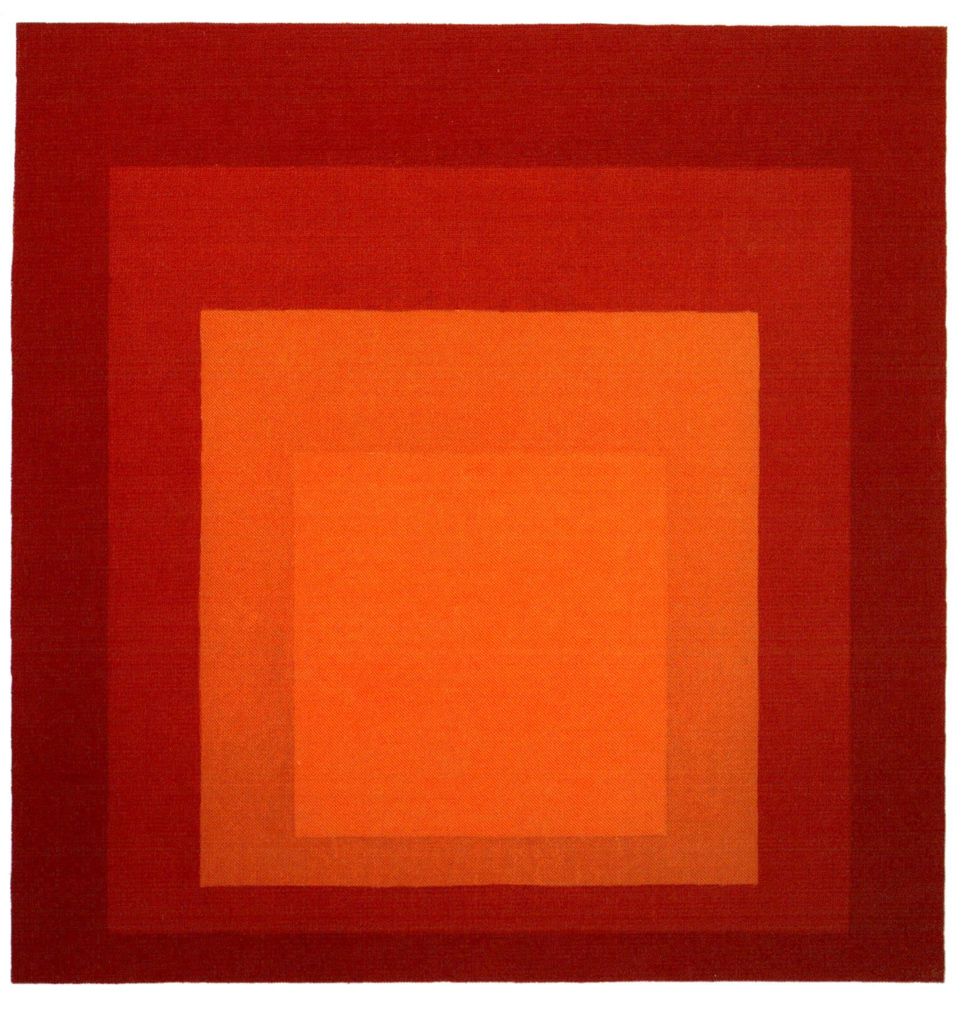

Josef Albers
Hommage au carré [Homage to the Square], 1972

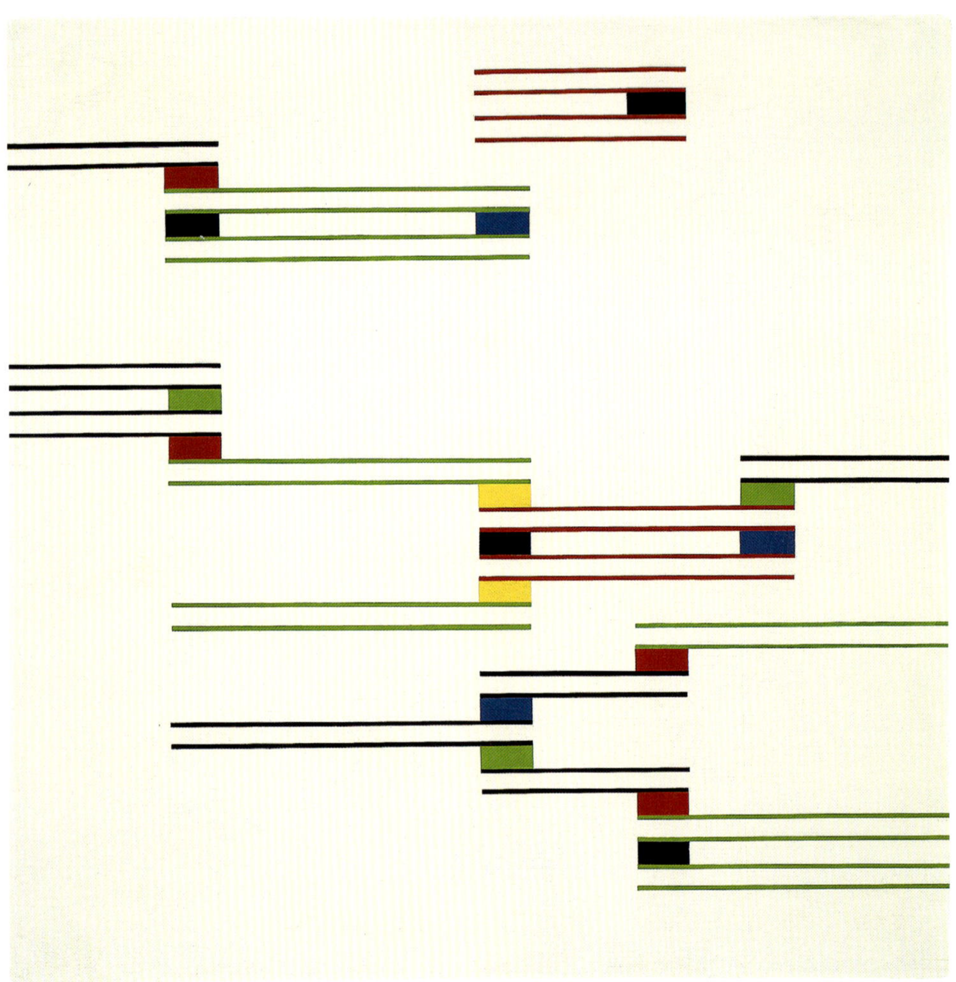

Alfredo Hlito
Ritmos cromáticos II [Chromatic Rhythms II], 1949

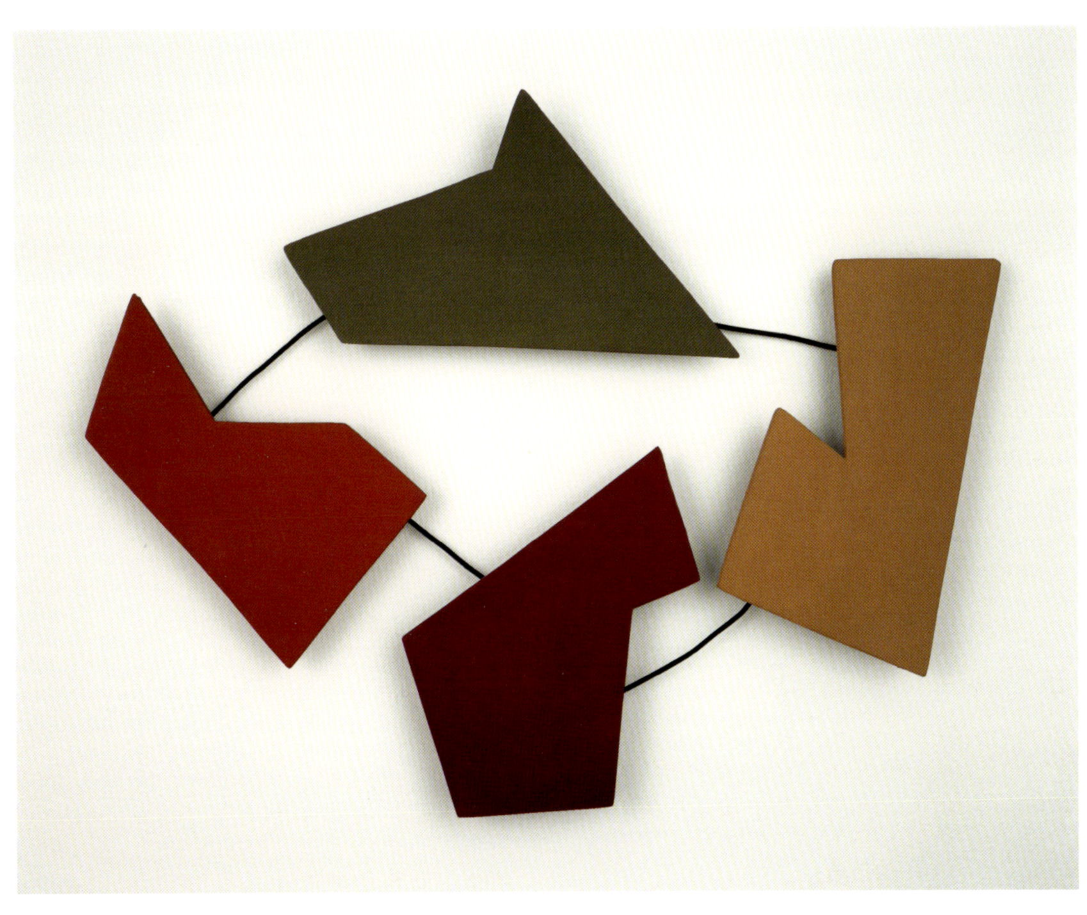

Raúl Lozza
Relieve n.º 30 [Relief No. 30], 1946

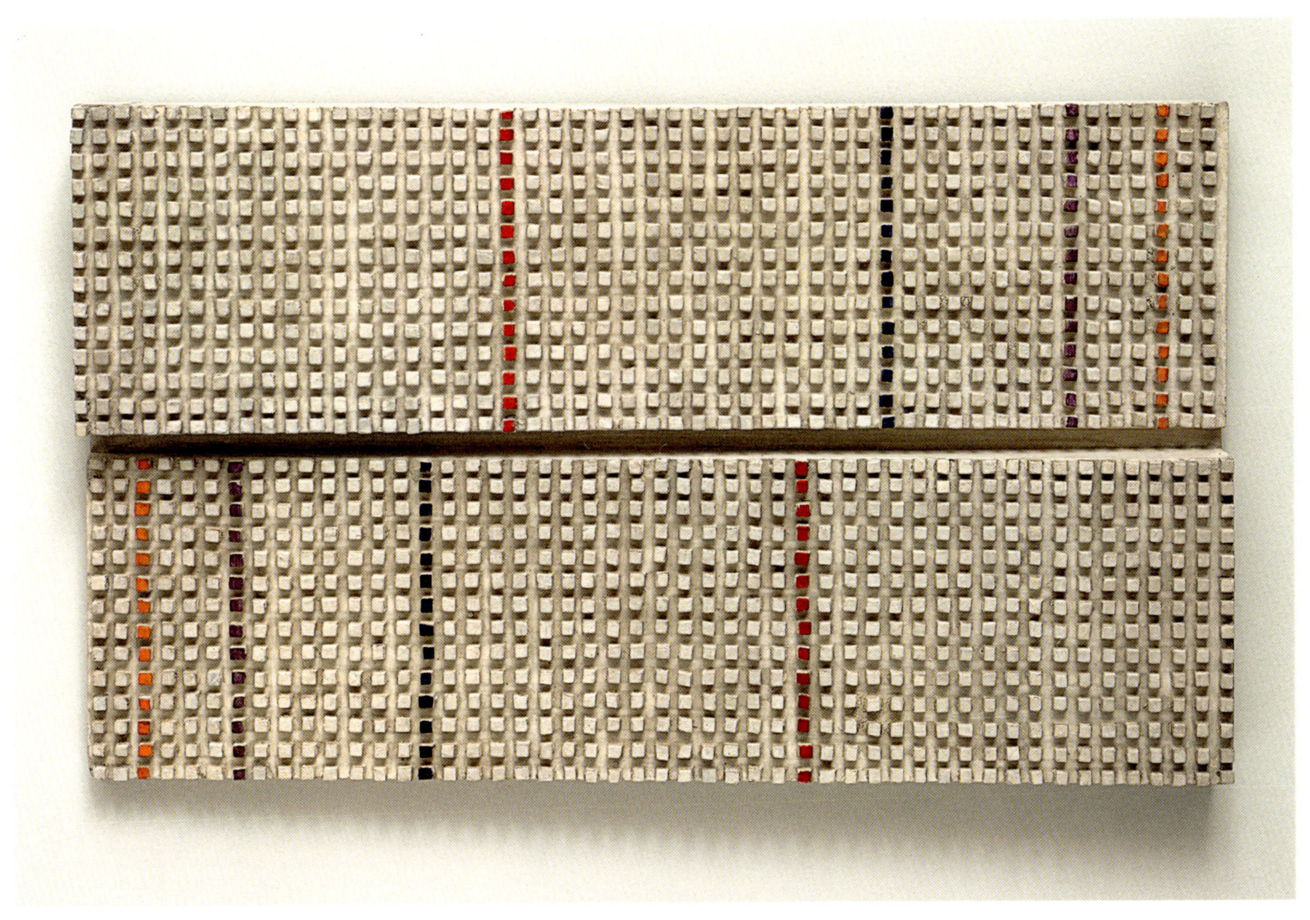

Jesús Soto
Untitled (Maquette for a mural at Universidad Central de Venezuela), 1952–53

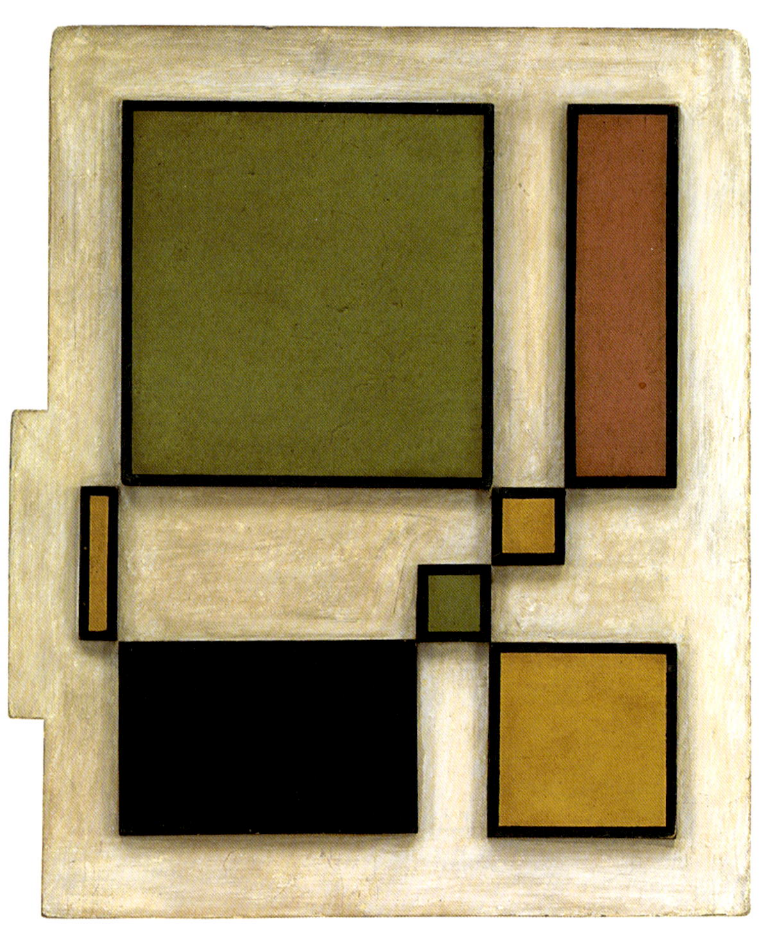

Rhod Rothfuss
Cuadrilongo amarillo [Yellow *Cuadrilongo*], 1955

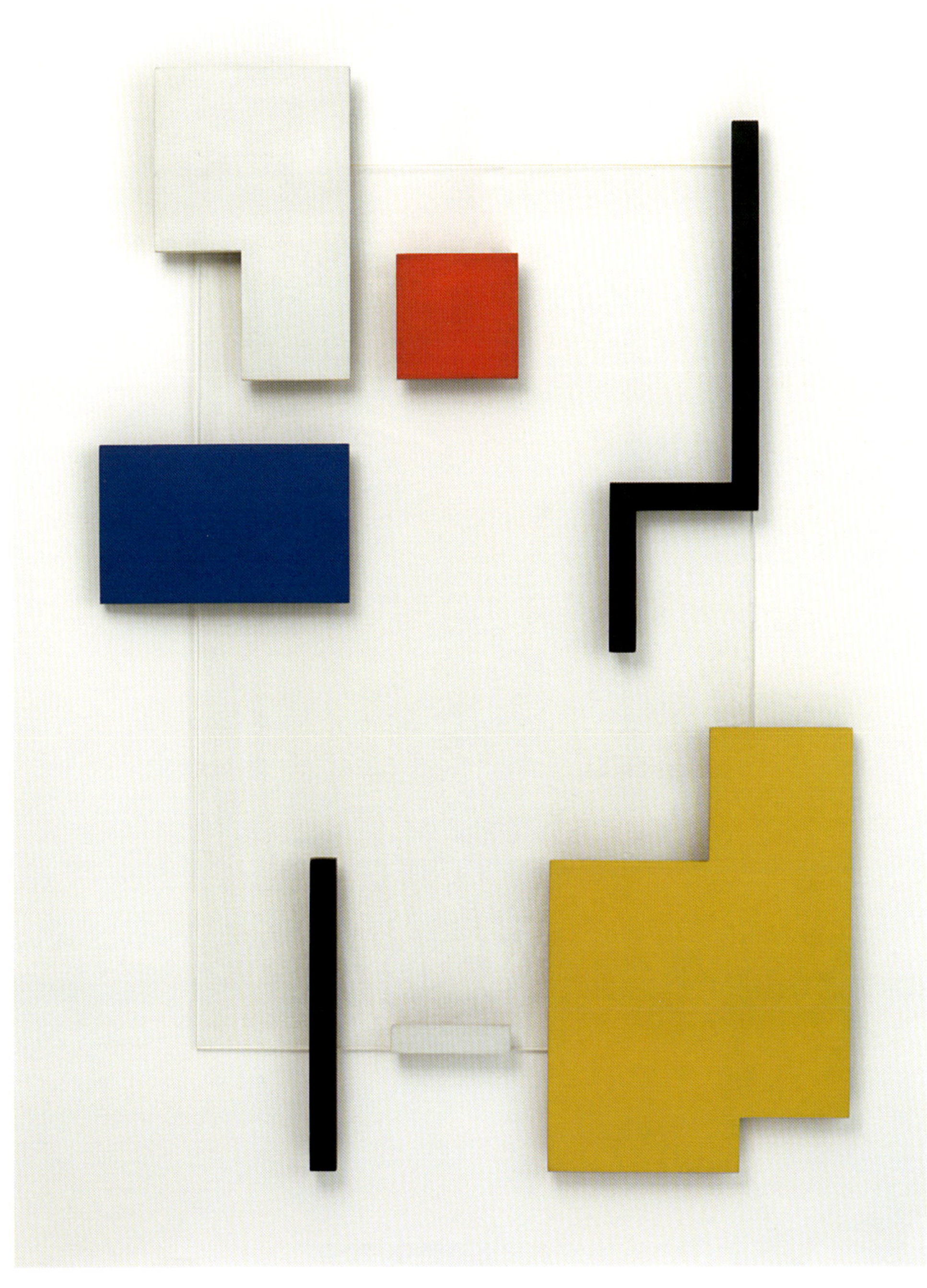

Juan Alberto Molenberg
Composición [Composition], 1946

Willys de Castro
Objeto ativo [Active Object], 1959

the intimate boundlessness
steve roden

the center of the universe

in the opening scene of bela tarr's film *werckmeister harmonies*, the main character valuska enters a pub and is instantly greeted by a friend who says softly, "show us." as both men walk to the center of the pub, the friend shouts to the other patrons, "lets make some room for valuska to show us!" after the tables are pushed off to the side, valuska places his friend in the center of the empty room. "you are the sun," he says, "the sun doesn't move…"

valuska brings another man to the center of the room, telling him that he is the earth as he sets him into motion, following a circular path around the man who is the sun. watching the two men, valuska says, "we'll have an explanation that simple folks like us can also understand about immortality…. all i ask is that you step with me into the boundlessness… where constancy… quietude… peace… and infinite emptiness reign…. just imagine that in this infinite sonorous silence… everywhere is an impenetrable darkness…. and how, at first, we don't notice the events we are witnessing…"

soon, another man is guided to the center of the room, and he begins to spin around the sun and earth as if he were following the orbit of the moon. the entire scene is a beautiful moment of choreography—humans performing the movements of planets, their synchronized motion reminiscent of those ancient wind-up children's toys of tin gears and swirling orbs called planetariums.

a few weeks ago i was standing in a museum, looking at willys de castro's 1961 *objeto ativo*, and as i moved around the object continuously as well as back and forth, i felt as if i were performing tarr's dance of the planets. after a few minutes of looking, de castro's object provoked my body into motion, so that the viewer became active, rather than the object.

confronted with de castro's object, i continued to reflect upon valuska's words, and plucked a few that felt like connective tissue… allowing me to wonder if "boundlessness" was a quality not only reserved for universes, but for a sculpture as well. i thought about the potential of "silence" as more than a mute emptiness of refusal, offering generously a confrontation between two things without distraction. lastly, there is "noticing," that moment when a gaze arrives at the humility of the object—rather than its spectacle. "noticing" is proof that "silence" can be a framing device for focus.

as i continue along these lines, d.h. lawrence, in his short poem "the white horse," offers more:

is a formal activity, while holding an object in one's hand is an intimate activity. looking at the yellow plane of *objeto ativo*, 1959–60, i notice an edge, where blue and yellow meet, and because of the nature of wet paint and human hands the yellow edge has a slightly muddy, greenish cast. this edge reveals to me that willys and i could have been friends, because it is clear that on this edge he did not use tape—this edge tells me that de castro, like agnes martin, understood that human precision and mechanical precision have very different voices.

when i was a child, my mother was aghast at my penchant for crossing out words rather than erasing them. forty or so years later, i feel the necessity as an artist to acknowledge my mistakes, accidents, and imperfections… for it would be dishonest to suggest i never make bad decisions. imperfections are human qualities, emphasizing humility to both the maker and viewer. imperfection levels the playing field, allowing the artist and viewer to converse as equals, and in this muddy green i see willys de castro's work as being imbued with humanness.

<u>in the realm of the poetic shelter</u>

in 1960 lygia clark created a sculpture titled *poetic shelter* (see p. 96), and while i love the artwork, the title tends to work on me even more. a shelter is neither a home, nor a prison. it offers protection from rain on top, but might allow water to run over one's feet. in a shelter one is generally half inside and half out, protected from some elements and open to others. in this way, a shelter can be seen as a contradiction.

so what can a poetic shelter be? perhaps a situation that protects poetry from rationalization or academic reproach.

standing in central park, i see a small area of tall red and white flowers, suggesting to me the presence of de castro's 1961 red and white *objeto ativo* that i had seen in a museum a few days earlier. thinking about de castro's work while being surrounded by nature rather than culture, his approach to the making of art feels connected to francis ponge's approach to the making of poetry. both subvert tradition through subtlety… hiding big ideas beneath humble veneers… both offer experiences that must be read via numerous "views"… and most importantly, both offer a deceptive feeling of happenstance which has been conceived and executed with an unbelievable level of focus and rigor.

when ponge says, "vegetable expression is written down once and for all. there's no way of retracting it; second thoughts are ruled out: revision is only by addenda,"[8] he could be speaking about de castro's work as much as he speaks of his own. making art and living life are continuums, and once a path has been taken, one can't help but continually find addendums along the way…

<u>graphic notations and "unit structures"</u>

de castro's tiny geometric works on paper are made up entirely of triangular forms. like architecture and music, these works use a series of similar units to form larger structures through various permutations. when i look at de castro's gouaches, i see not only a series of triangles arranged on a flat plane, but a relationship that has existed for centuries between color, shape, and sound. from the "illuminated" nature of some of the earliest musical manuscripts, to františek kupka and wassily kandinsky's interest in music, arnold schoenberg's interest in painting, and alexander

8. francis ponge, "flora and fauna," from *le parti pris des choses*, in idem, *selected poems*, ed. margaret guiton (winston-salem, NC: wake forest university press, 1984), 75.

scriabin's interest in color—the arrangement of musical notes and the arrangement of shapes and colors are in constant conversation. knowing that de castro worked with both graphics and music, it is no great stretch to see his small untitled gouaches not only in relation to abstract painting, but to the kinds of graphic notation explored by composers such as morton feldman, john cage, and cornelius cardew—allowing me to view de castro's small arrangements of forms and colors as scores, where the placement of triangular units suggest the placement of fingers on piano keys, and thus, eventually, the sounding of notes...

cecil taylor, in the notes to his seminal 1966 recording *unit structures*, wrote that "form is possibility"—reminding me of the time i saw the graphic designer jack stauffacher trying to convince a room of groaning design students that "rules equal freedom." while no two men were ever further apart in their ways and works, both exploited limitations to provoke experimentation. for these men, as well as willys de castro, there can be no possibilities without form, just as there are no freedoms without rules.

the seventeenth-century philosopher pascal wrote in his *pensees* that "the last step that reason takes is to recognize that there is an infinity of things that lie beyond it,"9 offering not only a perfect evocation of de castro's works, but a perfect user's manual on how to approach them.

9. pascal, *pensées*, trans. h. f. stewart (new york: pantheon books, 1950), 31.

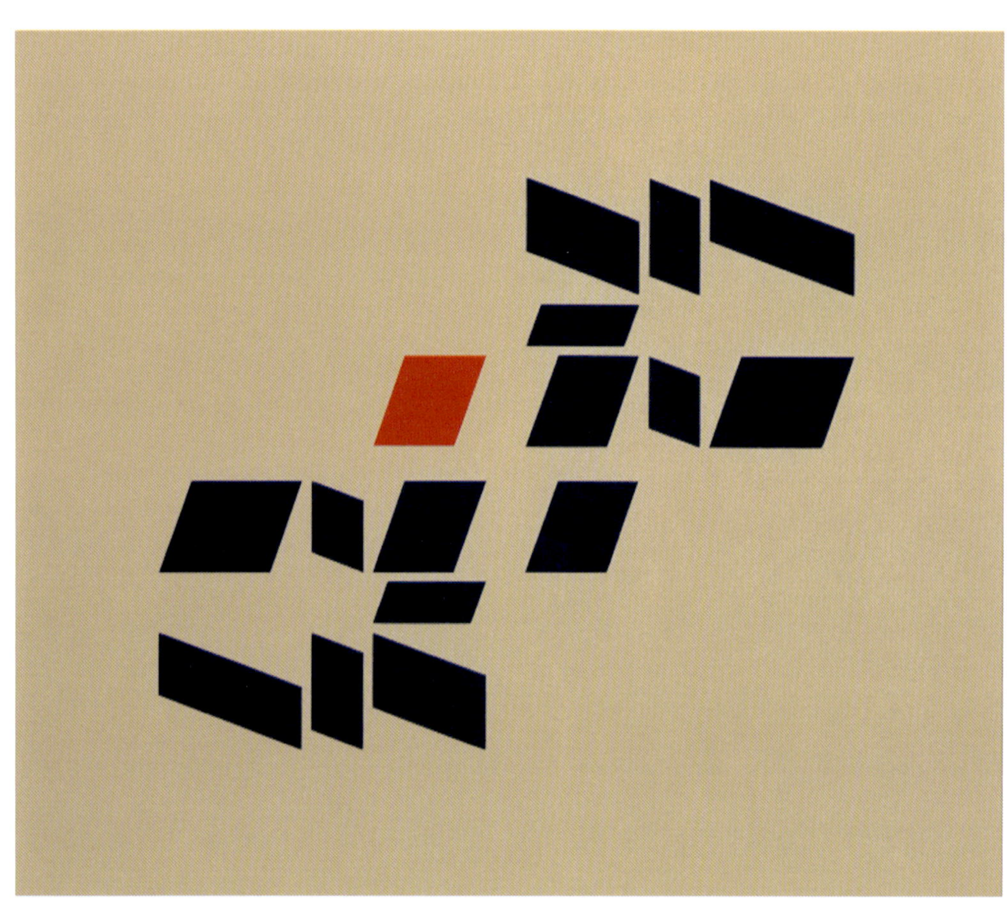

Hélio Oiticica
Metaesquema [Metascheme], 1957

A Tenebrous Exactitude
Reinaldo Laddaga

During a conversation with one of the curators of this exhibition, we agreed that when I sat down to write the text you are now reading, I would concentrate on the notion of "intentionality." It seemed fitting that I should, since the implicit mobilization of that concept is one of the fundamental operations in the framing of our experience of art. Quite simply, we approach works of art as things made by someone with some intention.[1] Somebody wants to show us something, even if what they want to show us is little more than the usefulness of executing some minimal maneuver. More usually, however, we think that what artists are trying to suggest to us is something weightier, more complex, and more important. That, we believe, is art: a place where critical questions are raised. But can questions be received as critical when they are raised through the composition of rectangles, squares, cubes, colors? Can they be critical for someone who does not form part of the *métier*, or this is an art intended just for artists?

It is possible that an exhibition like this is harder to view for the spectators we have become than exhibitions that display older works of art. Take, for instance, an exhibition of fifteenth-century portraits: we know that the artists and patrons of that time were very different men and women from us, and our admiration, if the work inspires it, is infused with the awareness of the distance between their artistic culture and ours. But what about an exhibition that shows us pieces much closer to us? When the distance is rather slight and yet, as in this case, unavoidable?

The majority of us have certainly lost a capacity that the artists in this show undoubtedly had. This is the capacity to observe the world in a certain way. Or, better said, the capacity to observe a particular fragment of the world in a certain way. In the realm of observation, there are talents that are won and lost. There are talents that are won and lost in worlds that possess definite but ever-changing attributes. Worlds, for instance, in which there are different proportions of abundance and poverty—abundance and poverty of information. We live at present in a world vastly more populated with information than the world in which these works were conceived, and a world where it is thus harder for them to generate the kind of silence they were meant to generate. Every time that they made a sculpture, a painting, the artists intended to add a new entity to the world and, at the same time, extract from the world a fragment, no matter how small, of the tapestry of decipherable things.

When we view these works today, it is difficult for us to remember that they were conceived in a spirit of violence. I refer not only to the violence implicit to the common cult of "rupture," a word much abused throughout the period. Nor am I thinking of the violence that many regarded as necessary to provoke the coming of an era when art would at last be exempt from the most servile tasks, such as provoking pleasure or representing a reality that everyone could recognize. I am referring mainly to the determination, then more or less widespread among artists, that each singular artwork

1. An excellent formulation is that proposed by Niklas Luhmann: "Observing works of art as art, rather than as worldly objects of some other type," he writes, "succeeds only if the beholder decodes the work's structure of distinctions and infers *from* this structure that the object could not have emerged spontaneously, but owes its existence instead to the intent of conveying information." Niklas Luhmann, *Art as a Social System* (Stanford: Stanford University Press, 2000), 39.

should violate the space in which it appeared, and shatter the habitual experiential framework that viewers brought to their every act of observation. This, it was thought, would induce in them a singular form of ecstasy. "What else," they thought, "can it be for? Why else bother with a practice that nobody, in any case, has any justification for or expectations of?"

A rushed examination may lead us to conclude that these are the works of artists with a simple passion for exactitude and cleanliness. But how, then, is it possible that an artist whose early work consisted of simple, colored rectangles hanging in various positions from the ceiling was at the time fascinated by the collective fervor of the samba schools? Might not the artist in question, Hélio Oiticica, have considered the rectangles to possess secret, non-obvious qualities? There is a phantasmagorical dimension to geometry, an underworld or overworld populated by geometric forms: this was a common belief among the artists whose works in this exhibition are messages perhaps more obscure than we tend to believe. That is why it is useful to reread the texts written by them and the critics of, say, half a century ago; not because we will find in them the last word on the art, but because those records of their ideas and intentions allow us to measure, even if in an incomplete way, the distance that lies between us and, perhaps, help us to tune more sharply our reception. Let us then dwell briefly on one of the best articulated positions of those years, that of the Brazilian poet and critic Ferreira Gullar, a central figure in the development of the Brazilian variant of abstract art that came to be known, partly thanks to his work, as "Neoconcrete Art." Let us linger in particular over the "Neoconcrete Manifesto," a 1959 text written in order to present (and even justify) an exhibition by the group of Rio de Janeiro artists that included, among others, Lygia Pape and Lygia Clark. The text is canonical, invariably appearing in critical anthologies on the art of the region.

The polemical objective of the manifesto is to play off one way of making geometric, abstract art to another, contrasting the manner of the "Neoconcrete" artists with that of artists who propose an impoverished interpretation of tradition. This interpretation, which Ferreira Gullar saw at the time as exemplified by Max Bill and the Ulm School, understands the artist's work as the production of compositions of appearances destined to generate visual sensations. This production, they thought, should be governed by the "objective" laws of perception. Ferreira Gullar is not convinced. Even if it were possible to successfully and comprehensively ascertain these laws, he nevertheless doubts they would be able to give us particularly useful instructions when it comes to making art. The task of the artist is not simply to invent "natural mechanisms" that might produce effects fully anticipated through calculation. Ferreira Gullar writes:

> We conceive of the work of art as neither "machine" nor "object," but rather as a quasi-corpus—that is, a being whose reality is not utterly consumed by relationships that are external to its elements. Divisible in parts via analysis, it is a being that only offers itself fully to direct phenomenological encounter. We believe that the work of art surpasses the material mechanism on which it rests, not because of any extraterritorial virtue: it surpasses it by transcending those mechanical relations (as Gestalt attempts to do) and by creating a tacit signification for itself (M. Ponty) which flourishes for the first time in the work. If we were obliged to locate something to which to compare the work of art, we would therefore not be able to find anything—not in the mechanical nor in things taken objectively; rather, like S. Langer and W. Wleidle [sic], it could only be in living organisms. That comparison, however, would still not be sufficient to express the specific reality of the aesthetic organism.[2]

2. Ferreira Gullar, "Manifesto neoconcreto," *Jornal do Brasil* (Rio de Janeiro), March 22, 1959; translated in *Ferreira Gullar in Conversation with Ariel Jiménez*, trans. Jen Hofer (New York and Caracas: Fundación Cisneros, 2012), 37. This is one of the volumes in an extraordinary series of recent conversations between critics (in the volumes I will be citing, Ariel Jiménez) and artists, which, together with the present volume, might be said to form the textual pendant to the exhibition. I shall shortly have occasion to cite them again.

Further on, he continues:

> This is because the work of art transcends mechanical space; in art the notions of cause and effect lose all validity, and notions of time, space, form, and color are integrated—by the very fact that they did not, as notions, preexist the work—in such a way that it would be impossible to speak of them as terms that might decompose. Neoconcrete art, asserting the absolute integration of those elements, works from the belief that the "geometric" vocabulary it employs can take on the expression of complex human realities, as is proved by many of the works of Mondrian, Malevich, Pevsner, Gabo, Sofía Tauber-Arp [*sic*], etc. If even these artists at times confused the concepts of mechanical form and expressive form, it is thus urgent to clarify that in the language of art, the forms that are called geometric lose the objective character of geometry in order to become a vehicle of imagination. Gestalt, even as a rationalist psychology, is also insufficient as a way to understand the phenomenon that dissolves space and form as realities that were originally determinable and presents them as time—as a spatialization of the work. By spatialization of the work we might understand the idea that the work is always in a process of making itself present, is always commencing anew the impulse that generated it and of which it was already the origin.[3]

Let us remove the theory from this passage. Let us forget the names of the philosophers Ferreira Gullar invokes in his support, infinitely more familiar to the readers the writer had in mind, his contemporaries, than they are to us. What is left? The description of an experience. The experience is that of someone observing something they know to be just a composition of materials, colors, and lines, an object that hangs from the wall or is placed on a pedestal, a material arrangement and nothing more, yet which seems all the same to be in another dimension, entirely quiet and, at the same time, ever-changing. Motionless and in transformation: this combination is one the critic finds fascinating (and it cannot be ruled out that this is so because it turns out the critic was and is a poet: the poetry published around that time by José Lezama Lima, Jorge Luis Borges, and João Cabral de Melo Neto often employs similar metaphors).

How is it possible for an inert object to present itself as if it were in perpetual flux? It happens when the object emerges "by creating a tacit signification for itself which flourishes for the first time in the work." Tacit? Yes, because it is insinuated but not fully stated. Something is being said through the mediation of that material configuration we confront in a gallery, a hall, a museum, but that something is incommensurable with the horizon established in the world where it happens to appear, so that we can never conclude the impulse we are incited to begin, and the certainty of that "never" is a component of the experience. The artwork presents itself as an expression of something we are unable to determine. What we observe, therefore, has the form of a promise whose fulfillment is insistently postponed, a pact the clauses of which are never fully articulated. It is thus that the work is "spatialized."

This is one of its ways of attracting us and capturing our attention. Another way to attract us is suggested by Ferreira Gullar when he writes that in the type of work he finds desirable, "notions of time, space, form, and color are integrated—by the very fact that they did not, as notions, preexist the work—in such a way that it would be impossible to speak of them as terms that might decompose." The work possesses a very high degree of integration: its parts cannot be separated. They are not even parts in the usual sense of the word: they did not exist before the work. "As notions," the writer adds as clarification. What can that mean? That a particular quality of blue or red, a basic profile like that of a circle or a square, a common format like that of the rectangular canvas, are what they are in each case—this color, this profile, this format—precisely because they are parts of this combination that nobody (not even the artist) could have anticipated, and which is an utter novelty. The red is the red it is because it is the red of this square, which is the square it is because it stands in such and such a relation to the edges of a canvas, which is what it is because it houses this red square. Changing just one of the components would modify the nature of all the others, so much so that we have the impression when perceiving it that we have never seen such things before: this color that we would almost prefer not to call "red," this form we are tempted not to call "square."

Integration, then. Fanatical integration. The observer of a painting, if the work behaves (as the artist would like), is a fanatic. This word occurs to me because there is an excellent description of the kind of experience that motivates Ferreira Gullar's text in an earlier piece of writing, "Narrative Art and Magic" by Jorge Luis Borges. "Magic," says Borges:

> is not the contradiction of the law of cause and effect but its crown, or nightmare. The miraculous is no less strange in that world than it is in the world of astronomers. All of the laws of nature as well as those of imagination govern it. To the superstitious mind, there is a necessary link not only between a gunshot and a corpse but between a corpse and a tortured wax image, or the prophetic smashing of a mirror, or spilled salt, thirteen people ominously seated at the same table.

> This dangerous connection, this frenzied and clearly defined cause and effect, also holds good in the novel. Saracen historians, whose writings are the source of Jose Antonio Conde's *Historia de la dominación de los árabes en España*, do not write of a king or caliph that he died, but that "He was taken to the rewards and gifts," or that "He passed into the mercy of the All-Powerful," or that "He awaited his fate so many years, so many moons, and so many days." This fear that a terrible event may be brought on by its mere mention is out of place or pointless in the overwhelming disorder of the real world, though not in a novel, which should be a rigorous scheme of attentions, echoes, and affinities. Every episode in a painstaking piece of fiction prefigures something still to come. Thus, in one of Chesterton's phantasmagorias, a man suddenly shoves a stranger out of the road to save him from an oncoming truck, and this necessary but alarming violence foreshadows the first man's later act of declaring the other man insane so that he may not be hanged for a murder. In another Chesterton story, a vast and dangerous conspiracy consisting of a single man (aided by false beards, masks, and aliases) is heralded with tenebrous exactitude by the lines:

> *As all stars shrivel in the single sun,*
> *The words are many but The Word is one.*

> which is later deciphered, with a permutation of capitals:

> *The words are many, but the word is One.*[4]

"The words are many, but the word is One": the parts (the quasi-parts) of the object are many, but the artwork is One, perfectly integrated, so that the slightest change in its composition changes the nature of the whole. In the world that constitutes the background to our everyday actions, where the position, let's say, of our kitchen chairs with respect to the table they surround does not seem particularly worthy to us of interpretation: things are arranged the way they are for no particular reason. But this is not the case for the one who believes in magic. Or, for that matter, the detective. We know the affinity Borges (and not only him) thought to exist between the reader and the

4. Jorge Luis Borges. "Narrative Art and Magic," in *Borges: A Reader; A Selection from the Writings of Jorge Luis Borges*, ed. Emir Rodríguez Monegal and Alastair Reid (New York: Dutton, 1981), 37–38; originally published in Spanish as "El arte narrativo y la magia," in *Discusión* (Buenos Aires: Gleizer, 1932). The translation has been slightly modified.

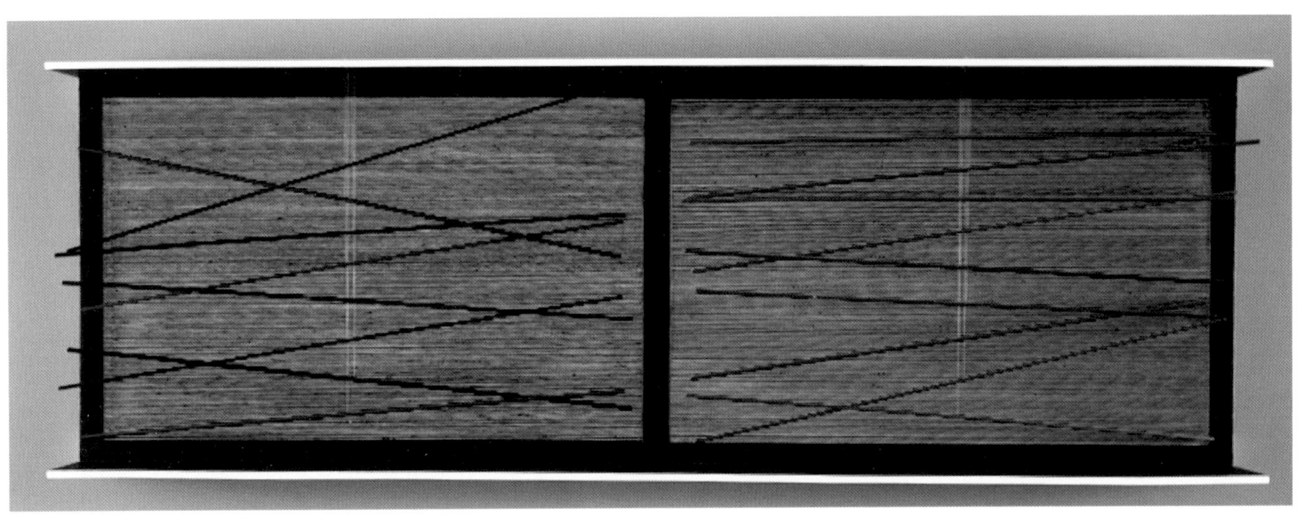

Jesús Soto
Baguettes rouges et noires [Red and Black Rods], 1964

detective. If there had been a crime in our kitchen, the detective would approach its arrangement as a stage setting populated with clues. A chair is in the exact position it is in because the other objects are in the positions that they occupy, and each one of them tells us something of what we want to discover.

Ferreira Gullar's language is above all that of phenomenology. We, on the other hand, are more likely to feel inclined to use that of information theory. In these terms, the work of art is a point of extremely high information density. The information is generated at the points where things make contact, in the relations between the parts when the parts cannot be other than what they are without modifying the nature of the whole. And works of art ("The words are many, but the word is One") are objects that render visible an infinity of relations among their components. Consider some of the compositions in wire, metal, and wood that were produced by Jesús Soto around 1960. If someone asked us to do it, we could probably count the number of lines and filaments that comprise them. But what about the number of relations between those components? No. The work confronts us with a perpetually full and always changing virtual entity that, even if it exists by virtue of the composition of the materials of the object that is its condition, seems like something detached.

"Vibration" is the word used by Jesús Soto to describe what his compositions are supposed to generate, and the word, in Soto's discourse, is insistently accompanied by another expression: "spatial ambiguity." The aim of his art, he tells us, is to compose phenomena whose decisive character is that while appearing in such and such a place, they do not let us determine completely what their exact relationship with the place in question is. In an interview with Ariel Jiménez, Soto spoke of the work of those years: "My intention," Soto says, "was to put color in a state of motion, not as chromatic harmony, which is another academic vestige that I was running away from, just as I ran from composition and balance. What I was looking for was and is a long way from the achievement of a beautiful harmony of colors. I only want to achieve those combinations where the color has the greatest vibratory force, and where the spatial ambiguity resulting from its superimpositions is evident."[5] In the same interview, a few pages further on, Soto talks about *Trapecio* (Trapeze), 1957, saying: "There you get quite a strange situation. When you confront this picture, you feel as if it were breathing. It expands and contracts like an accordion. It's an essential work, and maybe some day I'll study the challenges it poses me in depth."[6]

Is it necessary to underline that the same elements are found here as in Ferreira Gullar's text? An entity that seems alive detaches itself from the space in which it appears (and, let us add, this occurs in a cultural context where biological metaphors are widespread and prevalent). The movement is oscillatory, not a form of displacement but of growth. That movement generates a form of beauty, not the beauty of a well-composed form but that of a singular intensity. Similar figures are found in an account by Carlos Cruz-Diez of the origin of his own work. Cruz-Diez tells us his work was unleashed the moment he discovered that his mission as a visual artist was to create, through the arrangement of material parts, phenomena that would detach themselves from the spaces they appeared in. In this narrative, a painful indecisiveness weighing on the artist is resolved when he is designing a catalogue for the New York Philharmonic. By placing a red page next to a white page, he finds that the white page is tinged with pink, and that the levels of intensity of this pulsating color vary with the distance between the pages. He continues:

> At that moment I realized that a piece like *Doble animación del plano* could only be executed in space, and only by working with reflected light. At that time I called this

5. *Jesús Soto in Conversation with Ariel Jiménez* (New York and Caracas: Fundación Cisneros, 2011), 161.

6. Ibid., 166.

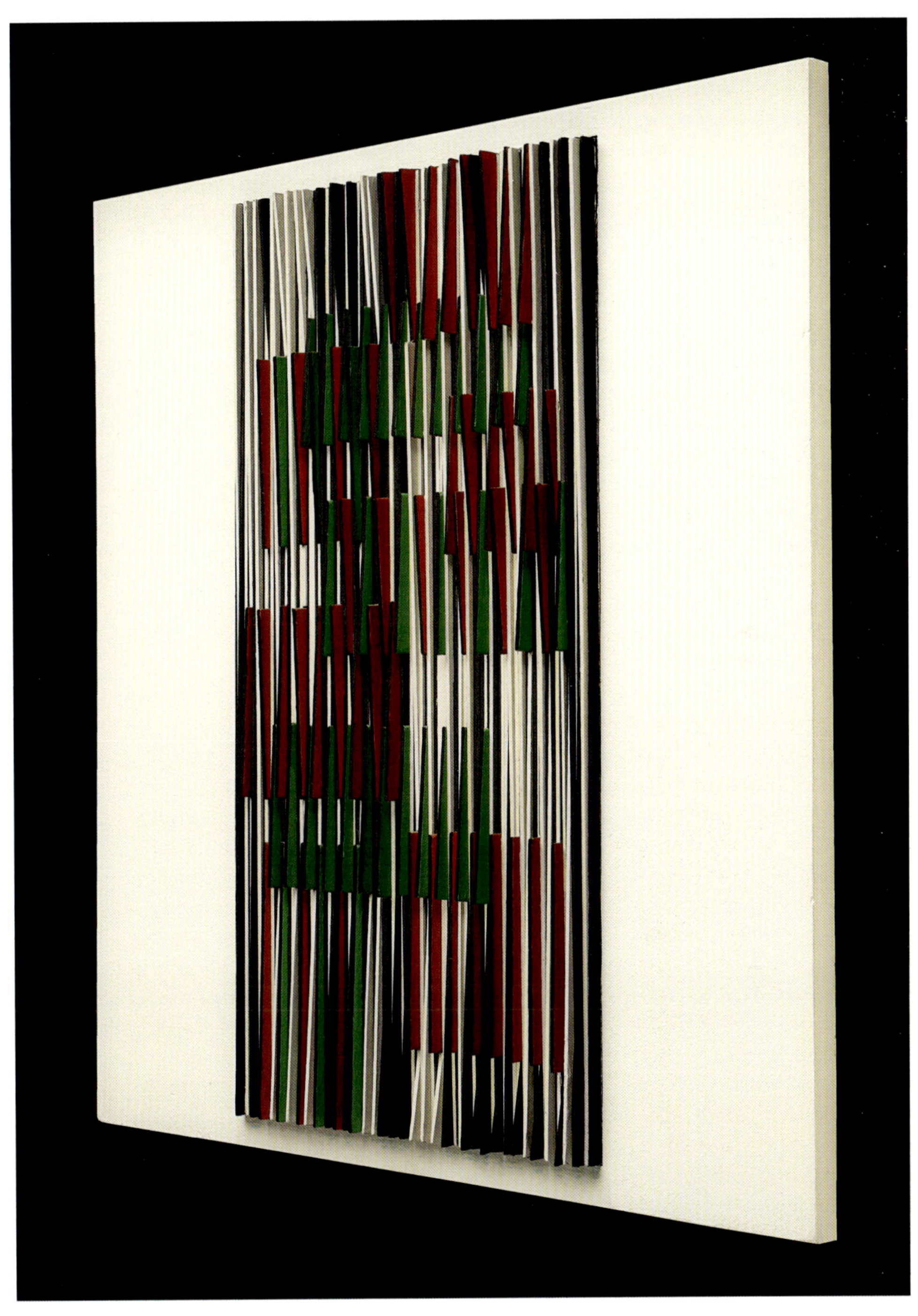

Carlos Cruz-Diez
Physichromie No. 6, 1960
Caseine on board on wood, 74.6 x 74.6 x 5.1 cm
Fundación Cruz-Diez (Not in exhibition)

an "indirect reading" because the color is radiated rather than produced on the support. If that color radiation was handled properly, the color would only be perceived in space and not on the painted surface. This was hardly an extraordinary observation, but it did give me the solution I was looking for so that I could completely saturate the space with color, just as the valley of Caracas is saturated when the sky is bathed in the colors of the sunset. This is what I achieved directly afterward, with my *Physichromies*.[7]

Commenting afterwards on these *physichromies*, he says:

I have always talked about realities, not to imitate them but to provoke them. The *Physichromies* are something I invented so that I might express myself with the joy of a painter in action, of painting in the process of being created, stripped of traditional concepts and techniques. In traditional painting, the artist's work instantly becomes part of the past, and what the viewer contemplates and deciphers is an action that exists in the past. The color that reaches the viewer's gaze "was painted," is frozen in time. The *Physichromies*, on the other hand, force us to deal with an event of color in the process of occurring in the moment, without past or future. But I am definitely a painter. You could say that a *Physichromie* contains painting in its purest form. All the effects and pleasures of painting are there: the harmonies, the glazing, the transparencies, even though it has nothing to do with the painting of the past.[8]

Here, once again, is the declaration of a fundamental intention: the objective of the painter's actions is to construct an object that, once situated, gives rise to the unfolding of a process. The *painter*, he said, because the means are those of painting, and one of the objectives is clearly to produce painting that exhibits what painting and nothing but painting can do. This art, after all, belongs to a period that celebrated with peculiar enthusiasm the figure of the expert, the technician, the man or woman who controls the materials and techniques proper to the area where they have resolved to concentrate their energies. What can a painter do that only a painter can do?

He or she can show what objects usually hide. Or rather, show what in our daily dealings with objects we are liable to ignore: that the stability of the things we move among is a surface effect, and that there are whirlwinds, sometimes slow and sometimes fast, lodged inside everything. That the world passes. And if something ought to remain with us from the observation of one or another of these nameless things artists propose to us, it is an increased ability to observe the constant passage of the world "in the process of occurring in the moment, without past or future." To see, in the things that exist, their existence.

This is the way the strongest and most ambitious artists of the period covered by this exhibition thought of the connection between a specialized practice—which proposes exploring the properties of a particular manner of proceeding, the explicit or tacit knowledge that gives its particular identity to a given discipline (Ferreira Gullar refers to its "language")—and the type of universal message that art in the conditions of modernity regards as its ultimate obligation and the thing that gives it its exalted nature. By doing nothing but paint, painters communicate something of capital importance to the viewer: that the world exists. They reveal the presence that insists in the nucleus of the present.

I do not say that all of the artists in the exhibition had this ambition, but many of them did. And most of them moreover resisted the temptation in the long run, if not

7. *Carlos Cruz-Diez in Conversation with Ariel Jiménez* (New York and Caracas: Fundación Cisneros, 2010), 52–53.

8. Ibid., 53.

immediately, to abandon painting, sculpture, drawing, and the disciplines others would call "traditional," a temptation that became very strong from the sixties on. Oiticica and Clark are, of course, the great exceptions. That is why it is interesting, before concluding, to read what Ferreira Gullar has to say about the late work of these two Brazilians:

> So the Neoconcrete proposition takes as its starting point an aesthetic experimentation born out of Cubism and is, to some extent, the final consequence of that process. The problem is that the experiences of Neoconcretism would later unleash the destruction of art. The things Lygia Clark was doing at the end of her life are perhaps a new form of therapy, as she said, but they don't have much to do with art. And what is Hélio Oiticica's much-celebrated *parangolé*? It's simply an element present in any samba school, which he took and imitated, without ever reaching any great expressive component, from the point of view of artistic creation. These examples represent the end of a process, and wind up being an exclusively sensory exercise.[9]

This "end of a process" is also the limit of the main body of the exhibition. The overwhelming majority of the pieces included were made in the belief or confidence that art's capacity to induce a decisive experience (even the most decisive experience of all, the experience that the world passes) is linked to a production aimed at making material structures that are more or less fixed, or whose movement is very restricted (forms oscillating with the air, rods moved by the viewers). Of course, this capacity depends on the powers of the observer, and especially on the power of the observer to place himself or herself at a distance from the world, in silence, until the phenomenon emerges in front of him or her in all its "spatial ambiguity." The ambition of these artists was immense. They had the highest expectations. They expected to reach viewers who would consecrate themselves (the religious resonances are quite apt) to the fulfillment of their role in the process with a devotion that present-day artists are unlikely ever to command. The placidity of spatial distributions, the rectangles, squares, tangents, and curves in these pieces, which sometimes seem to result from sheer calculation, should not make us forget that many of these paintings, sculptures, and objects were meant to induce a particular form of ecstasy. A triangle (no, what arises, in particular circumstances, from a triangle) raised to the power of mystery.

Is this superstition? Perhaps. But if we wanted to view this exhibition in such a way that the potentialities it contains will exhibit themselves and reach their fullest dimension, we should (we must) recover, if only for an instant, certain superstitions: there is a spectral dimension to geometry. In certain conditions, its exactitude is tenebrous. This is what was being explored.

9. *Ferreira Gullar in Conversation with Ariel Jiménez*, 44.

ruptura

charroux — cordeiro — de barros — fejer — haar — sacilotto — wladyslaw

a arte antiga foi grande, quando foi inteligente.
contudo, a nossa inteligência não pode ser a de Leonardo.
a história deu um salto qualitativo:

não há mais continuidade!

então nós distinguimos

- os que criam formas novas de princípios velhos.
- os que criam formas novas de princípios novos.

por que?

o naturalismo científico da renascença — o método para representar o mundo exterior (três dimensões) sôbre um plano (duas dimensões) — esgotou a sua tarefa histórica.

foi a crise   foi a renovação

hoje o novo pode ser diferenciado
precisamente do velho. nós rompemos com o velho por isto afirmamos:

é o velho

- tôdas as variedades e hibridações do naturalismo;
- a mera negação do naturalismo, isto é, o naturalismo "errado" das crianças, dos loucos, dos "primitivos" dos expressionistas, dos surrealistas, etc. . . . ;
- o não-figurativismo hedonista, produto do gôsto gratuito, que busca a mera excitação do prazer ou do desprazer.

é o novo

- as expressões baseadas nos novos princípios artísticos;
- tôdas as experiências que tendem à renovação dos valores essenciais da arte visual (espaço-tempo, movimento, e matéria);
- a intuição artística dotada de princípios claros e inteligentes e de grandes possibilidades de desenvolvimento prático;
- conferir à arte um lugar definido no quadro do trabalho espiritual contemporâneo, considerando-a um meio de conhecimento deduzível de conceitos, situando-a acima da opinião, exigindo para o seu juízo conhecimento prévio.

arte moderna não é ignorância, nós somos contra a ignorância.

Lothar Charoux, Waldemar Cordeiro, Geraldo de Barros, Luiz Sacilotto, and others, "Manifiesto Ruptura" [Rupture Manifesto], São Paulo, 1952. Published on the occasion of the first Grupo Ruptura exhibition at the Museu de Arte Moderna de São Paulo, 1952

Illusion

"We conceive of the work of art as neither 'machine' nor 'object,' but rather as a quasi-corpus—that is, a being whose reality is not utterly consumed by relationships that are external to its elements. Divisible in parts via analysis, it is a being that only offers itself fully to direct phenomenological encounter."

Neoconcrete Manifesto

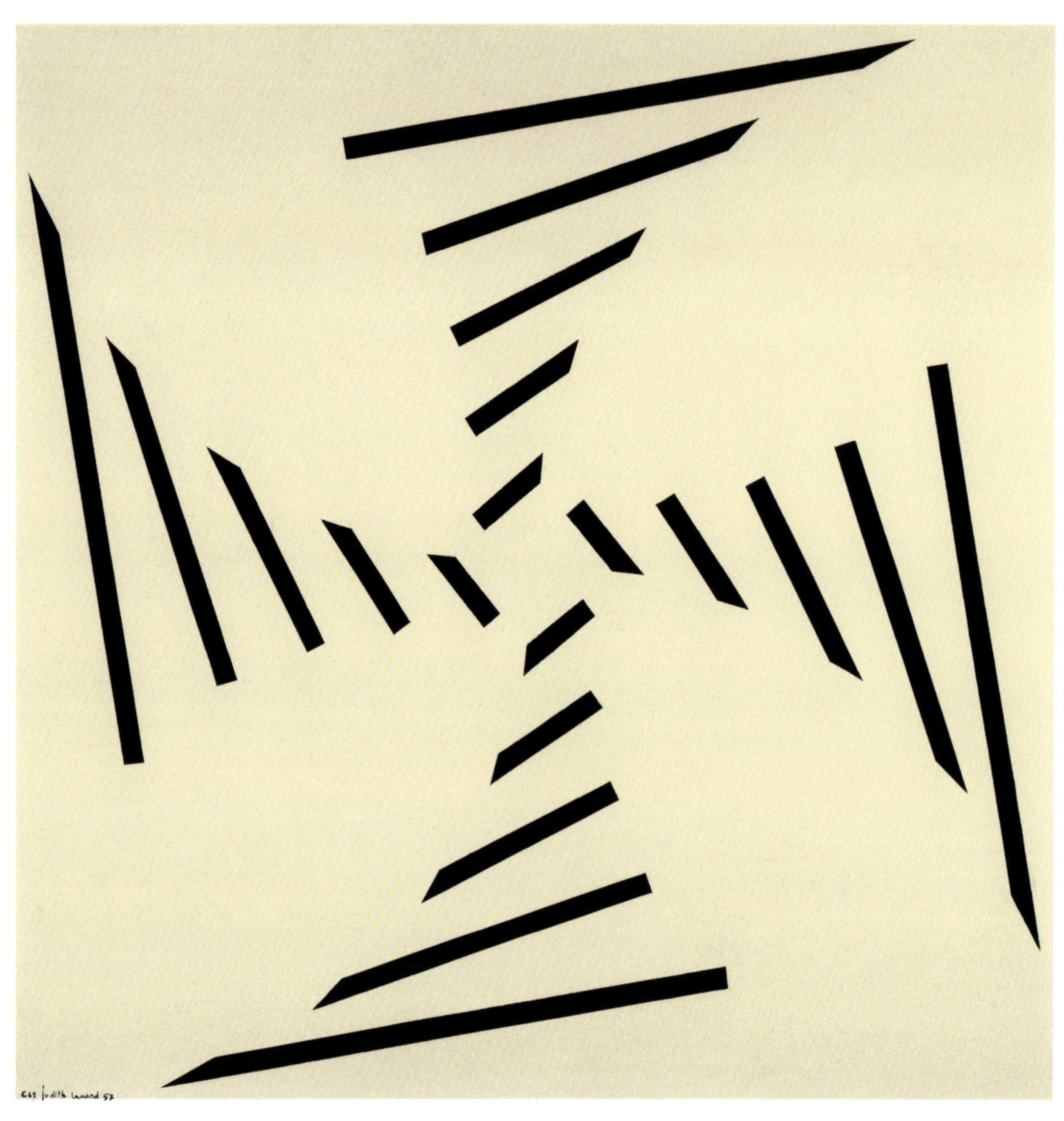

Judith Lauand
Concreto 61 [Concrete 61], 1957

64

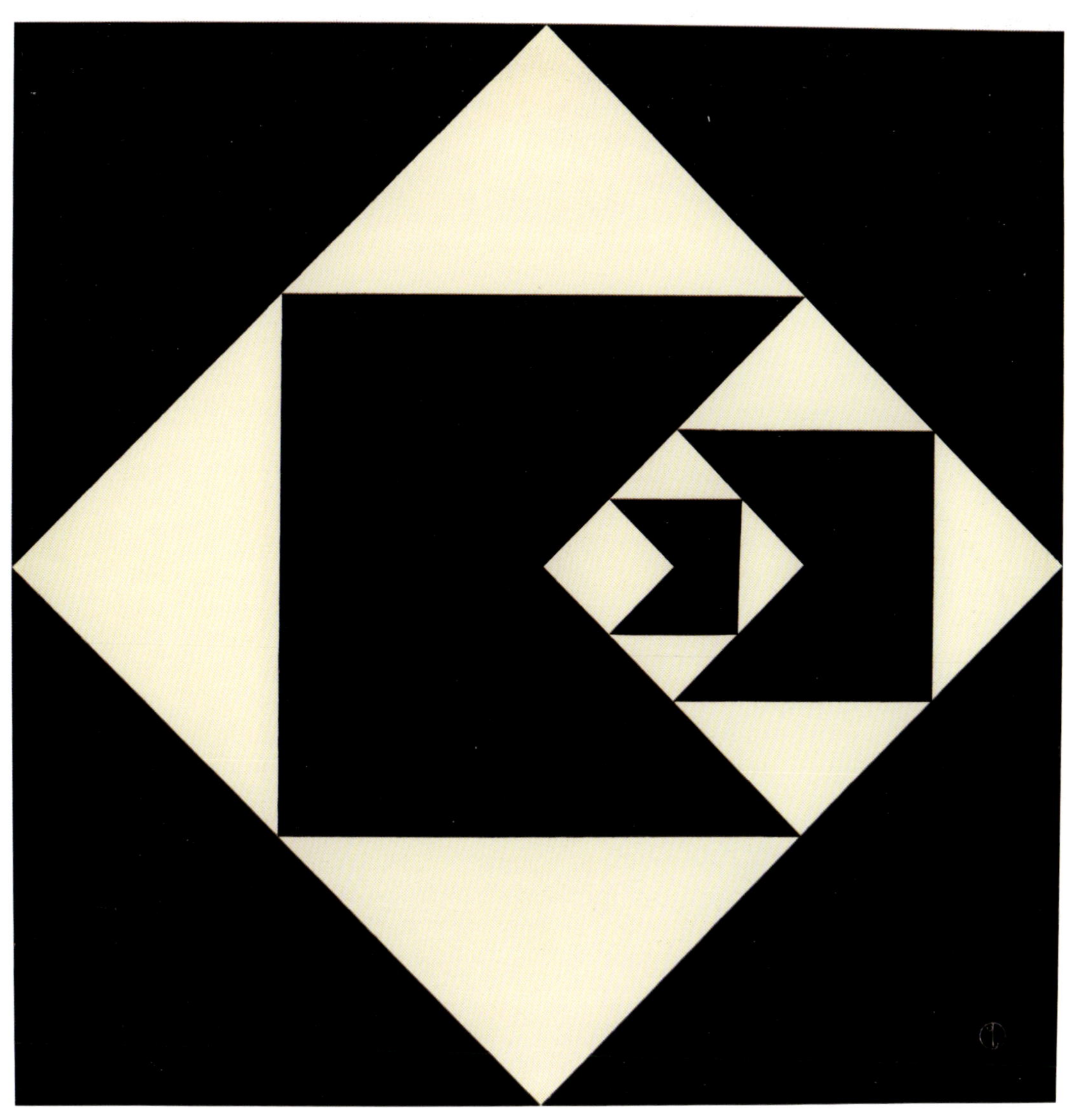

Geraldo de Barros
Função diagonal [Diagonal Function], 1952

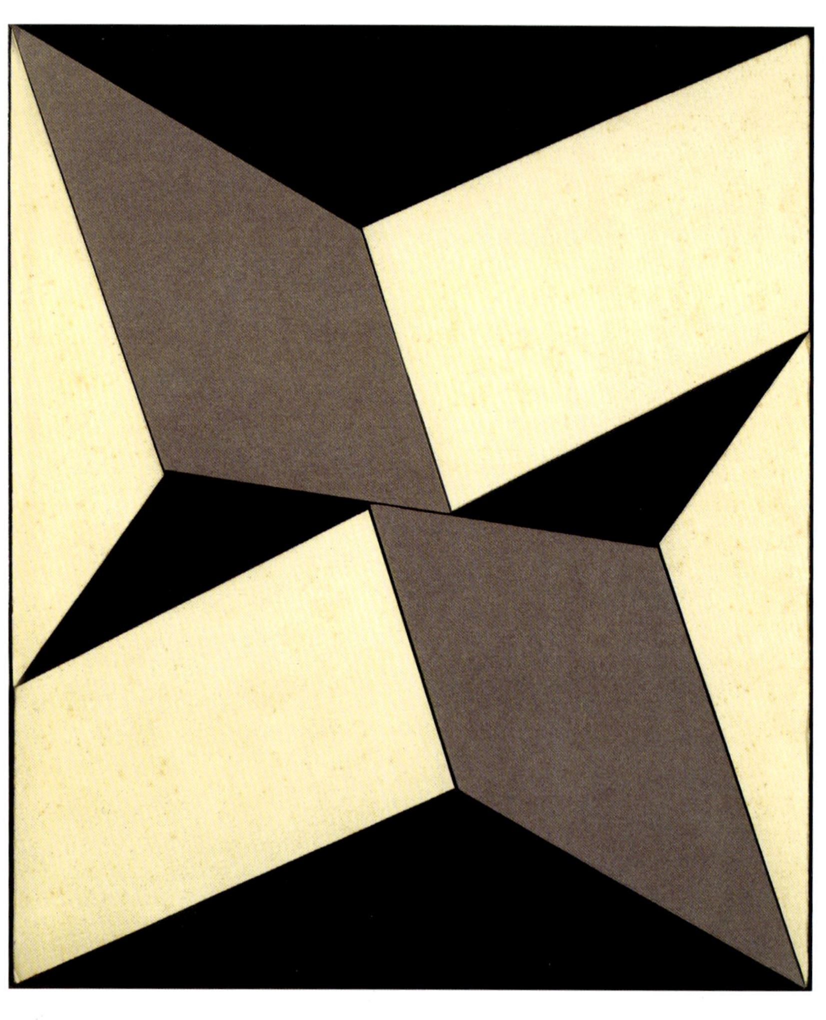

Lygia Clark
Estudo para plano em superfície moduláda [Plane on Modulated Surface (Study)], 1957

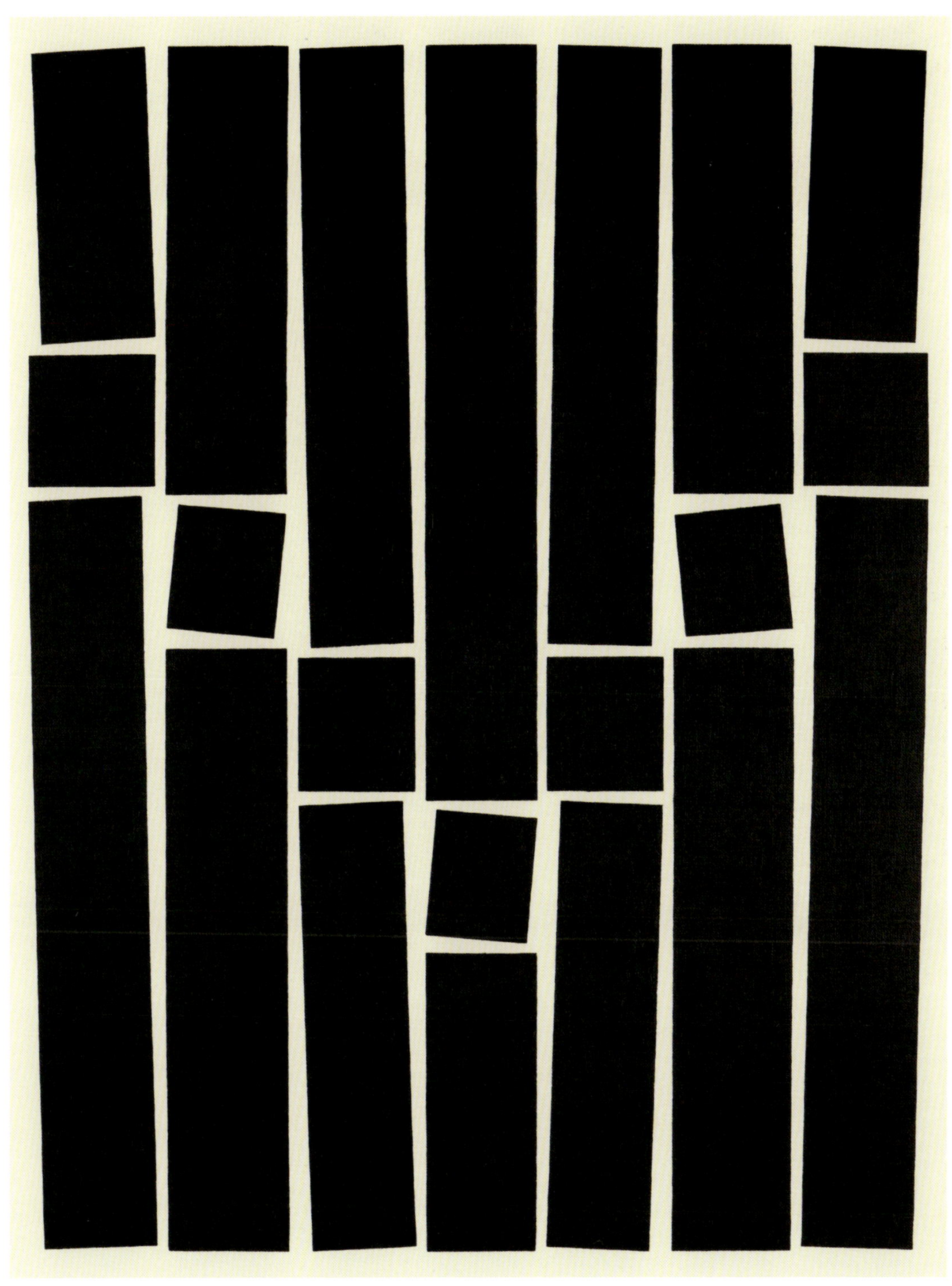

Hélio Oiticica
Pintura 9 [Painting 9], 1959

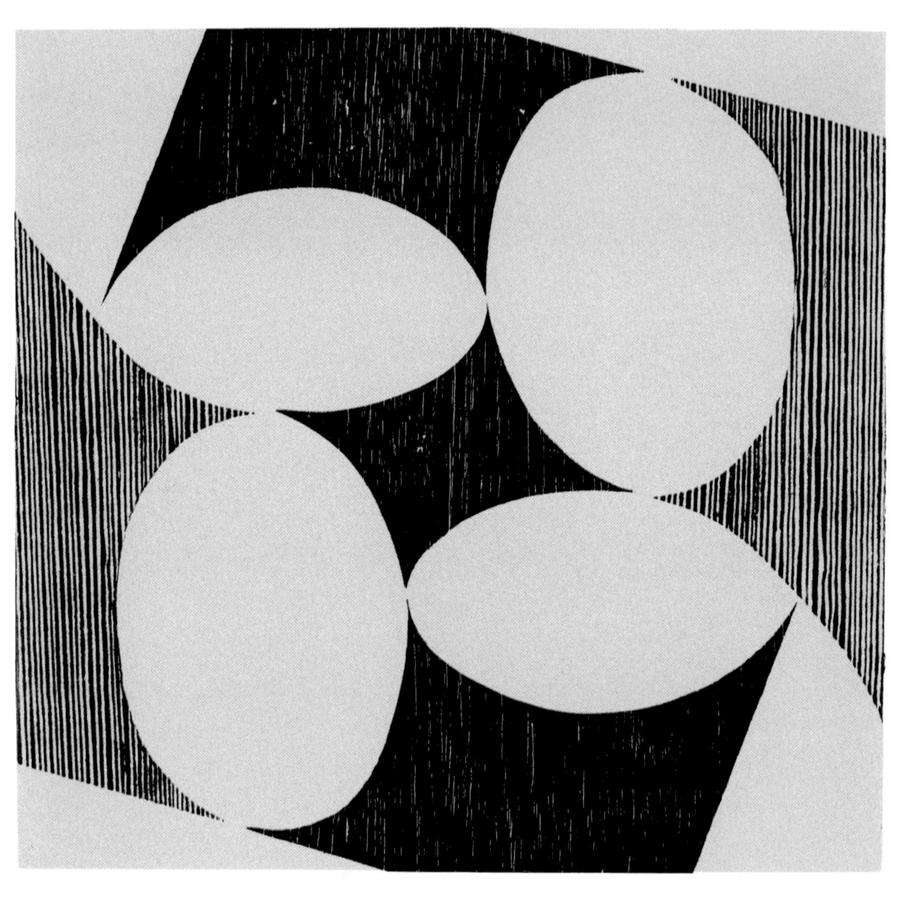

Lygia Pape
Sin título. *Tecelar* [Untitled. Weaving], 1959

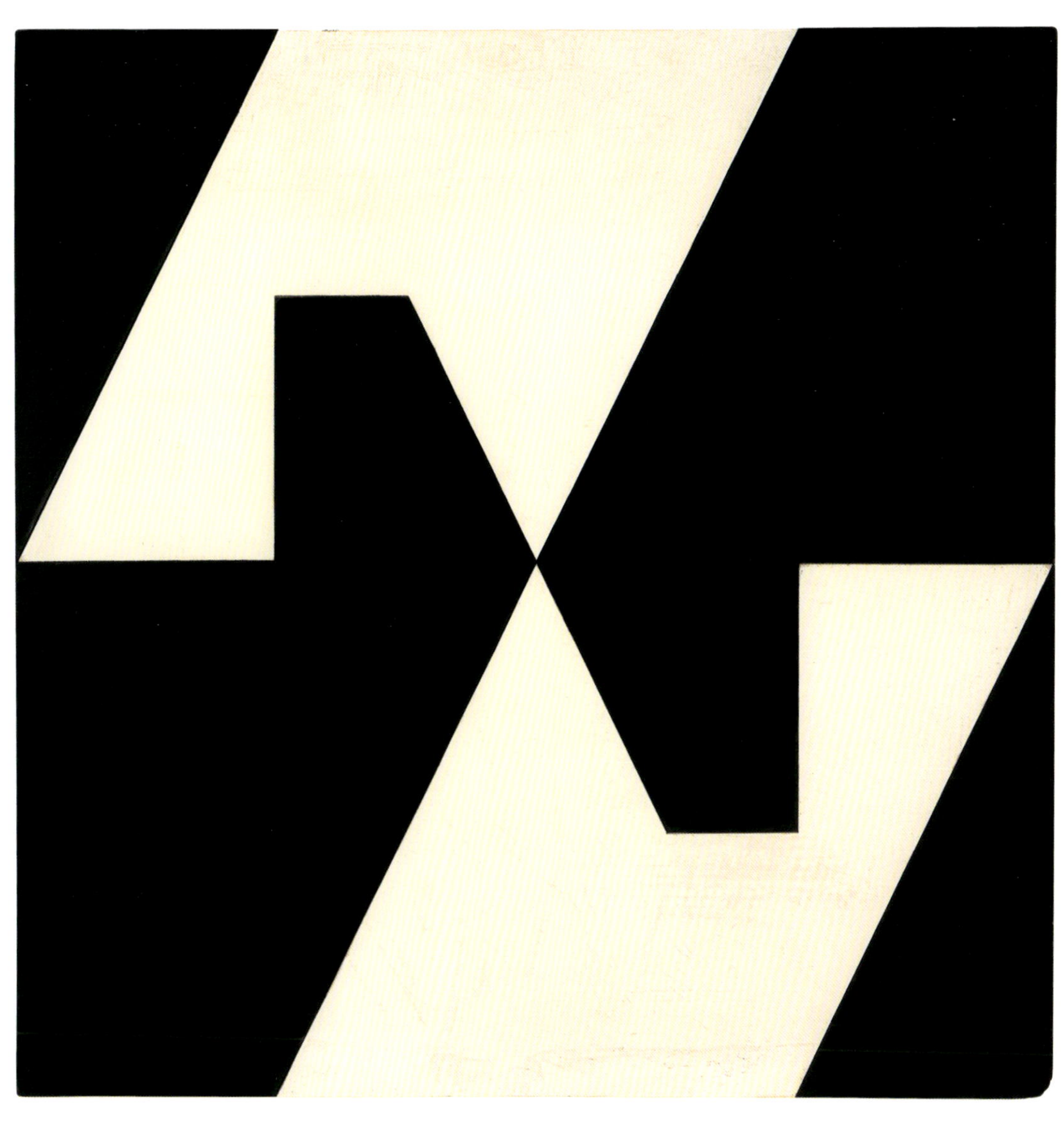

Lygia Clark
Planos em superfície modulada n.º 4 [Planes on Modulated Surface No. 4], 1957

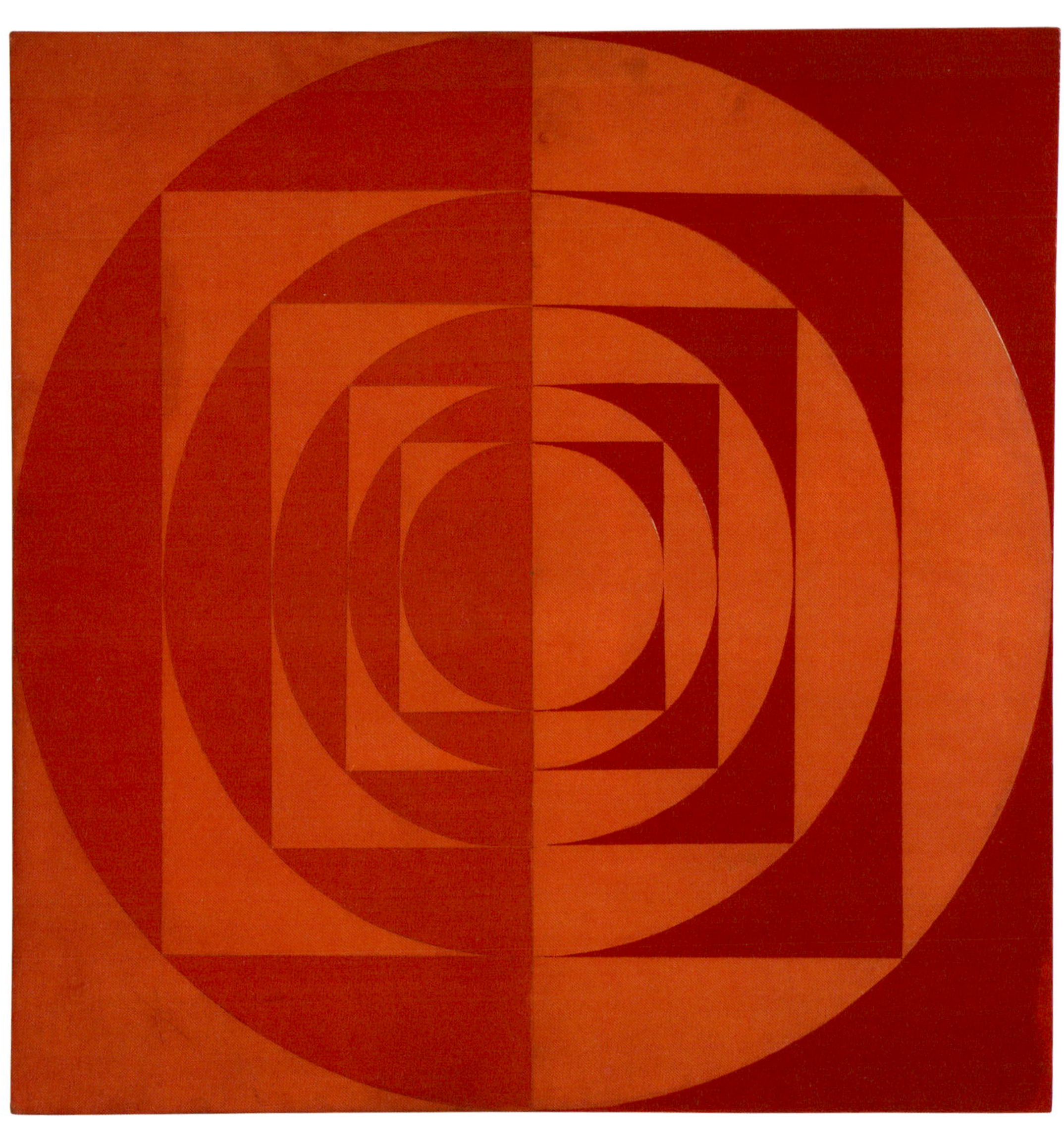

Hermelindo Fiaminghi
Seccionado n.º 1 [Sectional No. 1], 1958

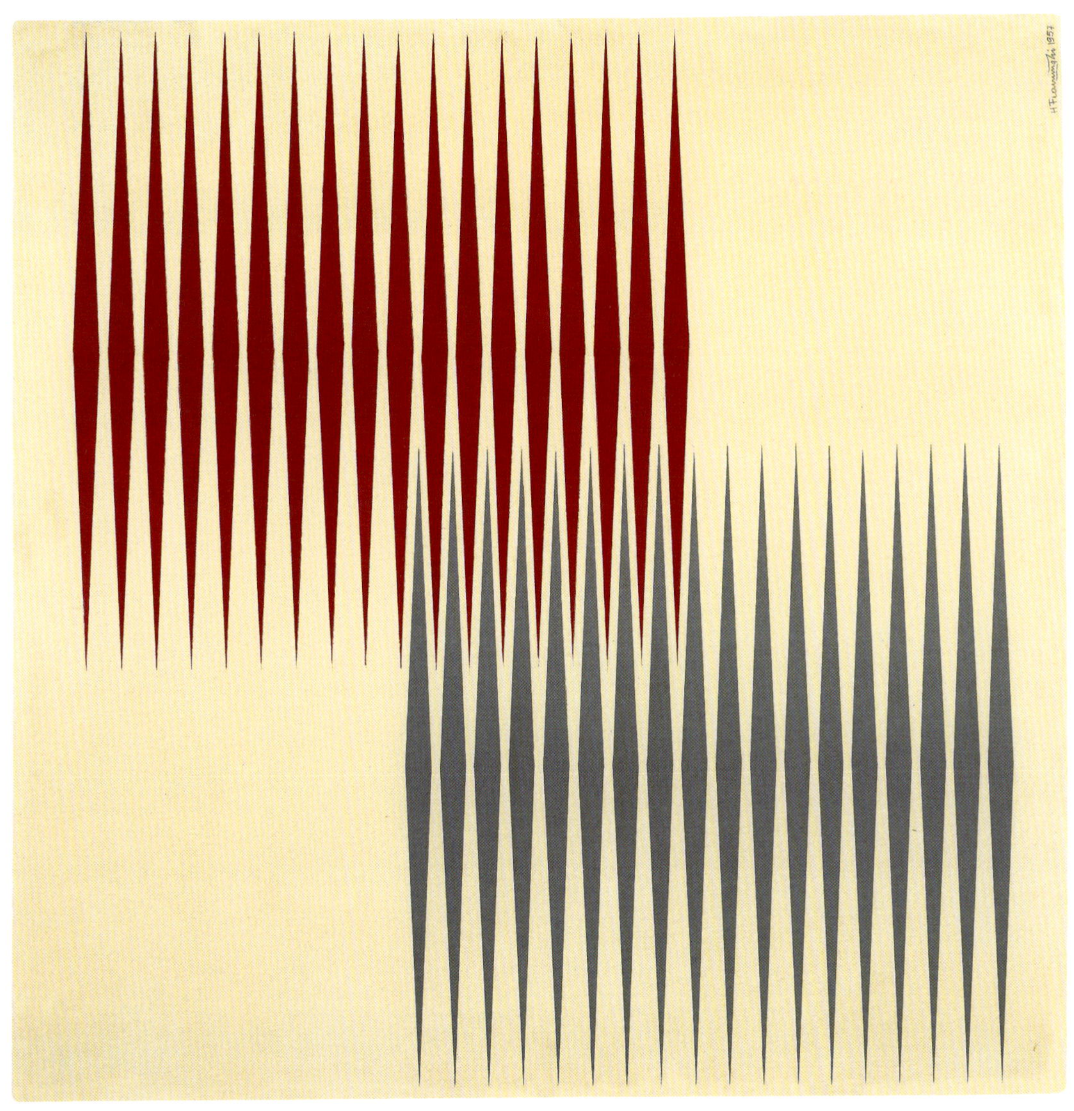

Hermelindo Fiaminghi
Alternado 2 [Alternated 2], 1957

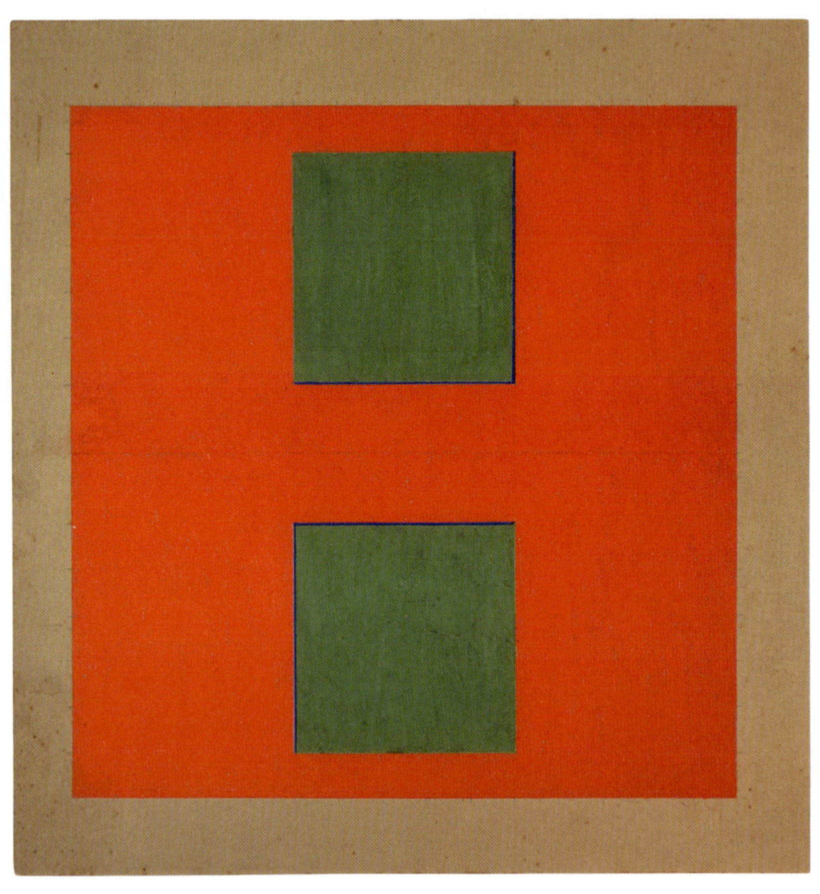

Hélio Oiticica
Sin título (*Grupo Frente*) [Untitled (*Frente Group*)], 1955

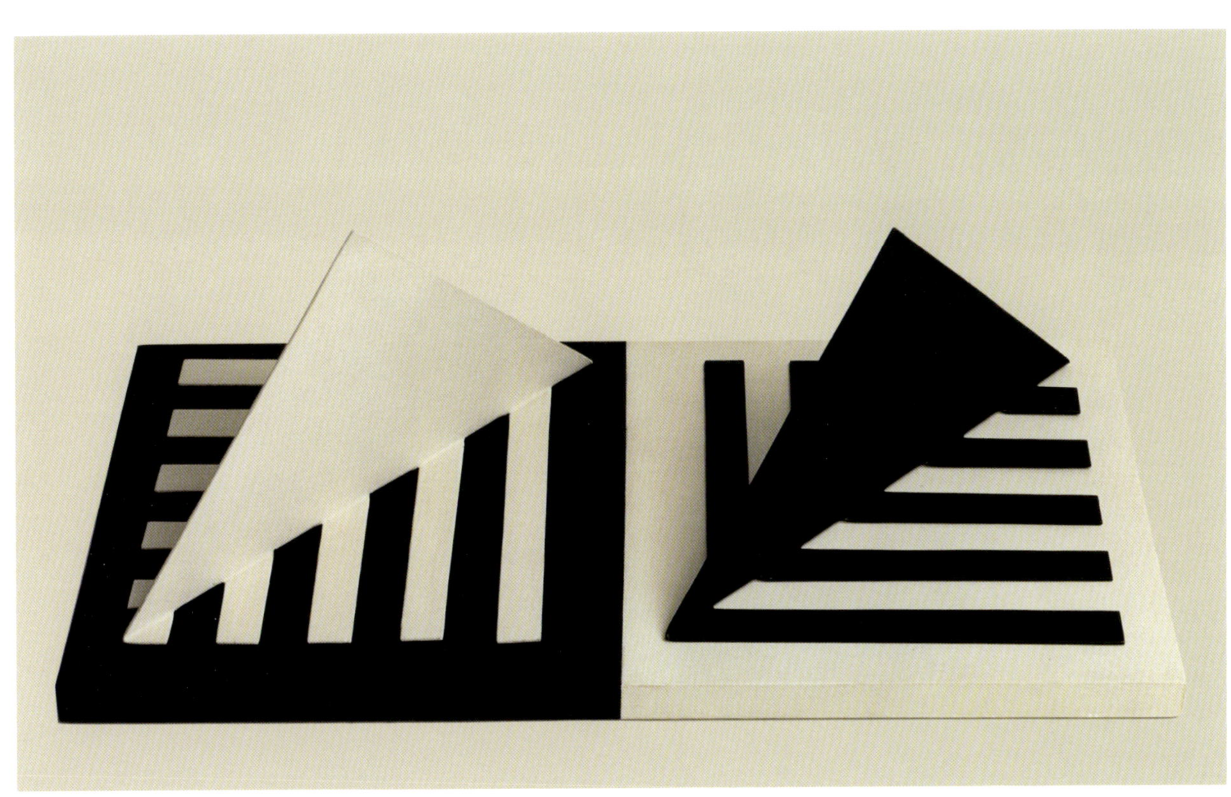

Luiz Sacilotto
Concreção 58 [Concretion 58], 1958

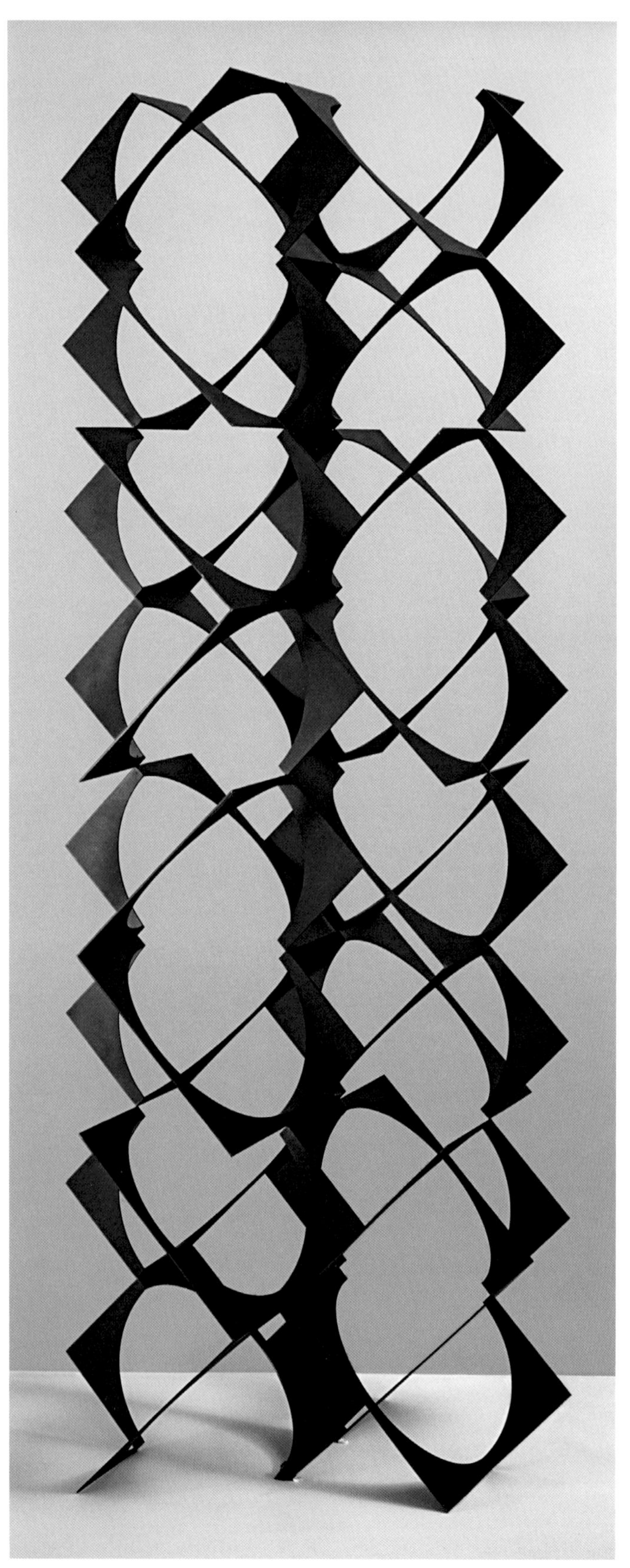

Franz Weissmann
Coluna neoconcreta [Neoconcrete Column], 1957

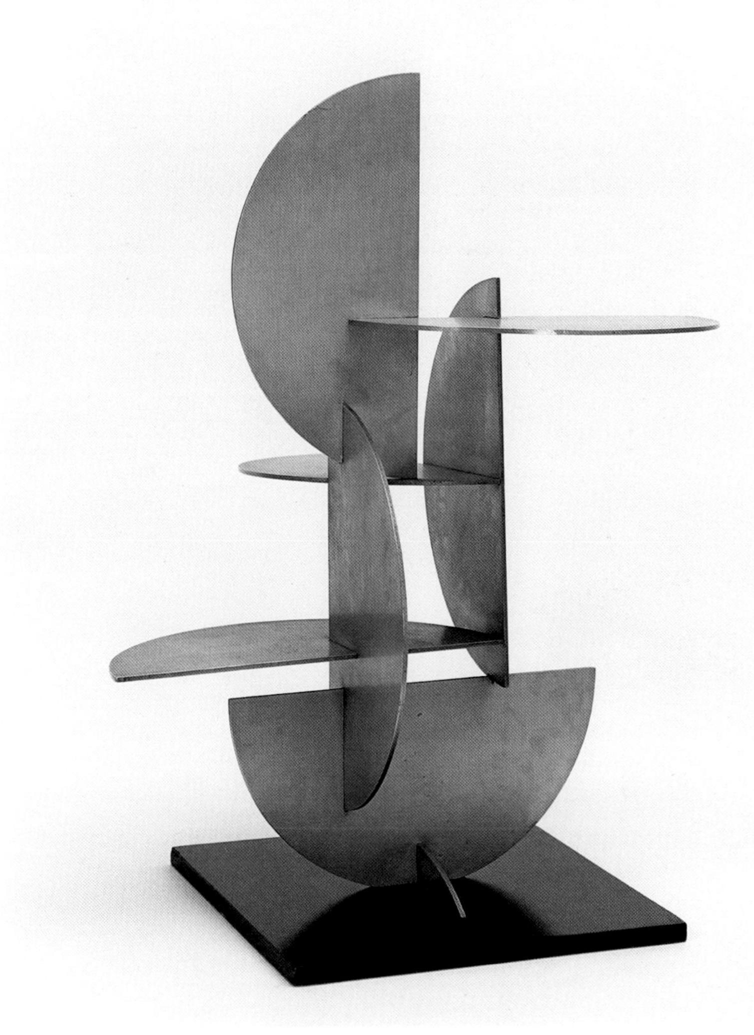

Franz Weissmann
Composição com semicírculos [Composition with Semicircles], 1953

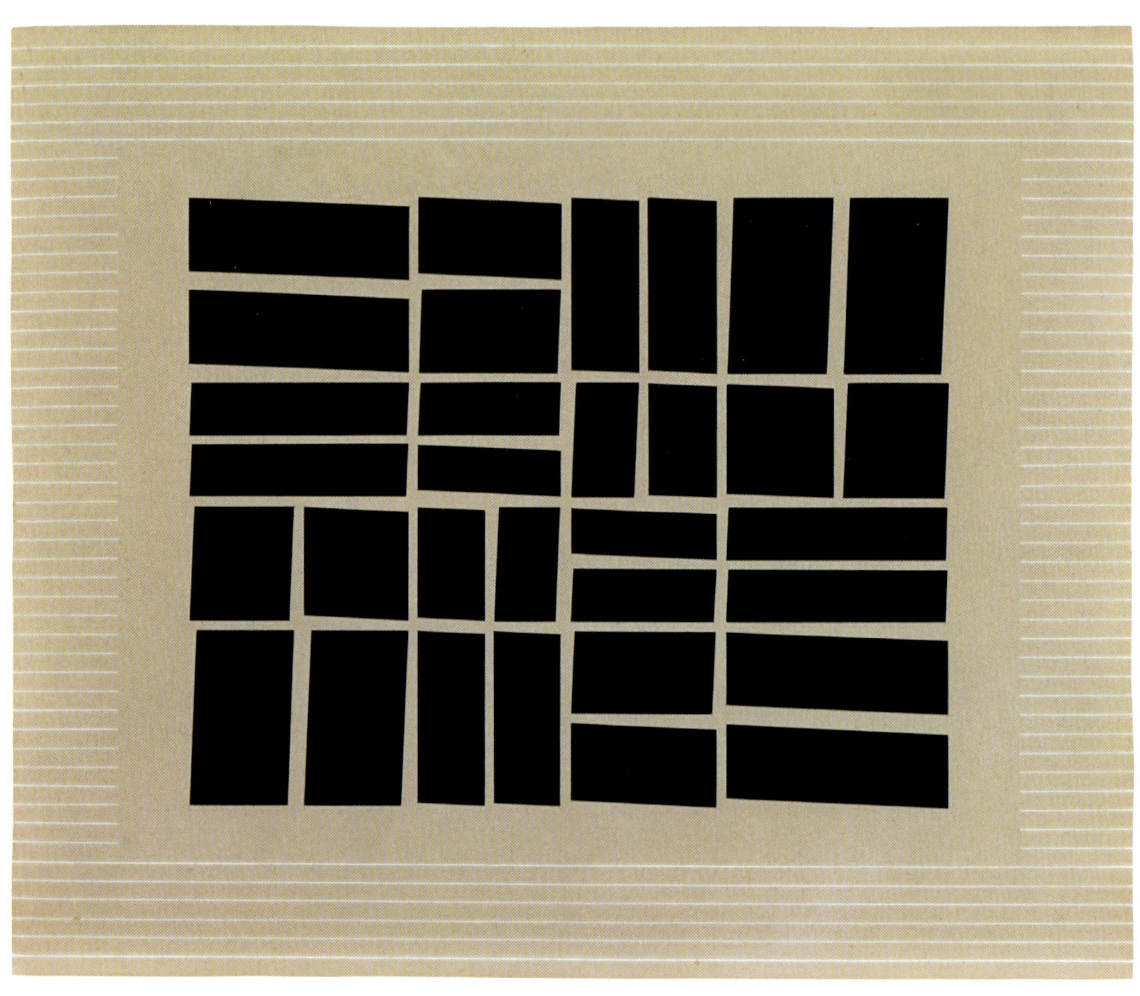

Hélio Oiticica
Metaesquema [Metascheme], 1958

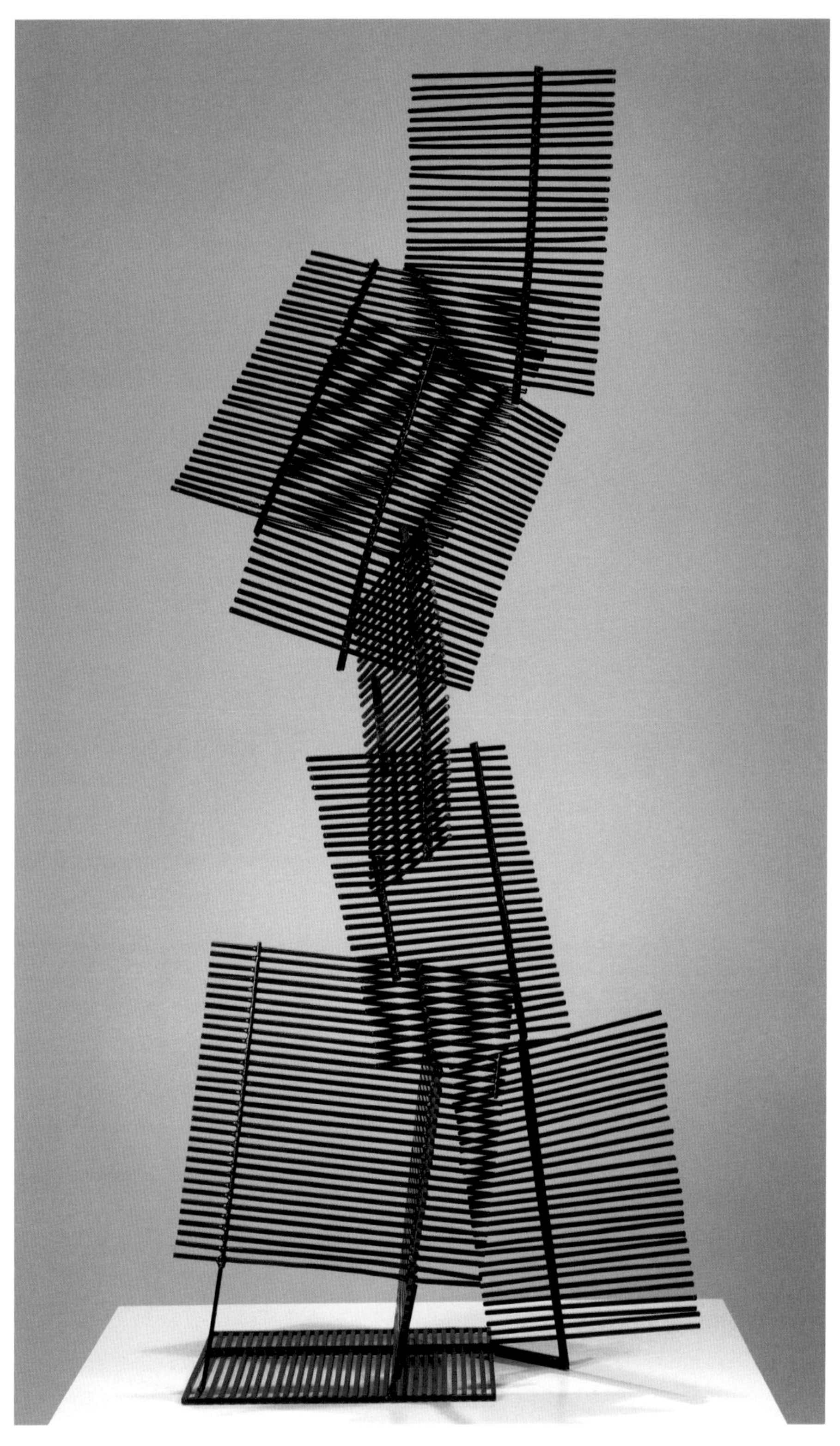

Gego
Ocho cuadrados [Eight Squares], 1961

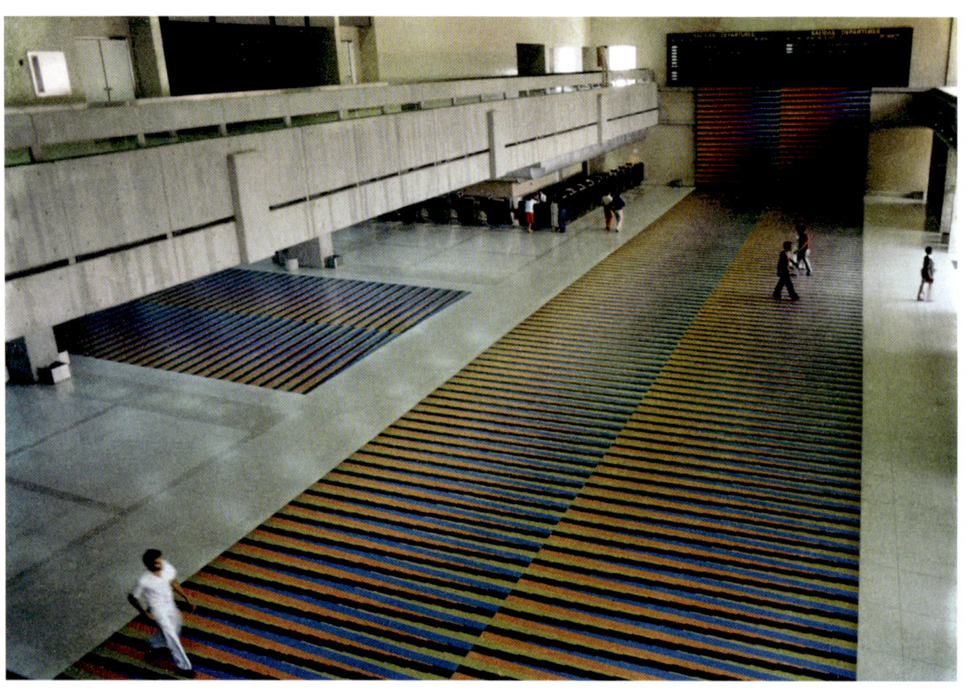

Carlos Cruz-Diez
Simón Bolívar International Airport of Maiquetía, Caracas, 1974

The Appearance of a Ghost
Jorge Pedro Núñez

At Seoul Airport, I found myself standing in front of the display window of Louis Vuitton. Drawn (serigraphed) all over the immense extension of the shop window, I saw parallel vertical lines delimited and grouped into sets by squares that multiplied all over the surface of the glass. These groups of parallel lines were seconded by another layer of glass, also serigraphed with the same motif, but slightly offset from the first. The back wall was a sheet of opaque white Plexiglas hiding a series of white fluorescent tubes that illuminated the whole display. On exhibit inside the window were bags and cases, the brand's emblematic products. The whole thing gave the impression of being a giant video screen activated by the viewer's movement and the reaction of the retina. The spectacle was assured. People walked from right to left and from left to right. Passers-by had photos taken of themselves in front of the window, but *souvenir* photography would never be able to capture what the human eye perceived in its physical interaction with the material universe of the optical illusion.

After formally analyzing the "phenomenon," I was immediately struck by its resemblance to Jesús Rafael Soto's superimpositions of printed lines on Plexiglas, such as *La cajita de Villanueva* (Villanueva's Little Box), 1955. The image creators of the great luxury ready-to-wear brands like Prada and Louis Vuitton were using the optical techniques developed by Soto and Cruz-Diez in the sixties as a catalogue of forms feeding the world of glamorous lifestyles with motifs lending themselves to optical illusion.

But could we read the meaning of a work from the use it is put to in the same way as the meaning given to it by the artist? Were this so, then in standing before Prada's Kinetic window displays in twenty-first-century Communist China, we would be observing something rather like Marcel Duchamp's *Reciprocal Readymade* (a project that was never realized) and its "use [of] a Rembrandt as an ironing board," which, mistakenly read, seems to sum up the very nature of the contemporary global economy.

In the "planetary aesthetic war," as Maurizio Lazzarato calls it, "A war that takes place over the ready-to-wear worlds created by capital, in the ferocious competition between machineries of expression rivaling with each other to conquer the market of subjectivities thrown into crisis. For it is not enough to create image worlds; they must also have the power to seduce, so that the subjectivities choose them as models for their remapping and concretize them in their everyday life."[1]

Today's processes of image production go through a great many phases of "swallowing" and digesting forms. The result is a displacement that has to do with the new exoduses of cultural forms and their deformation in translation.

In 1955, in a text by Pontus Hultén on the work of Jean Tinguely that looked back at the origins of Kinetic Art, attention was drawn to the ideological gap between the

1. Suely Rolnik, "Politics of Flexible Subjectivity: The Event Work of Lygia Clark," in *Antinomies of Art and Culture: Modernity, Postmodernity, Contemporaneity*, ed. Terry Smith, Okwui Enwezor, Nancy Condee (Durham, N.C.: Duke University Press, 2008), 104.

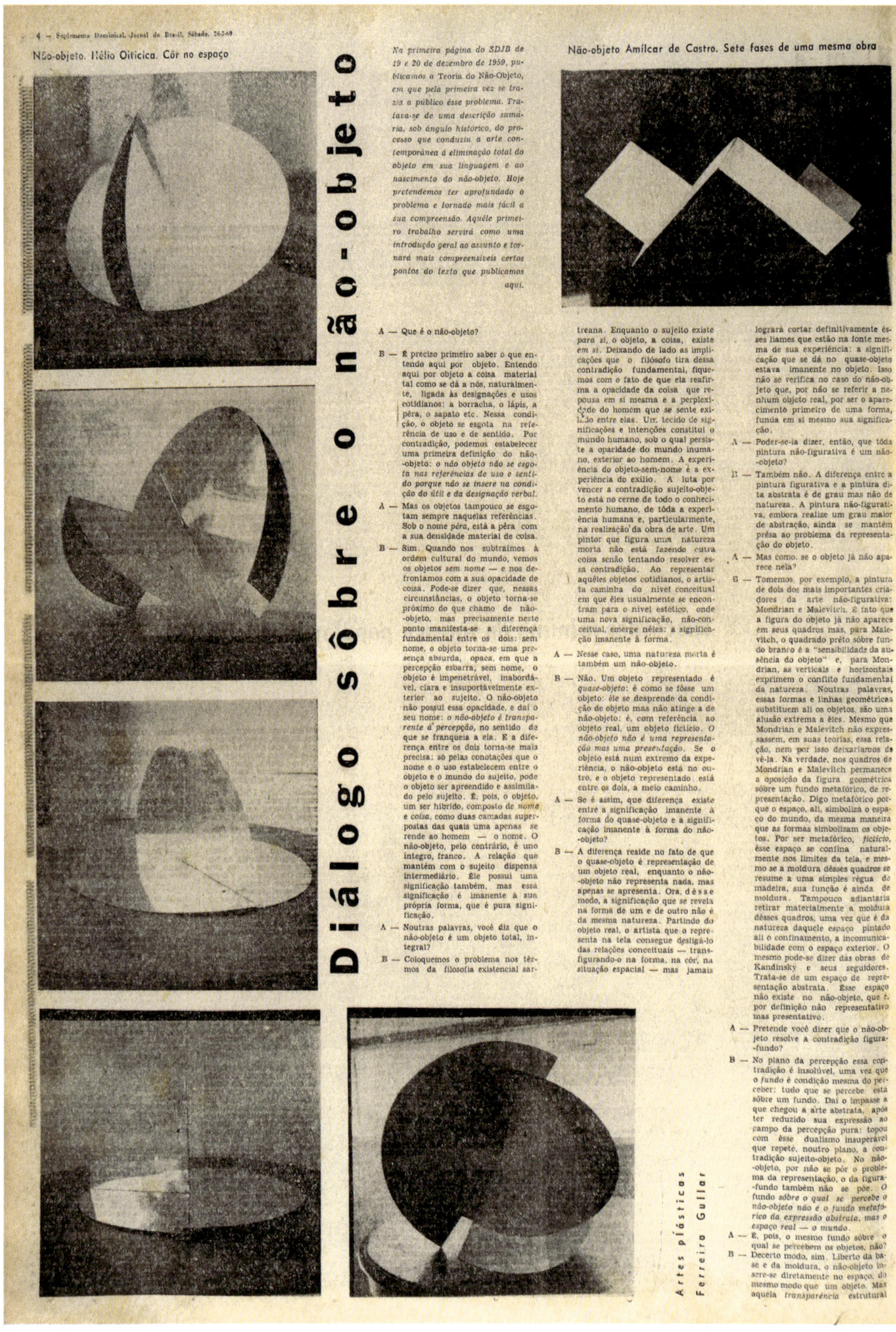

Não-objeto. Hélio Oiticica. Côr no espaço

Não-objeto Amílcar de Castro. Sete fases de uma mesma obra

Diálogo sôbre o não-objeto

Na primeira página do SDJB de 19 e 20 de dezembro de 1959, publicamos a Teoria do Não-Objeto, em que pela primeira vez se trazia a público êsse problema. Tratava-se de uma descrição sumária, sob ângulo histórico, do processo que conduziu a arte contemporânea à eliminação total do objeto em sua linguagem e ao nascimento do não-objeto. Hoje pretendemos ter aprofundado o problema e tornado mais fácil a sua compreensão. Aquêle primeiro trabalho servirá como uma introdução geral ao assunto e tornará mais compreensíveis certos pontos do texto que publicamos aqui.

A — Que é o não-objeto?

B — É preciso primeiro saber o que entendo aqui por objeto. Entendo aqui por objeto a coisa material tal como se dá a nós, naturalmente, ligada às designações e usos cotidianos: a borracha, o lápis, a pêra, o sapato etc. Nessa condição, o objeto se esgota na referência de uso e de sentido. Por contradição, podemos estabelecer uma primeira definição do não-objeto: *o não objeto não se esgota nas referências de uso e sentido porque não se insere na condição do útil e da designação verbal.*

A — Mas os objetos tampouco se esgotam sempre naquelas referências. Sob o nome *pêra*, está a pêra com a sua densidade material de coisa.

B — Sim. Quando nos subtraímos à ordem cultural do mundo, vemos os objetos *sem nome* — e nos defrontamos com a sua opacidade de coisa. Pode-se dizer que, nessas circunstâncias, o objeto torna-se próximo do que chamo de não-objeto, mas precisamente neste ponto manifesta-se a diferença fundamental entre os dois: sem nome, o objeto torna-se uma presença absurda, opaca, em que a percepção esbarra; sem nome, o objeto é impenetrável, inabordável, clara e insuportàvelmente exterior ao sujeito. O não-objeto não possui essa opacidade, e daí o seu nome: *o não-objeto é transparente à percepção*, no sentido de que se franqueia a ela. E a diferença entre os dois torna-se mais precisa: só pelas conotações que o nome e o uso estabelecem entre o objeto e o mundo do sujeito, pode o objeto ser apreendido e assimilado pelo sujeito. É, pois, o objeto, um ser híbrido, composto de *nome* e *coisa*, como duas camadas superpostas das quais uma apenas se rende ao homem — o nome. O não-objeto, pelo contrário, é uno íntegro, franco. A relação que mantém com o sujeito dispensa intermediário. Êle possui uma significação também, mas essa significação é imanente à sua própria forma, que é pura significação.

A — Noutras palavras, você diz que o não-objeto é um objeto total, integral?

B — Coloquemos o problema nos têrmos da filosofia existencial sartreana. Enquanto o sujeito existe para si, o objeto, a coisa, existe em si. Deixando de lado as implicações que o filósofo tira dessa contradição fundamental, fiquemos com o fato de que ela reafirma a opacidade da coisa que repousa em si mesma e a perplexidade do homem que se sente exilado entre elas. Um tecido de significações e intenções constitui o mundo humano, sob o qual persiste a opacidade do mundo inumano, exterior ao homem. A experiência do objeto-sem-nome é a experiência do exílio. A luta por vencer a contradição sujeito-objeto está no cerne de todo o conhecimento humano, de tôda a experiência humana e, particularmente, na realização da obra de arte. Um pintor que figura uma natureza morta não está fazendo outra coisa senão tentando resolver essa contradição. Ao representar aquêles objetos cotidianos, o artista caminha do nível conceitual em que êles usualmente se encontram para o nível estético, onde uma nova significação, não-conceitual, emerge nêles: a significação imanente à forma.

A — Nesse caso, uma natureza morta é também um não-objeto?

B — Não. Um objeto representado é *quase-objeto*: é como se fôsse um objeto: êle se desprende da condição de objeto mas não atinge a de não-objeto: é, com referência ao objeto real, um objeto fictício. O *não-objeto não é uma representação mas uma presentação*. Se o objeto está num extremo da experiência, o não-objeto está no outro, e o objeto representado está entre os dois, a meio caminho.

A — Se é assim, que diferença existe entre a significação imanente à forma do quase-objeto e a significação imanente à forma do não-objeto?

B — A diferença reside no fato de que o quase-objeto é representação de um objeto real, enquanto o não-objeto não representa nada, mas apenas se apresenta. Ora, dêsse modo, a significação que se revela na forma de um e de outro não é da mesma natureza. Partindo do objeto real, o artista que o representa na tela consegue desligá-lo das relações conceituais — transfigurando-o na forma, na côr, na situação espacial — mas jamais logrará cortar definitivamente êsses liames que estão na fonte mesma de sua experiência: a significação que se dá no quase-objeto estava imanente no objeto. Isso não se verifica no caso do não-objeto que, por não se referir a nenhum objeto real, por ser o aparecimento primeiro de uma forma, funda em si mesmo sua significação.

A — Poder-se-ia dizer, então, que tôda pintura não-figurativa é um não-objeto?

B — Também não. A diferença entre a pintura figurativa e a pintura dita abstrata é de grau mas não de natureza. A pintura não-figurativa, embora realize um grau maior de abstração, ainda se mantém presa ao problema da representação do objeto.

A — Mas como, se o objeto já não aparece nela?

B — Tomemos, por exemplo, a pintura de dois dos mais importantes criadores da arte não-figurativa: Mondrian e Malevitch. É fato que a figura do objeto já não aparece em seus quadros mas, para Malevitch, o quadrado prêto sôbre fundo branco é a "sensibilidade da ausência do objeto" e, para Mondrian, as verticais e horizontais exprimem o conflito fundamental da natureza. Noutras palavras, essas formas e linhas geométricas substituem ali os objetos, são uma alusão extrema a êles. Mesmo que Mondrian e Malevitch não expressassem, em suas teorias, essa relação, nem por isso deixaríamos de vê-la. Na verdade, nos quadros de Mondrian e Malevitch permanece a aposição da figura geométrica sôbre um fundo metafórico, de representação. Digo metafórico porque o espaço, ali, simboliza o espaço do mundo, da mesma maneira que as formas simbolizam os objetos. Por ser metafórico, fictício, êsse espaço se confina naturalmente nos limites da tela, e mesmo se a moldura dêsses quadros se resume a uma simples régua de madeira, sua função é ainda de moldura. Tampouco adiantaria retirar materialmente a moldura dêsses quadros, uma vez que é da natureza daquele espaço pintado ali o confinamento, a incomunicabilidade com o espaço exterior. O mesmo pode-se dizer das obras de Kandinsky e seus seguidores. Trata-se de um espaço de representação abstrata. Esse espaço não existe no não-objeto, que é, por definição não representativo mas presentativo.

A — Pretende você dizer que o não-objeto resolve a contradição figura-fundo?

B — No plano da percepção essa contradição é insolúvel, uma vez que o *fundo* é condição mesma do perceber: tudo que se percebe está sôbre um fundo. Daí o impasse a que chegou a arte abstrata, após ter reduzido sua expressão ao campo da percepção pura: topou com êsse dualismo insuperável que repete, noutro plano, a contradição sujeito-objeto. No não-objeto, por não se pôr o problema da representação, o da figura-fundo também não se põe. O fundo *sôbre o qual se percebe o não-objeto não é o fundo metafórico da expressão abstrata, mas o espaço real — o mundo.*

A — É, pois, o mesmo fundo sôbre o qual se percebem os objetos, não?

B — Decerto modo, sim. Liberto da base e da moldura, o não-objeto insere-se diretamente no espaço, do mesmo modo que um objeto. Mas aquela *transparência* estrutural

Artes plásticas — Ferreira Gullar

Ferreira Gullar, "Diálogo sôbre o não objeto" [Dialogue on the Non-Object], *Jornal do Brasil,* **Sunday supplement, Rio de Janeiro, March 26, 1960**

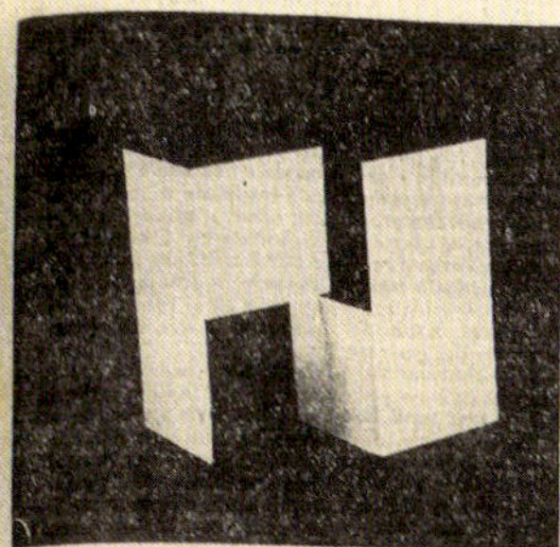
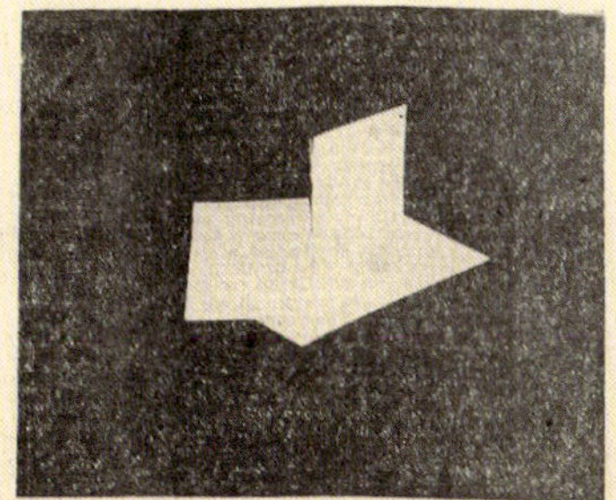
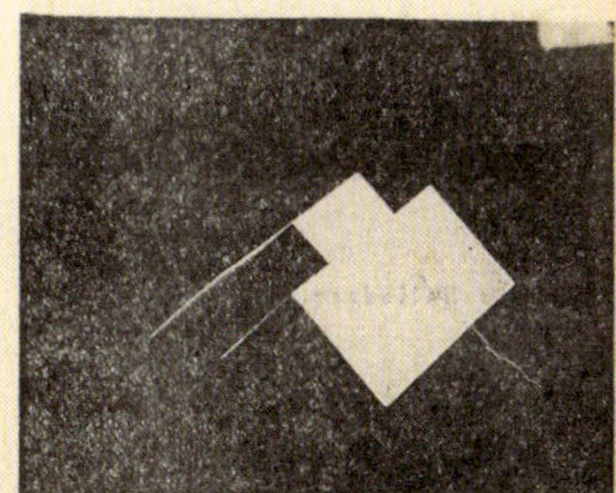

do não-objeto, que o distingue do objeto, permite-nos dizer que êle transcende o espaço, e não por iludi-lo (como faz o objeto), mas por nêle se inserir radicalmente. Nascendo diretamente no e do espaço, o não-objeto é ao mesmo tempo um trabalhar e um refundar dêsse espaço: o renascer permanente da forma e do espaço. Essa transformação espacial é a própria condição de nascimento do não-objeto.

A — Você falou em moldura e base. Basta eliminar êsses elementos para fazer um não-objeto?

B — Não, da mesma maneira que não bastava eliminar a figura para fazer um bom quadro abstrato. Não se trata da presença ou ausência material da moldura ou da base. Trata-se de criar sem o apoio dêsses elementos. A moldura e a base, na pintura e na escultura respectivamente, condicionam a expressão do artista e são, também, os marcos de uma determinada posição em face da arte. O que importa, pois, não é fazer um quadro sem moldura ou uma escultura sem base, mas resolver os novos problemas que se põem quando a expressão já não conta com aquêles elementos.

A — Que significam a moldura e a base?

B — Significam que a linguagem da obra é representativa, mesmo se as formas são abstratas (falo da base e da moldura como elementos pressupostos na expressão). Quando o problema da representação é ultrapassado, a moldura e a base perdem a função. Mas não basta simplesmente retirá-las da obra. No caso da escultura, a base indica uma posição privilegiada, e se a escultura não possui base (materialmente falando) mas detém aquêle privilégio, o problema da base continua inerente a ela. Não se trata, portanto, de um não-objeto.

A — Conclui-se daí que a não-representação é um caráter básico do não-objeto. E êle ainda pintura ou escultura?

B — As considerações a que nos obriga o aparecimento do não-objeto, conduziu-nos a ver a representação como elemento inerente à pintura e à escultura. Ao contrário do que se vem afirmando há pelos menos 50 anos, só em alguns casos excepcionais a arte contemporânea ultrapassou o problema da representação. Essas exceções — os contra-relevos de Tatlin, as arquiteturas, suprematistas de Malevitch — estão fora das definições do que seja pintura, escultura, arquitetura. O mesmo se dá com os trabalhos do grupo neoconcreto — e daí o nome de não-objeto. Acredito que uma arte realmente não-representativa repele as noções acadêmicas de gênero artístico. O próprio conceito de arte vacila, se não o tomamos na acepção fundamental de experiência primeira.

A — Quer dizer que, na sua opinião, pintura e escultura acabaram...

B — Ou talvez nunca tenham, de fato, existido. Pelo menos na época moderna, todo artista trabalha no limite de sua arte, tentando ultrapassá-lo. Trata-se sempre de uma antiarte. O que importava para Brancusi — quer êle o soubesse ou não — não era fazer escultura, mas a escultura. Contraditòriamente, para fazer a escultura, êle se distanciava cada vez mais de tudo o que se conhecia como escultura. O mesmo pode-se dizer de Pevsner, de Vantongerloo, de Picasso, de Mondrian, de Kandinsky, de Malevitch, de Pollock etc. O artista busca, na pintura ou na escultura, a experiência primeira do mundo, mas a própria pintura (ou escultura) já é um mundo conceituado, que é preciso ultrapassar. E finalmente chegou-se ao momento atual, em que o artista já não se preocupara em fazer pintura ou escultura, para através delas reencontrar a experiência primeira do mundo: tenta precipitar diretamente essa experiência. É uma redescoberta do mundo: as firmas, as cores, o espaço não pertencem a esta ou àquela linguagem artística mas, antes, ao mundo mesmo, a experiência viva e indeterminada do homem. Lidar diretamente com êsses elementos, fora dos quadros institucionais da arte, é lidar diretamente com o mundo, é formulá-lo pela primeira vez. E aqui, observa-se outra diferença fundamental entre um quadro e um não-objeto: aquêle nasce de um esfôrço do artista para, gradativamente, romper o mundo já conceitual da linguagem artística — vem-se de

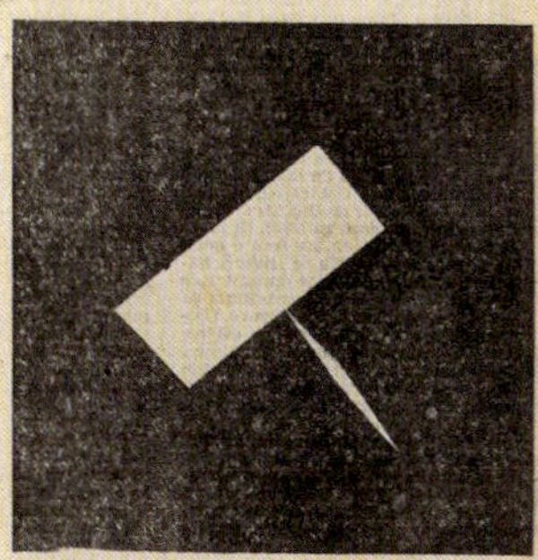
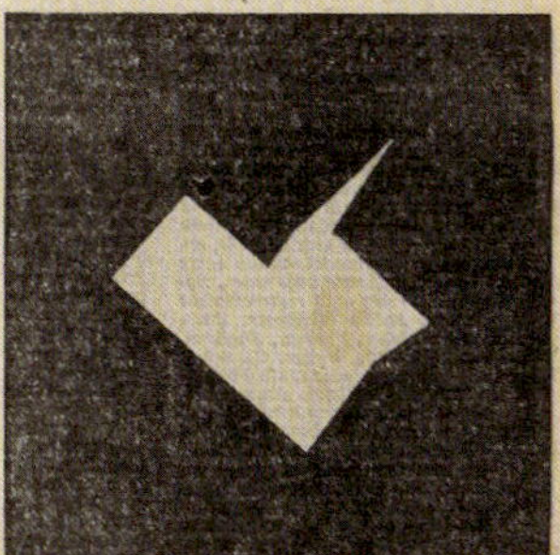
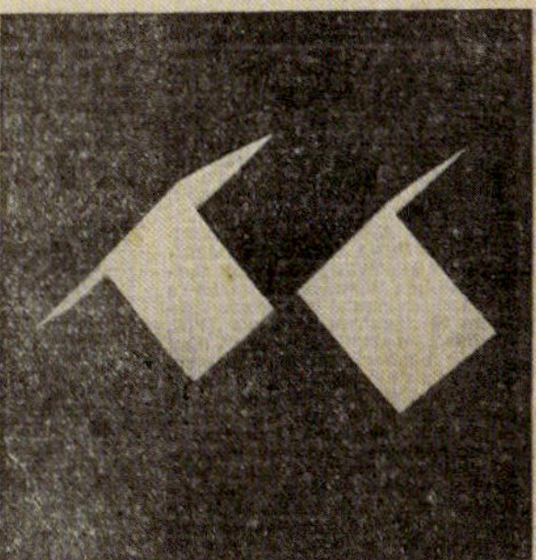

fora para dentro, da significação usual para uma nova significação; o não-objeto irrompe de dentro para fora, da não-significação para a significação.

A — Dentro da teoria do não-objeto, como se coloca precisamente o problema da poesia?

P — Também o poeta busca a experiência primeira do mundo, também êle trabalha no limite da linguagem poética. Na época moderna, vimos a destruição das formas fixas de estrofe, de verso, para chegar-se ao verso livre. Mas, depois, o verso livre também tornou-se um instrumento estereotipado: rebentou-se a sintaxe e chegou-se à palavra como elemento primeiro. Da mesma maneira que a côr libertou-se da pintura, a palavra libertou-se da poesia. O poeta tem a palavra mas já não tem um quadro estético preestabelecido onde colocá-la hàbilmente. Êle se defronta com ela desarmado, sem nenhuma possibilidade definida mas com tôdas as possibilidades indefinidas. O que importa não é fazer um poema — nem mesmo fazer um não-objeto — mas revelar o quanto de mundo se deposita na palavra.

A — Você já escreveu que, no que se refere à poesia, o não-objeto é a procura de um lugar para a palavra. Que quer dizer isto?

B — É que a palavra ou está na frase — onde perde sua individualidade — ou no dicionário, onde se encontra sòzinha e mutilada, pois é dada como mera denotação. O não-objeto verbal é o antidicionário: o lugar onde a palavra isolada irradia tôda a sua carga. Os elementos visuais que ali se casam a ela têm a função de explicitara, intensificar, concretizar a multivocidade que a palavra encerra.

A — Há, então, uma fusão de pintura, relêvo, escultura e poesia?

B — Creio que não. Planos, formas, cores, são elementos da realidade, antes de serem elementos de uma linguagem artística. No não-objeto os elementos plásticos não são usados com o mesmo sentido que na pintura ou na escultura. Já são escolhidos segundo um propósito verbal, isto é: da mesma maneira que um poeta tradicional elabora seu poema convocando e repelindo palavras, o poeta neoconcreto convoca, além das palavras, formas, cores, movimentos, num nível em que a linguagem verbal e a linguagem plástica se interpenetram. Ninguém ignora que nenhuma experiência humana se limita a um dos cinco sentidos do homem, uma vez que o homem reage com uma totalidade e que, na "simbólica geral do corpo" (M.-Ponty), os sentidos se decifram uns aos outros.

A — O não-objeto deve ter movimento?

B — Nessa altura, cabe esclarecer que não digo como deve ser o não-objeto, mas apenas defino o que já existe, o que está feito. A maioria dos não-objetos existentes implicam, de uma forma ou de outra, no movimento sôbre êle do espectador ou do leitor. O espectador é solicitado a usar o não-objeto. A mera contemplação não basta para revelar o sentido da obra — e o espectador passa da contemplação à ação. Mas o que a sua ação produz é a obra mesma, porque êsse uso, previsto na estrutura da obra, é absorvido por ela, revela-a e incorpora-se à sua significação. O não-objeto é concedido no tempo: é uma imobilidade aberta a uma mobilidade aberta

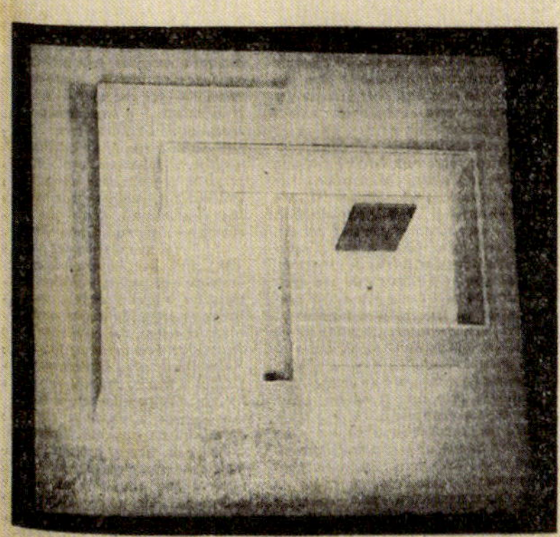

Não-objeto. Amilcar de Castro. Sete fases de uma mesma obra

a uma imobilidade aberta. A contemplação conduz à ação que conduz a uma nova contemplação. Diante do espectador, o não-objeto apresenta-se como inconcluso e lhe oferece os meios de ser concluído. O espectador age, mas o tempo de sua ação não flui, não transcende a obra, não se perde além dela; incorpora-se a ela, e dura. A ação não consome a obra, mas a enriquece; depois da ação, a obra é mais que antes — e essa segunda contemplação já contém, além da forma vista pela primeira vez, um passado em que o espectador e a obra se fundiram: êle verteu nela o seu tempo. O não-objeto reclama o espectador (trata-se ainda de espectador?) não como testemunha passivo de sua existência mas como a condição mesma de seu fazer-se. Sem êle, a obra existe apenas em potência, à espera do gesto humano que a atualize.

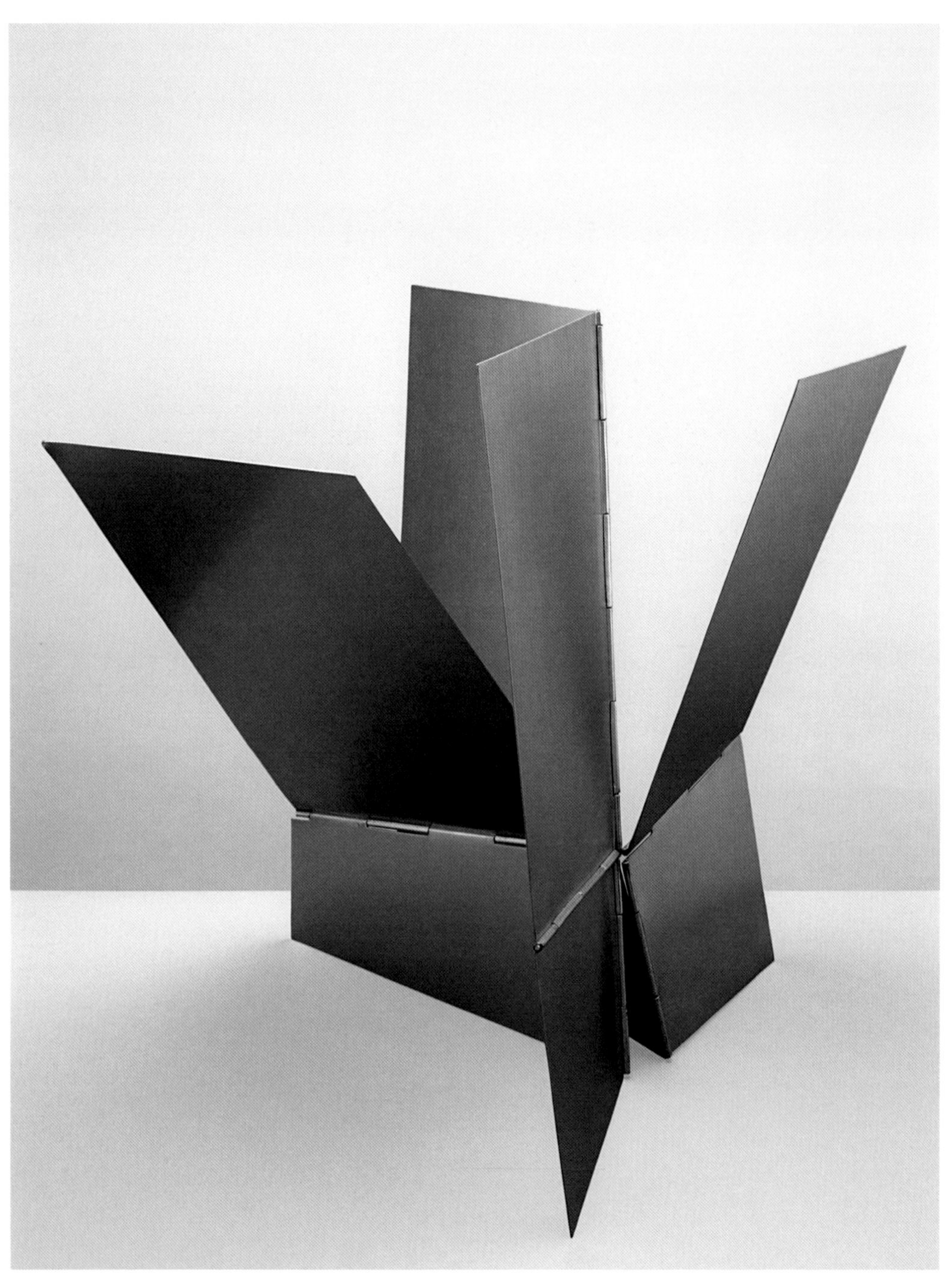

Lygia Clark
Monumento a todas as situações [Monument to All Situations], 1962

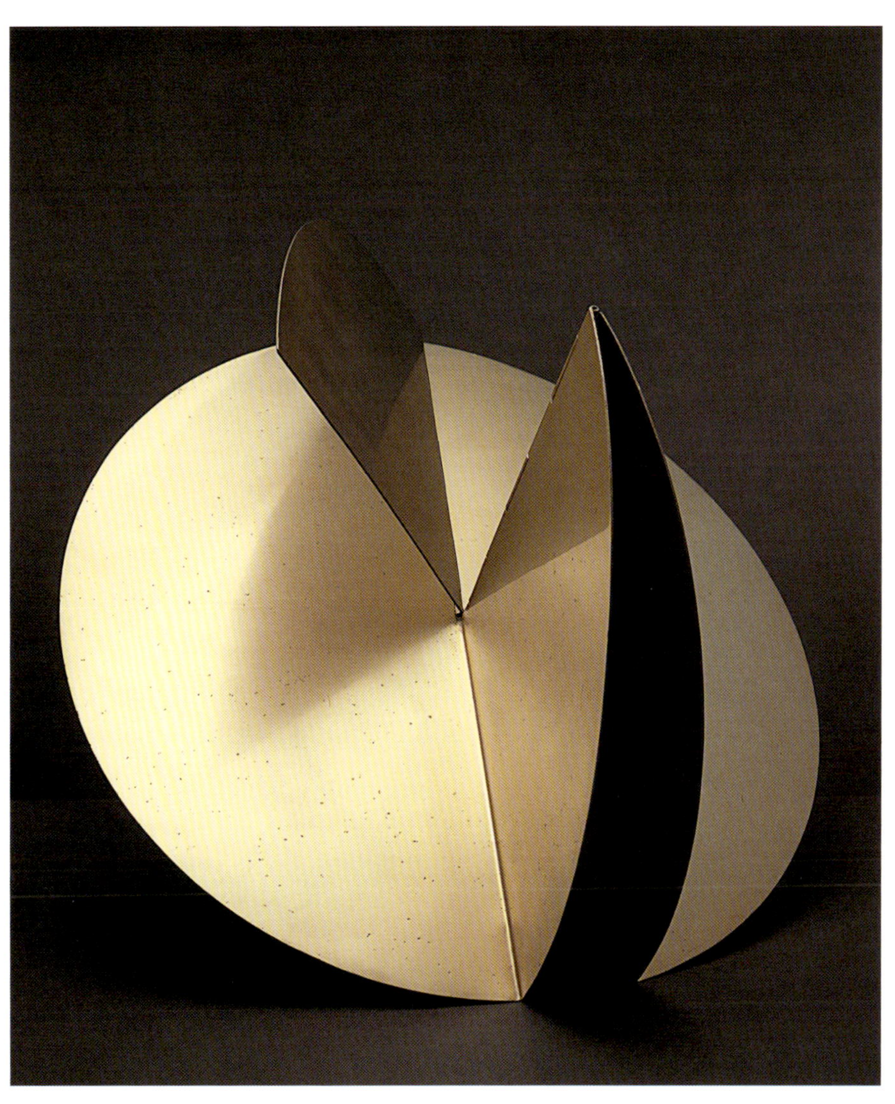

Lygia Clark
Relógio de sol [Sundial], 1960

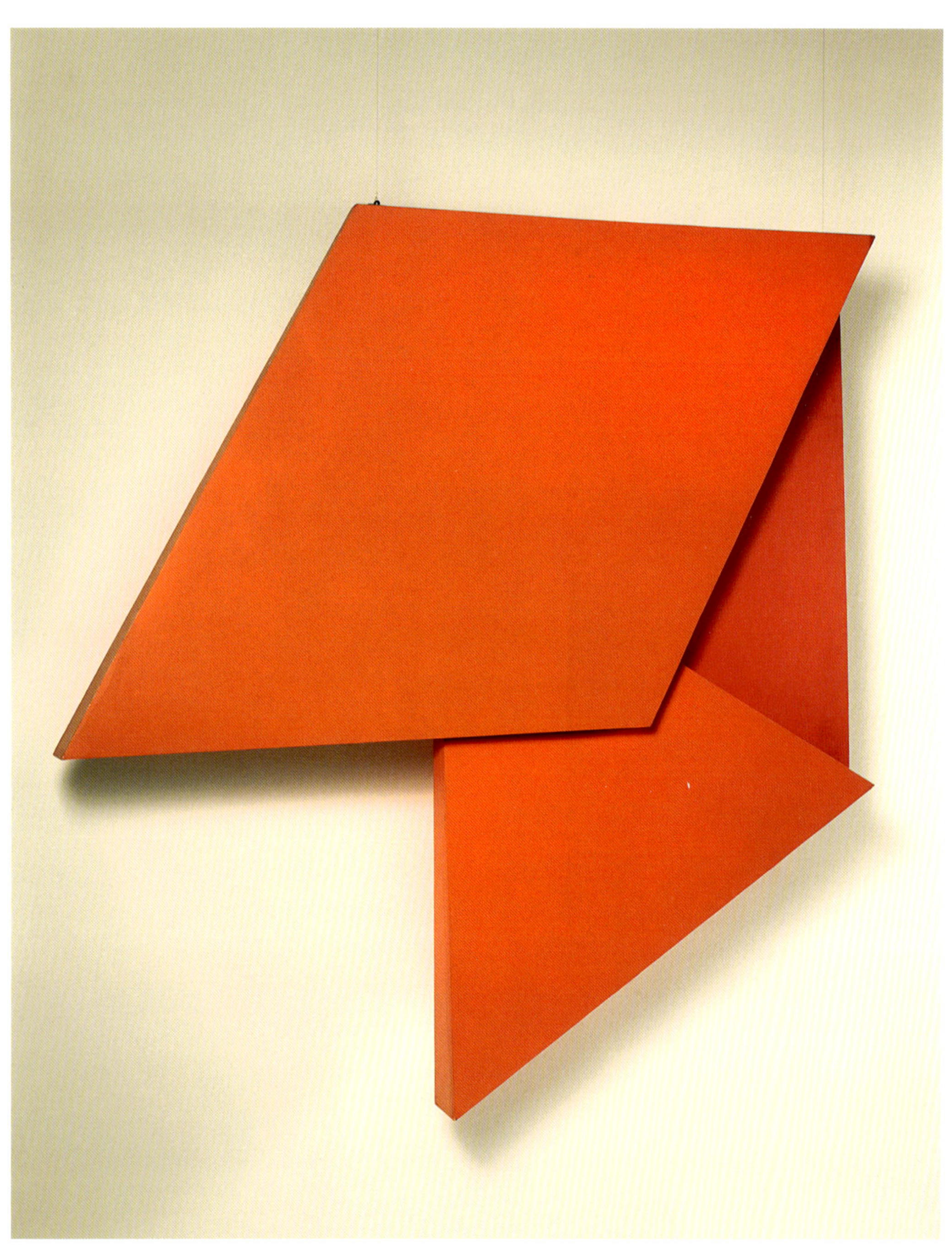

Hélio Oiticica
Untitled, from the series *Relevos espaciais* [Spatial Reliefs], 1959. Reconstructed in 1991

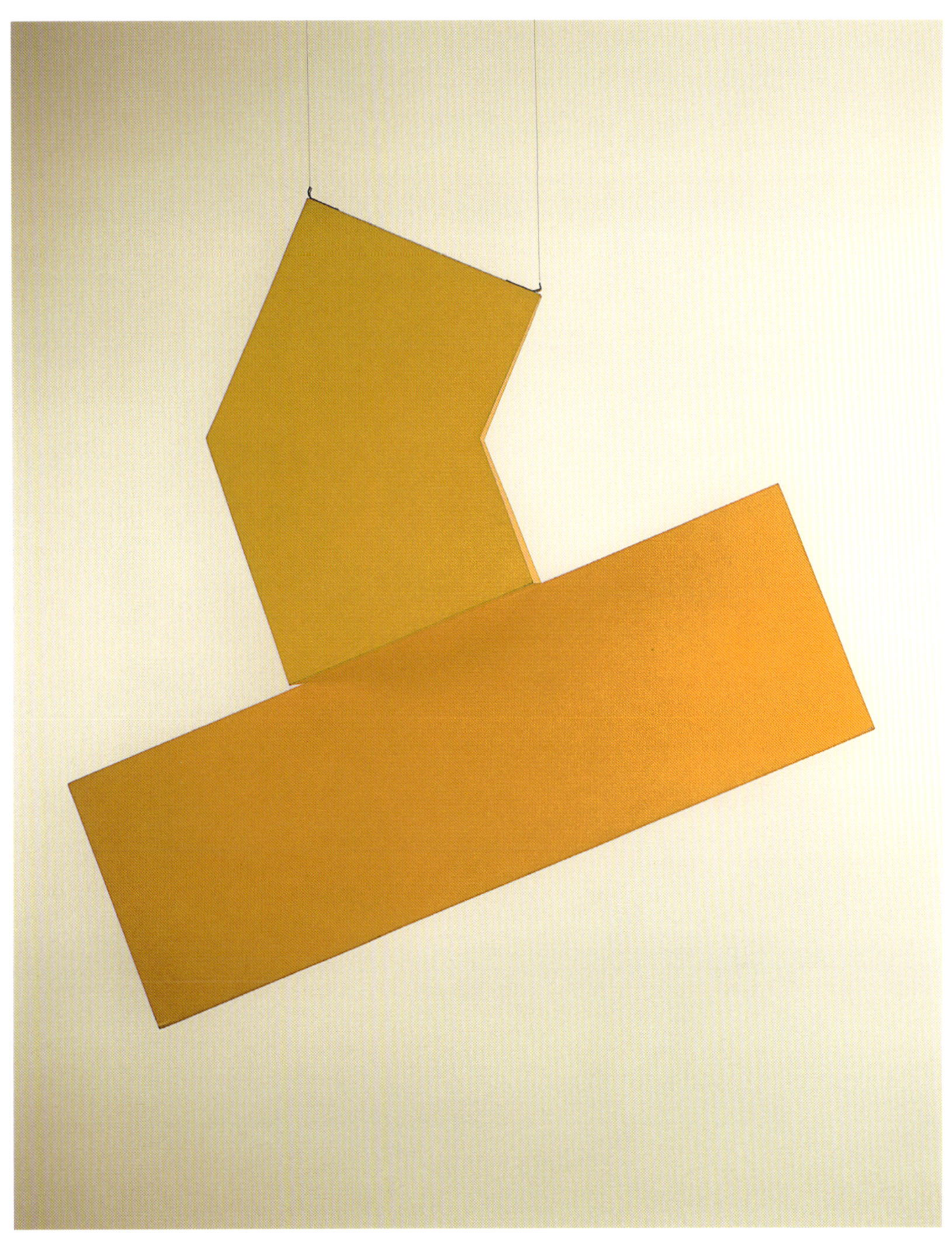

Hélio Oiticica
Untitled, from the series *Relevos espaciais* [Spatial Reliefs], 1959. Reconstructed in 1991

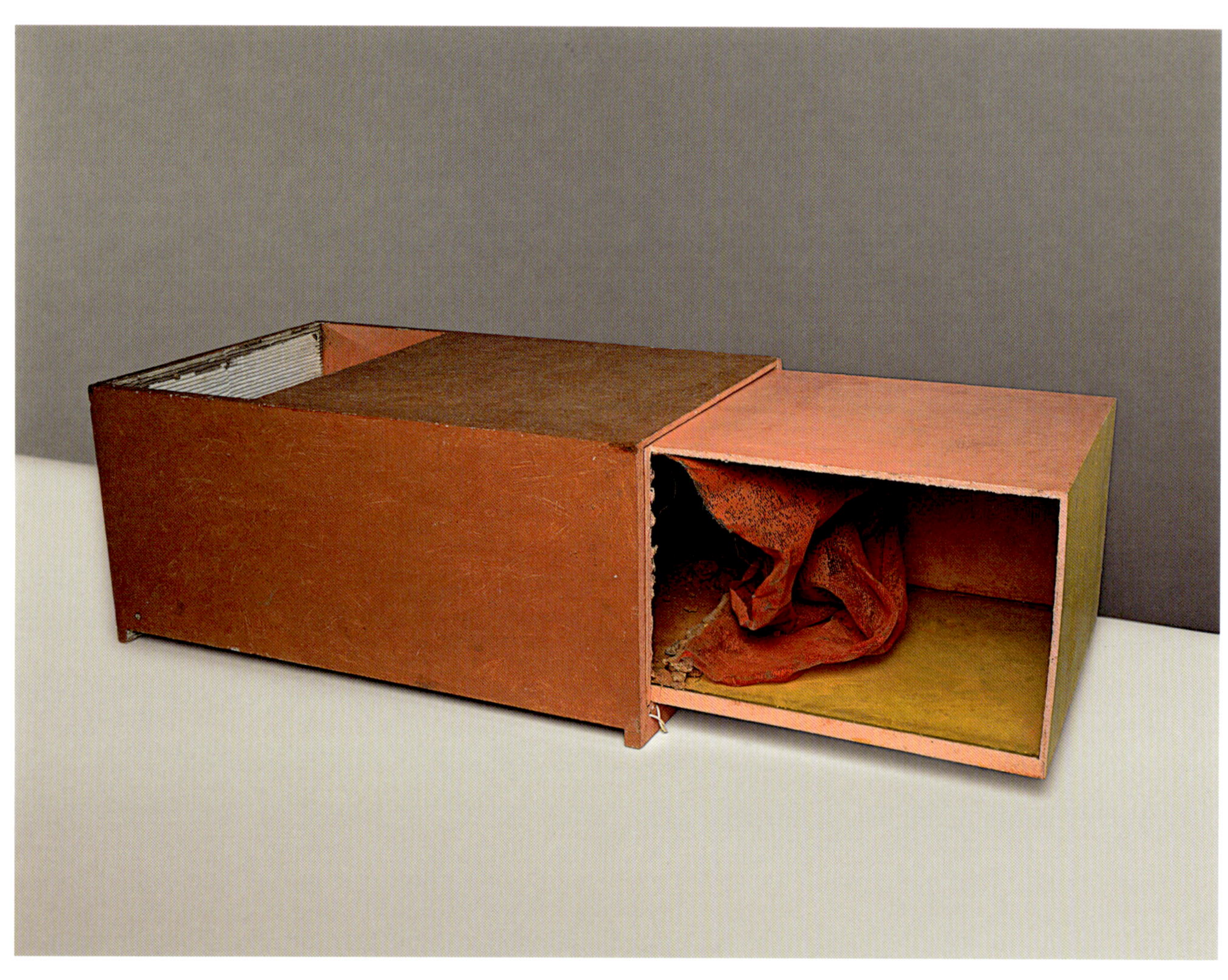

Hélio Oiticica
Box bolide 12, 'archeologic', 1964–65

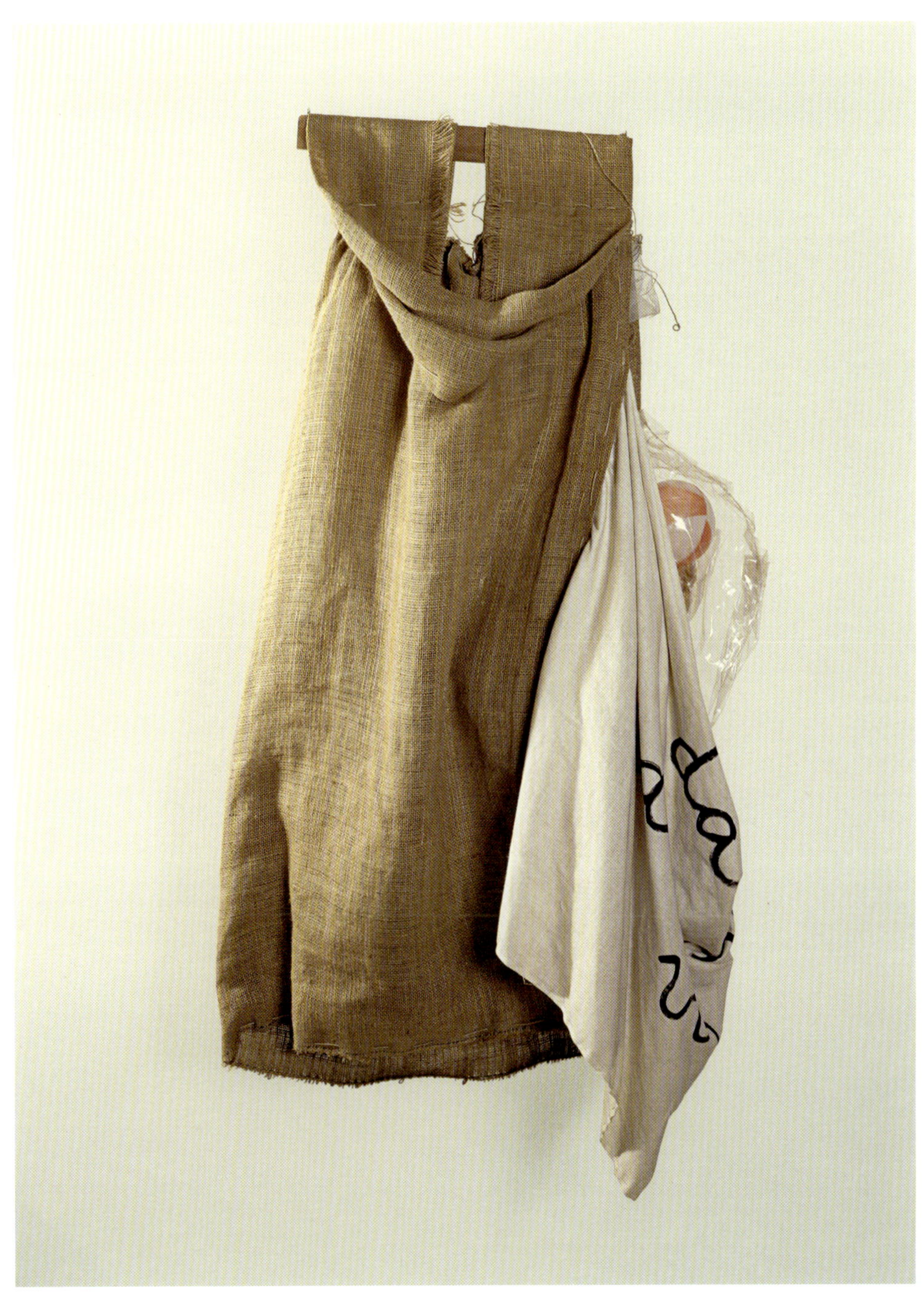

Hélio Oiticica
P 16 Parangolé capa 12 "Da adversidade vivemos" [P 16 Parangolé Cape 12:
"We Live from Adversity"], 1965. Reconstructed in 1992

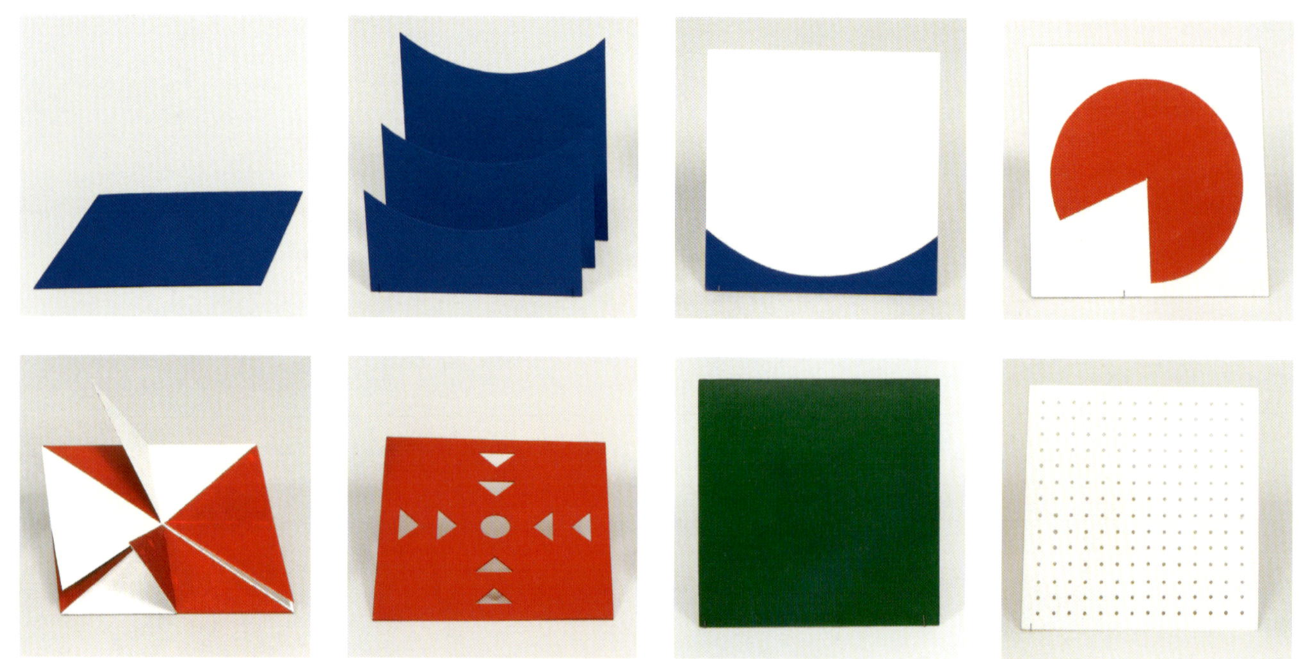

Lygia Pape
Livro da criação [Book of Creation], 1959–60

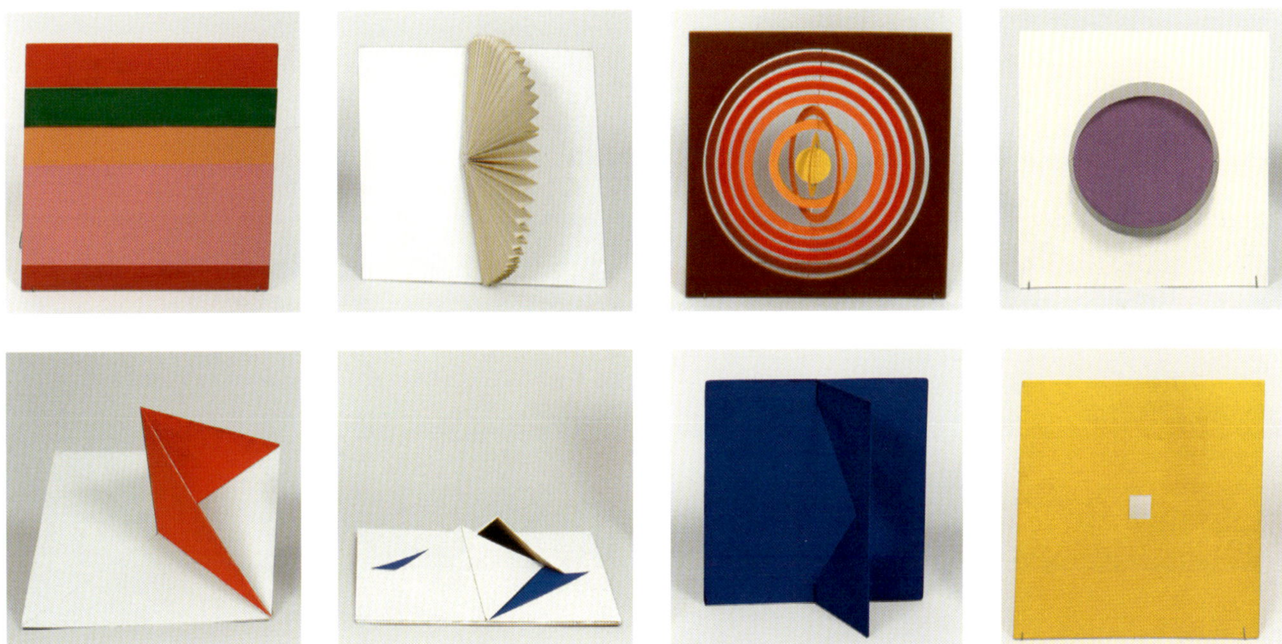

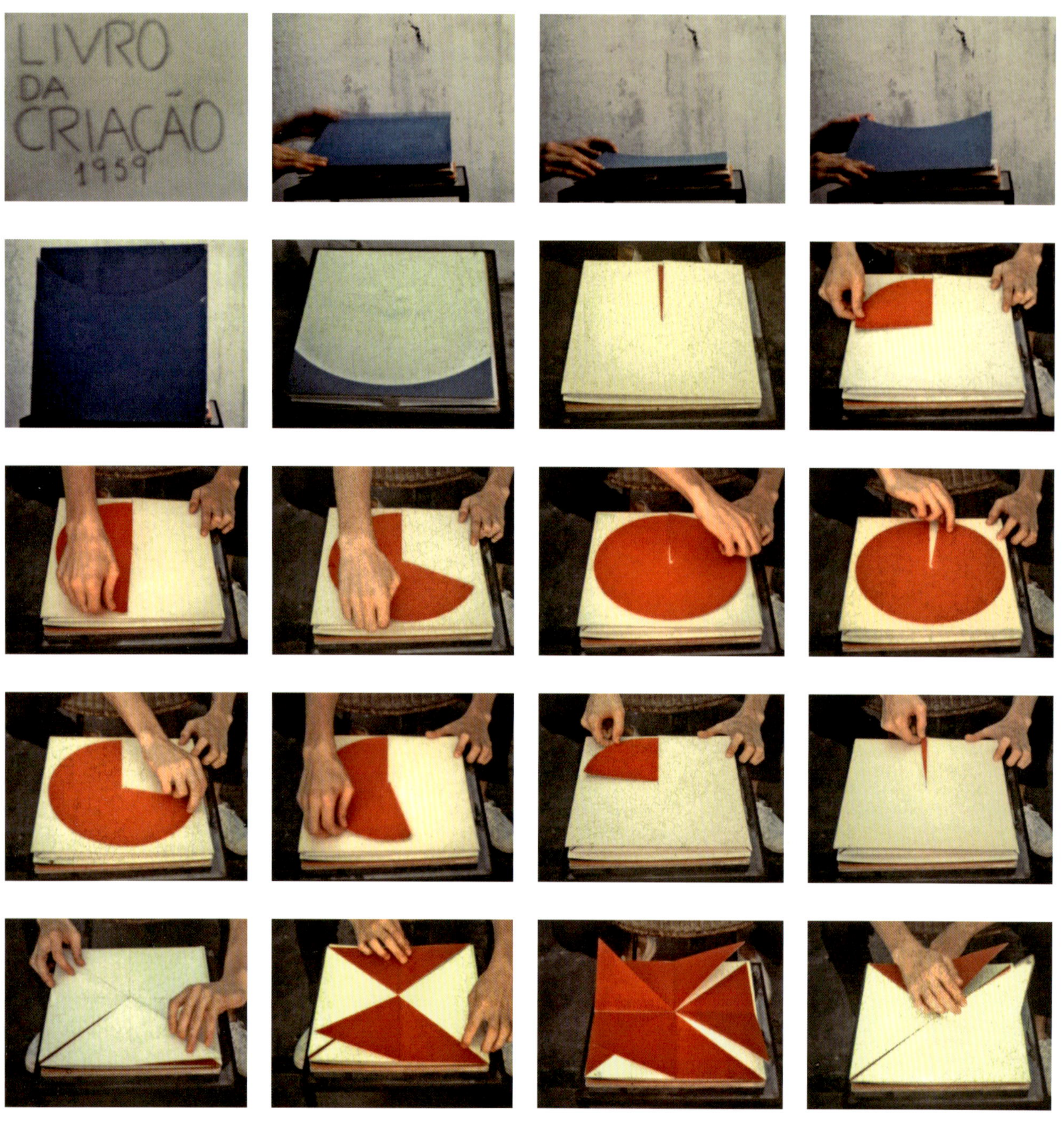

Lygia Pape
Stills from the film *Livro da criação* [Book of Creation], 1959

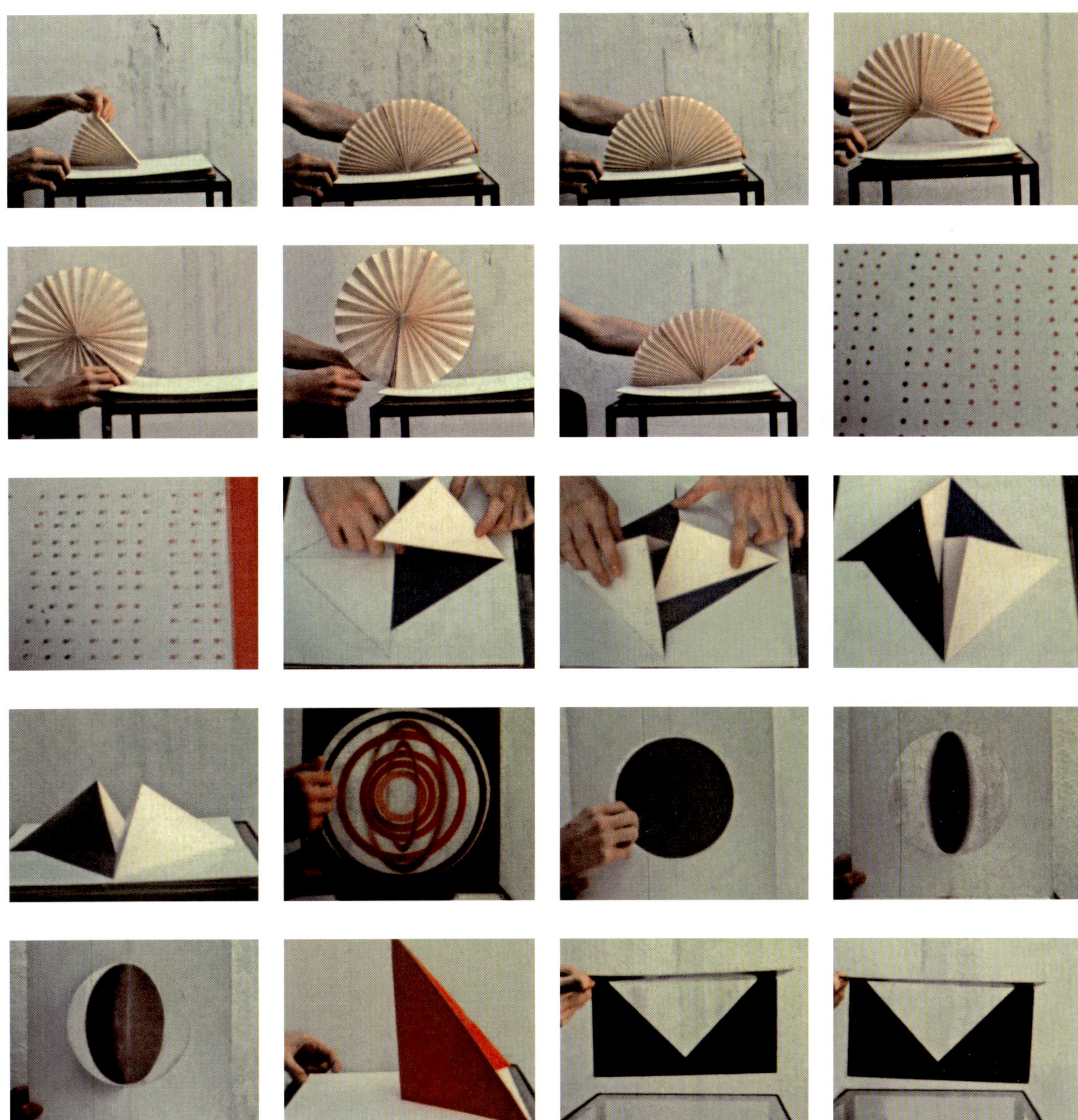

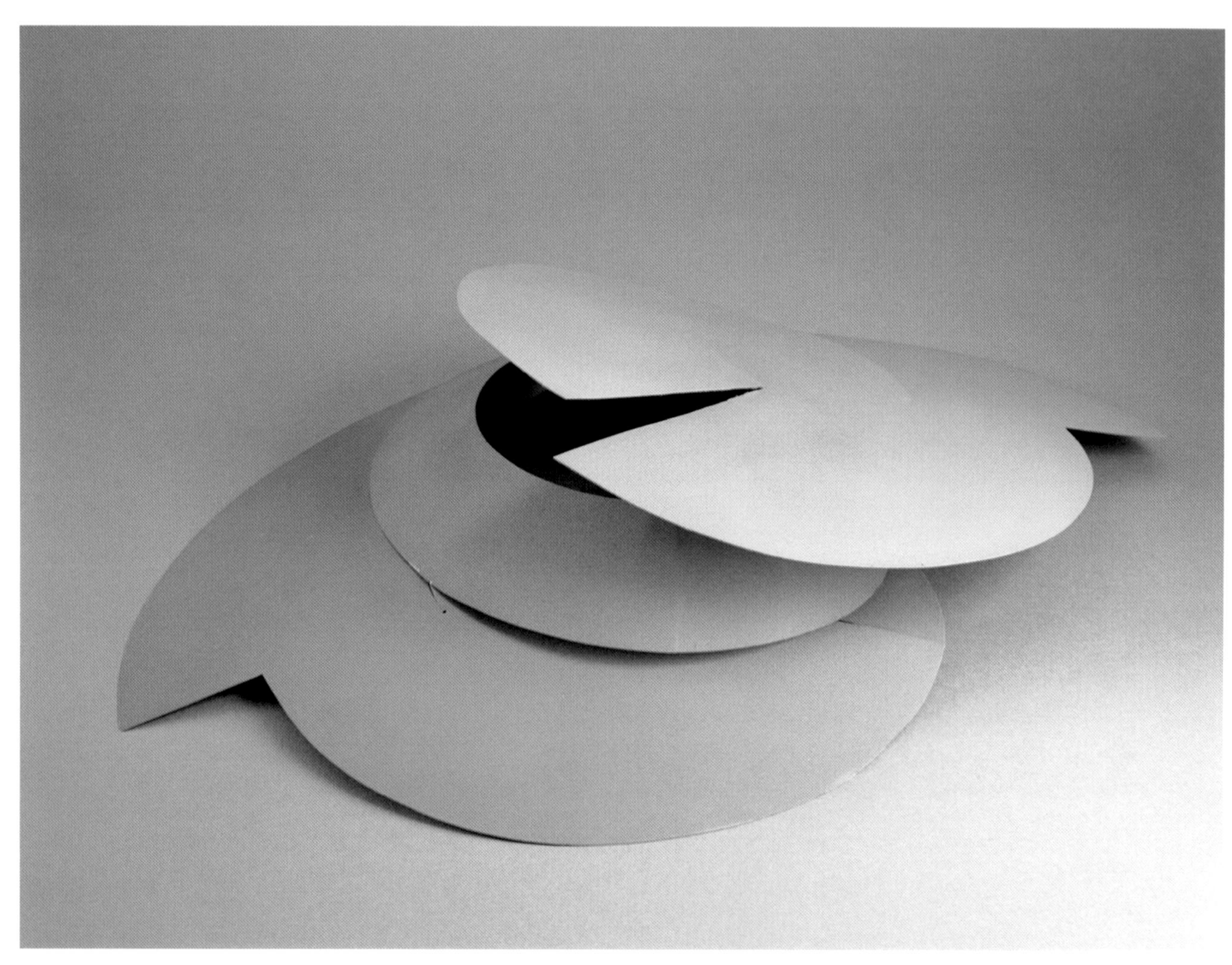

Lygia Clark
Abrigo poético [Poetic Shelter], 1960

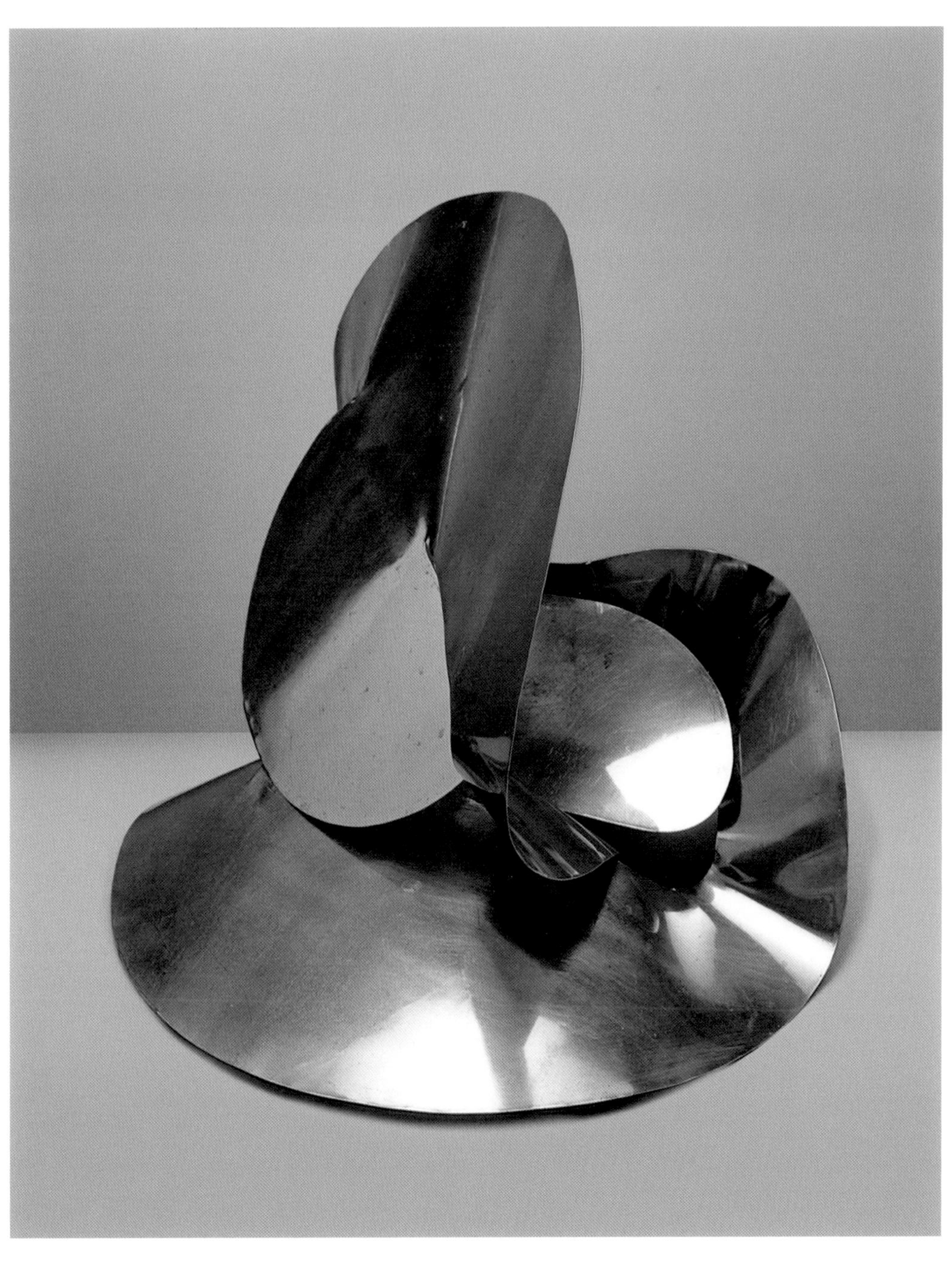

Lygia Clark
O dentro é o fora [The Inside Is the Outside], 1963

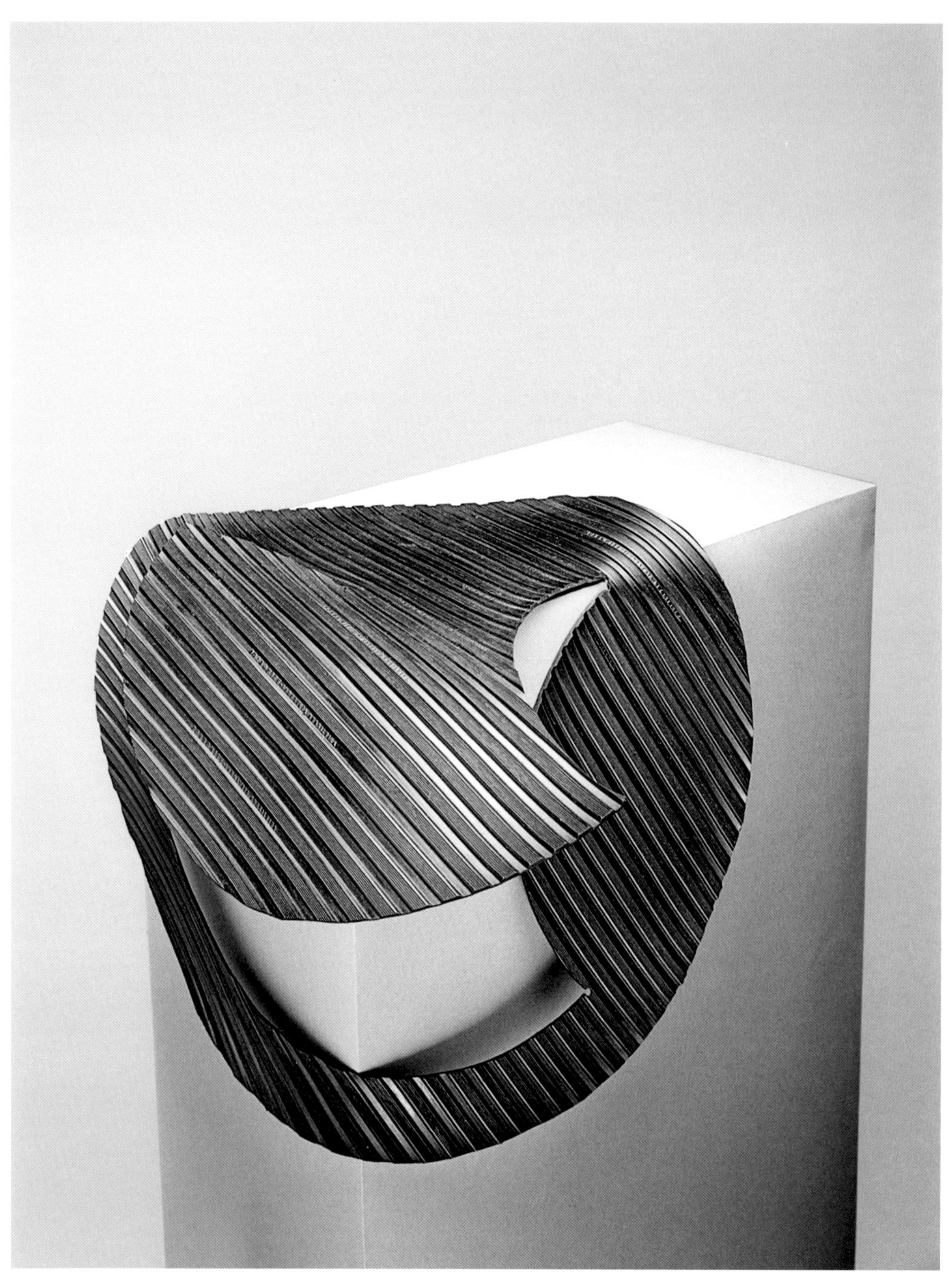

Lygia Clark
***Estudo para Obra mole* [Study for Soft Work], 1964**

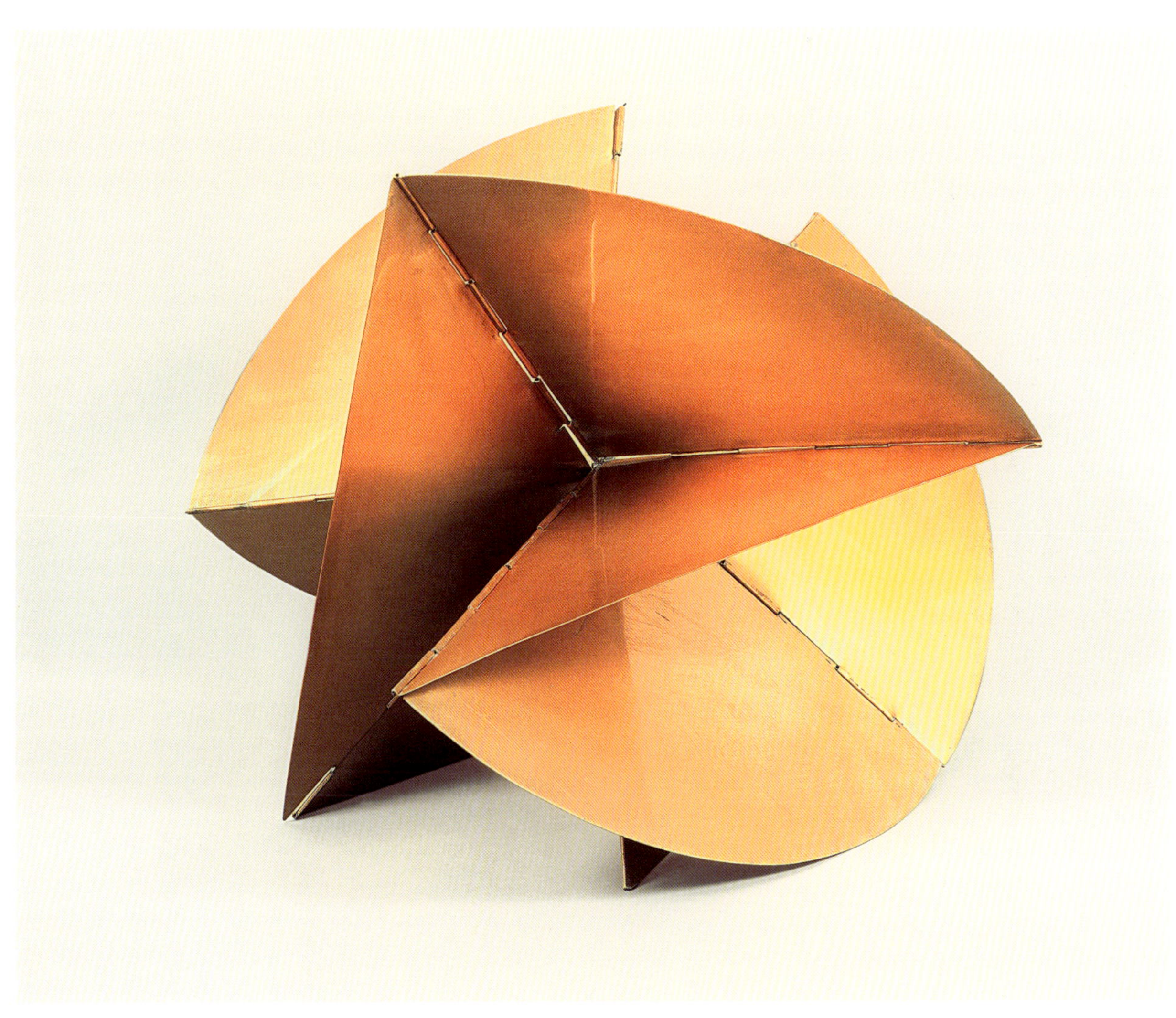

Lygia Clark
Máquina-Md [Machine-Md], 1962

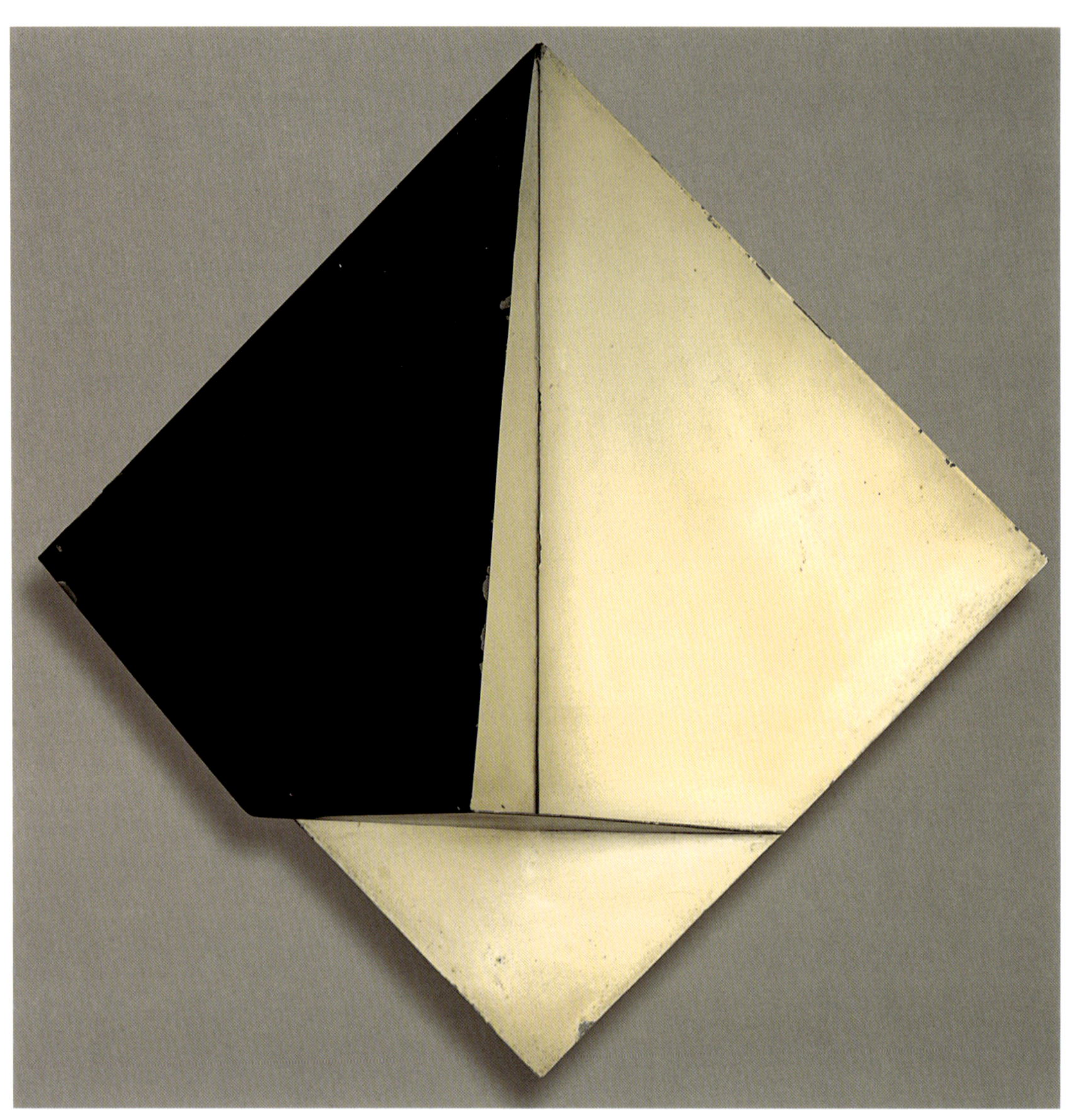

Lygia Clark
Casulo n.º 2 [Cocoon No. 2], 1959

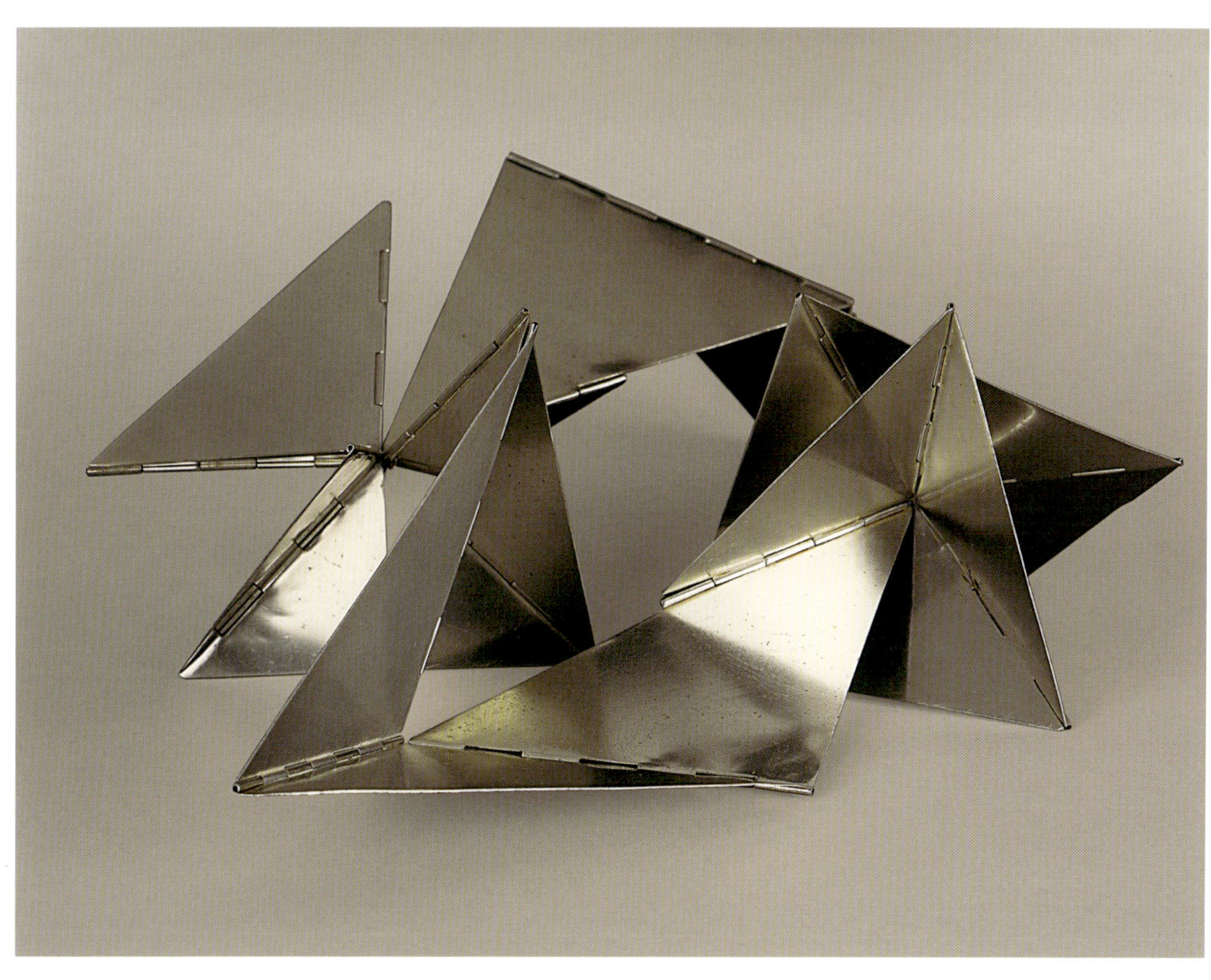

Lygia Clark
Radar-Pq., 1960. Executed in 1984

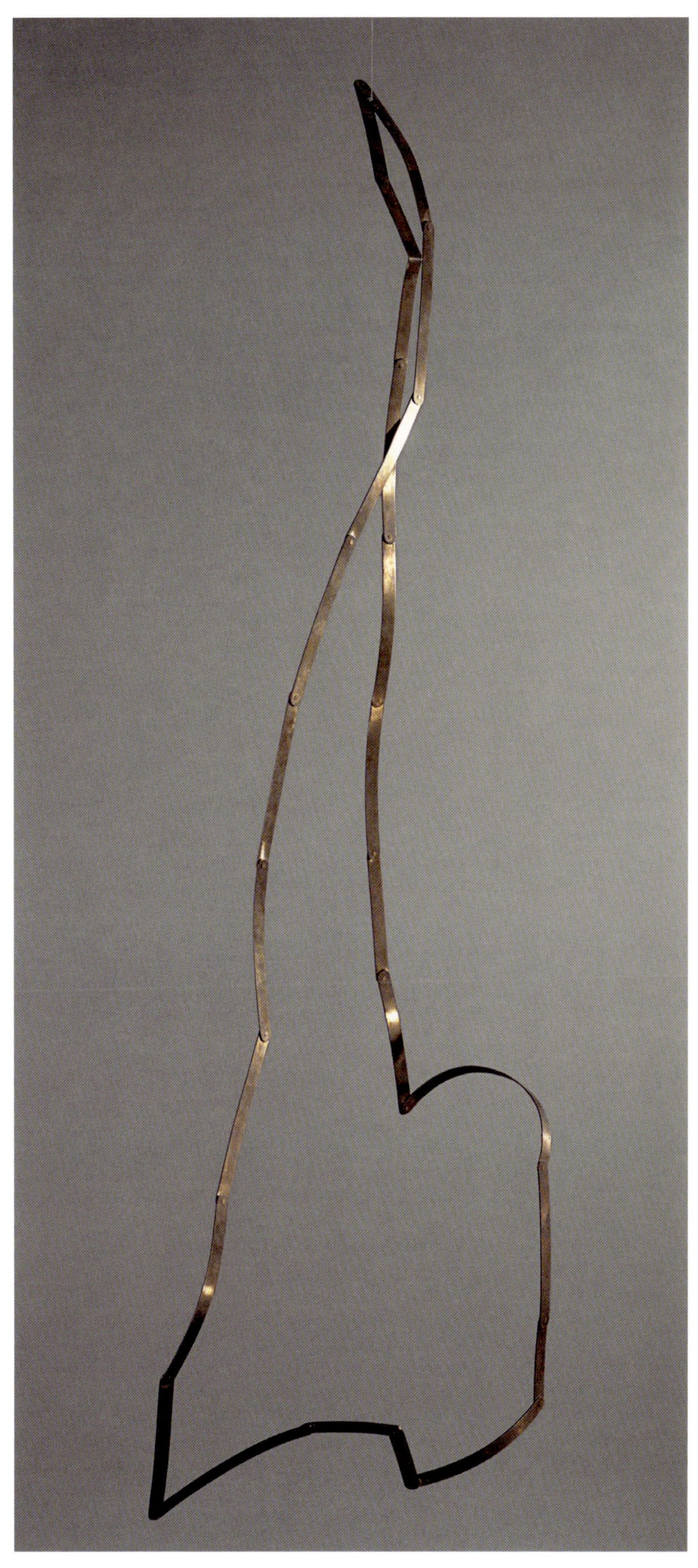

Gyula Kosice
Escultura móvil articulada
[Mobile Articulated Sculpture], 1948

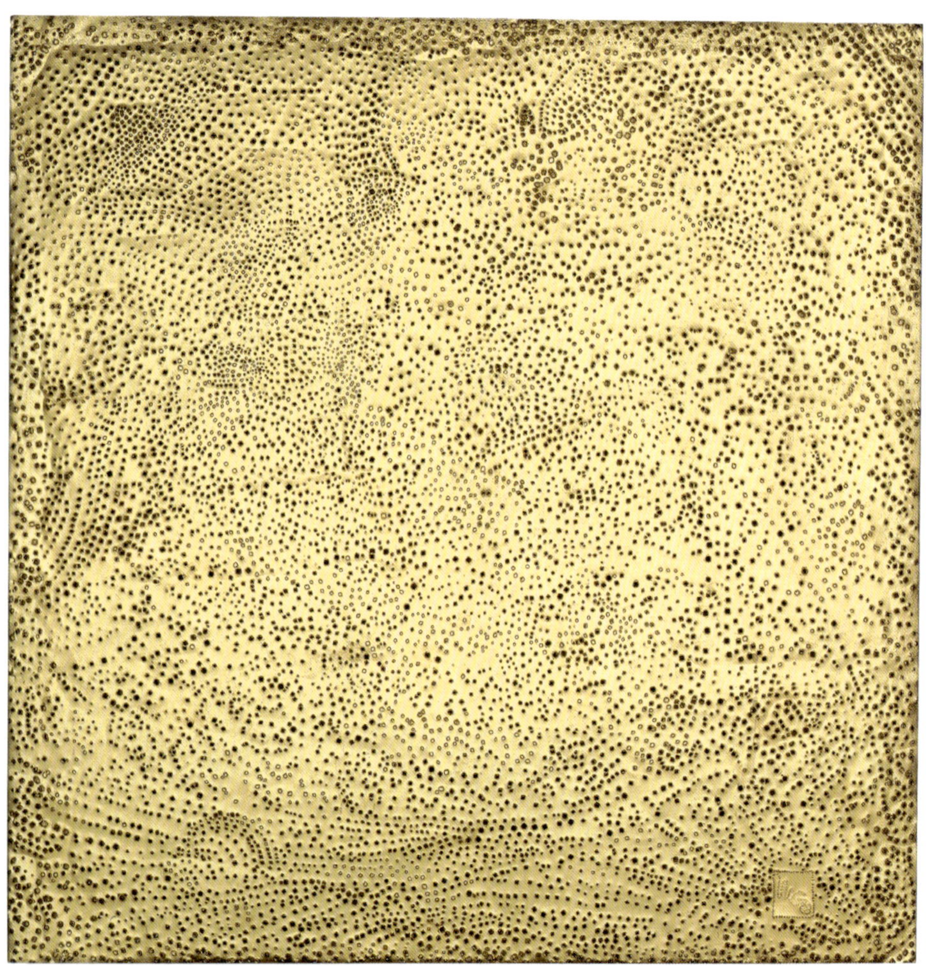

Mathias Goeritz
Untitled, 1960

Farewell to the Periphery
Avant-Gardes and Neo-Avant-Gardes in the Art of Latin America*

Andrea Giunta

When we take a European or North American colleague with a grounding in the story of modern art around a Latin American museum to show him or her something of local art, we always hear similar remarks. Instead of showing curiosity about the characteristics of the works, the artists, the movements, or the contexts out of which they emerged, their observations smack of a type of attribution that classifies each work and each artist, whose name they are hearing for the first time, as an heir or imitator of some celebrated European avant-garde artist. The repertoire is classic and recurrent: Piet Mondrian, Max Ernst, Joan Miró, Theo van Doesburg, Georges Vantongerloo, Paul Klee. And, of course, Pablo Picasso and Marcel Duchamp. Where we see Alfredo Hlito, they see Vantongerloo, and where we see Joaquín Torres-García, they see Mondrian. This tension could be extended to postwar painting in the United States by claiming that Picasso or Miró are to be seen in the work of Arshile Gorky. Such a pattern of classifications and affiliations is not organized solely from an outsider's perspective, since it has also permeated the art histories of the Latin American countries, themselves organized on the basis of the innovations of the European avant-gardes.[1]

It is not that the formal relationship does not exist. But we know it to be no more than one fact among many in understanding how the images intervene in the dynamics of culture. In this text, I sustain that a productive and at the same time critical relationship with the historical avant-gardes was established after World War II in every artistic milieu, even in the European and North American movements. Certain material and historical conditions of reading affected the international course of the avant-garde, tracing out a global scene that, in many cases, revised and radicalized the proposals of the historical avant-gardes, leading them toward degrees of productivity or consequences that had been left until then in suspense. From this perspective, some doubt is cast upon the traditional identification of New York as the hegemonic center to which the Parisian avant-garde moved during World War II. It might be said that at that point, from the standpoint of the evolutionary logic of modern art, we were all in the same place. Rather than a date or a fact, the cutoff point of World War II implies the articulation of a global scenario in which a generalized and simultaneous reactivation of avant-garde strategies became visible, and in which something that these strategies had previously taught is again revealed: that art can activate—that is to say, unsettle, transform, subvert—the present.

I shall be basing this argument on artists who allow us to reconsider the traditional relationship between production centers of novelty and spaces of reception and imitation. Nevertheless, the rereading of the historical avant-gardes allows only some of the plot lines of the postwar transformation of visual culture to become perceptible and thereby significant. It must not be forgotten that these avant-gardes and neo-avant-gardes, which we shall approach through certain specific examples in Latin

*In 2012, I presented preliminary versions of this essay in Madrid, Buenos Aires, and Mexico City. The comments I received from Paulo Herkenhoff, Suely Rolnik, María Amalia García, Cuauhtémoc Medina, and Gabriel Pérez-Barreiro helped me to identify the problems of my initial arguments.

1. For an alternative approach to the relationship between European and Latin American avant-gardes, see Marcelo Pacheco, "La Argentina y una mirada travestida. Emilio Pettoruti entre los espejos," in *Arte, historia e identidad en América: Visiones comparativas*, ed. Gustavo Curiel, Renato González Mello, and Juana Gutiérrez Haces (Mexico City: Instituto de Investigaciones Estéticas, UNAM, 1994), 789–802. Although it does not actually employ the terminology, the text analyzes structures of internal colonialism.

America from the immediate postwar years to the seventies,[2] were activated on the basis of forms originating in a wide diversity of complex visual materials and cultural strategies, including not only avant-garde culture but also pre-Hispanic and colonial culture, mass culture and media culture, slum culture from the Argentinean *villa miseria* to the Brazilian *favela*, and the culture of political activism. In the same way, these movements developed in contact with other disciplines ranging from literature, poetry, and music to psychoanalysis and philosophy. It must therefore always be borne in mind that every work produces a burst of response that is particular and unique, and cannot be straitjacketed within the patterns of affiliation, genealogies, or evolutionary models that structure fetishized readings of art objects.[3] That is to say, every cultural contact or strategic appropriation of a visual or conceptual arrangement generates a field of theories and experiments that acts as a subversive element at a specific time and place.

I am going to concentrate on four scenarios: the Argentine Concrete artists of the immediate postwar period; the initial phase of Mathias Goeritz, between Guadalajara and Mexico City; the passage from Concretism to Neoconcretism in Brazil; and a proposed rereading of Conceptual Art. In the course of this survey, I hope to retrieve some hidden strands of the past, and in so doing to review the power of certain personal relationships.

* * *

At the end of World War II, Europe was exhausted and disoriented. The art scene not only lacked the strength to envisage the future, but the very future that had confidently been anticipated up until the thirties, when successive fronts were formed in Paris in opposition to Surrealism,[4] had been wiped out by the more brutal reality of the war. While there was a sensation in Europe that every artistic path so far explored had been exhausted, America started to be recognized as the place where Europe's great failures could be converted into successes. It was in this context that the avant-garde scenes of Latin America were reformulated. What they sustained, on the basis of texts and images, was that the art they represented restored the idea of the avant-garde to its dimension as an aesthetic renewal, and also to its relationship with life and politics.

In one sense, this discourse fit well into the narrative of modern Western art, where every new ism was explained as an answer to problems left unsolved by the previous one, like a dialogue in time where everything appeared to follow a master plan.

The year 1944 witnessed the appearance in Buenos Aires of the magazine *Arturo*, a seminal publication for understanding certain premises of postwar abstraction in Argentina.[5] I am not going to linger over an analysis of this publication, but I am interested in emphasizing three aspects that serve as a reference for a broader study of the Latin American avant-gardes. First, this was a regional platform that brought together contributions by Chileans, Argentineans, Brazilians, and Uruguayans. Second, it was one of the first publications to theorize the cut-out frame, to be understood as a forerunner of the formulations of European abstraction. Finally, the magazine contains one of the keys to an understanding of artistic culture in Latin America immediately after the war: the power of reproductions.

In 1945, Lidy Prati and Tomás Maldonado produced pivotal works in the development of the cut-out frame—the subdivision of an irregular perimeter with figures, as explained by Rhod Rothfuss in *Arturo*—and the coplanar frame—the structure of

2. Contemporary effects of certain avant-garde devices have been analyzed by Brian Holmes in "The Revenge of the Concept: Artistic Exchanges, Networked Resistance," presented in the context of the exhibition *Geography and the Politics of Mobility*, Generali Foundation, Vienna, January 18, 2003, and published in *Confronting Capitalism: Dispatches from a Global Movement* (Brooklyn, NY: Soft Skull Press, 2004), 350–68. He also referred to these practices as "post-avant-garde," setting them apart from an exclusive artistic context, in "Un sentido de *Tucumán Arde* lo encontramos hoy en el zapatismo," collective interview in *Ramona*, no. 55 (October 2005): 7–22. See also Andrea Giunta, "Activism," trans. Tamara Stuby, in *Contemporary Art: 1989 to the Present*, ed. Alexander Dumbadze and Suzanne Hudson (Oxford: Wiley-Blackwell, 2013), 234–44.

3. One example of the disarticulation of the reading of the work through the optic of sterilized legacies is that carried out by Suely Rolnik with the construction of the corporeal memory of the work of Lygia Clark and of the context from which it originates. See Suely Rolnik, "Archive for a Work-Event: Activating the Body's Memory of Lygia Clark's Poetics and its Context (Part 1)," *Manifesta Journal* 13 (December 2011): 72–80 http://www.manifestajournal.org /issues/fungus-contemporary# (accessed November 21, 2012).

4. I am referring to the successive alliances of abstract artists that were formed to counteract the influence of Surrealism under the leadership of André Breton. The Cercle et Carré group, founded by Michel Seuphor and Joaquín Torres-García in Paris in 1929, was followed in 1930, also in Paris, by Art Concret, the creation of the Dutch artist Theo van Doesburg, which replaced abstract art with Concrete Art, as defined in the "Manifesto of Concrete Art" published in the first and only issue of *Art concret* (signed by Jean Hélion, Otto Carlsund, Léon

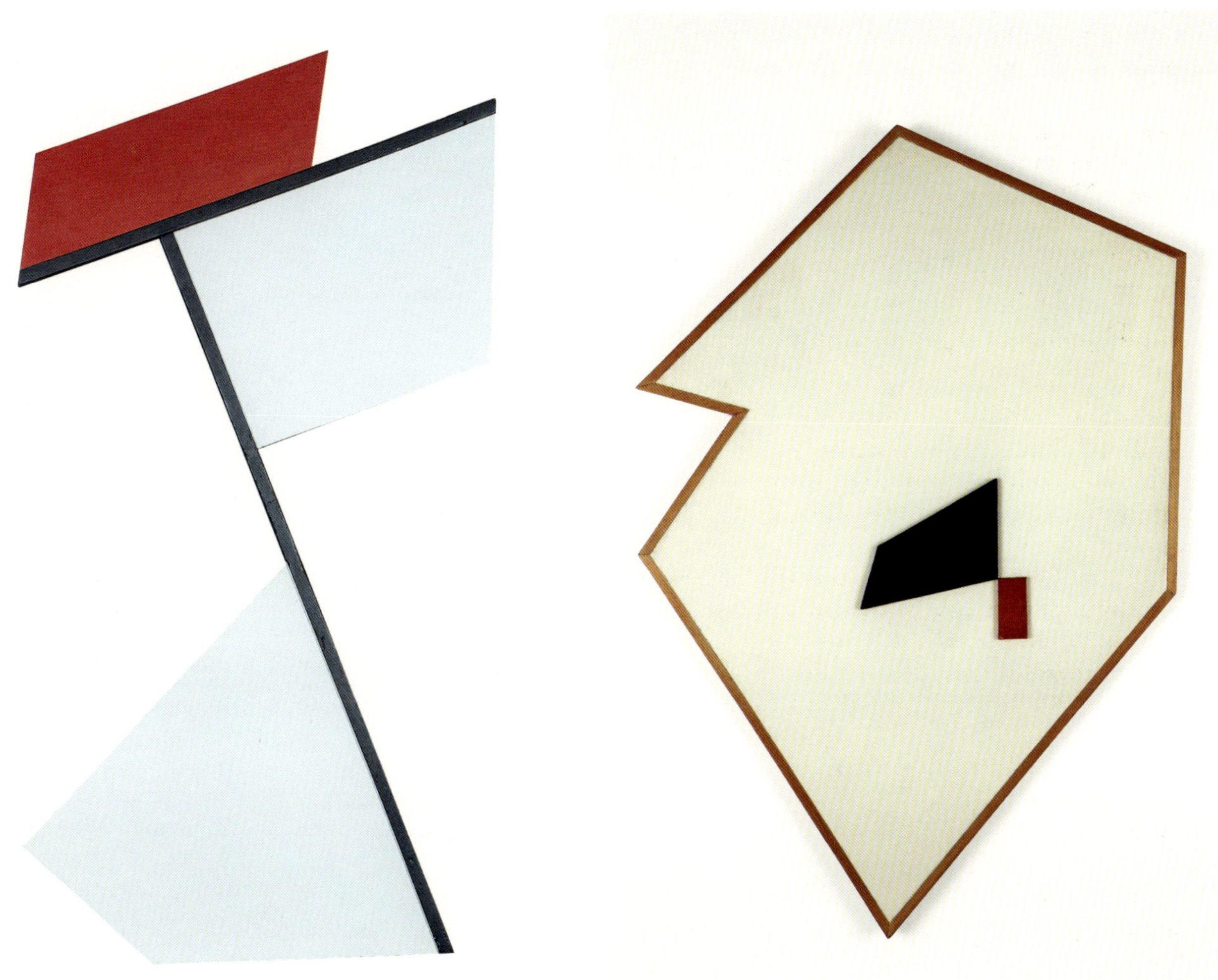

Lidy Prati, *Concreto* [Concrete], 1945
Oil on wood, 60 x 35 cm
Private collection (Not in exhibition)

Tomás Maldonado, Untitled, 1945
Polychromed wood, 77 x 55 cm
Private collection (Not in exhibition)

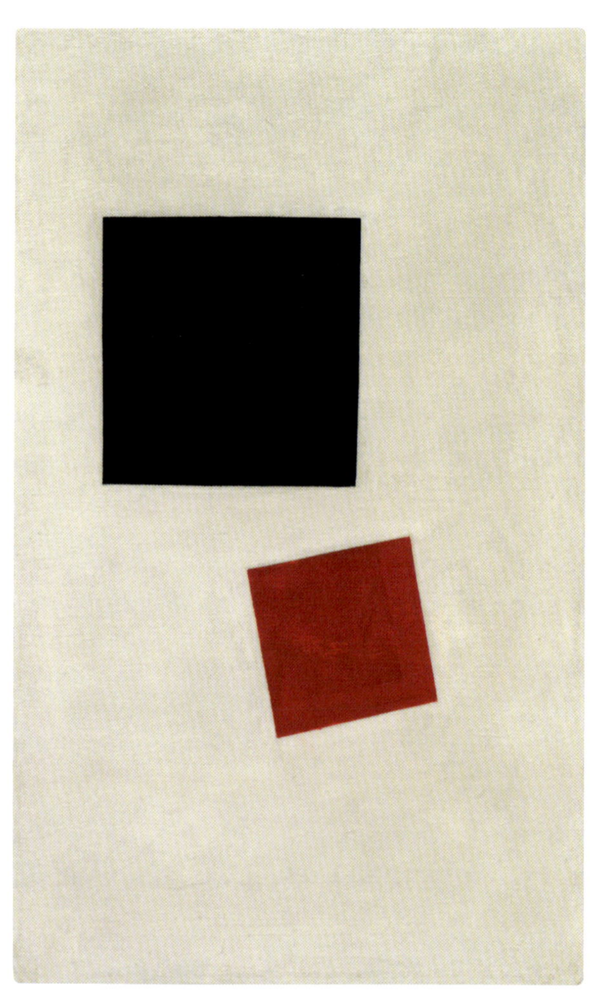

Kazimir Malevich
Black Square and Red Square or Suprematist Composition, 1915
Oil on canvas, 71.1 x 44.5 cm
The Museum of Modern Art, New York (Not in exhibition)

Arthur Tutundjian, and Marcel Wantz), itself a response to Cercle et Carré enunciated in the phrase: "real materials, real space." Finally, Abstraction-Création (1931–1936), founded in Paris, continued the ideas of Art Concret under the conception of a great international abstract front seeking to halt the onslaught of Surrealism. Its initiators were Theo van Doesburg, Auguste Herbin, Jean Hélion, and Georges Vantongerloo, and other artists involved were Albert Gleizes, František Kupka, Piet Mondrian, Jean Arp, Naum Gabo, Barbara Hepworth, Ben Nicholson, Kurt Schwitters, Wassily Kandinsky, and Bart van der Leck, among others. After the death of van Doesburg in 1931, his ideas were taken up toward the end of the decade by the Swiss artists Max Bill and Jean Arp.

5. See María Amalia García, *El arte abstracto. Intercambios culturales entre Argentina y Brasil* (Buenos Aires: Siglo XXI, 2011), 25–53.

6. See María Amalia García, "Lidy Prati y su instancia diferencial en la unidad del arte concreto," in *Yente / Prati*, exh. cat. Malba-Museo de Arte Latinoamericano de Buenos Aires (Buenos Aires: Malba-Fundación Costantini, 2009), 94–95.

7. Tomás Maldonado, "Lo abstracto y lo concreto en el arte moderno," *Arte Concreto-Invención* (Buenos Aires), no. 1 (August 1946): 5–7.

8. After taking part in Milan in the controversy between Elio Vittorini and Palmiro Togliatti (in the journal *Il Politecnico*, the semi-official organ of the Communist Party, Vittorini had proposed an escape from the impasse resulting from the dogma of Socialist Realism), and having witnessed the debate between André Breton and Tristan Tzara in Paris, Maldonado tried unsuccessfully to launch a viable alternative within the Party in Argentina. His immediate expulsion was

interrelated elements in which the surrounding space is woven into the form, so acquiring plastic relevance. For both of them, the collection of the Museum of Modern Art (MoMA) in New York appears to have been crucial. Their production fused Kazimir Malevich's *Suprematist Composition*, 1915, included in the famous exhibition on *Cubism and Abstract Art* held at the MoMA in 1936, with *Composition en blanc, noir et rouge*, 1936, by Piet Mondrian (see p. 113). The latter was reproduced in *Arturo* in black and white, and Lidy Prati filled in the work's single fragment of red by hand.[6] This underlines how important it was for them to make that red visible, since they could only imagine it from reproductions. (It should be mentioned that it was not until 1948, in Switzerland, that Maldonado first saw an original Mondrian.)

The palettes are the same, both artists were key figures in Concrete Art, and both pointed to limitations they hoped to overcome with their own structures. These compositions, enclosed within the frame in Malevich or unresolved in their expansive tension in Mondrian, were reformulated in the works of Prati and Maldonado by means of the cut-out and coplanar frame. This is the representation of art history that they subscribed to in their works and their texts. In 1946, Maldonado affirmed that the coplanar frame was the greatest discovery of his movement (also represented by artists like Alberto Molenberg and Raúl Lozza). It was a proposal in which the picture, as a "containing organism," was abolished.[7]

The objective was not, however, solely a formal one. Maldonado's itinerary, his relationship to the Communist Party and the conflict that culminated with his expulsion from it,[8] and his definition of the social significance of Concrete Art in relation to industrial design (especially after his work with the Ulm School) all point to the political and utopian dimensions inscribed within the discussion on language and forms.

The process of rereading works by Mondrian, Malevich, or Vantongerloo developed within a circulation of images marked by postwar conditions. The materials arrived only sporadically, the reproductions were poor (the colors had to be imagined or even painted in by hand), and the artists had to lend one another the few images they possessed. These conditions gave rise to an *intensive reading* of a corpus of images circulating in Buenos Aires, whose repertoire was renewed in fits and starts. Every image was thus analyzed and debated insistently, and complex formal consequences were drawn from it.

Through this reconstruction of a historical period on the basis of the images it gave rise to, I hope to draw attention to a central condition of the Latin American abstract avant-gardes. Given their understanding of the logic governing the development of modern art, these artists thought that innovation—the next step, the answer to an unresolved problem or even to one never envisioned by their predecessors—could arise anywhere. In a recent interview, Gyula Kosice said in this respect: "What I wanted was to be unlike anyone else."[9] What shines through here is the avant-garde imagination, characterized by the ideas of foresight, originality, and heroism. Kosice's major innovations include the cut-out frame, his manipulable metal structures, the sculpture *Royï* (kinetic, random, and participatory sculpture highlighting the centrality of the viewer who manipulates the sculpture), the sculpture of neon gas, Hydrokineticism, and the Hydrospatial City with its nomadic and interplanetary forms and its proposed hydrocitizens. The suspended city, capable of supplying itself with water, is offered as a solution to the problems he anticipated for the future of mankind. It is a cosmic utopia fed by an imagery of transparent houses capable of creating new societies and, at the same time, inscribed within the narrative of the space race. The forms of art proposed by the abstract avant-garde in Buenos Aires after 1944 served to inaugurate the idea of a future whose starting point was the final moment of European achievement. Metaphors of foresight and originality were in themselves enough to ignite the imagination and to establish valuation criteria. There was much of the emotional outburst in these representations. The artists did not regard themselves as students or followers. For them, the European avant-gardes were not debts they owed but toolboxes they could use to formulate their own avant-garde movements.

Their innovations were aimed at an audience far beyond the local. They were intended for the modern art audience of the West, and for anyone willing to recognize the solutions they proposed, which implied overcoming unresolved artistic issues in order to "advance" in the direction indicated by the idea of modern art.

* * *

After the war, the avant-gardes investigated the artistic capital that had been accumulated before the conflict. Was this a movement of continuity or regression? Were they going forward or back?

When analyzed on the basis of European modernism, the Latin American avant-gardes might well be conceptualized from the same perspective as that adopted by Benjamin Buchloh in referring to the New York School of the 1940s and 1950s: that is, as its *immediate extension* or its *logical development*.[10] In his distinction between avant-gardes and neo-avant-gardes, Peter Bürger argues that the first are innovative, critical, and skeptical of the established order, while the second are a repetition misappropriated by tendencies, and as such inauthentic.[11] His perspective is marked by melancholy for the loss of the innovative potential of the early avant-gardes. Buchloh introduced a contrary perspective by locating the rediscovery of Dada and Constructivism, the moment when their aesthetic productivity was rendered visible, in 1951. In contrast to the disenchantment of Bürger, who sees only failure in the art of the neo-avant-garde, Buchloh focuses on its capacity for resistance and its power to offer a critique of the spectacularization of culture.

From another point of view, Hal Foster also questions the residual evolutionism he sees in Bürger, and contributes additional material for assessing the productivity of the neo-avant-gardes. Foster inverts the notion of an imitative dispersal: "In postwar art to pose the question of repetition is to pose the question of the *neo-avant-garde*, a loose grouping of North American and Western European (and, I would add, Latin American) artists of the 1950s and 1960s who reprised such avant-garde devices of the 1910s and 1920s as collage and assemblage, the readymade and the grid, monochrome painting and constructed sculpture."[12] Instead of the symptoms of wear and tear, Foster emphasizes those of vitality. He grants visibility to the temporal and conceptual exchange between avant-gardes and neo-avant-gardes. Furthermore, he says that it is in the return of the neo-avant-garde that the avant-gardes become readable. It is a reflexive return rather than an operation of naïve pastiche, and it is a return that involves a critique of postwar society and an appeal for new audiences; in short, a dispute over the significance of culture. Foster's is a post-historical approach based on the central notion of *deferred action,* whereby an analogy is traced between modern art and the Freudian capturing of the psychic temporality of the subject read through the lenses of Lacan. From such a perspective, the avant-garde and the neo-avant-garde are constituted in Foster's opinion by "a complex relay of anticipated futures and

determined by a tribunal chaired by Alicia Penalba. His case is an example of the local purges in the Communist Party, another being the expulsion of the critic Córdova Iturburu.

9. *Gyula Kosice in Conversation with Gabriel Pérez-Barreiro* (New York and Caracas: Fundación Cisneros, 2012), 39.

10. Benjamin H. D. Buchloh, *Neo-Avantgarde and Culture Industry: Essays on European and American Art from 1955 to 1975* (Cambridge, Mass.: MIT Press, 2000), 24.

11. Peter Bürger, *Theory of the Avant-Garde* (Manchester: Manchester University Press, 1984).

12. Hal Foster, *The Return of the Real: The Avant-Garde at the End of the Century* (Cambridge, Mass.: MIT Press, 1996), 1.

reconstructed pasts—in short, in a deferred action that throws over any simple scheme of before and after, cause and effect, origin and repetition."[13]

In his theory of the avant-garde, Bürger points out that the criticism of art institutions (the self-criticism of the art system) is a central feature of the historical avant-garde movements, above all Dadaism. This criticism expresses itself as regards both the apparatus of distribution (institutions for the legitimation of art) and the status of art in bourgeois society (that is, its autonomy). The avant-garde wants to restore art's everyday praxis, its social effect.[14] In his essay on Conceptual Art, Buchloh foregrounds the neo-avant-gardes' critique of the traditional paradigms of visuality, above all after 1966 with the work of Marcel Broodthaers, Daniel Buren, and Hans Haacke, and also stresses their focusing on the logic of institutions, with power to determine the conditions of cultural consumption.[15] By that time, all these features were also visible in the work of León Ferrari, Pablo Suárez, Roberto Jacoby, Cildo Meireles, Antonio Manuel, Artur Barrio, Antonio Dias, Antonio Caro, and Luis Camnitzer.

I should like to return for a moment to certain specific articulations of the paths traced by images and by ideas about art. From the 1930s onward, the narrative of European artistic modernity circulated in texts that explained the order, characteristics, and genealogies of modern art, laid out in books and catalogues with complex indices and charts. A historiographical moment had come to an end. Civilizing narratives as they were, these pedagogical guides, which spread the idea that modern art was gestated in Paris but was valid for the rest of the world (this formed the central axis of their colonial project), could be used in another way. The forms, images, and explanations of modern art were assumed in their diffusion, forming the idea of an artistic past that could be assembled differently in new contexts as well as those from which it had arisen. If, as Foster maintains, the neo-avant-gardes did not cancel the avant-garde project but rather understood and completed it, such a development could take place wherever the lessons of modernism had been assimilated, and it could do so everywhere at the same time.

For this reading, situated in a context of rereading on a worldwide scale, the question is not one of revising the evolutionary patterns of artistic modernity in order to find a niche for surges of avant-garde activity on Alfred Barr's famous map. It is not a matter of completing the evolutionary model, but of suspending it so as to make historical simultaneity visible, and not only that of the investigation of artistic languages but also of the institutional critique they involve, together with other more overt and hostile forms of anti-institutionalism. The moment around 1968 traces out an international horizon through a multiplicity of artistic scenes, though these also shared contacts and agendas. Without wishing to evaluate the success or failure of these experiments, I am interested in showing how much light they can shed on the complex tensions between avant-gardes and neo-avant-gardes.

* * *

13. Ibid., 29.

14. See Bürger, *Theory of the Avant-Garde*, 33–38.

15. Benjamin H. D. Buchloh, "Conceptual Art 1962–1969: From the Aesthetic of Administration to the Critique of Institution," *October* 55 (Winter 1990): 105–43.

Mathias Goeritz arrived in Guadalajara in 1949. After a period in Spain marked by his experience of the war and by the Altamira School's attempt at an artistic renewal reaching down to primitive and abstract roots, he arrived to Mexico with the idea of implementing a detailed and ambitious scheme to update the university curriculum, a plan he envisaged as the emergence of a new Bauhaus. His activity fell under the influence of two movements. On the one hand, he wanted to modernize Guadalajara's cultural milieu through the introduction of modern art. To this end, he organized exhibitions (with originals or with photographs of the works) on artists like Klee, Henry Moore, Gorky, Wassily Kandinsky, Miró, and Picasso. We know that Goeritz did not find it easy to spearhead either an educational project or abstract art in general in Guadalajara. In Mexico City, he drew up plans for a museum, *El Eco* (1952–53), which in one sense represents the culmination of a modernist program guided, in this case, by the idea of integrating the arts through architecture, an architecture Goeritz called "emotional." This is an abstraction with spiritual and symbolic roots, different from the type of rational abstraction, obsessed with the impersonal logic of the brushstroke, that characterized the Concrete Art group in Buenos Aires. The same sense of spirituality is to be found in his gilded reliefs. Second, Goeritz proposed a method of teaching that was new to Mexico. In using the pedagogy of the Bauhaus, he was resorting to one of the formative experiments of European modernity. Nevertheless, Goeritz adapted these modernist guidelines to Mexican culture, appealing to specific materials with local connotations (like gourds or gold leaf), iconographic topoi (the serpent, including its more popular representation as a broken reed), and specific palettes (like that developed from his relationship with the painter Chucho Reyes, an expert in the colonial and folk objects from which he took the chromatic ranges whose influence can be seen in the towers of Ciudad Satélite).

In Goeritz's work, this tradition branches off in many directions. One is urban sculpture (the towers of Ciudad Satélite), where the program of abstraction is united with the public vocation also seen in his giant murals. It is a *logical development* of the abstract line enunciated since the earliest avant-gardes. Perceptible at the same time is the emergence of a neo-Dadaism that appears in some of his installations and performances of the early sixties. In this sense, one can speak of a return. In his own work, Goeritz effects a "dismantling of the avant-gardes"[16] represented by his manifesto, *¡Please Stop!*, written as a reaction to the *Homage to New York* presented by Jean Tinguely in the gardens of the MoMA in 1961. However, he did inscribe a personal variable of mystic Dadaism, a "prayer art against shit art." His statements expressed weariness of avant-garde provocations amidst a critique that introduced spirituality and religion. At the same time, they opposed Social Realism, the Rupture Generation, and French Nouveau Réalisme under the guiding light of Pierre Restany. Goeritz's proposal was reactive and reproductive. On the one hand, he proposed retrieving a spiritual legacy he believed to be extinct; on the other, he used the very neo-Dadaist and neo-avant-garde gestures he was questioning.[17] His critique of the art system was to lead him to abandon galleries after his 1962 exhibition in New York, but the public registration of his abstract propositions remained trapped in the political whirlwinds of the sixties. For one thing, Goeritz's meditative forms coincided with liturgical changes deriving from an ability to read the political force of abstraction. The most radical or iconoclastic renovation of the liturgy took place alongside an aesthetic transformation that found in works such as Mathias Goeritz's stained-glass windows for Cuernavaca Cathedral (1961) an image capable of reorienting popular piety through abstraction, a sort of return to a primitive Christianity free of ornamental or theological overload, Baroque or otherwise. As Luis Adrián Vargas Santiago points out, non-narrative forms participated in the administration of a doctrine that united Karl Marx and the Bible in the relationship between the guerrilla and religion.[19] They also allowed the unexpected consequences of images to be controlled. The invitation sent out to the artists who took part in the Ruta de la Amistad (Route of Friendship) established the use of a particular material (concrete) and a particular language (abstract).[19] Paradoxically, the term "concrete," the concept which had risen as a motto for the first postwar abstract movement in Buenos Aires, now referred to the construction material that oriented the form.[20] These conditions

16. See Francisco Reyes Palma, "Oratorio monocromático. Los Hartos," in *Los ecos de Mathias Goeritz*, ed. Ida Rodríguez Prampolini and Ferruccio Asta, exh. cat. Antiguo Colegio de San Idelfonso (Mexico City: Instituto Nacional de Bellas Artes, 1997), 123.

17. A precursor of this Dadaist attitude can be found in the "installation" he set up with his students in 1951, consisting of a vertical pile of chairs. Cristóbal Andrés Jácome Moreno regards this as his first tower in "Composiciones visuales: Mathias Goeritz en Guadalajara," *Estudios Jaliscenses*, no. 81 (August 2010): 56–67.

18. This historical outline and these hypotheses were proposed by Luis Adrián Vargas Santiago in "Imágenes, teología y guerrilla" at the symposium "Genealogías del arte contemporáneo en México 1952–1967," Instituto de Investigaciones Estéticas y Museo de Arte Contemporáneo, Universidad Nacional Autónoma de México, August 30–31, 2012.

19. Karel Wendl, who took part in the Ruta de la Amistad as coordinator, writes that "the particular problem the sculptors were to solve limited their artistic liberty by the following restrictions: the sculptures had to be made of concrete, monumental, and abstract." Karel Wendl, "Research Notes: The Route of Friendship; A Cultural/Artistic Event of the Games of the XIX Olympiad in Mexico City—1968," *OLYMPIKA: The International Journal of Olympic Studies* 7 (1997): 113–34. I am grateful to Jennifer Josten for this reference.

20. Although the building material concrete is referred to in Spain as "hormigón," the word "concreto," a borrowing from English, is employed in Latin America—ed.

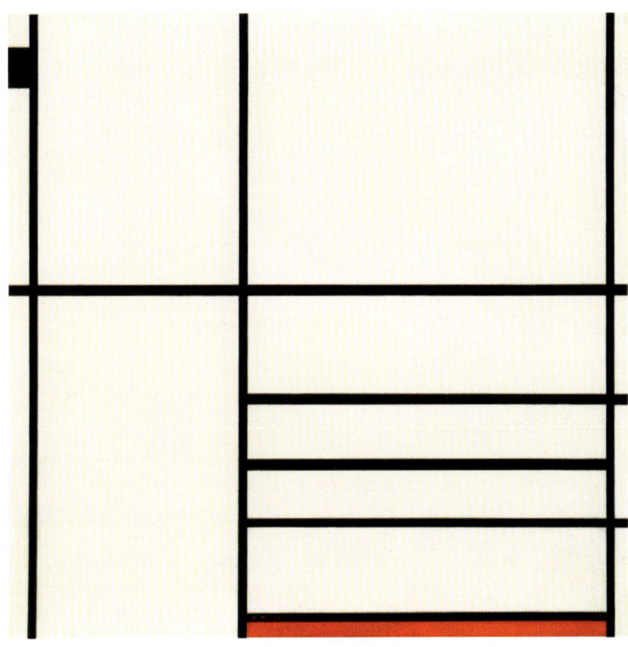

Piet Mondrian
Composition en blanc, noir et rouge [Composition in white, black, and red], 1936
Oil on canvas, 102.2 x 104.1 cm
The Museum of Modern Art, New York (Not in exhibition)

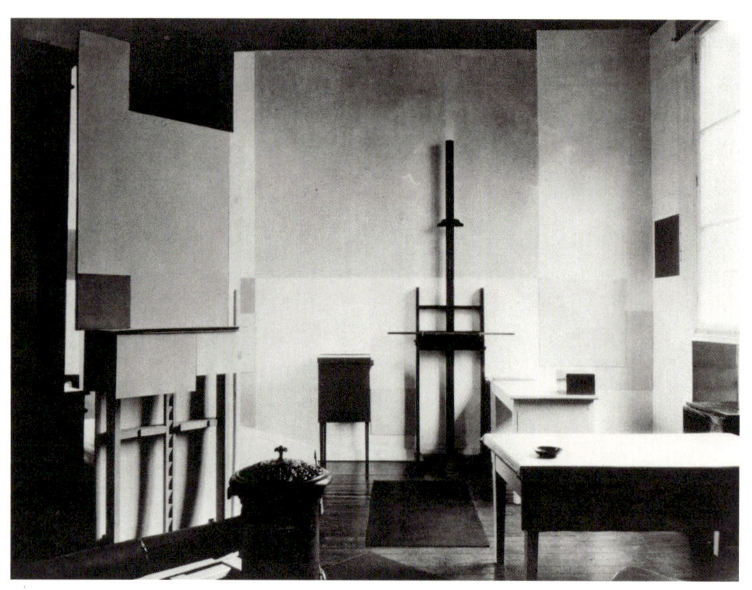

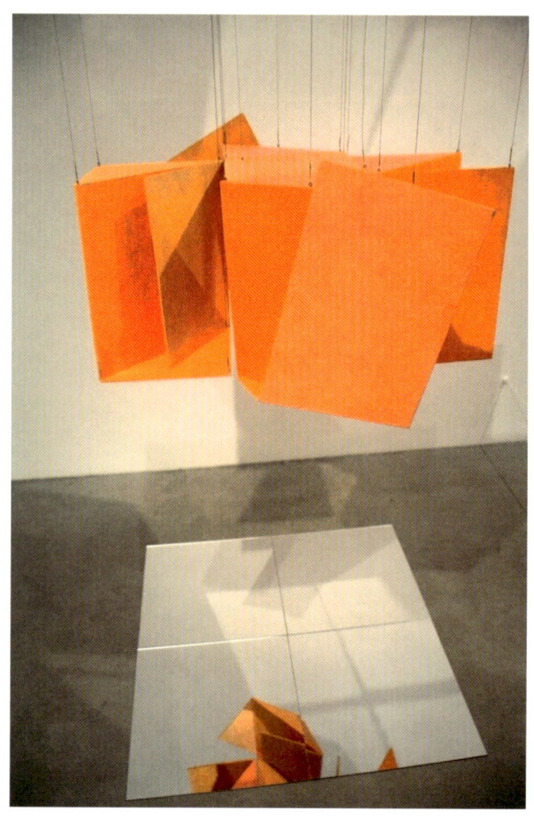

Paul Delbo
Piet Mondrian's studio, Paris, 1926

Hélio Oiticica
Grande núcleo NC3, NC4, NC6
[Grand Nucleus, NC3, NC4, NC6], 1960–63
Oil on wood, 1077 x 717 cm
Coleção César e Claudio Oiticica (Not in exhibition)

anticipated a potential insubordination of the themes that the country hosting the Games of the XIX Olympiad in 1968 could not permit.[21] Contrary to the established history of Latin American art, Mexico did have a moment of abstraction that can be understood as a kind of culmination of modernism, or as the political administration of forms.

* * *

In the Brazilian art of the late fifties, the inscriptional strategies of the avant-garde and the neo-avant-garde merged out of an internal logic defined by the specific itineraries of abstraction in São Paulo and Rio de Janeiro. At that moment, Mondrian was a model for the images and texts of Lygia Clark. Let us recall the letter Lygia Clark wrote to him in May 1959, in which she stresses the restorative meaning she finds in his work: "Mondrian, if your strength may serve me, it would be like the raw steak placed on that sore eye so that it may see again as soon as possible and may be able to face this reality which is often so unbearable—'The artist is a loner.'"[22] At the moment she was writing, the initial force of the Concrete movement had weakened, and in the intimate tone of this elegy addressed to the dead master, she asks him whether she should leave the group and follow her own path. It was in 1958, just a year earlier, that Lygia Clark's work had started to break loose from the plane. In *Unidades 1–7* (Units 1–7), 1958, her squares painted in industrial pigment are interrupted with cuts that draw awareness to a zone of ambiguity or transition between the wall and the plane of the work. The living line. A respiration. That is where the folds of the *Casulo* (Buds), 1959 (p. 100), series begin: with the death of the plane, and *bichos* (creatures) that double up in space. The goal is a formal one but also, and above all, performative, distancing itself from the arrested order of the painted abstract plane. It is acting on the plane in the same way as one acts on the line, as when Lygia cuts the paper in *Caminhando* (Walking), 1963, or a sheet of metal, or of rubber. Mondrian is only one possible point of contact that provides certain elements for envisaging the passage from plane to body, which, from that point on, would be the object of Clark's investigations that moved increasingly away from the institutional standard.[23] This escape from the plane and the wall toward experience, and the very notion of work as process, are incomprehensible without Maurice Merleau-Ponty and his phenomenology, introduced to Latin America by the likes of Mário Pedrosa and Ferreira Gullar. Philosophy, yes, but everyday life too: the *bichos* could also have been born by twisting a napkin during a family meal.[24]

Hélio Oiticica also sets the orthogonal grid in motion and creates spaces that emphasize the cracks or chromatic abysses residing between Mondrian's zones of pure color. Yellow, orange, red, or white on white are arranged on the wall or suspended and activated in space. These images are reminiscent of the arrangements of planes seen in the interiors of Mondrian's studios in New York and Paris. In both Oiticica's and Clark's work this invasion of space takes place between 1958 and 1959. Oiticica goes further than Mondrian, making the forms breathe and reflect one another. We might in this case talk of a *logical development* of the avant-garde. I wish in this way to differentiate a moment of modernist expansion in Oiticica's work, also found in that of Clark, from another that is critical of modernity. With Clark, this occurs with the introduction of nature and then the body. With Oiticica, it is when the forms and planes of color become body, movement, and dance, and when references to popular culture are introduced, displaced from the erudite canon onto the culture of the *morro* and the carnival. The great explanatory dilemma of Brazilian Neoconcretism is tensed between two models. On one side is that concentrated in the idea of the development of forms. From this perspective, the *parangolé* would be a mise-en-scène of the (modern)

21. Jennifer Josten pointed this out in her paper "Los Hartos en el contexto de los grupos de vanguardia," at the symposium "Genealogías del arte contemporáneo en México."

22. Lygia Clark, "Letter to Mondrian," in exh. cat. Fundació Antoni Tàpies, Barcelona et al. (Barcelona: Fundació Antoni Tàpies, 1997), 115.

23. Suely Rolnik, "The Body's Contagious Memory: Lydia Clark's Return to the Museum," *Traversal* (May 2007), http://eipcp.net/ transversal/0507/rolnik /en (accessed September 16, 2012).

24. As her son recalls her doing. See Renata Sant'Anna and Valquíria Prates, *Lygia Clark linhas vivas* (São Paulo: Paulinas, 2006). I am grateful to Paulo Herkenhoff for reminding me of this account.

Paris-14-1-51

Rafi and Lia

Dear friends:

I suppose that on more than one occasion you must have doubted whether
I remembered the two of you given my prolonged silence. One must be
in a situation like mine to understand the need for friends like you;
I remember you as often as I do my nearest and dearest. But Paris,
or any new life, produces crises that can only be overcome with the
passing of days. Today I am better; after three months of receiving
shocks, sensations, and lessons in immense proportions, from which
I often felt weak, I have begun a period of analysis and, to a certain
degree, calm from which to look at things and evaluate them. There
were terrible moments in which the good and the bad confused me as
if it were all improvised; painting was thirty years ahead of me
and it was those thirty years that crushed me when I arrived. Up to
Cubism, everything was familiar to me. From Cubism (1913) until now,
there were thirty-seven years of painting that I knew nothing about.
Abstract art had started in 1910 with Kandinsky, the same period in
which the Cubists were filled with the glory of that great revolution.
Mondrian began to prepare the great synthesis with Neoplasticism,
coming to resolve in the most un-objective way, with the sole use of
the vertical and the horizontal, the rigor of the orthogonal concept
that plagued Cézanne, and which Picasso, Braque, Delaunay, and Juan
Gris, etc. proposed in the Cubist conclusions. So then, abstract art
had stopped being the new thing twenty years ago only to become the
greatest revolution the history of art has ever witnessed, solving
problems that, having disappeared with the Italian Primitives, Cubism
would revive, thus laying the foundations for a new art.

Imagine the speed at which I needed to move in order to relate to my
own time. But for that there is Paris, to make up for the passage of
time.

I have taken my first steps in painting; my colleagues are a bit
puzzled as to how I have managed to assimilate everything and point
my form of expression toward new horizons; and it is because there
is no greater truth than the creative responsibility of the artist to
understand his own time, to express it and to represent it, and this
is only achieved by probing the mystery of the unknown until one
uncovers the connecting paths that indicate the road of progress.

You can write back to the mailing address.

Your friend always: Soto

In the margin: . . . school. A hug to Roberto, and from now on I will uphold my life as a
painter at all costs.

**Transcription of a letter sent by Jesús Soto to the Venezuelan sculptors Lía Bermúdez
and, most likely, Rafael Barrios. Paris, January 14, 1951**

Vibration

"I only want to achieve those combinations in which color has greater vibratory strength, and where the spatial ambiguity that results from its superimpositions is evident."

Jesús Soto

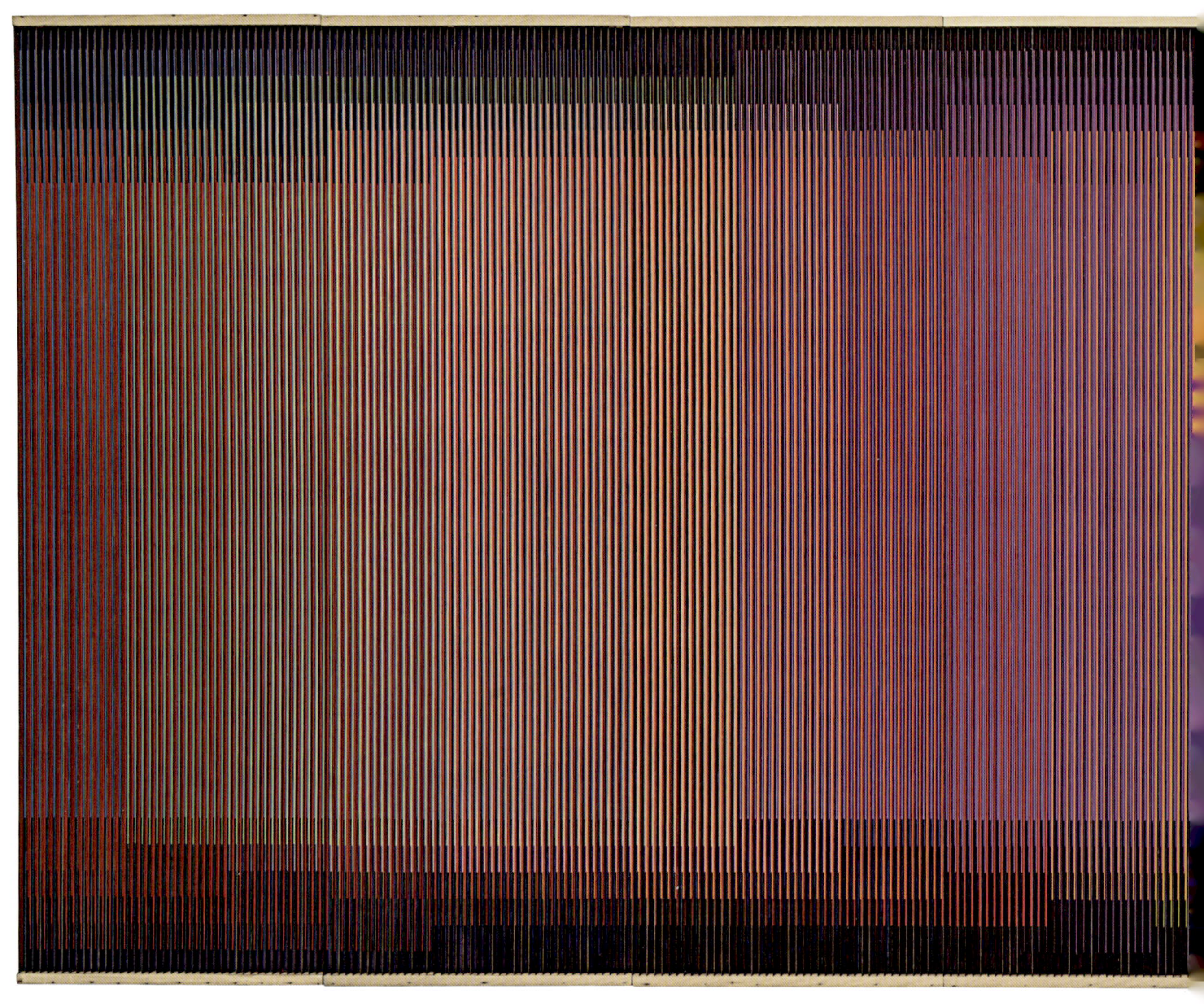

Carlos Cruz-Diez
Physichromie No. 500, 1970

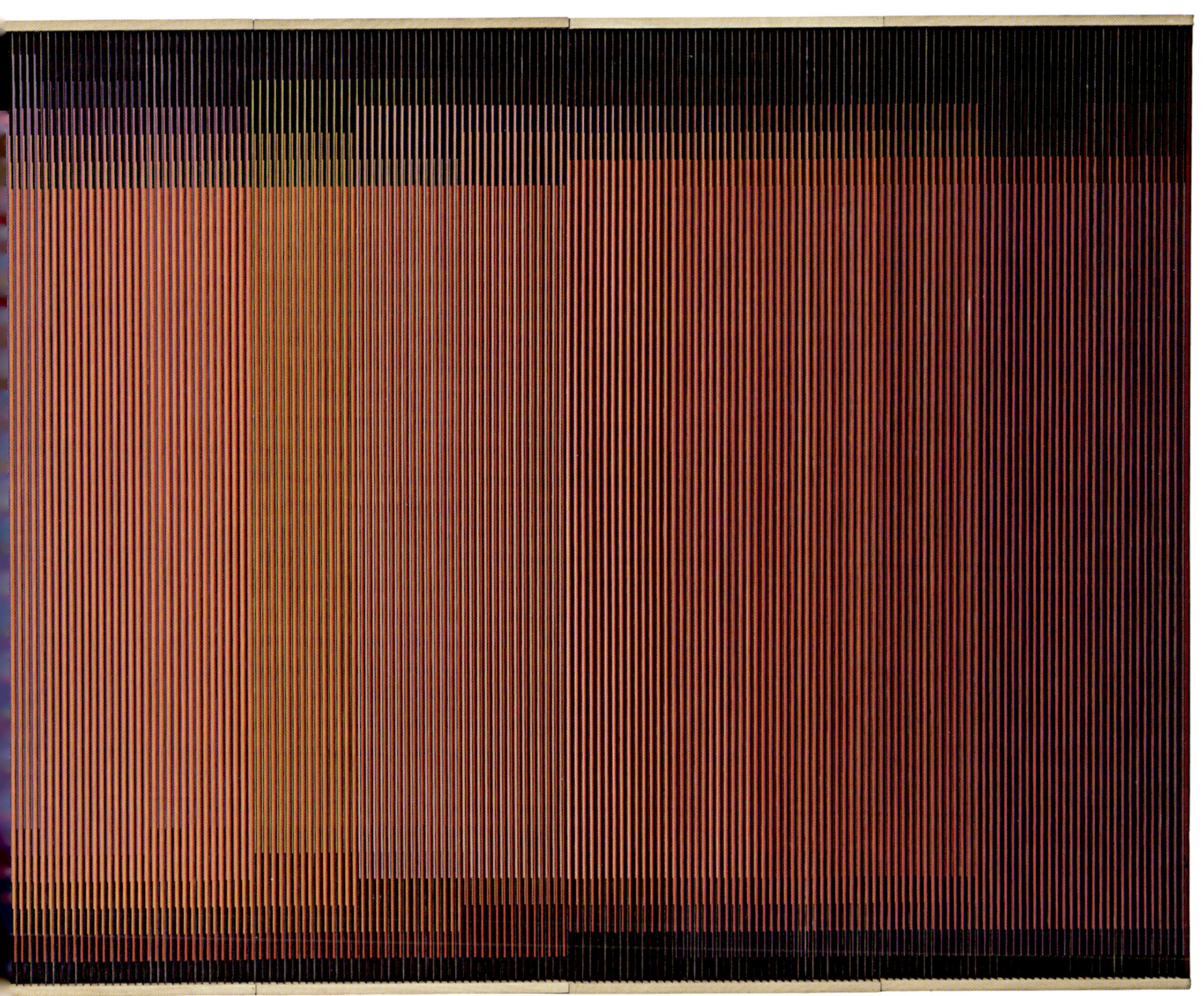

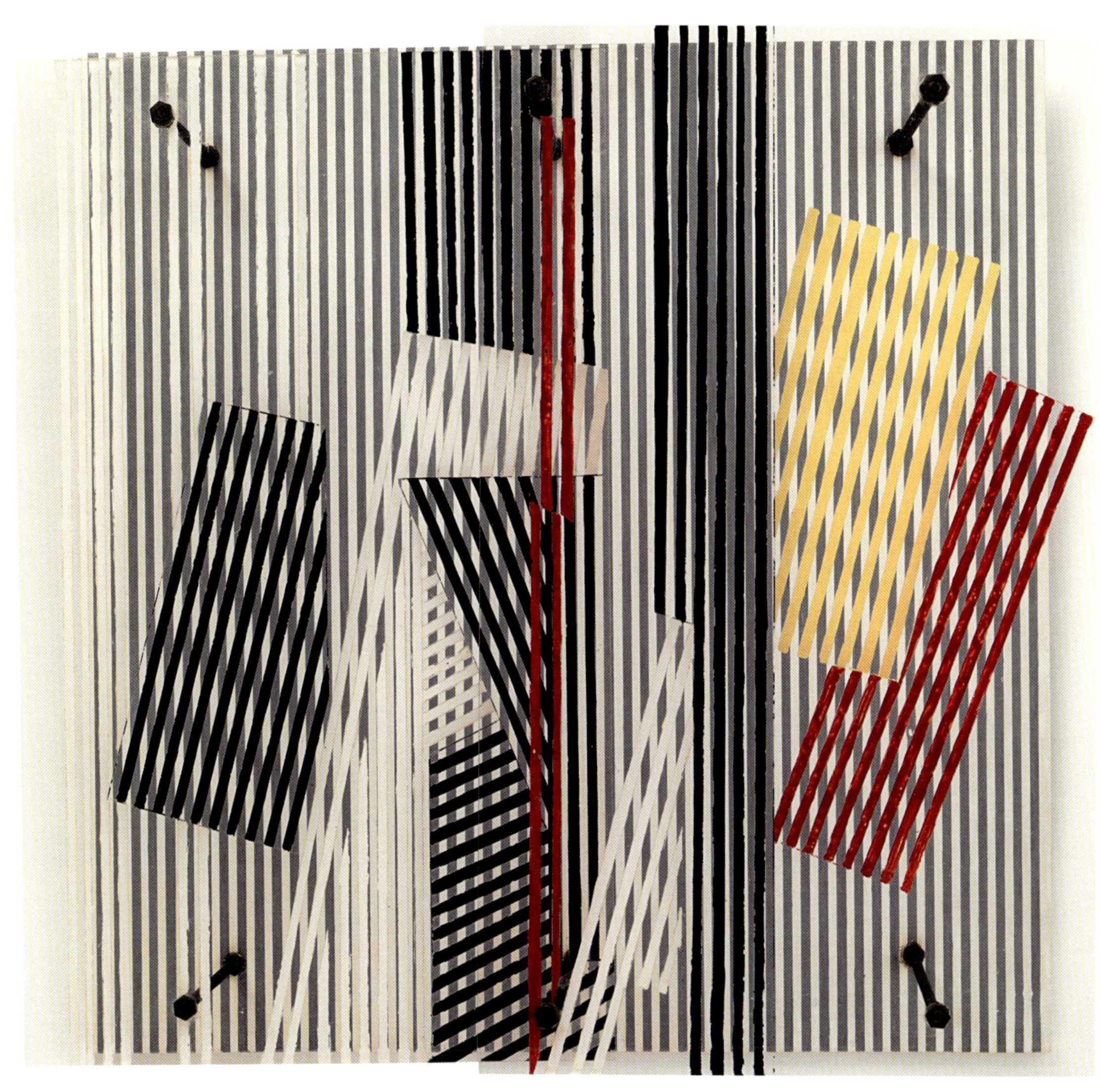

Jesús Soto
Doble transparencia [Double Transparency], 1956

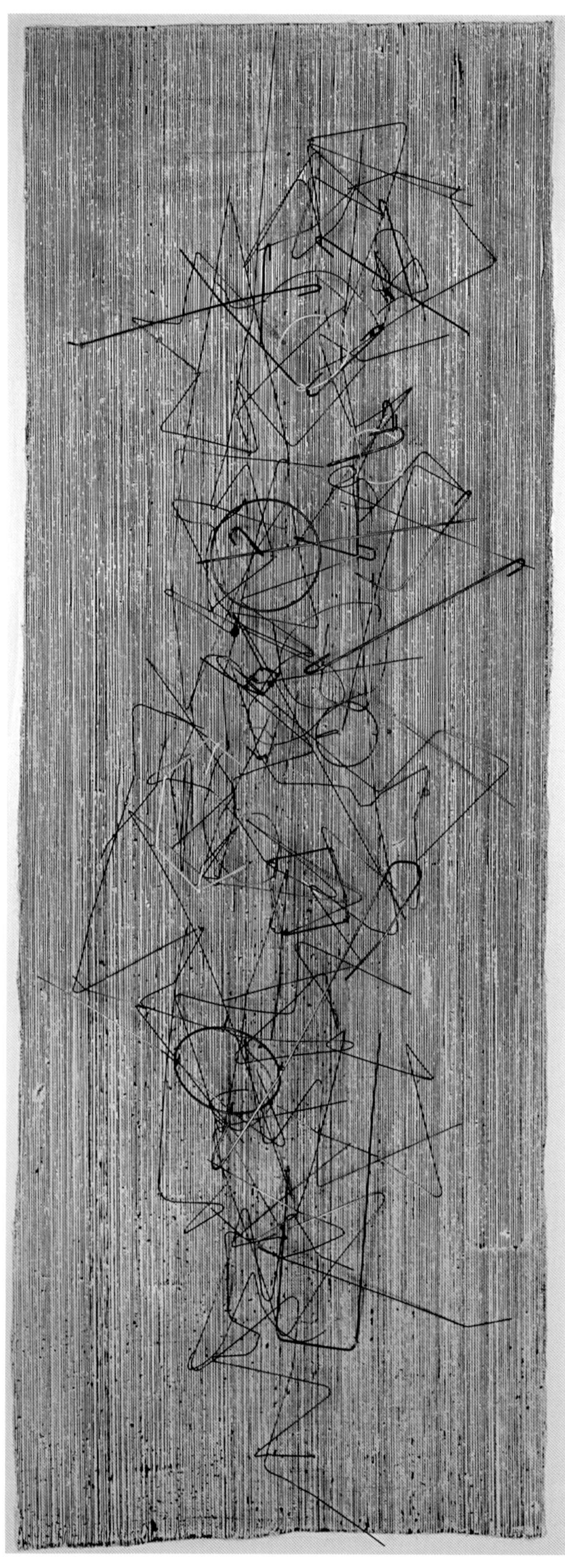

Jesús Soto
Vibración III [Vibration III], 1960–61

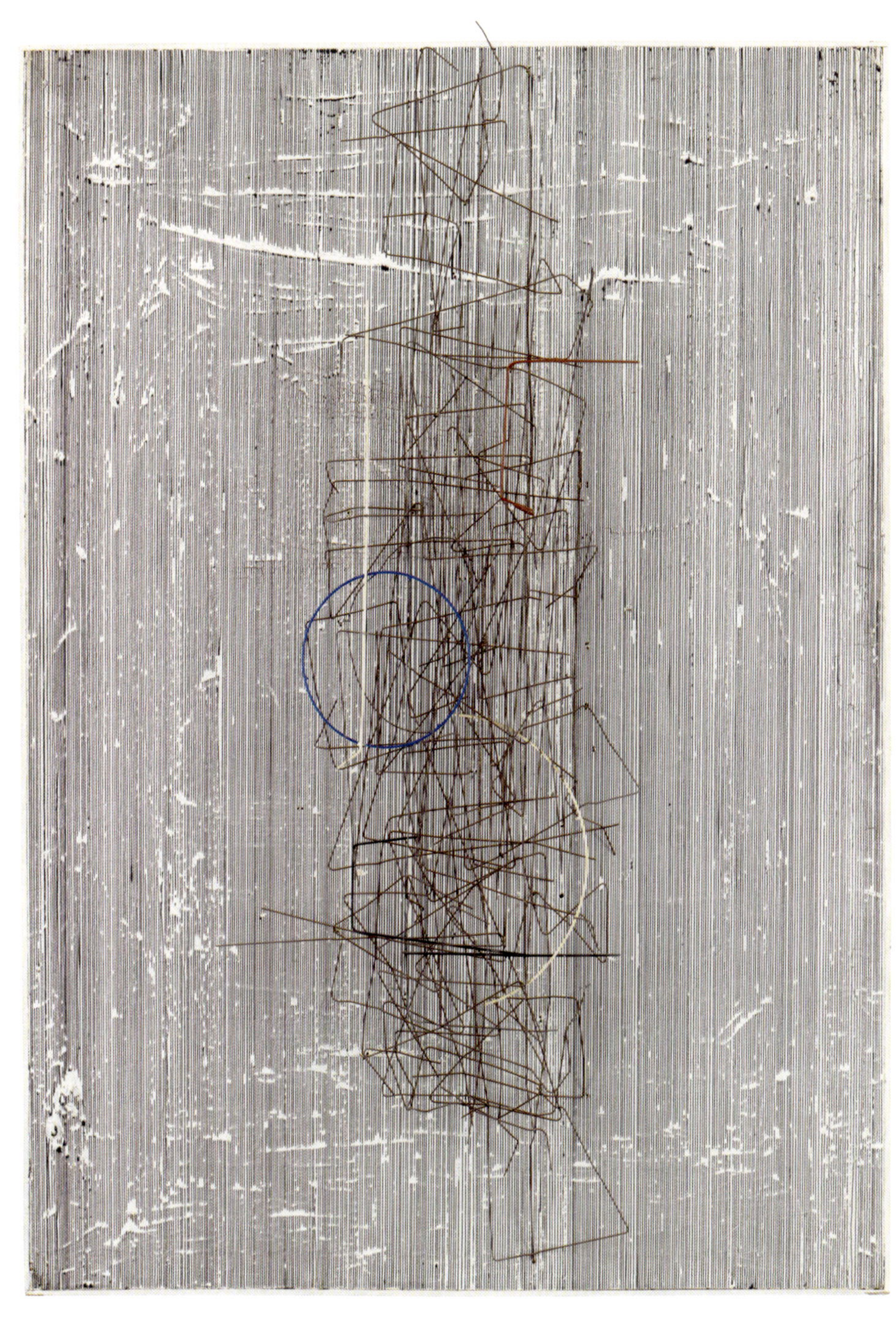

Jesús Soto
Vibración metálica [Metallic Vibration], 1962

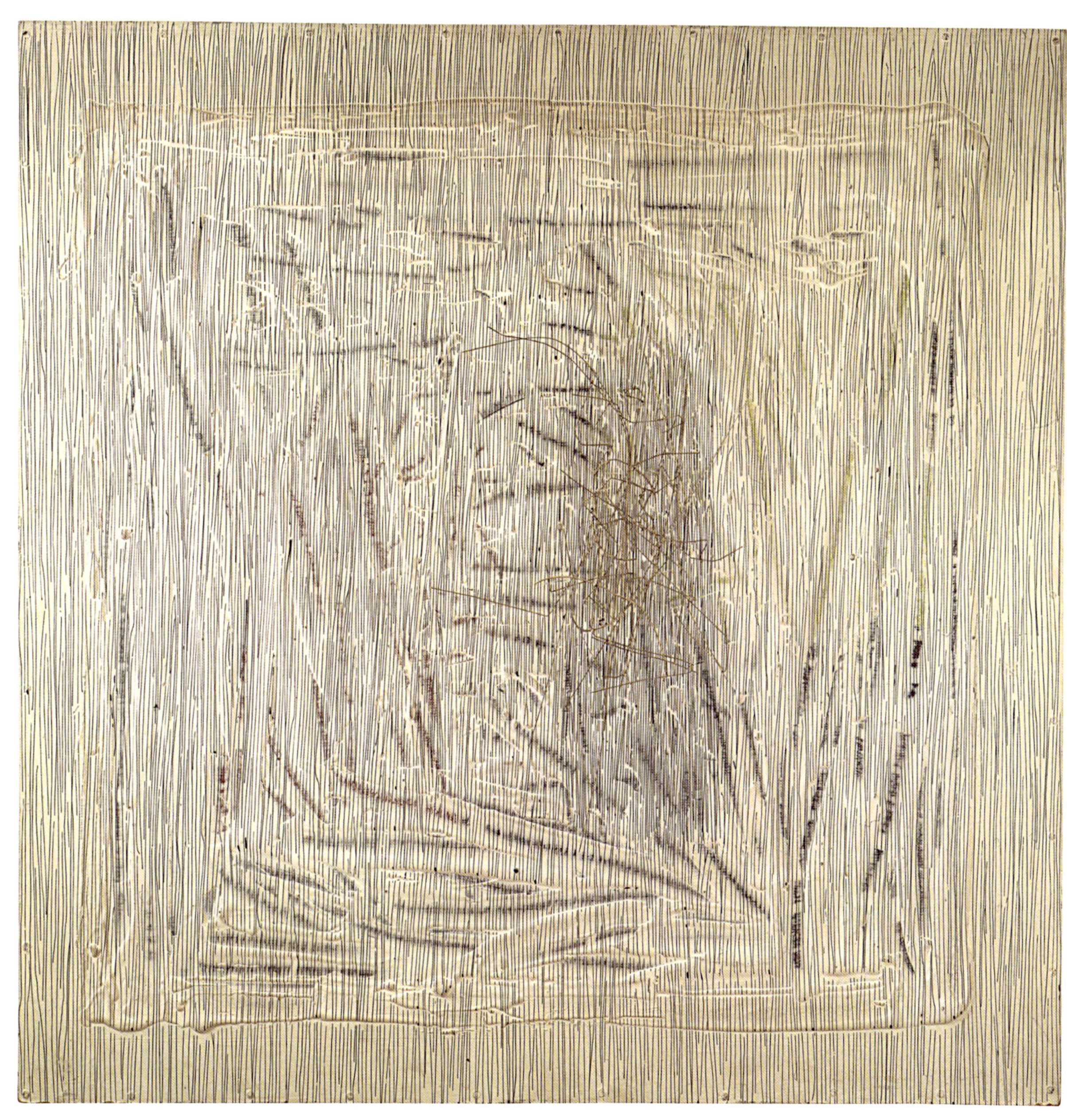

Jesús Soto
Vibration, 1960

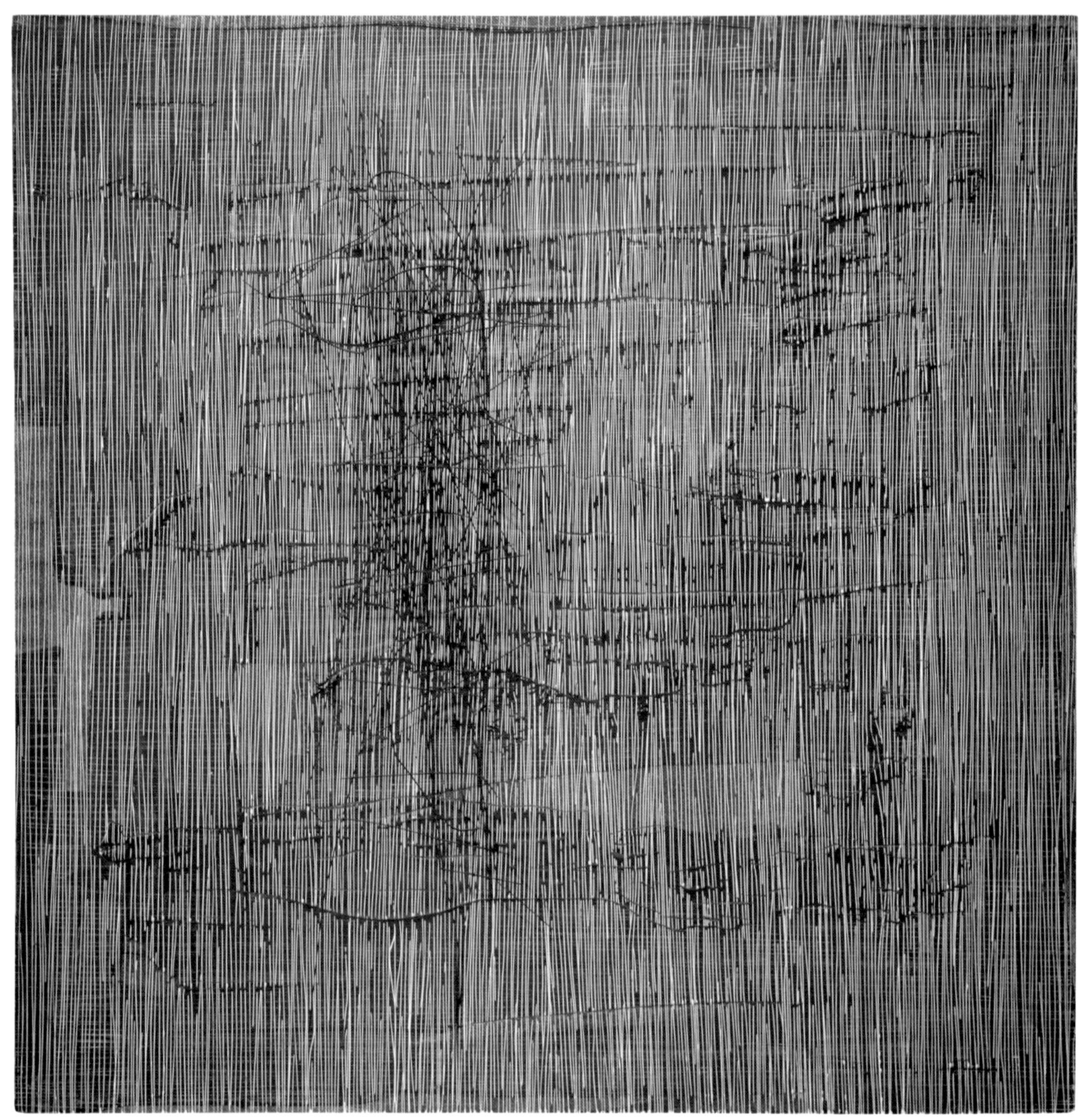

Jesús Soto
Vibración [Vibration], 1960

128

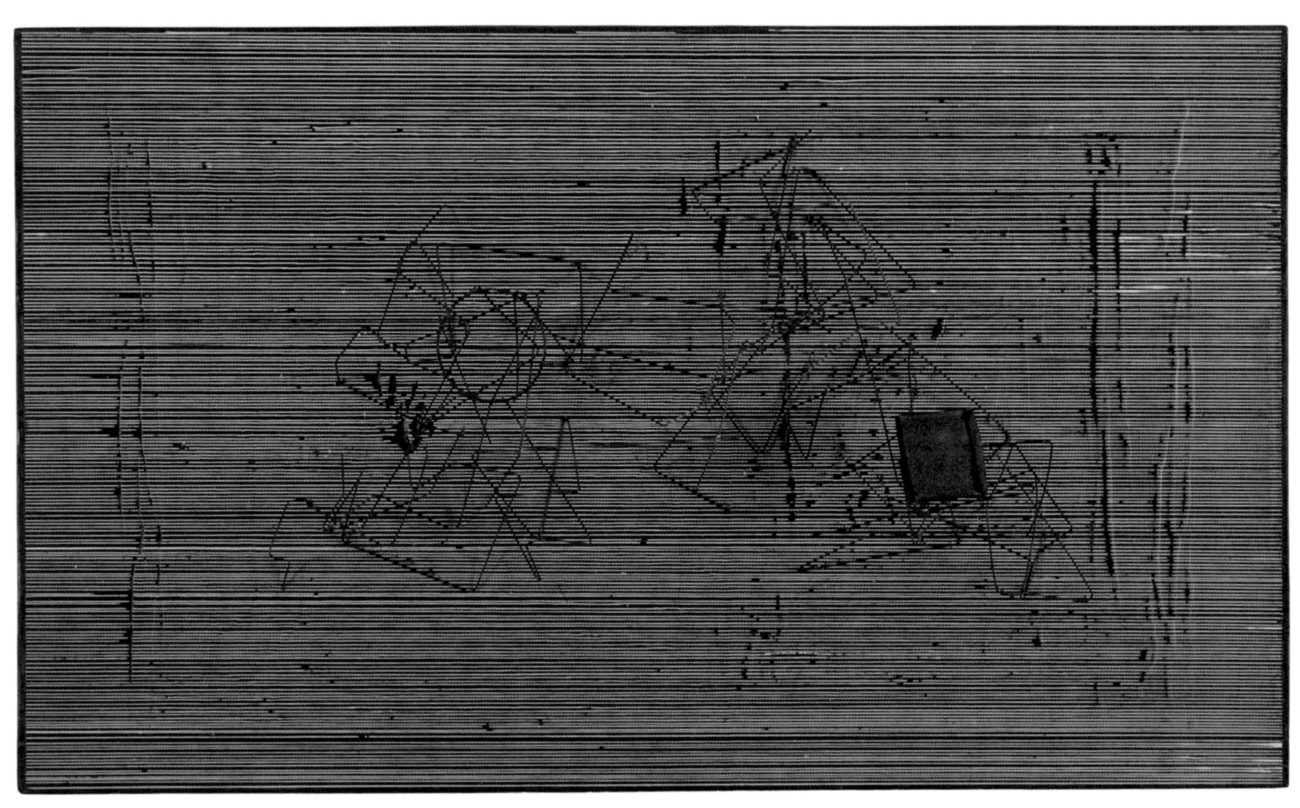

Jesús Soto
Hommage à Yves Klein [Homage to Yves Klein], 1961

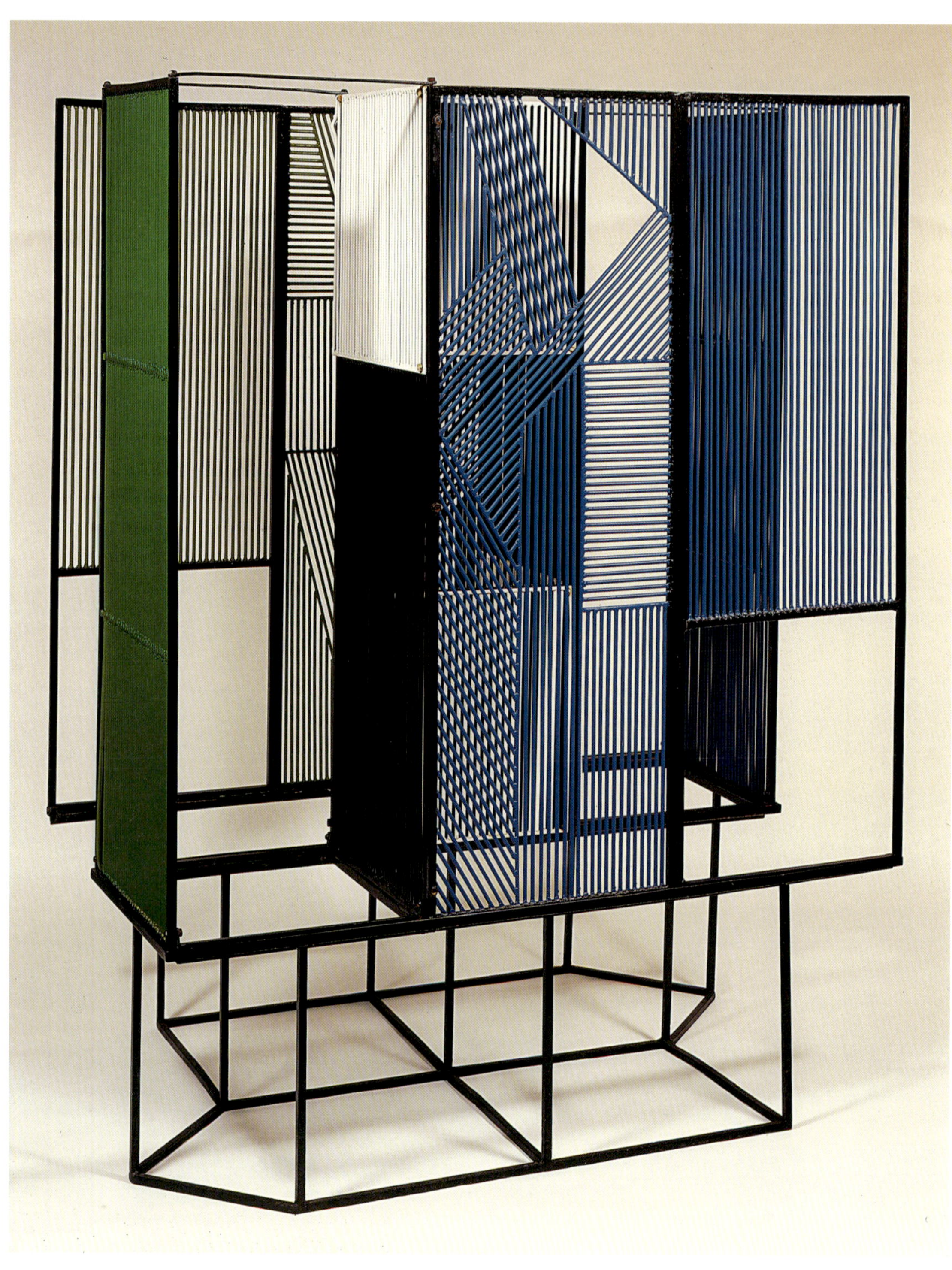

Jesús Soto
Pre-penetrable, 1957

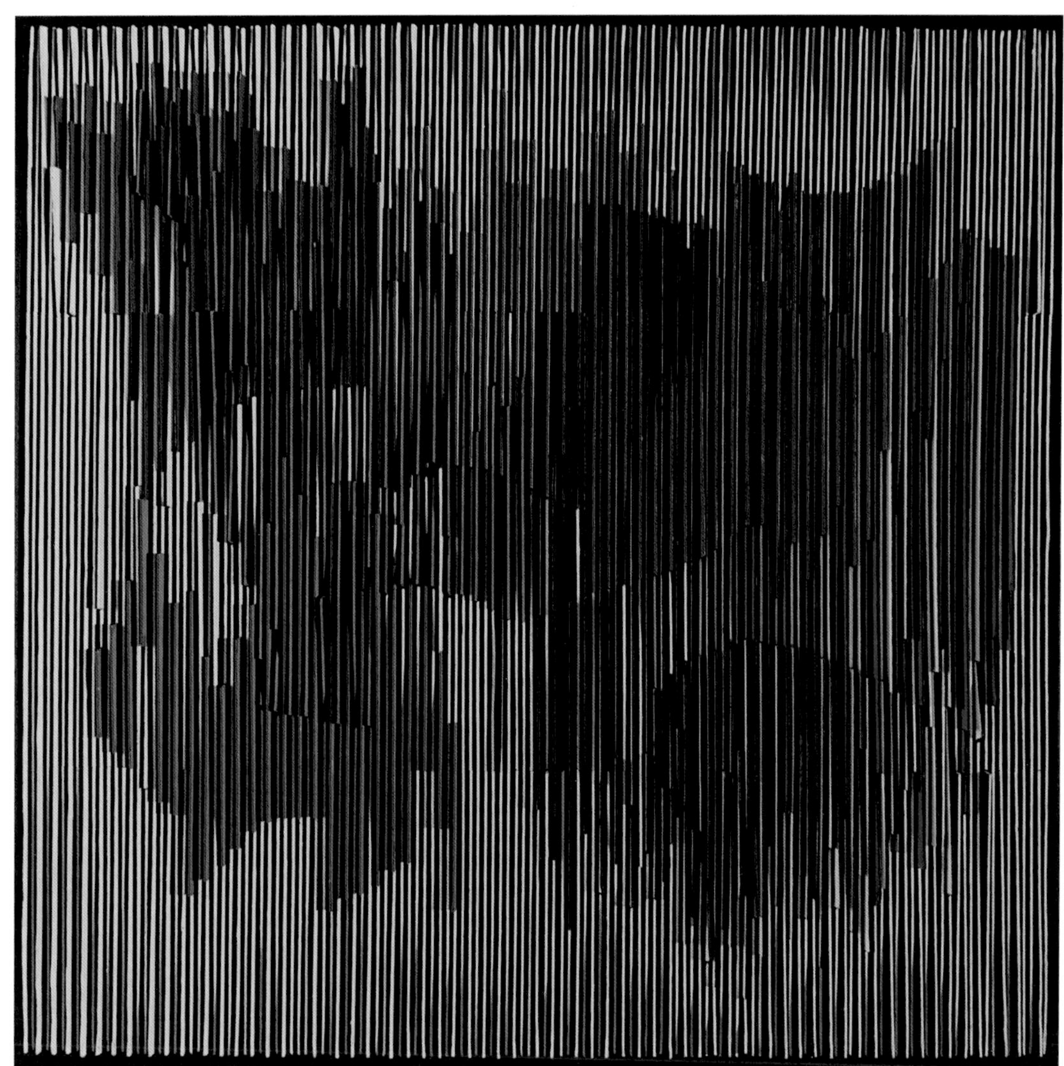

Carlos Cruz-Diez
Physichromie No. 21, 1960

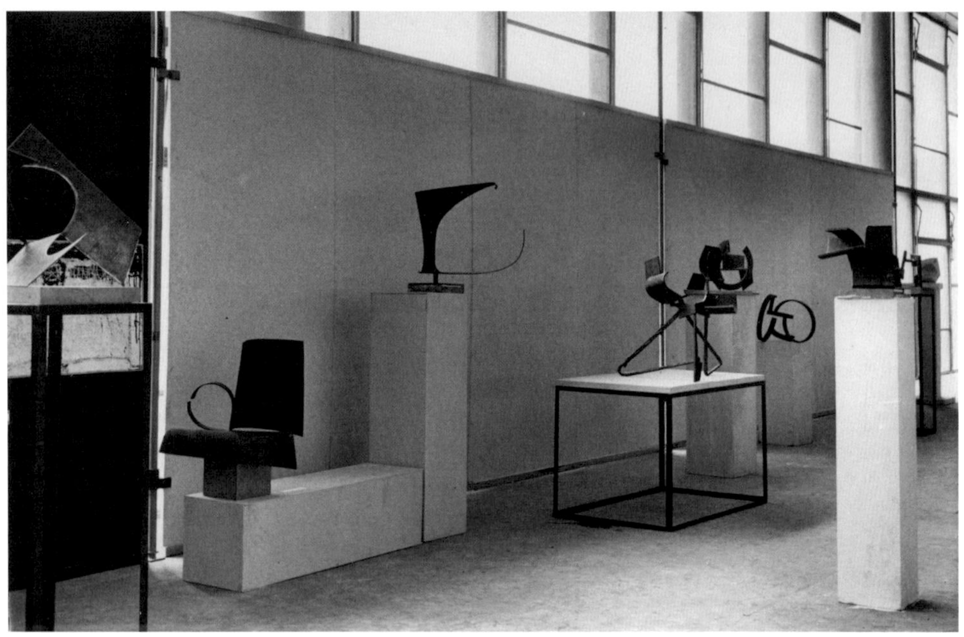

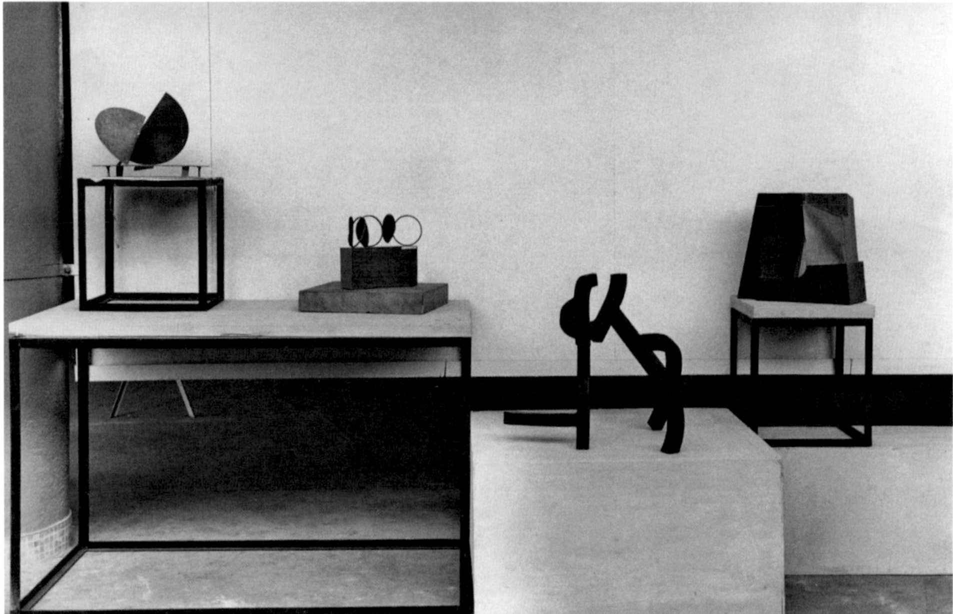

Works by Jorge Oteiza at the 1957 Bienal de São Paulo

From left to right (above): *Prueba de desocupación activa del espacio con la Unidad plana abierta en tres fases / Expansión espiral vacía* [Test for Active Disoccupation of Space with the Open Flat Unit in Three Phases / Empty Spiral Expansion]; *Desocupación del cilindro / Apertura del cilindro* [Disoccupation of the Cylinder / Opening of the Cylinder]; *Suspensión vacía (Estela funeraria Homenaje al constructor aeronáutico René Couzinet)* [Empty Suspension (Funerary Stele, Homage to the Aeronautical Engineer René Couzinet)]; *Expansión espacial por fusión de Unidades abiertas* [Spatial Expansion by Fusion of Open Units]; *Ordenación de un espacio definido / Control hiperespacial* [Ordering of a Defined Space / Hyperspatial Control]; *Desocupación de la esfera / De la serie de la desocupación de la esfera* [Disoccupation of the Sphere / From the Series of the Disoccupation of the Sphere]; *Rotación espacial con la Unidad Malévich abierta / Homenaje a Malévich* [Spatial Rotation with the Malevich Unit Open / Homage to Malevich]; *Primera variante Vacíos en cadena / Construcción vacía con cuatro Unidades planas positivo, negativo* [First Variant, A Series of Empty Spaces / Empty Construction with Four Flat Units, Positive-Negative].

Works by Jorge Oteiza at the 1957 Bienal de São Paulo

From left to right (below): *Par espacial ingrávido / Par móvil* [Weightless Spatial Pair / Moving Pair]; *Respiración espacial* [Spatial Breathing]; *Núcleo en contracción* [Contracting Nucleus]; *Fusión de sólidos abiertos con núcleo vacío* [Fusion of Open Solids with Empty Nucleus].

Jorge Oteiza/Lygia Clark: Life after Formalism
Txomin Badiola

In the last chapter of his book on conceptualism in Latin America, the artist and writer Luis Camnitzer included a quotation by the Cuban filmmaker Julio García Espinosa: "Art will not disappear into nothingness. It will disappear into everythingness."[1] Although the quotation appeared in the context of a critique of the role of the artist as specialist in the late 1960s, it is particularly evocative if its context is broadened to the late fifties, when there was a sense of an urgent need to pass from the purely intralinguistic problems of art to a greater fusion with life. If we wished to narrow the boundaries further, the quotation would be particularly apt for a discussion of the transition during those years between formalism,[2] evidently on the verge of exhaustion, and artistic activism in the social sphere.

Formalism had had a cleansing effect on artistic language by liberating it from subjectivism and its litigations with appearances. Its practices were characterized by the reduction of reality to a limited set of conventional linguistic units and by the creation of an autonomous reality defined by internal dependences. Nevertheless, this autonomy necessarily had to be relativized, since formalist language was forced in most cases to seek legitimacy outside itself, either from esoteric positions like that represented by theosophy in Piet Mondrian, the Rosicrucian brotherhood in František Kupka, or transcendentalism in Kazimir Malevich, or else by assuming the instrumental nature of its position. That is what occurred with the mutation of Constructivism into Productivism, overcoming the idea of "laboratory art" by intervening in the mass production of utensils for the new revolutionary reality, or with the redirection of Suprematism, Neoplasticism, and the Bauhaus toward applied art and architecture, finding themselves going off, so to speak, on a tangent that evidenced how difficult they found it not to succumb to a mere "decorative avant-garde," to use Joseph Kosuth's expression.[3]

After the initial avant-garde experiments, the thirties saw the rebirth in France of movements reacting against Surrealism, such as Cercle et Carré (1929), Abstraction-Création (1930), and Art Concret (1930). Characterized by an eclectic formalism, they included a motley group of artists from different generations and national and artistic origins whose sole nexus was an ample and diffuse idea of the abstract. Two of their most illustrious participants, the Uruguayan Joaquín Torres-García and the Swiss Max Bill, had a decisive influence on the resurgence of formalism in its third phase, whose most successful form was Concretism, developed with particular intensity in South America from the mid-forties onward. Its key representatives included two Argentine groups, Madí and Arte Concreto-Invención (1946), the latter the brainchild of Tomás Maldonado, who had just been the director of the Hochschule für Gestaltung founded by Max Bill in Ulm, Germany. Also of importance were the Brazilian groups Ruptura (São Paulo, 1952) and Frente (Rio de Janeiro, 1954–56), both created in the wake of the work of Max Bill, who took the first prize at the 1951 Bienal de São Paulo.

1. Luis Camnitzer, *Conceptualism in Latin American Art: Didactics of Liberation* (Austin, TX: University of Texas Press, 2007), 262. The quotation originally comes from an essay by Julio García Espinosa "Por un cine imperfecto," in *Una imagen recorre el mundo* (Havana: Editorial Letras Cubanas, 1979), 16.

2. By formalist artistic practices, we understand here those which come down in favor of linguistic reduction. Formalist language would thus be one articulated on the basis of the oppositions and differences of elementary units designed to function within a combination whose framework is autonomous, anti-referential and anti-illusionist. Stylistically, it is associated fundamentally with abstract and geometric works.

3. Joseph Kosuth, "*Art after Philosophy*," *Studio International* (London) 178, nos. 915–17 (October–December 1969).

The rigidity of the Concretist approach, with its cold, impersonal, systematic, and programmed character, devitalized and scientistic, began to be questioned in Brazil in 1957 after dissensions between the São Paulo and Rio groups. The second of these, which included artists like Lygia Clark, Willys and Amílcar de Castro, Franz Weissmann, and others, called for a more intuitive art that would be more attentive to human capacities and incapacities and to the contingencies of ordinary life, as well as to the spatiotemporal experiences of the viewer as a participant in the formation of the artworks. This rupture was sealed two years later, in 1959, with the drawing up and signing by the aforementioned artists of the "Neoconcrete Manifesto," which, despite the continuity implied in its nomenclature, assumed an openness toward new notions of artistic creation.

The year these disagreements began, 1957, was the year of a Bienal de São Paulo of great importance for the debate, since the German pavilion had presented an exhibition on the Bauhaus that included not only the classic artists but also various others who had distinguished themselves in the specific problematics of Concrete Art, such as Joseph Albers, Johannes Itten, and Max Bill. Furthermore, the Argentine pavilion showed artists with similar interests belonging to a variety of groups, including Abstraction-Création, Madí, and Arte Concreto-Invención. The Brazilian pavilion meanwhile included a fair number of the artists in confrontation: Alfredo Volpi, Samson Flexor, Lothar Charoux, Waldemar Cordeiro, Geraldo de Barros, Ivan Serpa, Lygia Pape, Lygia Clark, Weissmann, Willys de Castro, Hélio Oiticica, and so on. However, the artist who was to make a fundamental difference in the debate on formalism was Jorge Oteiza, the winner of the International Prize for Sculpture at the same biennial. The impact made by his presentation of twenty-eight sculptures and his evident experimental roots in the tradition of Constructivist formalism, but at the same time the heterodoxy of his approach and his thirst for polemic—expressed in the text that accompanied his display, "Propósito Experimental, 1956–57" (Experimental Proposition, 1956–57)—all had an undeniable effect on the ongoing debate.

Although his work has become definitively associated with the Constructivist tradition,[4] Oteiza was actually a sculptor whose natural expression moved more comfortably in the realm of statuary. As an artist conscious of his social and cultural mission, however, his lack of interest in problems of personal expression prompted him at a given moment to renounce the sculptor he had been and to turn into another, more suited to the nature of the experimental proposition he was committed to.

The beginnings of his work in the early thirties are linked to research into archaic cultures and the ability of the statue to purge beings of all that is temporal in them, producing a physical entity, a sign of the eternal, that is situated outside the contingencies and arbitrariness of life, and so definitively outside death. These initial investigations, where art is completely bound to the existential, gave way in the thirties and forties to contacts with vitalist sculpture, contributing to its interrogation from the perspective of scientific advances regarding multidimensional spaces, non-Euclidian geometries, and the space-time continuum. In the works of these years, the "statue"[5] appeared as the result of a hyperspace that ruled its three-dimensional developments, subsequently proceeding in others to empty out the mass of the statue and so convert the sculpture into a generator of energy. When he took part in the International Sculpture Competition for a Monument to the Unknown Political Prisoner in London in 1953, Oteiza presented a project where the concurrence of two light masses generated a great spatial activation that constituted itself as the true, albeit immaterial, sculpture. The sculptor thus had the opportunity to confirm what he

4. If we regard Oteiza's properly productive phase as the years from 1929 to 1959, so ignoring the occasional pieces of the seventies and the nineties, the vast majority of which are materializations of earlier *modelli* and *maquettes*, we could say that his work in a constructivist language boils down to a period of four years, from 1955 to 1959, out of a total of thirty.

5. Oteiza was faithful throughout his sculpting life to the idea of the "statue" as a transcendent dimension of the sculptural, on occasions provocatively confronted with a modern sculpture that had become a mere formal game.

regarded as an error in the tendency of most sculptors who feel the need for a light and fundamentally spatial sculpture, which is to resort to the easy exercise of using light materials and anecdotal thematic resources to denote that lightness. For Oteiza, on the other hand, the problems of lightness and spatiality were of a strictly structural order. He also rejected those practices based on physical materializations of mathematical concepts, since these confused mathematical with phenomenological space. Increasingly aware of the limitations for his interests implied by working on an idea of statuary, Oteiza regarded the Constructive sculpture of a gestural nature then emerging in Europe and North America, based on the tradition of "drawing in space" established by Julio González and updated by sculptors like David Smith, as just as unviable as that of the Concrete artists in the line of Max Bill:

> An obelisk, a sphere, a pyramid, a column—these aren't a statue, although they may signify a symbolic sign that the sculptor may convert into a statue. Nor is a Möbius strip or a hyperboloid sufficient today, nor are any of the figures that contemporary scientific thinking imagines in the private nature of their domain, just as a chair, or a wire mesh, or a tree, a head, an antenna, or a radar dish are insufficient to fabricate a statue without a rigorous plastic system of conversion, without a close awareness of the molecular and structural nature of the new statue.[6]

The solution emerged in 1956, following a typical path of late modernity that was described by the critic Hal Foster and characterized by a particular "return"[7] to works of a not very distant past—like Louis Althusser's return to Marx, or Jacques Lacan's to Freud—in which, "We return to those empty spaces that have been masked by omission or concealed in a false and misleading plenitude. [These are] rediscoveries of an essential lack."[8]

Oteiza returned to Mondrian and Malevich, artists invested with an experimental aura that in his opinion did not correspond, beyond the genius of their formal intuitions, to a full experimental consciousness. The rereading to which he subjected these pioneers was an attempt to extract a spatial logic where it seemed to be denied, to exhaust it and verify it at a limit where the very artwork is placed in question. In the case of Oteiza, the adoption to this effect of a truly experimental formalist language foresaw both a conclusion (as objective) and a set of conclusions (as application), which, in his opinion, would also imply the destruction or dissolution of formalist language itself. Formalism is overcome to gain life, which would expel the artist from art so that he could pronounce himself politically in reality. For Oteiza, confronting the political failure of the avant-garde and searching for a way out becomes the great revisionist act, but the mere will is not enough. It was not sufficient to feel the need for an exit from art toward life, but life ought to be the logical consequence of an operation within art. In this sense, in Oteiza's vision, García Espinosa's opening sentence would be reformulated as follows: "Sculpture should disappear into nothingness so that art can appear in everything."

Such an approach, exemplified by the works presented in São Paulo, explicit in the text accompanying them, and widely publicized after he was awarded the prize, necessarily had an impact on the South American situation, especially in Brazil. During his stay in that country, Oteiza never shunned discussion and even argument. The accounts written for the press by Mário Pedrosa, the cofounder of the Frente group and secretary of the biennial, relate how Oteiza visited the patriarch of modern Brazilian painting, Alfredo Volpi, and energetically criticized his pictures to the stupefaction of many. He also tells of his discussions with Waldemar Cordeiro and other Concretists,

6. Jorge Oteiza, "Protest of the Sculptor Oteiza," in Joseba Zulaika, ed., *Oteiza's Selected Writings*, trans. Frederick Fornoff (Reno: Center for Basque Studies, 2003), 214; originally published as "Protesta del Escultor Oteiza," *Revista Nacional de Arquitectura* (Madrid), no. 138 (June 1953), 45–46.

7. "The method of these returns is similar: to focus on the 'constructive omission' crucial to each discourse. The motives are similar too: not only to restore the radical integrity of the discourse but to challenge its status in the present, the received ideas that deform its structure and restrict its efficacy. This is not to claim the final truth of such readings. On the contrary, it is to clarify their contingent strategy, which is to *reconnect* with a lost practice in order to *disconnect* from a present way of working felt to be outmoded, misguided, or otherwise oppressive." Hal Foster, *The Return of the Real: The Avant-Garde at the End of the Century* (Cambridge, Mass.: MIT Press, 1996). 2–3.

8. Michel Foucault, "What is an Author?" (1969), in *Language, Counter-Memory, Practice* (Ithaca: Cornell University Press, 1977), 135; originally published in French as "Qu'est-ce qu'un auteur," *Bulletin de la Société française de Philosophie* 63, no. 3 (1969), 73–104.

whom he accused of providing merely optical solutions amounting to trompe l'oeils, and with the visual poets, whom Oteiza believed to be entwined in a vacuous formalism whose main reference was the Stéphane Mallarmé of *Coup de dés*. The alternative championed by Oteiza was the process of dissolution of language found in another poem by Mallarmé, *Igitur*, but this was regarded by the visual poets as a dangerous process of "humanization." Despite the tone of these arguments, Pedrosa, who was among the reticent, recognized that:

> The Concretists who judged him unsympathetically were to admit at the end of the discussion that the Spaniard's ideas were not without their uses, and they promised to adopt them for their next experiments.[9]

Where Oteiza found the most receptive attitude was beyond a doubt in the Rio de Janeiro group, and particularly with Lygia Clark and Franz Weissmann, who led the debate on "Concretist" orthodoxy. According to Pedrosa:

> In Rio, Oteiza was well received, especially by Lygia Clark, who gathered a group at her home to present the sculptor to them. Oteiza was enthusiastic about Lygia Clark's most recent investigations, and returned to her studio several times to look, criticize, praise, discuss, theorize. When their friendship had advanced to a certain point, Lygia Clark said to the Spaniard, "Let's go for a walk, so that I can show you the nice things in Rio and its landscapes." Oteiza was furious: "What do you mean, landscapes? I hate that academic nature! I want to go to Weissmann's studio." And there they went, and Oteiza looked, commented, criticized, judged, theorized, praised. And he fell silent only once, when an equally sincere observation by Lygia somewhat disconcerted him. They say he responds unhesitatingly to the slightest question, and that he hurls words like darts of lava. But he's a nice guy.[10]

Although Oteiza had lived between 1935 and 1947 in various Latin American countries, such as Argentina, Chile, and Colombia, and despite the fact that he had his greatest professional success in Brazil and later, more turbulently, in Uruguay, Oteiza's influence in Latin America is still unjustly underrated. As Luis Camnitzer states:

> During his extended stays in Latin America he strongly interacted with the intellectual world.... During this second visit, he affected curricular thinking in both art and architecture schools in Montevideo.... His talks, more than his work..., directed at least some of us toward conceptualization and dematerialization and to an understanding of the separation of art as craft from art as creation.[11]

It is always risky to speak in terms of influence, which often flows through unexpectedly labyrinthine twists and turns. What is beyond all doubt is the effect of Oteiza's presence in São Paulo in 1957 on the development of Brazilian Concretism at the moment when it was starting to question itself. This is obvious in the case of Weissmann, the winner of the national prize at the biennial, who went so far as to move to Irún with his wife so as to live near Oteiza. It is also possible to trace the effect of the Basque sculptor on Clark in the progressive discrediting of orthodox formalist positions.

The paintings presented by Clark at the biennial, where she was also rewarded with some acquisitions, concentrated intensively on the spatial interaction of contrasted surfaces that was proper to Concretism. However, after the "Neoconcrete Manifesto" of 1959, and throughout the early sixties, she created her now very famous series of

9. Mário Pedrosa, *Jornal do Brasil* (Rio de Janeiro), October 20, 1957. Press articles on Oteiza in Brazil compiled by Macarena Cebrián and Marcelo Rivera.

10. Ibid.

11. Camnitzer, *Conceptualism in Latin American Art*, 142, 144.

bichos (creatures), constructions formed by the flat elements typical of Neo-Constructivist sculpture, but joined with hinges that prevented the sculpture from forming itself definitively, ultimately configuring it as a field of formal and spatial possibilities in the viewer's own hands.

Precisely in 1959 Oteiza paid another visit to Clark, in the course of which he asserted, "Sculpture conceived as such is finished."[12] At that time, regarding the process of the emptying of sculpture in his "Experimental Laboratory" as complete,[13] Oteiza had put an end to his project and was abandoning artistic practice:

> I'm no longer a sculptor, nor have I anything interesting to do in sculpture. Art flows out into life, it's a spiritual and practical knowledge for integrating man into true reality. The political relations of the artist with education and life should be intimate ones.[14]

Both artists shared the conviction of the inefficacy of the artwork in its merely contemplative function, but at the same time vindicated the need to introduce the creative logic of their production into life through education and activism. Progressively, this idea seeped through more thoroughly into the work of Clark, where the role of the artwork broadened its functions to become *objetos sensoriais* (sensorial objects), 1966–68. At the same time, her authorship was diluted as priority was given to the relational quality of those works as propitiators of individual and collective corporal experiences. One paradigmatic example of this new manner of proceeding, almost an "anti-Concretist" manifesto, is the piece *Caminhando* (Walking, 1963), which consisted of the action of cutting a Möbius strip longitudinally. Inaccessible save to purely mental mathematical reasoning, the topological space represented by the model of the strip, an emblem of Max Bill's Concrete Art, was transformed by the participant in the action of Clark's work into pure experience of a space-time continuum. Persisting in a constant exercise of artistic radicalism, Clark went on to concentrate after a given point on the therapeutic dimension of her artistic practice and its component of self-knowledge, revelation, and liberation, so rescuing it from the specialization of the artist and handing it over to the people.

Oteiza and Clark exemplify the possibilities of a set of practices that manage to differentiate themselves from the conventionality of the artistic mainstream, even though—or precisely because—they are conditioned by their status as "minor art,"[15] meaning resulting from positions that are in principle incomprehensible within hegemonic discourses yet whose declarations occur within those same hegemonic artistic discourses. The relevance of their proposals gains in intensity as their cases are studied, helping to sanction the viability of alternative behaviors within the stultified world of artistic creation.

12. *Jornal do Brasil* (Rio de Janeiro), February 23, 1959.

13. Oteiza fundamentally carried out his experimental work on the basis of countless tiny maquettes and modelli fashioned in materials like plaster, wood, tin, wire, glass or paper. The full set of these, part of which is currently exhibited at the Fundación Oteiza in Alzuza, Navarre, is called *Laboratorio Experimental* (Experimental Laboratory).

14. J. Luis Seisdedos, "Tres famosos artistas en una casa de la Avenida de Francia en Irún. Reunión con Weissmann, Oteiza y Basterretxea" *El Diario Vasco* (San Sebastián), April 7, 1961.

15. The notion of "minor art" is employed here in the same sense as the use of the term "minor literature" by Gilles Deleuze and Félix Guattari: "A minor literature doesn't come from a minor language, it is rather that which a minority constructs within a major language." See their book *Kafka: Toward a Minor Literature* (Minneapolis: University of Minnesota Press, 1986), 16; originally published in French as *Kafka: Pour une litterature mineure* (Paris: Les Editions de Minuit, 1975).

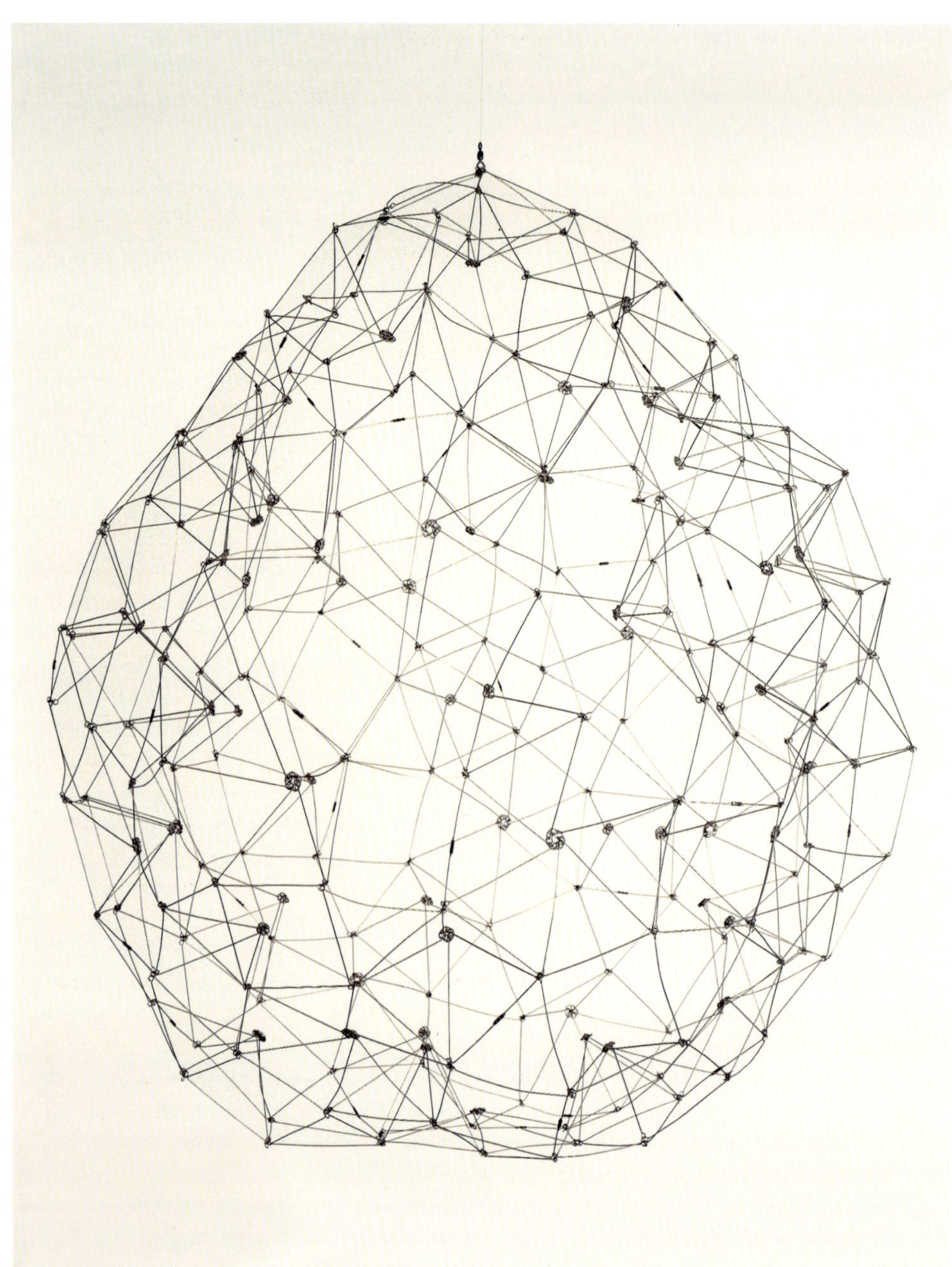

Gego
Esfera [Sphere], 1976

Symmetries and Slight Anachronisms:
Speculating on Modern Art in Latin America

Olga Fernández López

The tragic destiny Jorge Luis Borges lays in store for Juan Dahlmann in the short story "The South," traversed by the conflict of identity between the protagonist's European and Argentine lineages (a duel that is above all a struggle with himself), is suspended in the interpretive oscillation between the liberation of a reckless death, in the *south*, and the fantasy of a delirious death, in the hospital. Neither option, however, saves him from dying, although only in dream, in fiction, can the two deaths be reconciled. The story/dream splits Dahlmann in two, and superimposes two realities, parallel to each other and scarcely touching, by means of a form that never quite makes clear whether it is specular or symmetrical. In one of his most celebrated lines, the narrator remarks that "reality favors symmetries and slight anachronisms," and the same is true not only of reality but also of the structure with which Borges endows the tale. As a narrative, history can sometimes deploy itself in symmetries and anachronisms, relations that can also be explored in the possible histories of modern art. Always assuming, that is, that anachronism is not confused with essentializing archaism, but that, as Walter Benjamin proposes, it is understood as a possible site for the emergence of dialectical images.

The End of Modernism

Despite the momentum and undeniable spread of its use in historiography, modernism (or, at least, modernist artistic forms) is starting to be seen by many artists as an anachronism or, at best, as a set of forms contaminated by a certain nostalgia, and now burdened by history. In the last decade, a growing caesura has thus inserted itself between a language that signifies the modern and another that is recognizably contemporary. Some of these artists have opted to incorporate or re-elaborate apparently exhausted forms, stepping aside from the dynamics of progress established by modernity itself, and perhaps searching for a new sense of the experience of the modern from the distance of the present. A number of artists have even taken advantage of the rift to imagine the history of modernism as if it were a myth, a naturalized version of historical facts that is nonetheless explanatory of only one possible version of them.[1] In parallel with this, artists absent from this history have started to be reappraised in the wake of new explanatory demands, generated either from within the "myth" itself in order to enlarge it from the inside, or by deconstructing the mythology and trying to put other histories into circulation. This panorama gives rise to multiple symmetries in which several histories seem to run parallel to one another.

The widespread use of the word "modernism" may make us forget that as a concept or label it masks a great lack of definition that extends to its adjective, "modernist." The term sometimes appears to refer to the art produced over a long historical period ("modernity"), blending on occasions with "modern art." This type of culturalist usage emphasizes its dimension of progress and its opposition to what preceded it (tradition,

1. This game is played out, for example, in the exhibition catalogue *What is Modern Art? (Group Show)*, ed. Inke Arms, exh. cat. Künstlerhaus Bethanien, Berlin (Berlin: Museum of American Art, 2006).

the academy). At other times, it is used to signify an expanded artistic movement of somewhat vague chronology (like romanticism), tending to confuse itself with the "avant-garde." As an agglutinative yet diffuse formula, it appears with particular frequency in Anglo-Saxon (American and British) historiography, above all when trying to cordon off the art produced on their territory in the twentieth century, and it has significantly determined the vocabulary used to organize a narrative that has become hegemonic. European and Latin American historiographies, on the other hand, have been rather more reluctant to use the word, and have proved more inclined to establish a territory, likewise diffuse, between "new art," "modern art," and the "avant-garde."

It should not be forgotten, however, that the word "modernism" was a term placed in circulation by the Nicaraguan Rubén Darío at the end of the nineteenth century, that it was quickly adopted in Spain, and that it gave its name there to a poetic, artistic, and architectural movement linked to the fin-de-siècle aesthetic. This meant it was discarded as a signifier for subsequent movements, and the more general European terms "new art" and "avant-garde" were consolidated instead. In the meantime, "modernism" was used to characterize the change that was taking place in literature in English at the start of the twentieth century. In art criticism, the term was popularized only after the early 1960s with the aesthetic thought of Clement Greenberg, who, together with Alfred Barr, has been viewed as a key figure in the construction of the "myth." The expansion of its use outside English-language historiography occurred relatively late, no earlier than the 1990s, and was brought on by the critical examinations of it by a new generation of historians, and by the expansion of the term "postmodernism."[2]

In Spanish, the word "modernismo" thus became swamped with confusion when it came to retranslation, since it incorporated an interpretation of artistic practices that proves unsatisfactory for an explanation of twentieth-century art in either Europe or Latin America. It should also be added that the imprecision of the term "modernism" affects not only its chronological and geographical identification, but also the thing it is trying to characterize, since this is not a question of a style, an ism, or a method. In actual fact, the term promotes a critical (rather than historiographical) paradigm, a prescriptive model that not only leaves out certain contemporary practices in the United States, but also much of the postwar artistic production around the world, since it is hard to make it fit neatly in the paradigm.

A refutation of its principles and conclusions was therefore necessary, but the arguments used, heavily dependent on the original "modernist" premises, do not appear to have led to a new narrative, but rather to a narrative improved through attention to its contradictions and the incorporation of some new additions. The modernist canon explains the history of art since 1945 on the basis of the critical model of a successive chain of movements (Abstract Expressionism, Pop Art, Post-Painterly Abstraction, Minimalism, Post-Minimalism, Conceptual Art, and so on), taking a genealogy of artists and movements from the United States as its paradigm. Superimposed on this is a historiographical model that does not question the underlying canon but tries instead to move beyond it by establishing a dialectic, opposing modernism to an "antimodernist" genealogy. This rereads some of the modernist works and includes some practices (fundamentally in the US and Europe) that had been left out of the original explanatory model (rather like the "others" of modernism). The process of overcoming the dialectic is consummated in postmodernism, which is arrived at from a considerably Eurocentric canon.[3]

One of the greatest achievements of the new historiography, however, has been an enlargement of the discipline beyond formalism, which acted simultaneously as both

2. The modernism/postmodernism dialectic was to be defended by authors like Rosalind Krauss, Douglas Crimp, Craig Owens, Hal Foster, and others. See Thomas Crow, "The Practice of Art History in America," *Daedalus* 135 (Spring 2006).

3. The model for this version would be the survey by Hal Foster, Rosalind Krauss, Yve-Alain Bois, and Benjamin H. D. Buchloh, *Art Since 1900: Modernism, Antimodernism, Postmodernism* (London: Thames & Hudson, 2004).

the object and the medium of study. This expansion has meant a refounding of the history of art, which now has a new conceptual repertoire at its disposal for tackling artistic phenomena. Nevertheless, the *modernism-antimodernism-postmodernism* model, which, as we have pointed out, is established on the basis of a single paradigmatic (and yet local) genealogy, has started to be applied, without ever questioning the underlying genealogy, to other scenarios trying to adapt themselves (as modernist, antimodernist, or postmodernist) to the new historiographical canon. At this point, there is little need to remark on the pertinence of this discussion for the art produced in Latin America, whose historiography is usually debated in this context.

The operative problems of the model of modernist origin are clearly shown in descriptions of university courses on art produced after 1945, which can be seen as an indication of hegemonic historiography, especially in the academic milieu of the United States. They evidence a general acceptance of the model of successive movements in which the genealogy of the US constitutes the backbone, while the Europeans are intercalated along it. In the European case, the movements and artists of Western Europe (Fluxus, Nouveau Réalisme, Arte Povera) share protagonism with the artists of the US, while those of Eastern Europe are left out, as are the Latin Americans.[4] Artistic practices pertaining neither to the US nor Europe are situated off this axis, with specific courses tracing parallel or alternative genealogies.[5] It would seem easier to register geographically than to go down in history.

This occurs, for instance, with courses on the art produced in Latin America that are presented in an autonomous and symmetrical fashion. Instead of a chronological division, it is usual to employ national/geographical criteria (Mexico, Argentina, Brazil, the Caribbean), with topics leaping from one country to another in accordance with their "strong" moments. This model consolidates a paradox that presents a label of "Latin American" art that is nevertheless explicable only in terms of countries. As a perception, it moreover tends to reinforce the nationalist view of the avant-garde movements that the various states presented publicly by means of cultural policy throughout the postwar period. Despite a proliferation of these specific courses, the fact is there remains a symbolic division between a canonical reference model and a myriad of "other" genealogies traversed by a regime of difference.[6] While the alternative of remaking an inclusive narrative with the addition of certain specific artists or movements does not seem very stimulating, the idea of constructing a single comprehensive narrative is also impracticable, bearing in mind that it is not modernism but modernity itself, and the colonial processes that make it possible, which have to be questioned. To rewrite a plural narrative, it would also be necessary to perform a parallel operation of decentering the supposed centers.

In the context of this discussion, it is also interesting to note how the course descriptions are brought to a conclusion. There are some variations in this respect. Some end up by organizing their final components into decades (the 1980s, the 1990s, and 2000s), while others identify the eighties with postmodernism, go straight from postmodernism to the art of the twenty-first century, or finish with different versions of "art and globalization" (sometimes passing through postmodernism, and sometimes not). What seems clear is that the criteria that articulated the modernist narrative are invalid for an understanding of the art of the last few decades, and still more curiously, there is no way, apart from a supposed postmodernism, to articulate the transition or explain the caesura. It is surprising, for instance, that postmodernism, understood in principle as the surpassing of modernism, is summarily dispatched as "eighties art" and thus becomes a mere ism, identified moreover with the artists of that moment in the United States. In this way, the

4. The Spring 2011 course "20th-Century Art II" at Hunter College CUNY is described in the following way: "This course will examine the history of American and European art from 1940 to about 1975, with an emphasis on the art in America. Through the study of such popular movements as Abstract Expressionism, Pop Art, Earth Art and Minimalism, structured around a selected group of core artists, recurring themes and topics will be examined in conjunction with current issues and events." See http://www.hunter.cuny.edu/art/art-history/course-descriptions/spring-2011 (accessed December 9, 2012).

5. One example of these "other genealogies" might be the course on Multiple Modernities offered by Columbia University in 2006, 2007, and 2009. See http://www.columbia.edu/cu/arthistory/courses/ Multiple-Modernities/index.html (accessed December 9, 2012).

6. Parallel courses tend to be structured around difference (Feminist Art, Identity and Politics of the Body, African-American Art), or around the "other" new media like photography and performance, something that both complements and reinforces the modernist interpretive model.

promised methodological opening is deactivated. The close of the cycle is resolved in an inevitable "art and globalization," which tries to respond descriptively to an expanded map in which the United States has ceased to be the sole reference point.

The modernist narrative, with its characteristics as a teleological myth naturalizing the hegemony of the US, does not have the expected ending. In the meantime, the new cartography is made visible as if the broadening of centers of artistic production had been generated out of nothing, and as if contemporary art were a product of the new geopolitical scene, the expansion of markets, or a simultaneous dissemination of contemporary languages, with no apparent connection to the "other" genealogies. All these contradictions, which are hard to resolve within the current divisions of academic opinion, have become more visible with the mounting of a series of exhibits that have revealed the unsustainability of the modernist narrative, not by showing how it has supposedly been surpassed but by questioning the established interests behind its symmetries. Given that the term "modernist" is hard to apply outside the English-speaking world, the new readings situate themselves within a revision of the development and legacy of the historical avant-gardes, something especially apt in the case of the art produced in Latin America.

Inverted Curating

It is frequently supposed that the crisis of the modernist historiographical model facilitated the entry through its "cracks" of non-European and non-US artists during the 1980s. However, the fact is that such an opening, originating in the Anglo-Saxon environment, continued to reproduce a regime of differences. This is especially evident in the transition from the eighties to the nineties, when the multicultural version of postmodernism served to perpetuate regionalist essentialism. This is what happened, for example, in exhibitions, a medium that was expressly used by the United States during the Cold War to control and fix "Latin American" art under its political and economic tutelage.[7] In the late eighties, with the re-establishment of democracies in Central and South America and the advance of neoliberalism, exhibitions like *Art of the Fantastic: Latin America, 1920–1987* reawakened old phantoms, though this time the new geopolitical scenario favored a reaction less mediated by anti-imperialist thought, resituating the battle for the control of image visibility on its own terrain, especially within the curatorial framework.[8] The idea of counter-representing from within exhibitions thus already appears in 1992, when it is regarded by Mari Carmen Ramírez as a programmatic axis:

> A rethinking and revamping of curatorial practices along these lines should open up the possibilities of apprehending the complex issues posed by Latin American/Latino art that the exhibition phenomenon of the 1980s buried under such artificial constructs as the "fantastic."[9]

It was precisely a group of Latin American and Latino curators who managed to clear a space for articulate debate in reaction to a pair of circumstances. One was the pro-identitarian, essentialist, and otherizing position promoted from the United States in exhibitions like that mentioned, and the other was the readiness shown by Spain to celebrate the fifth centenary of Columbus's arrival in America.[10] Between 1987 and 1994, there was thus not only a concentration of commemorative exhibitions traveling around the United States and Europe, but also a fierce critical reaction to them and the initiation of a series of critical exhibitions, curated by Latin Americans, that tried to

7. Mari Carmen Ramírez speaks of three waves of concentrations of exhibitions on "Latin American art," during the periods 1940–45, 1959–70, and the late eighties to early nineties, in Mari Carmen Ramírez, "Brokering Identities: Art Curators and the Politics of Cultural Representation," in *Thinking about Exhibitions*, ed. Reesa Greenberg, Bruce Ferguson and Sandy Nairne (London: Routledge, 1996), 21–38.

8. *Art of the Fantastic: Latin America, 1920–1987*, Indianapolis Museum of Art, 1987. Other exhibitions of the time were: *Latin American Artists in New York since 1970*, Archer Huntington Art Gallery of the University of Texas at Austin, 1987; *The Latin American Spirit: Art and Artists in the United States*, Bronx Museum of the Arts, 1988; *Hispanic Art in the United States: Thirty Contemporary Painters and Sculptors*, Houston Museum of Fine Arts and Brooklyn Museum, 1989; *The Decade Show: Frameworks of Identity in the 1980s*, Museum of Contemporary Hispanic Art, The New Museum of Contemporary Art and The Studio Museum in Harlem, New York, 1990; *Art in Latin America: The Modern Era, 1920–1980*, The Hayward Gallery, London, 1989; and *Latin American Artists of the Twentieth Century*, Estación Plaza de Armas, Seville and the Museum of Modern Art, New York, 1992–93.

9. The paths she signals are: (a) specific exhibits permitting an in-depth analysis of particular movements, groups, or artists, along with the establishment of comparative frames of analysis; (b) encouraging US curators to overcome the limitations imposed by the Europe-US framework; and (c) resistance by Latin American and Latino curators to the production of exhibitions that feed the perceptual parameters of the mainstream. See Mari Carmen Ramírez, "Beyond 'The Fantastic': Framing Identity in

U.S. Exhibitions of Latin American Art," *Art Journal* 51, no. 4, "Latin American Art" (Winter 1992): 60–68.

10. Held in Spain was the aforementioned *Latin American Artists of the Twentieth Century* and *Voces de Ultramar*, Centro Atlántico de Arte Moderno, Las Palmas de Gran Canaria and Casa de América, Madrid, 1992. We might add *America: Bride of the Sun*, Royal Museum of Fine Arts, Antwerp, 1992. One exhibition of a critical nature held in Spain was a public art exhibition project, *Plus Ultra*, curated by Mar Villaespesa and commissioned by the pavilion of Andalusia at EXPO '92.

11. Gerardo Mosquera defines "inverted curating" in the following terms: "the countries which host the art of other cultures are at the same time curating the shows; it is almost never the other way around, and it is regarded as the most natural thing to happen. The world is practically divided between curating cultures and curated cultures." The reference to the curating of the world comes from James Clifford. See Gerardo Mosquera, "Some Problems in Transcultural Curating," in *Global Visions: Towards a New Internationalism in the Visual Arts*, ed. Jean Fisher (London: Kala Press/InIVA, 1994), 105–12.

12. Gerardo Mosquera, ed., *Beyond the Fantastic: Contemporary Art Criticism from Latin America* (London: InIVA, 1996).

13. See Rafal Niemojewski, "Venice or Havana: A Polemic in the Genesis of the Contemporary Biennial," in *The Biennial Reader*, ed. Elena Filipovic, Marieke van Hal, and Solveig Ovstebo (Bergen: Bergen Kunstehall; Ostfildern: Hatje Cantz, 2010).

14. See Rachel Weiss, ed., *Making Art Global (Part 1): The Third Havana Biennial 1989* (London: Afterall Books, 2011).

15. Very influential at the moment is the book by Néstor

counteract what Gerardo Mosquera called "inverted curating" based on the "insatiable desire and power of the postmodern West to curate the world."[11] This reaction also had a clear reference point in *Beyond the Fantastic*, a book edited by Mosquera in 1994, which combined a position of discrepancy with the publication in English of texts by Latin American historians and critics on art in Latin America, proposing a plurality of narratives to confront the texts of Anglo-Saxon historians.[12] This critical vanguard eventually took concrete form in a series of exhibitions that were to have a greater impact on later historiography than the front opened with the publications, which itself is indicative of the capacity of exhibitions to project themselves discursively in the global era, with a vast potential to transform existing images, though also to neutralize or banalize them.

In any case, the new exhibition scenario was significantly prefigured at the Havana Biennial, whose third edition in 1989 has been regarded as a turning point in exhibition models linking globalization and contemporary art.[13] The third biennial was important for consolidating the south-south encounter initiated in earlier editions, so promoting alternative narratives to the European-US model. At the same time, the model of the biennial facilitated the transition from a notion of Third World art to one of proto-globalization of the periphery. Its theoretical articulation under the title *Tradición-Contemporaneidad*—developed in large part by its principal curator Gerardo Mosquera—tried to short-circuit a series of binary pairs in which "peripheral" art had become ensnared, such as old/new, art/craft, original/copy, and center/periphery, and resituate local productions under a postcolonial paradigm that questioned not only modernism but also, and above all, modernity as a colonial process.[14] From this position, resorting to the hybrid, to the cultural appropriation or "mismatch," took shape as a sign of identity and an escape route from the stereotyping essentialism of the indigenous or the fantastic.[15] This interpretive line was to resound in the nineties in the proposals of other curators, such as Mari Carmen Ramírez, Luis Camnitzer, and Paulo Herkenhoff.[16]

Nevertheless, this appropriationist flexibility was easily reappropriated as a multicultural element, especially in a demographically changing United States, if not as a commodifiable element of the new neocolonial scenario.[17] Although it was a process of differential appropriation whose advantage was that it made colonial and imperialist processes visible, working with the supposedly hegemonic references meant continued support for the hierarchical model, driving every possible attempt at irony into a double bind that returned again and again to the theme of identity. On the other hand, the attempt to collapse the premodern in the postmodern ended up providing culturalist alibis for the development of certain nationalist institutional policies, as Jorge Luis Marzo has pointed out.[18] In any case, the consolidation of the biennials of Havana, Porto Alegre (1997), and Lima (1997), and the new boost given to that of São Paulo, have been crucial for the establishment of new centers of production and enunciation.[19]

This broadening of the scope of exhibitions allowed several important shows to be mounted for the construction of a new narrative that tried to steer a course between questioning the "Latin American art" label and questioning national narratives, one example being *Ante América*.[20] It should be pointed out that many of them took place at US institutions and some at Spanish ones, indicative of what constitutes a space that is at the same time one of legitimization and of conflict, and significative of the difficulty of promoting challenging exhibitions in the territory of the artistic production itself.[21] Perhaps the most recurrent characteristic of the exhibitions of the nineties is the defense of the pluralism of artists and movements beyond the regionalist "Latin American" vision, and it is on the basis of this pluralism that attempts are made to establish connections, whether by employing imaginary and mobile cartographies (*Cartographies: 14 Latin American Artists*), searching for constellations of artistic sensibility (*Heterotopías. Medio siglo sin lugar, 1918–1968*), or rereading history through the geographical enlargement of apparently centered movements (*Global Conceptualisms: Points of Origin, 1950s–1980s*).[22] Recourse to cartography and the diffusion of geography and translation (and also constellations and networks) through the vocabulary of curatorial projects are symptomatic of a specifically curatorial approach that is already contaminated by new historiographical models of postcolonial and global influence.

Beyond the reductive gaze of the indigenist and the fantastic, which fixed Latin American production within a permanent Surrealism/Magic Realism, it now becomes possible to glimpse other proposals that were formerly obscured by the interests serving the narrative of modernist art. In this way, there now appears a conceptualism beyond the conceptual that questions the restrictive tautological model in both directions and allows linking paths to be opened up toward contemporary languages. This conceptualism, characterized as ideological, sought at first to identify itself with the political commitment of the seventies, and has now led to a broadening of the study of specific practices in relation to their precise historical contexts, making the diversity of approaches clearly manifest. The indisputable presence of an avant-garde or neo-avant-garde in Latin America (and simultaneously in other areas forgotten by historiography, like Eastern Europe and Japan) facilitates a general reconsideration of postwar historiography that is no longer articulated around the heavily mortgaged binary opposition of modernism and antimodernism but around the different ways in which the continuity of the avant-garde was imagined and theorized in postwar Europe and also in other centers, including the Americas. In this sense, we could say that this history is not specular but symmetrical.

The rereading of the historiographical model has been accompanied by a greater circulation of the artwork of the period, including works of Latin American geometric abstraction, especially from Brazil and Venezuela. The recurrent negation by art in the United States of its European Neoplasticist and Constructivist sources, and its continual nationalist declarations, are symptomatic of its need to belittle and refute European influence, to which a certain deficiency in the reception of some artists during the Cold War may also have contributed. This enforced obscurity of the European sources in their modernist projection has significantly and unjustifiably affected the reading of geometric practices in Latin America. In many American countries, however, the geometric avant-garde forms were consciously re-elaborated and redeveloped, for not only was such a continuation unaffected by trauma owing to these nations' non-participation in World War II, but it was linked, owing to the war itself, to a period of economic and social growth and of cultural enrichment thanks to those who were exiled there.[23] Exhibitions like *The Geometry of Hope*, centered more on practices than on geography, have tried to shun the cliché of identity and transfer the debate to a new history of postwar artistic practices.[24]

Paris School, New York School, School of the South

This process of rewinding brings us back to our starting point, and to the interrogation of the model of subordinate or deformed mirror symmetries, giving us an opportunity to reapproach the myth from other perspectives. While artistic discourse before World War II was shot through with the Europe-America relationship, it afterwards started to triangulate with a growing and clearly lopsided division between the United States, Latin America, and Europe. This process took place progressively, although it was not

García Canclini, *Culturas híbridas. Estrategias para entrar y salir de la modernidad* (Mexico City: Grijalbo, 1990). On the idea of the mismatch (*descalce*), see Gerardo Mosquera, ed., *Copiar el Edén. Arte reciente en Chile* (Santiago de Chile: Ediciones y Publicaciones Puro Chile, 2008).

16. Ramírez makes the following reflections: "At the core of these issues lies the notion of appropriation and the particular role it has played in the Latin American/Latino version of modernism to counteract the ethnocentric discourse of the West. . . . This has yielded a symbolic system based on hybridization and synthesis that has traditionally been condemned by Western authorities. And yet in this context appropriation assumes a positive function. Rather than leading to a pool of formal signifiers aimed at revitalizing a symbolic system or recreating its mirror-image, it may be considered, as Luis Camnitzer has observed, 'a process of enrichment that can generate syncretic work, helping to absorb and digest the impact of the imposed (or dominant) culture." In Mari Carmen Ramírez, "Beyond 'The Fantastic," 67. In 1998, Paulo Herkenhoff revisited Oswald de Andrade's concept of anthropophagy, whose cannibal substratum is also appropriationist, at the Bienal de São Paulo.

17. See, for example, a discussion of the case of Mexican in Anna Indych-Lopez, "Between the National and the Transnational: Aspects of Exhibiting Modern and Contemporary Mexican Art at the Americas Society," in *A Principality of Its Own*, ed. José Luis Falconi and Gabriela Rangel (New York: The Americas Society, 2006), 84–99.

18. Jorge Luis Marzo "Neo, post, ultra, pre, para, contra, anti. Modernidad, barroco y capitalismo en el arte contemporáneo mexicano" (2011), http://www.soymenos.net

/arte_contemporaneo_
mexico.pdf (accessed December
9, 2012). A similar line is
represented by the exhibition
*Ultrabarroco: aspectos de un arte
postlatinoamericano*, curated by
Elisabeth Armstrong and Víctor
Zamudio-Taylor, Museum of
Contemporary Art, San Diego,
2000.

19. Justo Pastor Mellado, "Nota
para redimensionar el debate
sobre arte y política" (2005),
http://www.justopastormellado.
cl/edicion/index.php?option=
content&task=view&id=208
&Itemid=28 (accessed December
9, 2012).

20. *Ante América* (curated by
Gerardo Mosquera, Carolina
Ponce de León, and Rachel Weiss,
Biblioteca Luis Ángel Arango,
Bogota, 1992) was a cycle of
exhibitions oriented toward
showing the complexity and
irreducible diversity of Latin
America. The exhibition
*Figuración Fabulación. 75 años de
pintura en América Latina 1914–
1989* (curated by Robert Guevara,
Museo de Bellas Artes, Caracas,
1990) also took a thematic model
for its approach rather than a
national or regional one.

21. See Justo Pastor Mellado,
"Apuntes para una delimitación
de la noción de curador como
producción de infraestructura"
(2001), at http://www.
micromuseo.org.pe/lecturas
/jpastor.html (accessed
December 9, 2012).

22. *Cartographies: 14 Latin
American Artists*, curated by Ivo
Mezquita, Winnipeg Art Gallery,
1993; *Heterotopías. Medio siglo
sin lugar 1918–1968*, curated by
Mari Carmen Ramírez and
Héctor Olea, Museo Nacional
Centro de Arte Reina Sofía, 2001;
*Global Conceptualisms: Points of
Origins, 1950s–1980s*, curated by
Luis Camnitzer, Mari Carmen
Ramírez, and Rachel Weiss,
Queens Museum of Art, 1999.

23. Significant in this respect is
the "recovery" of the European
origins of exiled artists from
Germany like Grete Stern, Gego,
and Mira Schendel in, for

until the late fifties that the US began to be recognized by Europe as a producer of
new forms. The European avant-garde had been configured as a cultural crucible
that proposed an art without geographical or disciplinary frontiers, and in which
artists from numerous European and also American countries had participated.
It was also configured as an experience of the modern in which mobility and cultural
transfer, the result of emigration and exile among the artists, had been decisive
elements in the formation of the new languages, as Raymond Williams points out.[25]
This internationalization occurred in and from Europe, and from there the rest of
the world was considered as a mere receiver of the new languages.

In spite of this hegemonic view, the fact is that the same conditions of growing
modernization, transnationality, and exchange (with local cultures too) were to be found
in the Americas. Since before the war, there had already arisen movements for cultural
autonomy, whether nationalist in inspiration (like anthropophagy in Brazil) or
universalist-regionalist (like those of Joaquín Torres-García). From the European
standpoint, it was hard to visualize these projects, which had moreover been forged
through exchange with Europe, as something originating and original. The metropolitan
interpretation of modern art understood its own processes as international and
universal, while the others were required to display a national, identitarian, or localist
differential from what the Europeans regarded as already fulfilled by their own history,
including their colonial history. The rest had to endow their projects for artistic
modernization with signs of their own identity, and to find, as Andrea Giunta indicates,
the perfect percentages for a mixture of international and local languages (a localist
internationalism).[26] In the Americas, this identitarian vocation was generally riddled
with nationalism, as in the Mexican and Brazilian cases. The first art in America to
achieve international legitimization was muralism in Mexico, which did so by combining
re-elaborations of international and local languages. Its model served as a reference
point for the continent and decisively influenced the art of the United States, exerting
an important effect on its first forms of modern art.

Immediately after World War II, the Europeans still found it difficult to see the
Americans, whether of the North or the South, as producers rather than receivers.
The first exhibitions taken from the United States to Europe were less imbued with the
hegemonic vocation they were to acquire shortly afterwards, and abstract art was even
viewed in the US itself as being under suspicion of communism. As the great power that
had just emerged from the war, the US meanwhile tried to present its art as equal in
quality to Europe's by means of a powerful machinery for producing one exhibition after
another, already displaying its imperialist purpose. Even so, the Europeans were
reluctant to give up their role, and critics responded to these necessarily eclectic
exhibitions with interest and curiosity, but also searching in the works for features that
would identify them as "American" (independence, vitality, freedom, and a certain
technical coarseness), and always emphasizing that America's art had reached less
interesting heights than its literature, which served as a touchstone.[27]

In 1958, a fundamental change took place in the appreciation of art from United States.
The Abstract Expressionists started to be shown on their own, and, with Europe in
reconstruction, the political and economic hegemony of the United States was
unstoppable. The works of the Abstract Expressionists, which were read as a clear
reaction to the refinement of European painting, began to be valued for the size of their
canvases and their expressive force as materializations of the energy and expansiveness of
the "American spirit."[28] This more or less identitarian acceptance was all the more
immediate for the United States when we consider that the works were presented as the

art of a single country (the US), a city (New York), and a school (the New York School), so establishing an automatic parallelism with the Paris School. This clearly simplified the formula. In Latin America, in the meantime, each country was trying to define its own national art, searching for a balance between avant-garde, modernization, and nationalism. The possibility of a School of the South was overwhelmed by Latin America's geographic, artistic, cultural, and political diversity.

From the United States, and above all through programmed exhibitions, an attempt was made to find a single formula fit for all "Latin American art," despite the diversity of its assimilation and conjugation of modern languages, its plurality of production centers, and the variety of its practices. The political, economic, and institutional instability induced in a Latin America fully exposed to the effects of the Cold War made it difficult, especially from the sixties onward, to deploy a sustained narrative. Although countries like Brazil created their own infrastructures of legitimization, such as the Bienal de São Paulo and various modern art museums, the different national modern arts started to seek legitimacy in the institutions of the United States. Here they ran up against the nascent critical paradigm that denied them any genealogy or development in connection with the avant-garde, and moreover saw them as derivative of their own version of it. The United States started to produce and reproduce the same monolithic history institutionally (in collections, museums, exhibitions, and critical and academic discourses), in a clear gesture of performative repetition of its own identity, always at risk. The North Americans reinforced themselves as equals, and reinforced the other as invariably different, in a well-known Western ritual of "otherizing" self-definition. Postwar Europe was trying to come to terms with its love-hate relationship with the US while attempting to retain its former cultural preeminence. And Francoist Spain was trying to actualize its colonial links through an odd policy of biennials, which it attempted to use to bolster up the regime's international standing under the notion of *Hispanidad*, a concept that tried to articulate the Spanish-speaking countries.[29]

Continuity of the Avant-Garde

Let us return once more to our starting point and establish new symmetries, even if such rewinding is tiresome. Once the narrative/canon is established, all the energy seems to be dissipated on its refutation, and twice as much effort is required for its reconstruction. Leaving historiographical hegemonies behind, we can very briefly re-examine artistic practices. After the war, questions raised by the historical avant-garde continued to be developed both in Europe and the Americas. There was a continuation of both the progressive detachment from mimesis and the constant (and perhaps impossible) desire for a radical elimination of representation. Some artists undertook research into the cognitive and perceptual aspects of the genesis of representation, eventually leading to its interrogation, to a (paradoxical) claim for its contingency, and to a destabilization of the perceiving subject. On the basis of such representative instabilities, different but not necessarily incompatible artistic strategies arose in an attempt to replace representation itself. These strategies overflow the bounds of the habitual classifications by movements, and are aimed at encouraging a new reading of twentieth-century art. In some cases it is a case of the construction of a new *real*, an objective, concrete, and autonomously significant artistic reality generated through the production of forms, images/words, and spaces in an exchange of reproduction for production. In other cases, what is proposed is the replacement of representation with presentation on the basis of the literalism of the object or text, or with practices informed by modes of theatricality and the presence of the body, sometimes as attempts

instance, the reception of the exhibition *Vibración: Modern Art from Latin America*, Bundeskunsthalle, Bonn, 2011. See "Exhibition of Modern Art from Latin America on View in Bonn," *Artdaily.org*, September 20, 2010, www.artdaily.org /index.asp?int_sec=11&int_ new=41002 (accessed December 9, 2012).

24. *The Geometry of Hope: Latin American Abstract Art from the Patricia Phelps de Cisneros Collection*, curated by Gabriel Pérez-Barreiro, Blanton Museum of Art, Austin, and Grey Art Gallery, New York, 2007.

25. Raymond Williams, *Politics of Modernism: Against the New Conformists* (London: Verso, 1989).

26. Andrea Giunta, *Avant-Garde, Internationalism, and Politics: Argentine Art in the Sixties* (Durham, NC and London: Duke University Press, 2007), 211.

27. On the reception of the art of the United States in Europe, which wavered between rejection and tempered enthusiasm, see Helen M. Franc, "The Early Years of the International Program and Council," in *The Museum of Modern Art at Mid-Century: At Home and Abroad* (New York: Museum of Modern Art, 1994), 108–49.

28. For example, Bernard Dorival writing in *Les Arts* on the exhibition *The New American Painting* at the Musée National d'Art Moderne, Paris, 1959: "Rather than the United States of standardization, system, and productivity, there are qualities here of Walt Whitman in these abstract paintings that burst forth with vigor and lyricism, full of vitality." Cited in ibid., 136.

29. These attempts were responded to with counter-biennials in Mexico City, Caracas, Havana, and Paris. See Miguel Cabañas, "Postrimerías de un instrumento de la política artística del franquismo. El final de las Bienales Hispanoamericas de arte," *Boletín del Seminario de Estudios de Arte y Arqueología de*

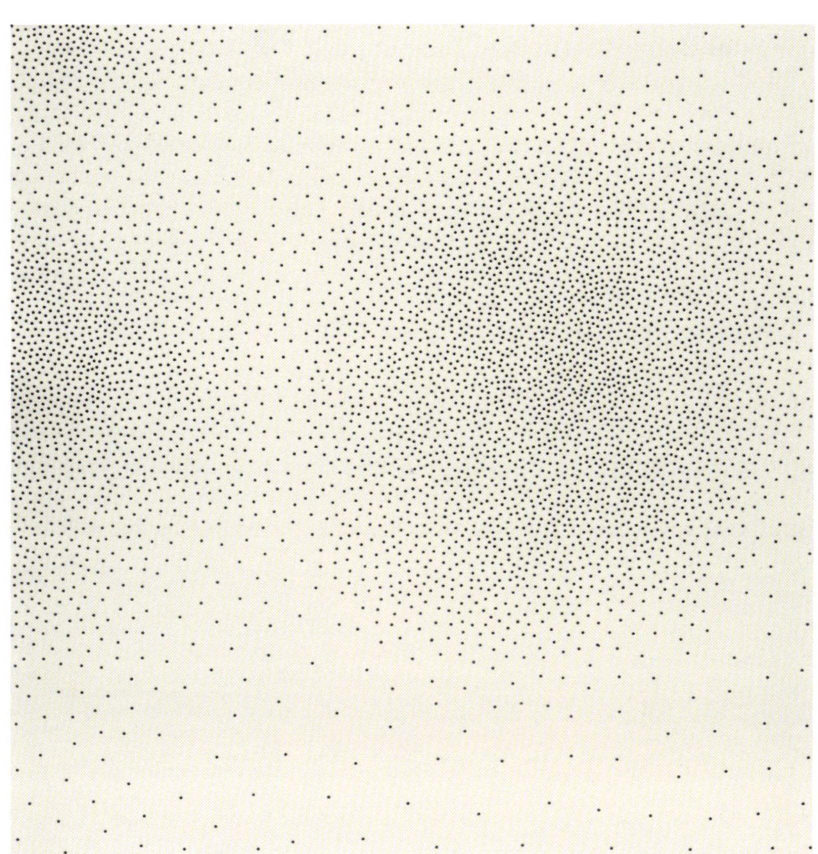

Mira Schendel
Perfurados I [Perforated I], n.d.

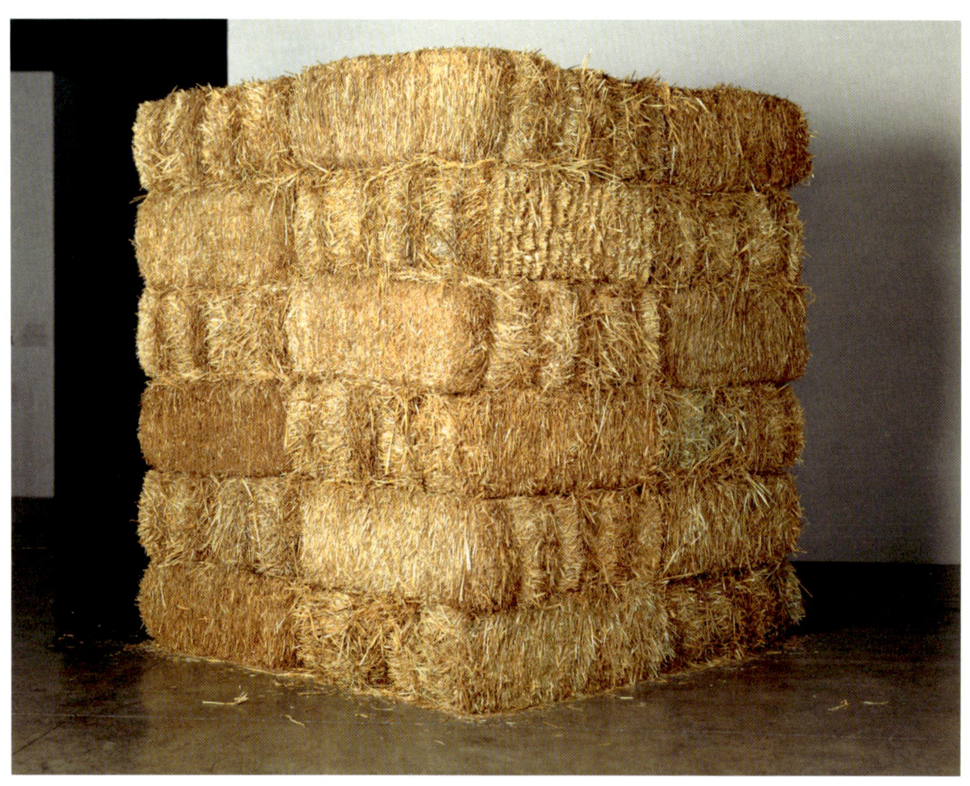

Cildo Meireles
Fio [Thread], 1990–95

to cipher and decipher subjectivity and otherness. And in further instances, it is manifested as the elimination of the frontiers between art and life, in a bid to fuse aesthetic experience and art together with intervention in reality.

It may seem hard to believe that these developments were brought about by a mere handful of artists, mostly men, located in New York, Paris, and a few German cities. When it comes to telling a story, of course, it is always easier to do so on the basis of an exemplary explanatory model that favors a version of facts as a continuum bonded together by a unity of times and spaces, and sustained by a critical paradigm that has emerged in a hegemonic nation. Nevertheless, various artists and groups in Latin America made significant contributions to the development of this legacy of the avant-garde. Among them, special attention is merited by those dedicated to a process whereby the artistic object ceased to be considered an end in itself and became instead a mediator of experience, in response to various formulations of the relations between painting/sculpture and object, architecture/space and object, and object and subject/body, producing new realms of experience straddling the object and the non-object. In these practices, it might be said that the nature of the artistic object went from that of an object to a model of an object. In other words, they could be considered as investigations that are objectified or dematerialized as demonstrative instruments.

If we consider *coplanares*, *bichos*, *nuclei*, *penetrables*, *reticuláreas*, *cromosaturaciones*, and even media art (to name only some of the best-known proposals, with every respect for the artistic specificities and poetics of their originators),[30] they could be seen as devices giving rise to a reflection on the perception, construction, or occupation of space, or on communication through an identity between content and method, cause and effect. To put it another way, they are practical devices that produce, in one and the same process, an object and a raising of awareness that may be perceptual, spatial, sensory, linguistic, or even ethical. This mediating "object," which is moreover situated between various artistic media, is inevitably differentiated from the prescriptiveness of the media-specific object, trapped in the cul-de-sac of the reification of Post-Painterly Abstraction or modernist sculpture.

This intermediate object, clearly avant-gardist, does not fit at all neatly into the Anglo-Saxon histories of painting or sculpture, constructed around a modernist object that is closed in on itself. It should be pointed out that there is a difference in the United States between the discourses and some of their practices, a case in point being the productive contradictions of minimalism.[31] The problem is that it is these contradictions that have been established as a universal model, above all when the European heritage is insistently denied. In histories written from postmodern premises, like that of Rosalind Krauss, the antimodernist characterization mentioned earlier and its postmodernist resolution help to prevent the continuum from being broken, but are not to be understood as universally applicable.[32] Their blindness toward the rest of the world, and the absence of Latin American artists in particular, is not only flagrant but can also be read as an indication of the impermeability of Krauss's model of an expanded field, partially restricted by a simplifying opposition between medium-specific and site-specific.[33] Eventually, by extension, this affects the histories of installations. In this case, the difficulty of propounding a history situated in a specific time and place, as New York was, encourages a thematic approach, where artists from outside the United States and Europe appear only sporadically, and those who do appear often tend to be contemporary artists.[34] Rewriting the history of twentieth-century art is not a simple matter. Narrative inertias still weigh heavily on the legitimizing institutions of museums and academia, and such hegemony means there is a permanent risk of falling into the trap of difference.

Valladolid 62 (1997). There were also some counter-biennials in opposition to "corporate" biennials in Latin America, like the First Argentine Festival of Contemporary Forms—the Anti-Biennial—held in 1966 to oppose the American Art Biennials organized in Córdoba by Industrias Kaiser.

30. I am thinking of mediating/demonstrative objects by Tomás Maldonado, Gyula Kosice, Lidy Prati, Lygia Clark, Hélio Oiticica, Gego, Mira Schendel, Carlos Cruz-Diez, Jesús Soto, Julio Le Parc, Grupo de los Medios, and Mathias Goeritz, among many others.

31. In this sense, it would be interesting to oppose these intermediate objects to the "specific objects" of Donald Judd. See Donald Judd, "Specific Objects," originally published in *Arts Yearbook* 8 (1965), and Michael Fried, "Art and Objecthood," *Artforum* 4, no. 10 (June 1967).

32. Rosalind Krauss, *Passages in Modern Sculpture* (Cambridge, Mass.: MIT Press, 1981).

33. Rosalind Krauss, "Sculpture in the Expanded Field," *October* 8 (Spring 1979).

34. For example, in Erika Suderburg, *Space, Site, Intervention: Situating Installation Art* (Minnesota: University of Minnesota Press, 2000); Julie H. Reiss, *From Margin to Center: The Spaces of Installation Art* (Cambridge, Mass.: MIT Press, 2001); or Claire Bishop, *Installation Art: A Critical History* (London: Tate Publishing, 2005).

Returning to some of the intermediate objects, and especially those that imply participation in the artistic process (like those of Lygia Clark, Hélio Oiticica, and Carlos Cruz-Diez, but also participation/raising of political awareness, as in Artur Barrio), it is interesting to note how they have been rapidly assimilated in recent years by a global scene where the revaluation of the spectator's role is proving essential. This movement toward participation, central to the European artistic scene since the 1990s and present in relational aesthetics, collaborative artistic projects, and the rise of performative practices, has been accompanied by a certain search for precursors. In the international panorama of exhibitions, from monographs to biennials, this has facilitated the recovery, if not the discovery, of a large number of Latin American artists, some of whose practices were situated, participative, or collaborative.[35] The new artistic sensibility owes fewer discursive debts to modernist interpretations, and moreover tries to be explicitly global.[36] The search for other precursors, and the rereading of the past from the standpoint of present necessities, helps to broaden historiographical horizons. Nevertheless, an excessively superficial parallelism risks ignoring the context in which practices of this type took place. The intersubjective encounters activated by art belong to the more general avant-garde project of emancipation, and there are great differences between the expectations of the 1950s and the 1990s, and in the ways they are materialized. Pointing out differences can be just as revealing as drawing parallels.

It is also pertinent to point out other risks of an accelerated circulation of artwork and artists. One would be the generation of a new canon, almost before the previous one had been dismantled. The procedure should rather be a deeper scrutiny of the interweaving of art in Latin America as a whole, an examination easily skewed by the preponderance on the art scene of certain countries like Mexico, Argentina, Venezuela, and Brazil.[37] On the other hand, practices that are less easily "exportable," such as visual poetry, or less well-known, like photography, performance, and the moving image, also form part of the development of the avant-garde. There is moreover a danger that the old canonical discourses might contribute to the creation of new signifiers of difference, such as a "vernacular geometry," an "activist conceptualism," or a misunderstood "satirical tropicalism," which would ultimately send the art of Latin America back from history to otherness. Problematical too is the attempt to convert avant-garde practices into antimodernist ones in order to insert them in the canonical history.

After more than three decades of revisionist exhibitions curated by Latin Americans and Latinos, increasing critical and academic dissemination from specialists, and enlarged collections and gradual attempts to consolidate institutions in Latin American countries (museums, foundations, biennials, independent spaces), it seems that efforts to move the debate beyond the identitarian cliché toward a more historical terrain have at least achieved greater circulation for certain artists and some practices from the Cold War period, paralleled by promotion for contemporary artists on the global map. Apart from the fantastic, as we pointed out earlier, the geometric abstract and conceptualist legacies (simplifying the labels) appear to have succeeded in establishing a parallel and equivalent imagery. It still remains to trace out the different paths, frequently intersecting, where bi-univocal vectors are to be apprehended on all three sides of the triangle (Europe, the United States, Latin America).[38] At the same time, and beyond the strictly art-historical debate, new paths of study are being opened, derived from the new tools that postmodernity (not postmodernism) has placed at the disposal of historians, and which try to formulate partial, plural, refractive, or thematic histories. Among them, we might signal approaches on the basis of postcolonial or decolonial thought, or of the political or transgendered body.

35. Besides those mentioned above, we might add Lygia Pape, Tucumán Arde, Víctor Grippo, the CADA group, and Cildo Meireles, among those that have appeared at biennials.

36. As in the "new critical paradigm" of relational aesthetics. See Nicolas Bourriaud, *Relational Aesthetics* (Paris: Les Presses du Réel, 2002).

37. This is one of the objectives of the research network Conceptualismos del Sur; see http://redconceptualismosdelsur.blogspot.com.es/ (accessed December 9, 2012).

38. One research project along these lines is "Meeting Margins, Transnational Art in Latin America and Europe 1950–1978," Universidad of Essex, Colchester and University of the Arts, London.

Coda

Now that the first decade of the twenty-first century is already past, the adjectivization of the terms "modernist" and "modern" seems to have been left behind in the progressive dynamics of modernity itself, which is formulated today out of languages and themes categorized as contemporary and global. We remain today with the (unfulfilled) promise of a modernity whose presumed universality is being insistently questioned, but also with an imagery of the modern and cultural forms that can be re-signified in new poetic and/or political practices. As we pointed out at the beginning— still some ways from the historiographical sifting and the proposing of new ways of looking at the past—certain contemporary artists, including some Latin Americans, are reflecting on various aspects of the construction of modernity, its expectations, its loose ends, its fractures, or its resistances, and to this end they are reusing, restaging, or reviving its sign-forms, its images, landscapes, spaces, or archives.[39] Instead of approaching the contemporary directly, they try to understand current reality by working on the immediate past or on the remnants of that past in the present.

For these artists, there are no hegemonic, derivative, or different forms because they have all been leveled by time. In some cases, always deliberate, the essentialisms have become "strategic," and there is an oscillation between identity, globalization, history, and the present. The original has lost much of its credibility, and the digital revolution merely increases the possibilities for rewriting. This apart, one notices a certain generational inclination to make fiction out of history through a superimposition of past and fiction, making it possible for heterogeneous times and spaces to coexist. This procedure implies neither a restrictedly formalist or historicist revaluation nor a melancholy exaltation. It is rather a matter of proposing new signifieds for old signifiers, and of using the imagination, together with investigation, to rewrite history.

39. Among many other artists who examine modernity from various angles, we find Armando Andrade Tudela, Carlos Garaicoa, Abraham Cruzvillegas, Fernando Bryce, Erik Beltrán, Ángela Bonadies and Juan José Olavarría, Tamar Guimarães, Raimond Chaves and Gilda Mantilla, Gabriel Kuri, and Mario García-Torres.

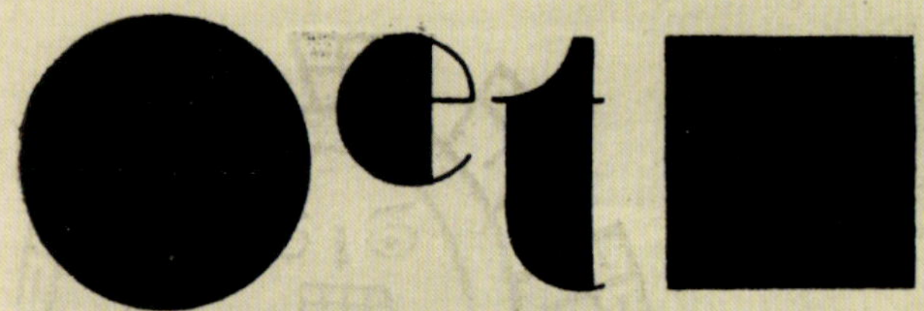

CIRCULO Y CUADRADO
SEGUNDA EPOCA - TRIMESTRAL
PRECIO DEL EJEMPLAR 0.25
SUSCRIPCION ANUAL 1.00

Montevideo, Setiembre 1938

REVISTA DE LA ASOCIACION DE ARTE CONSTRUCTIVO
DIRECCION: MERCEDES 1889-MONTEVIDEO-URUGUAY

TRADICION CONSTRUCTIVA DE AMERICA

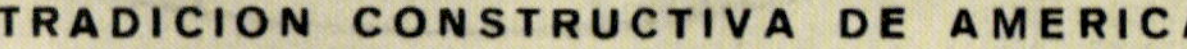

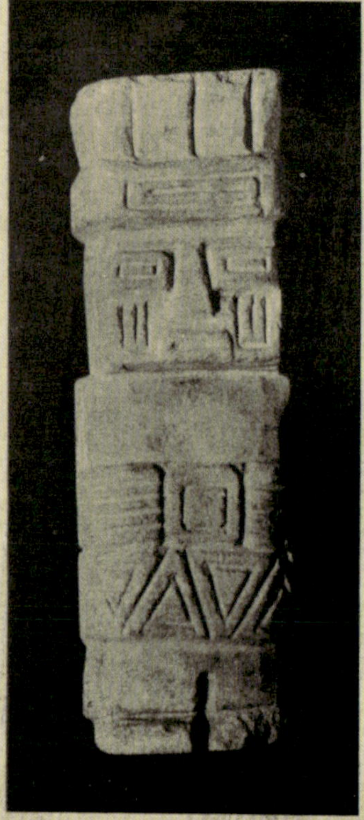

ARCILLA   **IDOLITO BOLIVIANO**

AMPLIACION DE ESTUDIOS

La Asociación de Arte Constructivo, al abrir una nueva serie de estudios sobre la **Tradición Constructiva en América**, es con el fin de poner en evidencia que, las teorías que hasta hoy sustentó, pueden equipararse a la cultura arcaica del Continente, y que por esto, al propugnar tales teorías, no es con el fin de formar una escuela más, sino de dar debida orientación, que sería la que unificaría, como ya lo hemos dicho en otras ocasiones, a todo el arte de América.

Muchas veces hemos señalado el parentesco existente entre el Arte Constructivo y el Arte Precolombiano que, en primer lugar, nos coloca en un mismo plano, pero sobre todo, y esto es lo más importante, en estrecha relación de teorías.

Nuestro objeto, al ampliar nuestra actividad con esta nueva serie de estudios, no es pues, con el fin de cambiar en nada nuestra base constructiva. Al contrario, lo que queremos, es poner eso en evidencia, en el grado actual de la evolución del arte americano propiamente dicho y, en cierto modo, explicar el presente por el pasado.

Pero hay que entenderse. No se trata de copia o de imitación, de parafrasear un arte admirable pero retrospectivo. Pues nuestra base, la regla de oro universal que rige asimismo nuestra filosofía y nuestro arte, la hallamos también en las antiguas culturas de América, y es, puede decirse, el lazo que nos une a ellas a través de los siglos.

Hemos pensado que sería útil señalar metódicamente y con estudios continuados, esa ligazón.

Y esto tendrá la doble virtud de poner aún más en evidencia que hasta el presente, la significación de nuestras teorías y de poner más de relieve, ante un público a veces mal informado, la profunda diferencia que existe, por ejemplo, entre nuestras concepciones y las de los Cubistas.

Por esto, nuestro programa constará de dos series paralelas de estudios. De una parte un estudio profundo de la arqueología y del arte precolombiano, y del otro su confrontación incesante con el construccionismo. Y esto se realizará por medio de conferencias, publicaciones, estudios de técnica constructiva, proyecciones, etc.

Y esperamos, gracias a estos nuevos temas de estudios, a la vez que enriquecernos con ideas nuevas, situar al Arte Constructivo, debidamente, en la historia del Arte Americano.

E insistimos en lo de otras veces: que nuestra actuación será ajena a toda tendencia social, política o religiosa.

A este fin pedimos que quieran significar su adhesión a nuestras actividades, las personas interesadas en dichos estudios directa o indirectamente, para cooperar a la realización de tan importante obra de cultura.

TRADITION CONSTRUCTIVE D'AMERIQUE

L'Association d'Art Constructif en ouvrant une nouvelle serie d'etudes sur la **Tradition Constructive d'Amerique**, a comme finalitée de mettre en évidence que la theorie qu'elle a toujours soutenue peut s'identifier a la culture archaique du Continent. Pourtant elle ne a pas repandue pour former une école de plus, mais au contraire pour donner une orientation qui unifierait, comme nous l'avons affirmé plusieurs fois, l'Art de l'Amerique.

Nous avons dejá bien souvent signalé la parenté qu'il existe entre le Constructivisme et l'art Precolombien. Parenté que crée un sol commun d'abord, mais surtout, et ceci est plus important, étroite parenté de théories.

Notre but, en prenant un autre nom pour nos études, n'est pas de changer quoi que ce soit a notre Art Constructif. Au contraire. Ce que nous voulons c'est le mettre bien en evidence au terme actuel de l'evolution de l'art americain proprement dit, et, en quelque sorte, expliquer le present par le passé.

Entendons nous. Il ne s'agit pas de copie ni d'imitation; jamais n'a été question de paraphraser un art admirable, certes, mais passé. Le Constructivisme est profondement original et entierement contemporain. Mais sa base, cette regle d'or universelle, qui régit aussi bien notre philosophie que notre art, on la trouve aussi dans les anciennes cultures americaines, et elle est pour ainsi dire le fil qui nous unit a elles a travers les siècles.

Nous avons pensé qu'il serait utile de signaler methodiquement et d'une façon suivie cette liaison. Cela aura le double mérite de marquer encore plus que jusqu'a ce jour la portée de nos theories, d'accentuer aux yeux d'un publique souvent mal informé, la profonde difference qu'il existe entre nos conceptions et celles des Cubistes, par exemple.

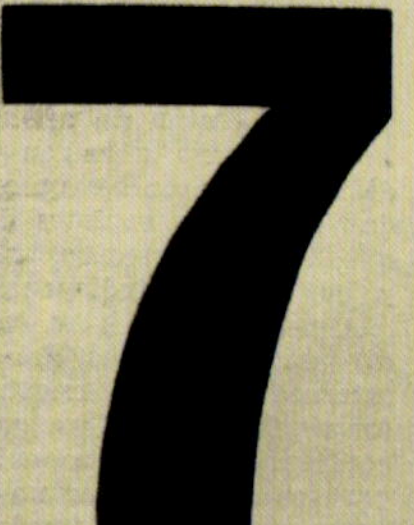

Universalism

"I insist that this kind of art must enter into the rhythms—not only into the fixed eternal plastic laws, but also into the system of proportions whereby through measure you achieve unity, i.e. harmony."

Joaquín Torres-García,
The School of the South

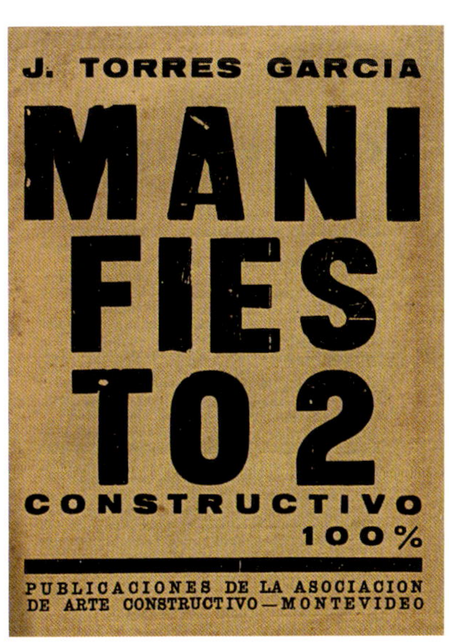

Joaquín Torres-García, *Manifiesto No. 2*, Montevideo: Asociación de Arte Constructivo, 1938

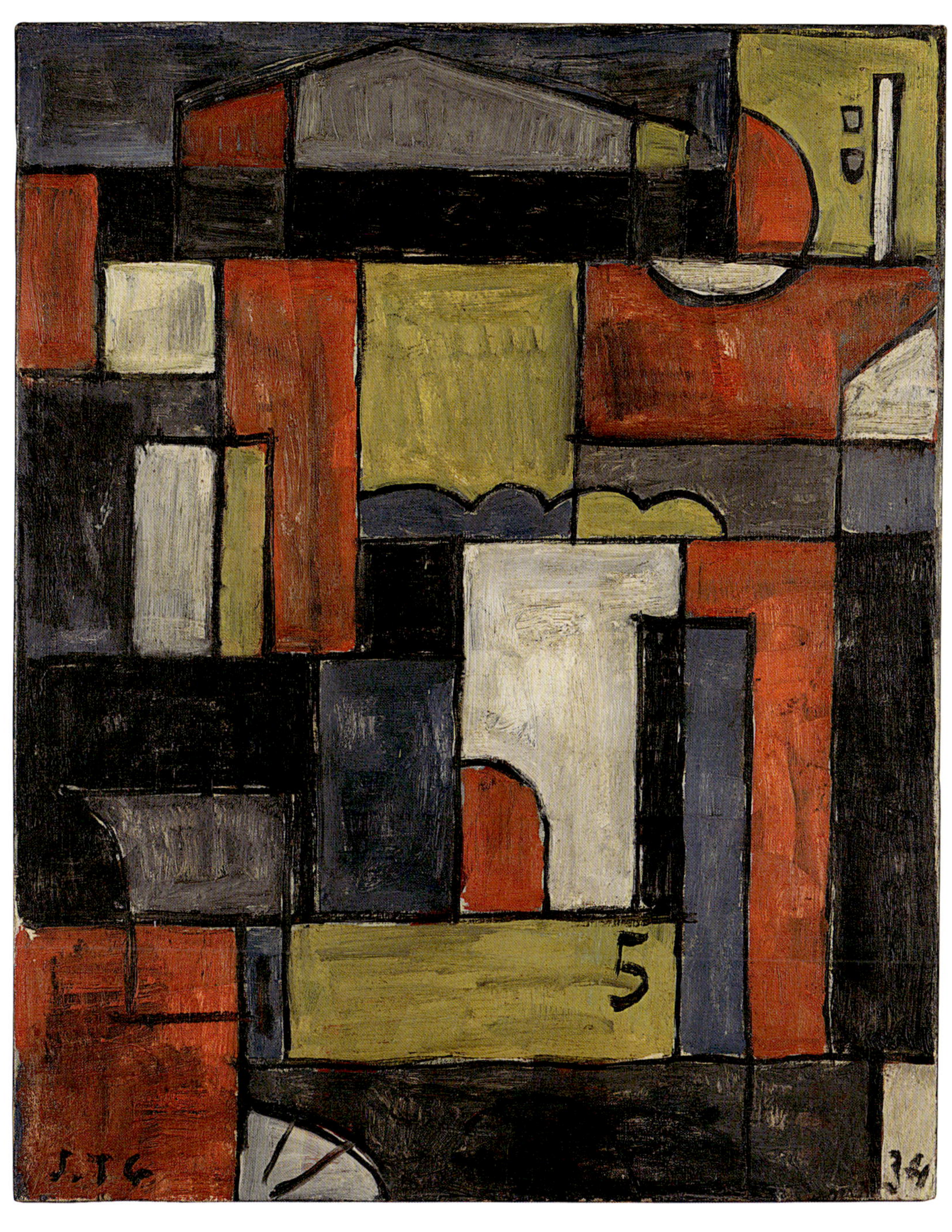

Joaquín Torres-García
Locomotora con casa constructiva [Locomotive with Constructive House], 1934

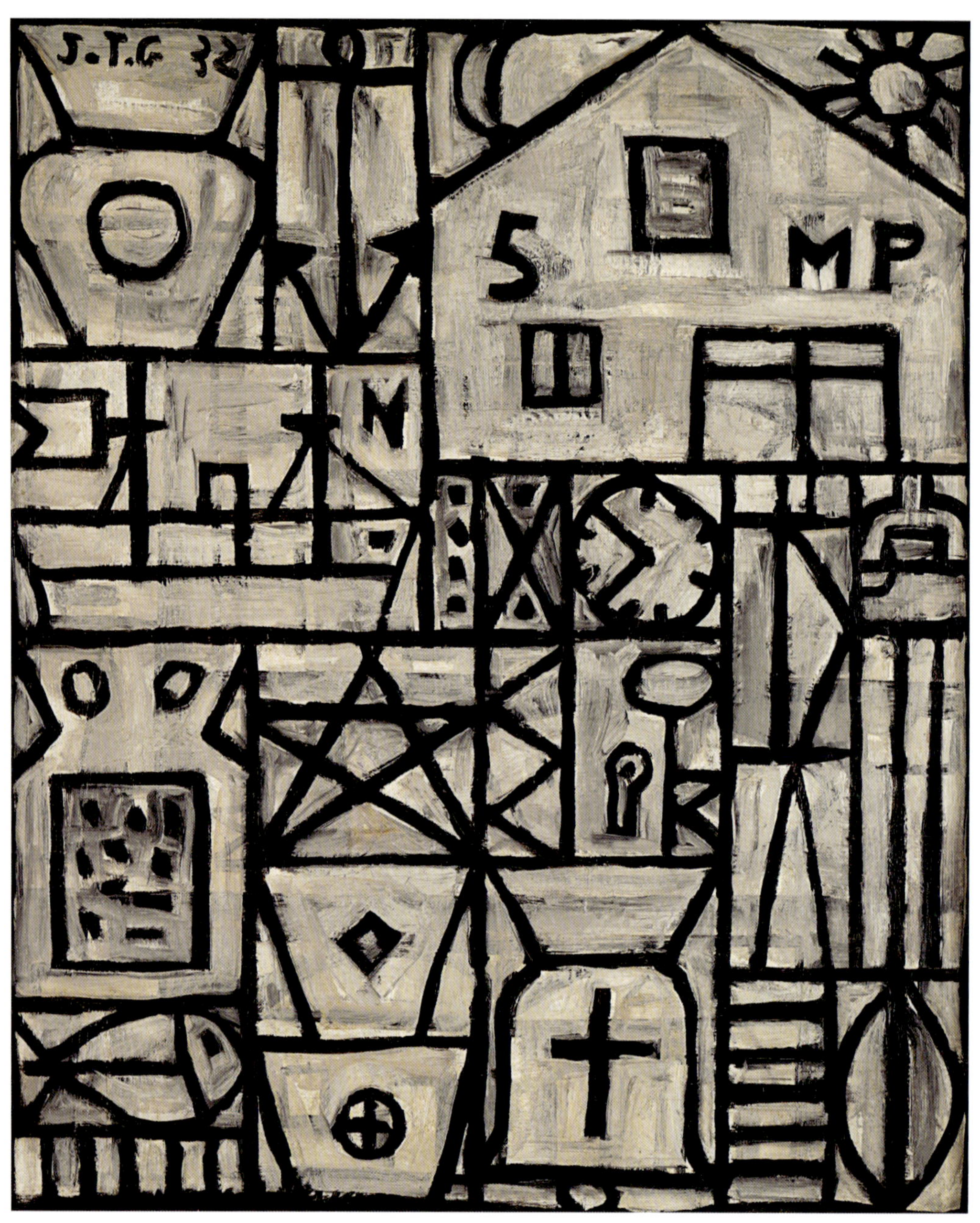

Joaquín Torres-García
Gare [Station], 1932

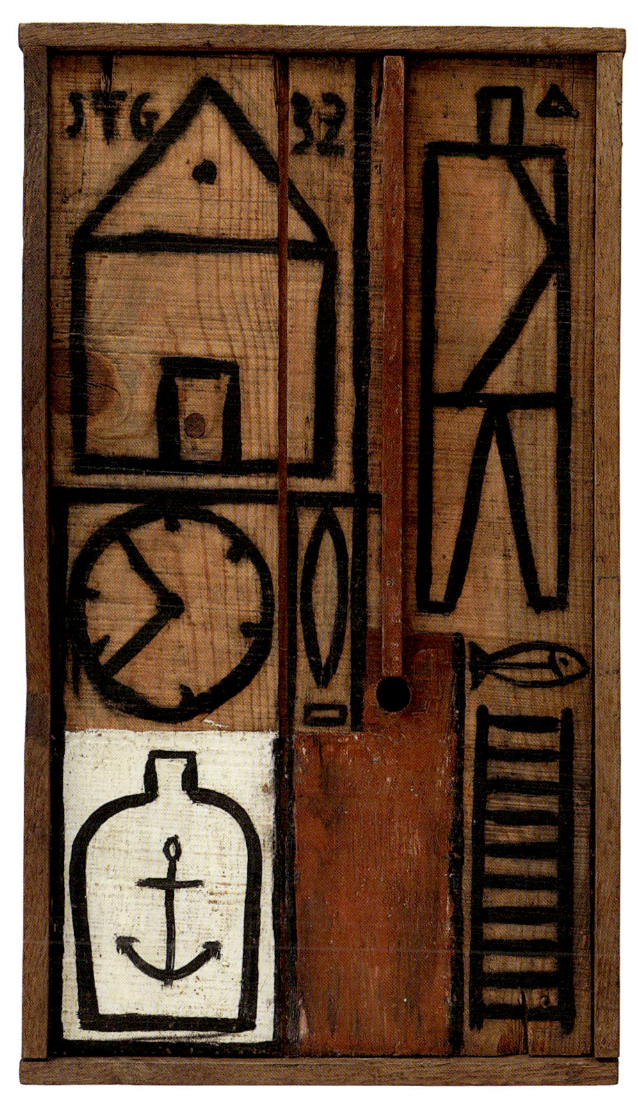

Joaquín Torres-García
Constructivo con madera superpuesta
[Constructive with Superimposed Wood], 1932

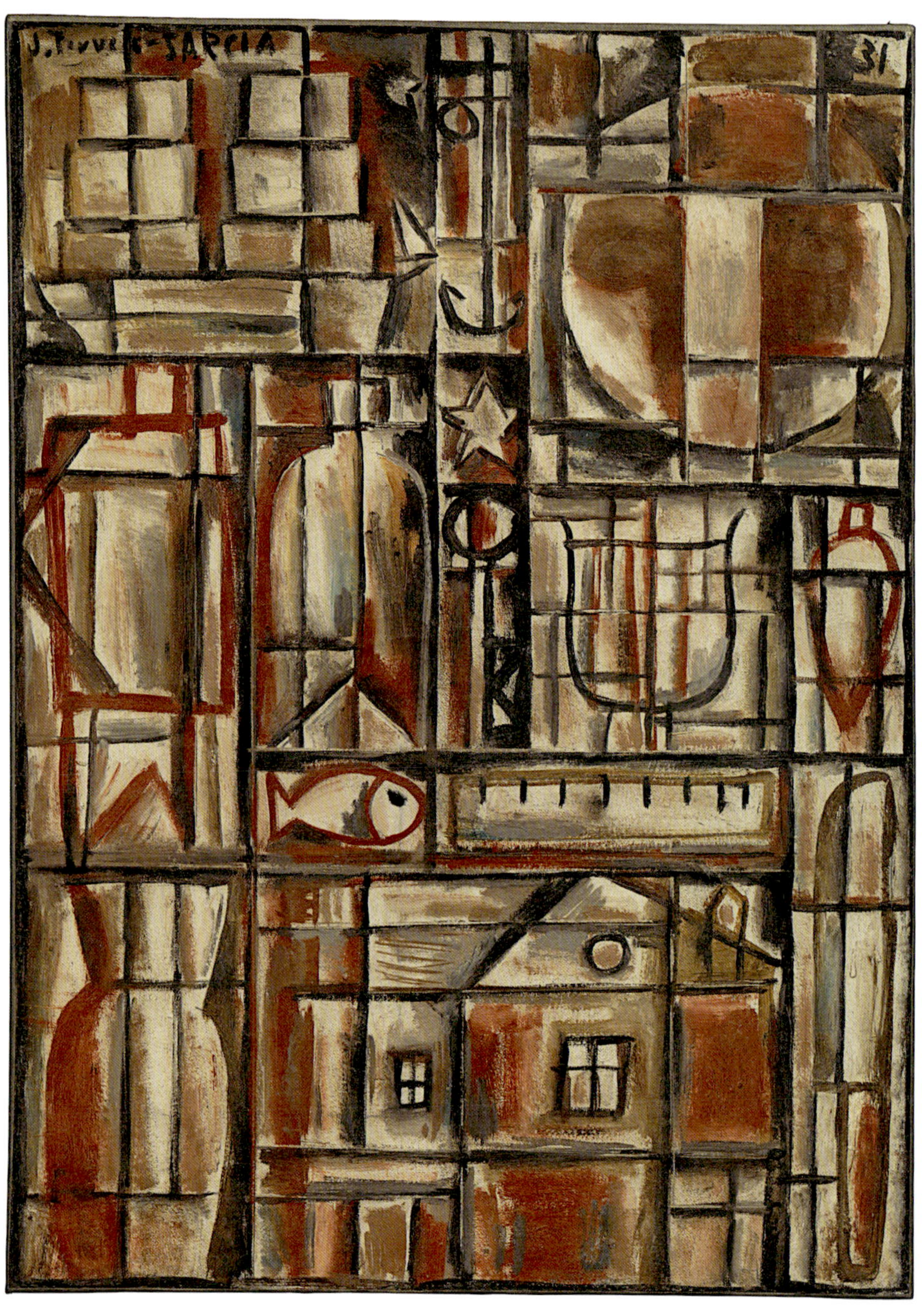

Joaquín Torres-García
Peinture constructive [Constructive Painting], 1931

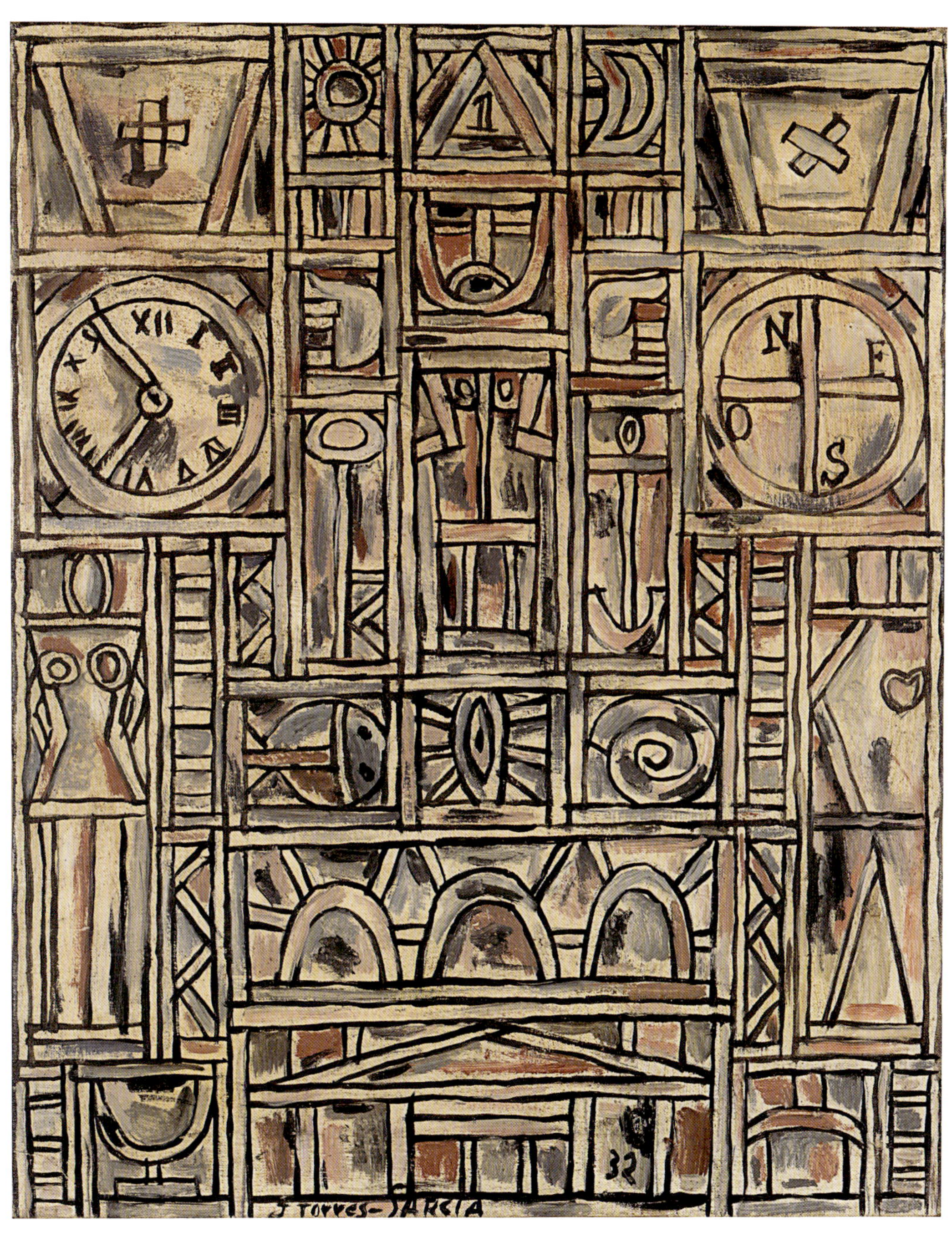

Joaquín Torres-García
Constructivo doble línea [Constructive with Double Line], 1932

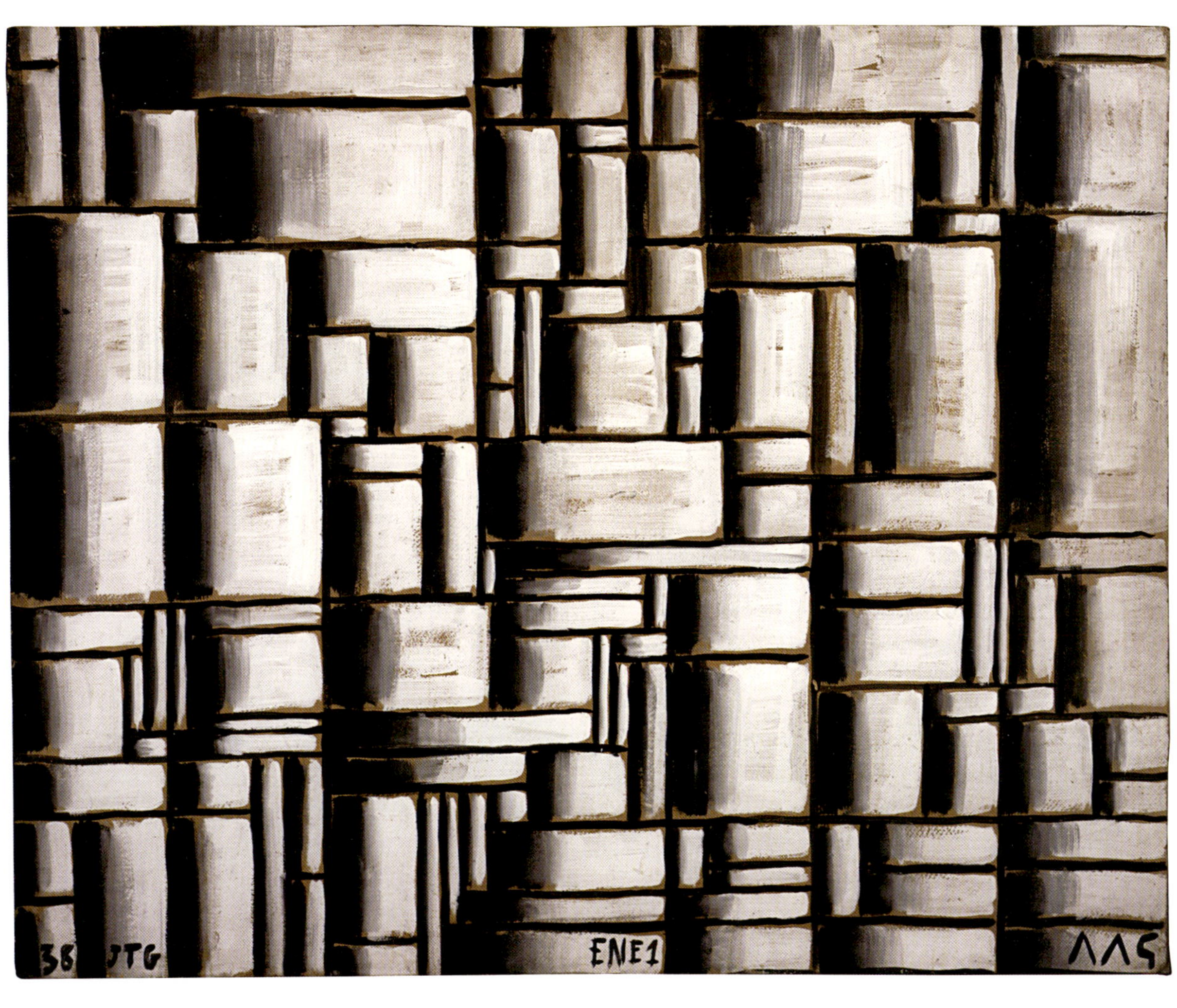

Joaquín Torres-García
Construcción en blanco y negro [Construction in White and Black], 1938

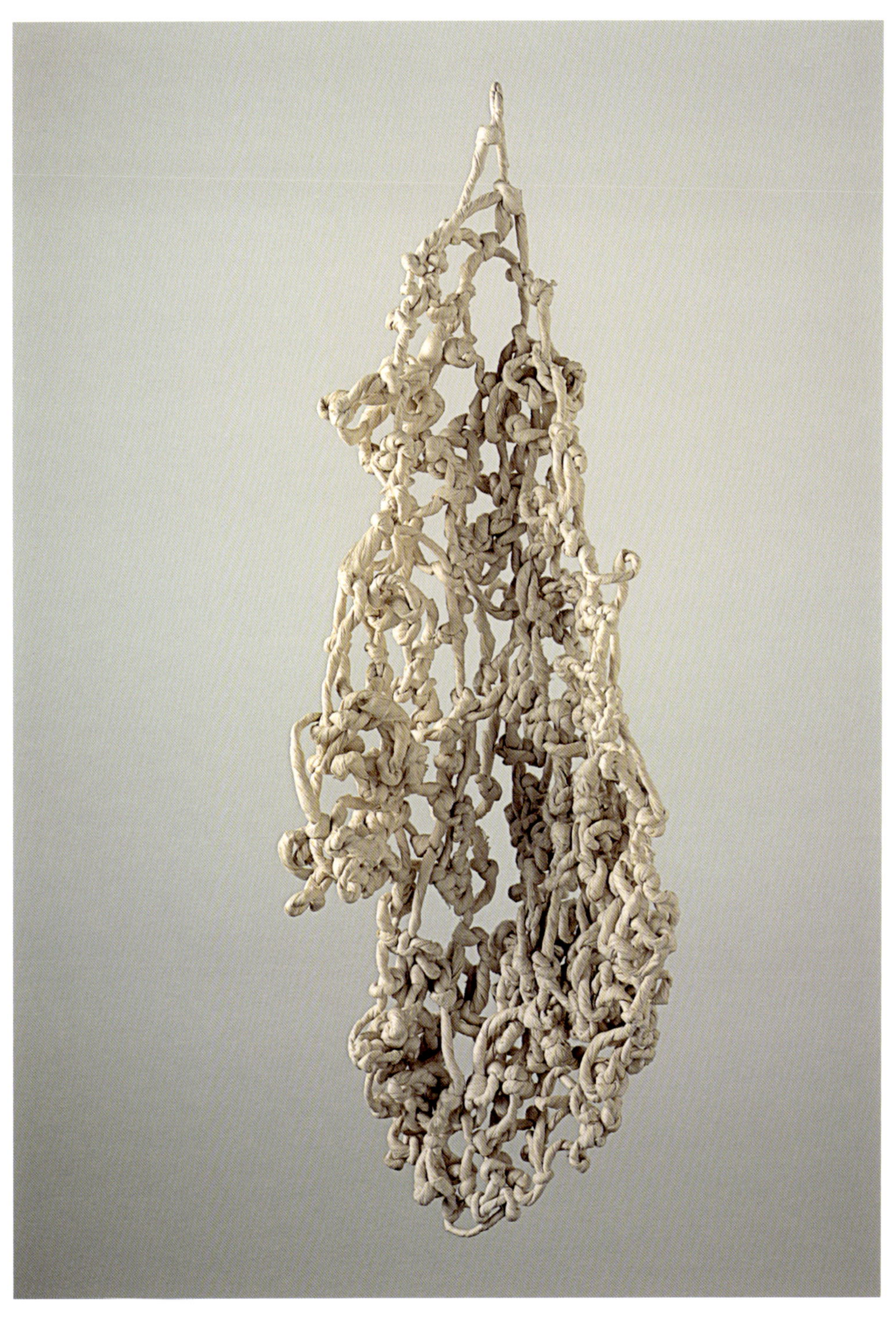

Mira Schendel
Untitled, from the series *Droguinhas* [Little Nothings], 1966

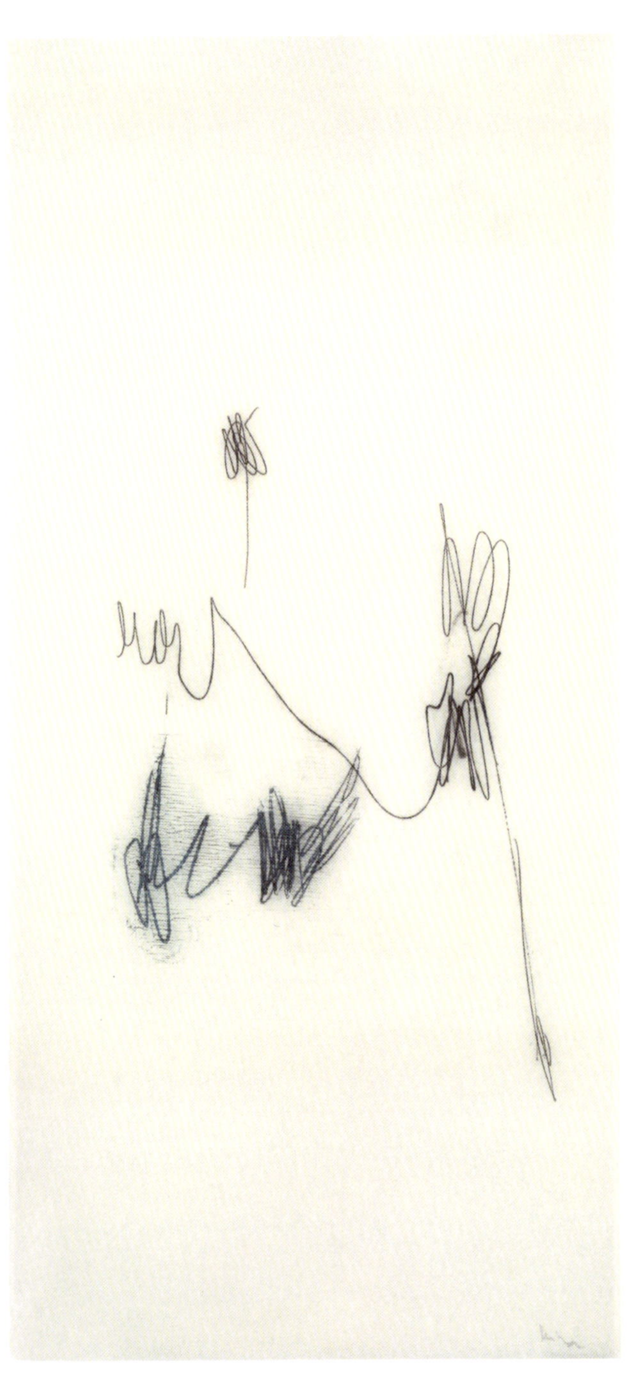

Mira Schendel
Untitled, c. 1964

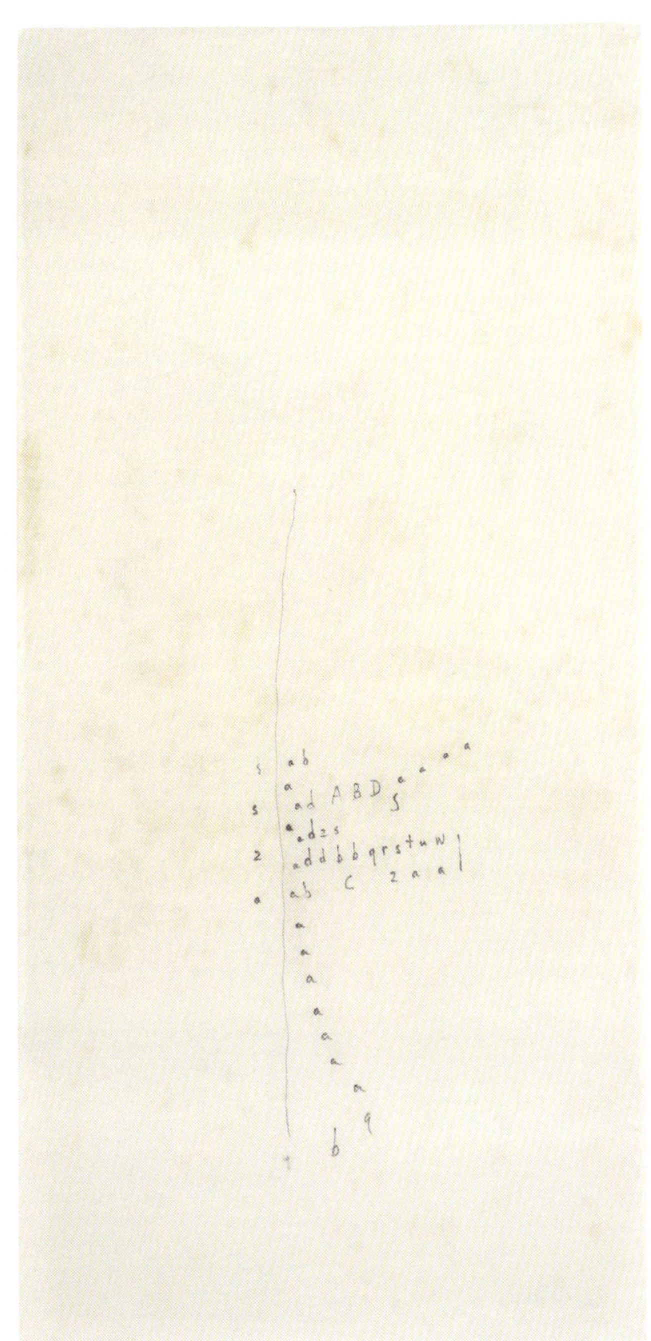

Mira Schendel
Untitled, c. 1965

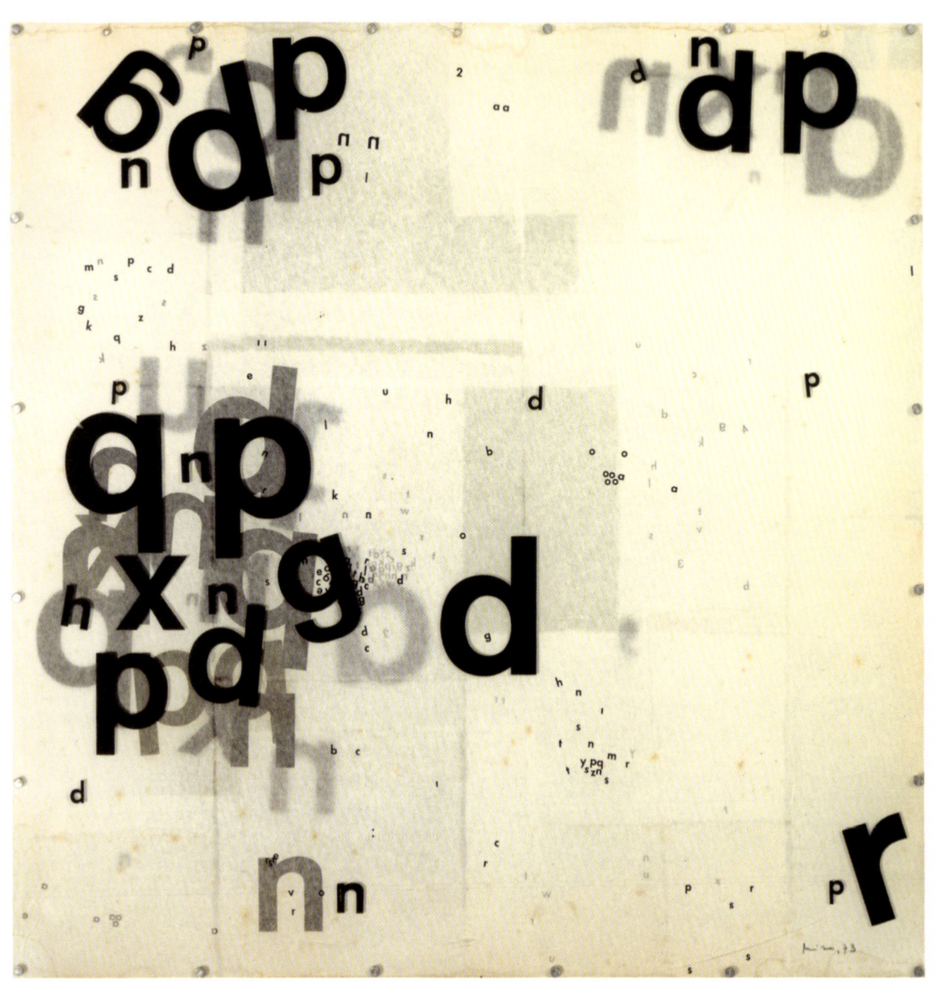

Mira Schendel
Untitled, from the series *Objetos gráficos* [Graphic Objects], 1973

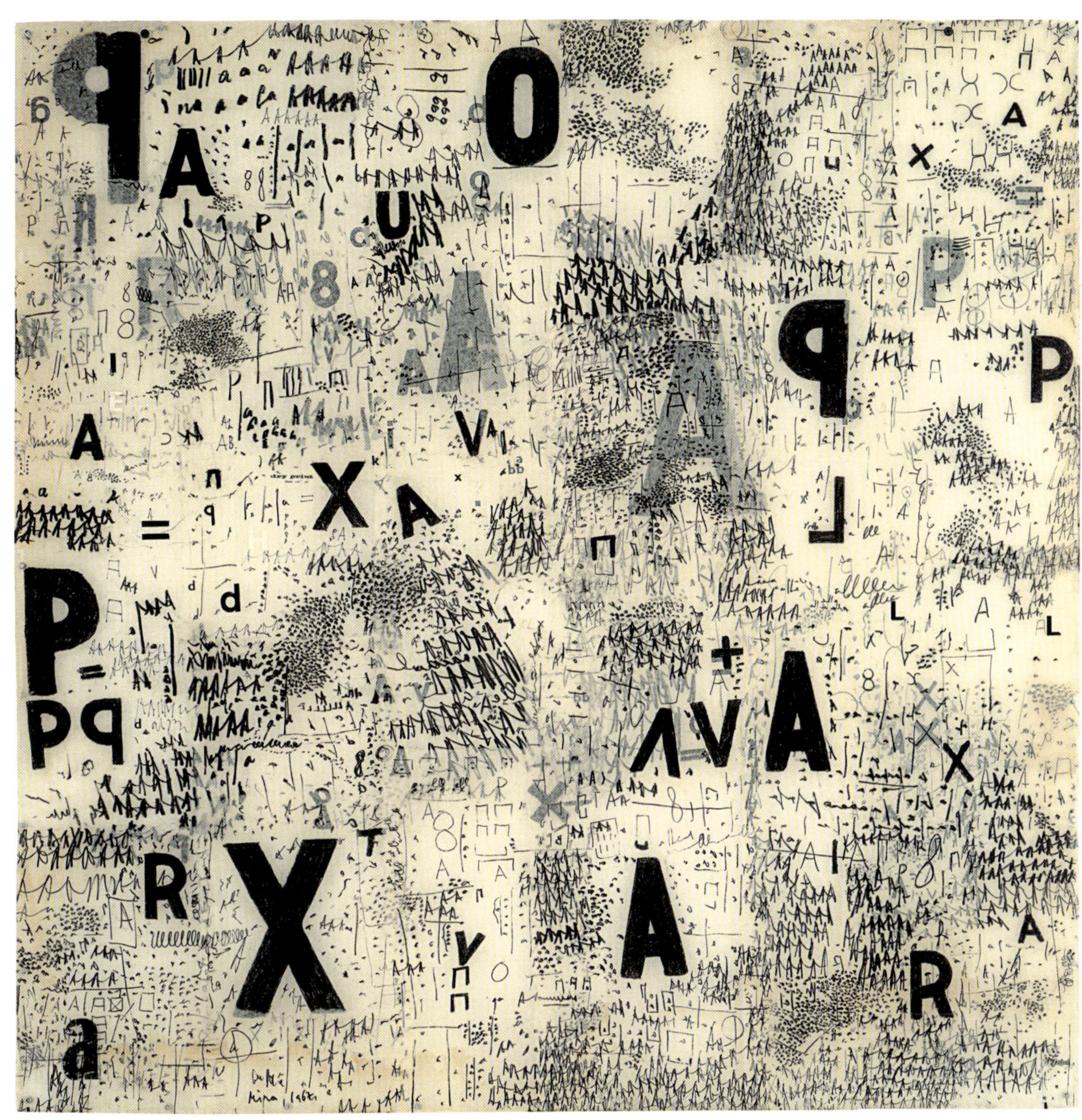

Mira Schendel
Untitled, from the series *Objetos gráficos* [Graphic Objects], 1967

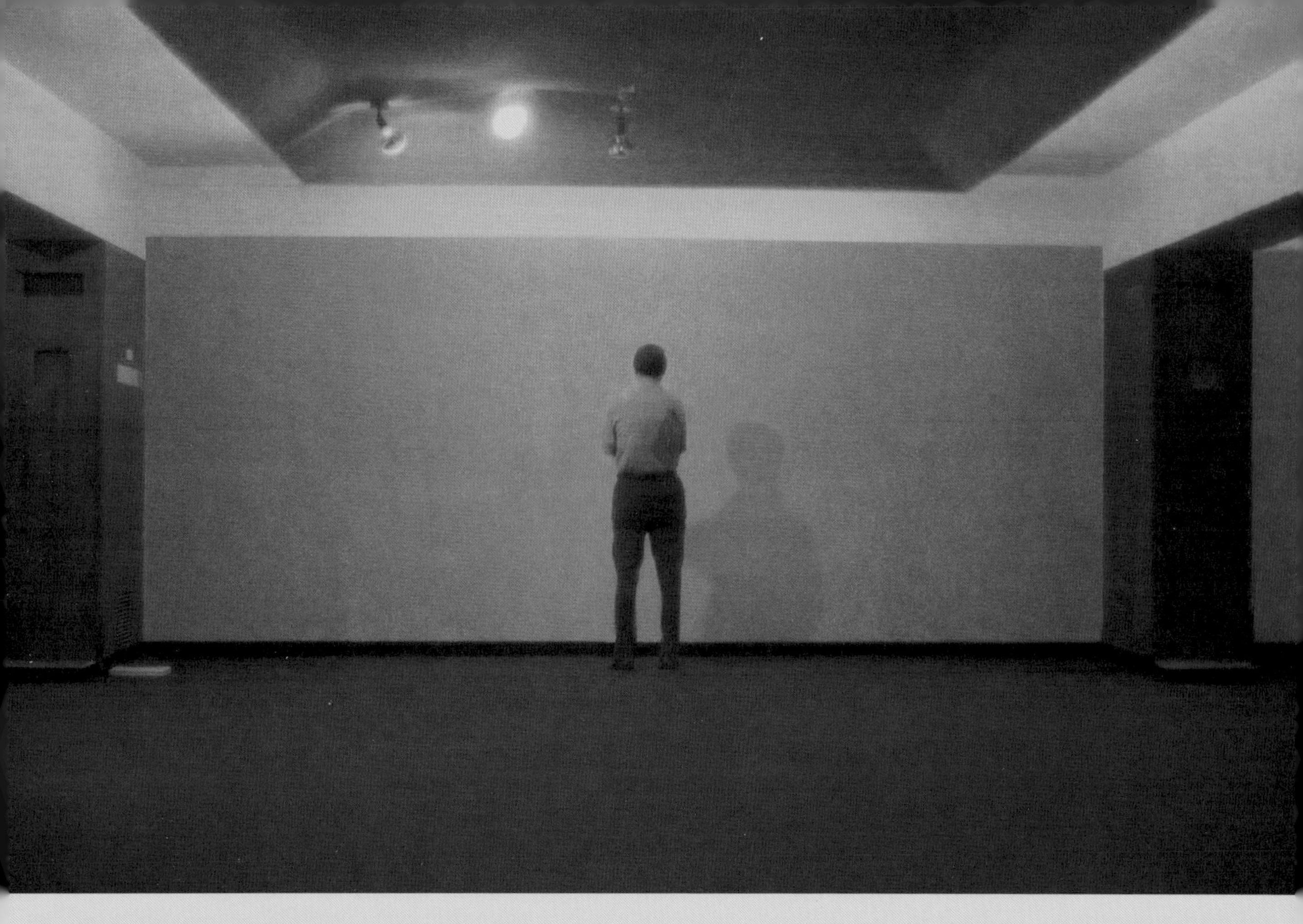

Héctor Fuenmayor
Citrus 6906 (originally Amarillo Sol K7YV68
[Sun Yellow K7YV68]), 1973

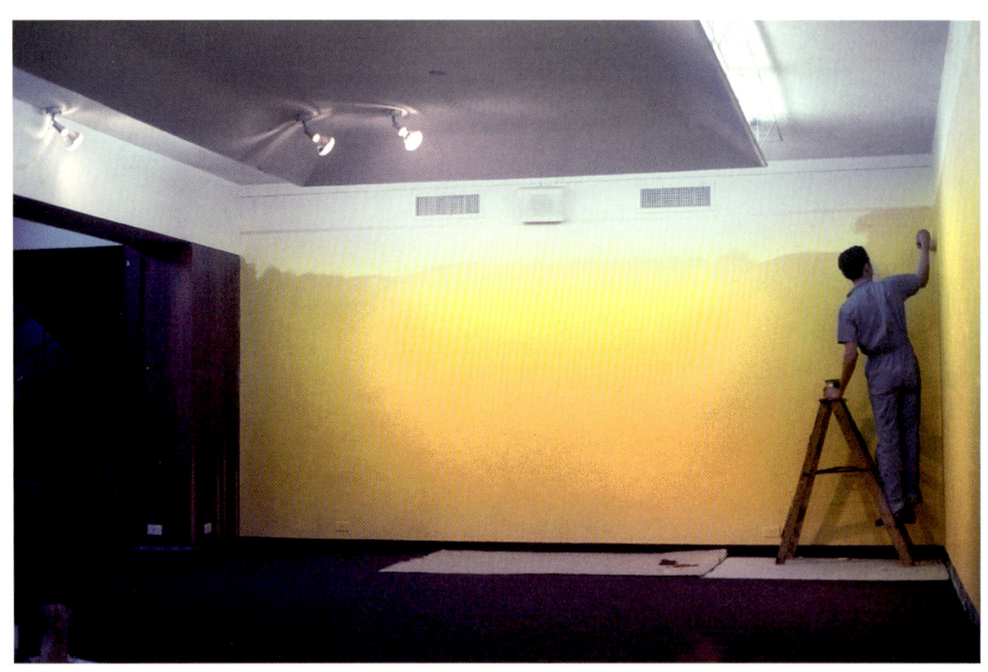

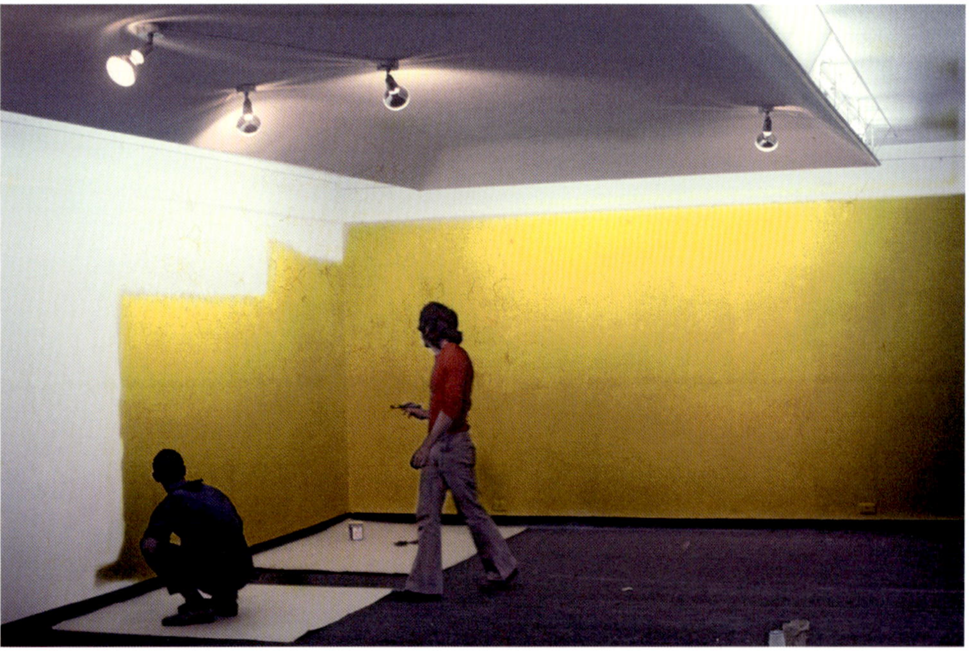

Citrus 6906 (originally *Amarillo Sol K7YV68* [Sun Yellow K7YV68]), 1973
Installation view at the Sala Mendoza, Caracas

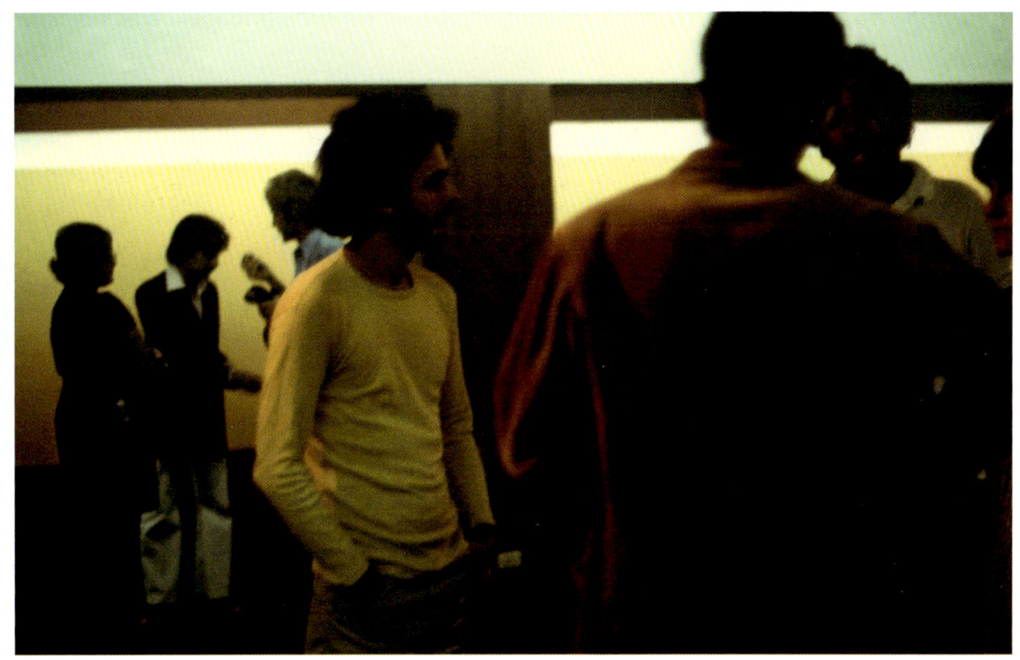

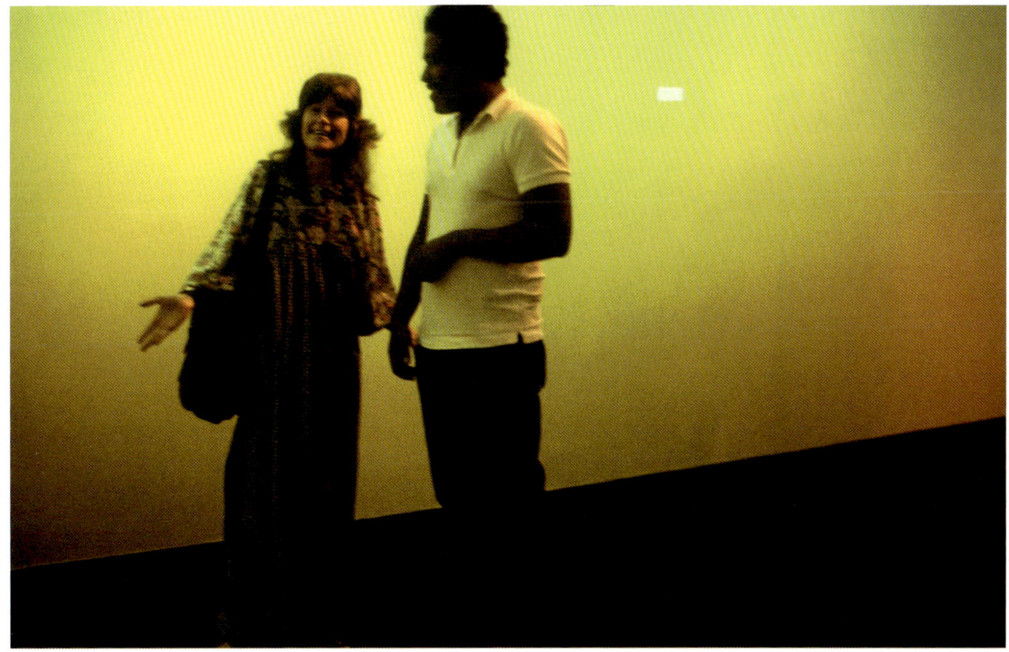

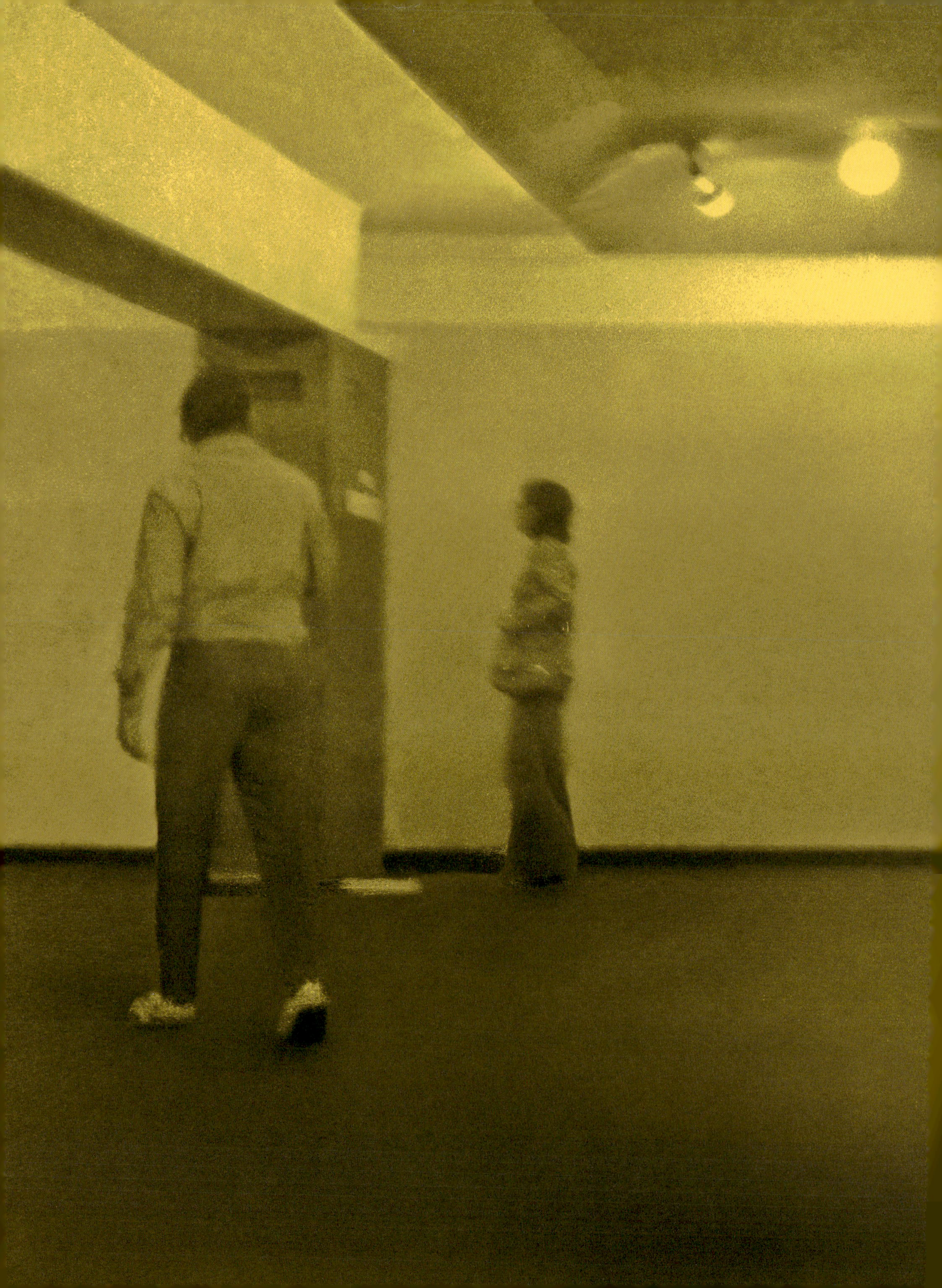

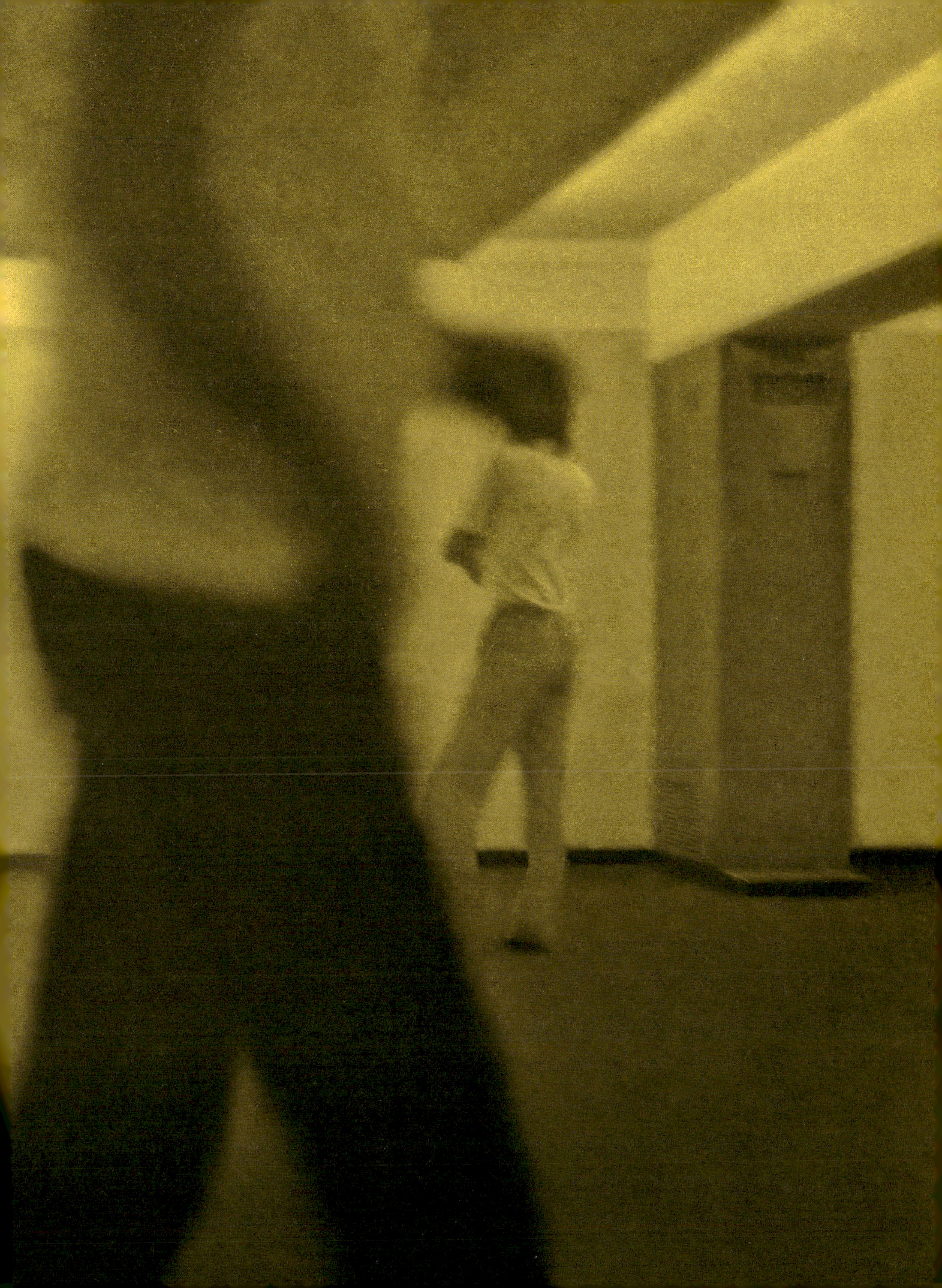

Questionnaire

1.

From your point of view, is there a continuity between Latin American geometric abstraction (1930–70) and the artistic movements that followed? Or is it rather a question of a rupture? Do you see some relationship between abstraction and Conceptual Art?

2.

Among the key values of the Latin American art that developed around Neoconcretism or Kinetic Art was its material and interpellative character. Nowadays, many of those artists have ceased to be *marginal* (to use Hélio Oiticica's expression), and their works fetch high prices on the market. As a historian or curator, what strategies would you suggest for preventing what appears to amount to their inevitable absorption?

3.

Recent years have seen a revival of interest in Latin American geometric abstraction and new studies of the period. Do you think it has had any influence on contemporary artistic production?

Luis Camnitzer

1.

To a large extent, it seems to me that stylistic ruptures
are much less important than they are usually made out
to be. There are things in art that look the same but
respond to totally different proposals, and also different
things that respond to the same investigation. In a
certain way, artistic styles, subject to a fundamentally
formalist typology, help the art historian but not the
comprehension of art. For one thing, it seems to me to be
an underlying error to speak of abstract art from 1930 to
1970 and then to go on to propose Conceptual Art as
starting after 1970, since many important conceptual
artists had already arisen in the mid-sixties. Secondly,
I think it is a mistake to try to cram very complex,
independent, and often politicized Latin American
conceptualist strategies into a schematic, formalist,
reductionist, and hegemonic category like "Conceptual
Art."

I therefore prefer to view artistic production in relation
to the problems that generated it in each case. While
much of European abstraction was based on theosophy
and anthroposophy, the formal shells that reached Latin
America were adapted to local necessities, sometimes
distorted by outside political agendas and sometimes
used as identitarian means of local affirmation. This
makes it very difficult to give generalizing answers.
I think that in Latin America, a certain figuration
probably had as much influence on conceptual art as did
a certain abstraction, and it is not possible to use the
simplistic hegemonic scheme of "Post-Minimalism."
There exist hybrid situations, as for example when Hélio
Oiticica adapted his abstract works of the fifties to
physical and emotional communication with the viewer.
Or when Waltercio Caldas used ideas taken from logic
and illogic to create works within an impeccable formal
aesthetic that in no way diminished the concept.

In other words, there are artists who continue with the
problematics that preceded them and artists who break
away from them, but this does not imply that they wrap
up their works in gift paper that is the same as or
different from the one earlier works came in. There

certainly are abstract conceptualisms, but there are also, for instance, figurative or expressionist conceptualisms.

2.

The fundamental strategy is to view the market as one thing and culture as another. While the two mutually inform each other in capitalist society, and the temptation is to fuse them into a "capitalist culture," there is still a need to differentiate art as a system of production of consumer goods on the one hand, and as a system of cultural and social activation on the other. As a historian or curator, I think the responsibility lies in helping to perceive those differences, and to make it clear when an artwork helps to acquire and broaden knowledge and when it limits itself to decorating walls or enhancing a collector's status. The good collector is not stupid, and will absorb any work of art he considers good, even if it is a work that marks him down as an enemy and attacks him. In this system of co-option, marginality, like subversion, is a temporary state, and so too is the state of innovation, which quickly dies in the conventional. All that is then left for the artist is to try to make new marginal or subversive artworks, and for the historian/curator to retrieve the data and the contexts that successfully gave rise at the time to what we might call a virginal state. For both, this means defining the locality and working on it, and ignoring the demands of the global market even when benefiting from its existence. The longer the artist lives and perseveres, the likelier it will be that he is eventually absorbed. I speak from experience.

3.

The question leads us back to the issue of style, and as such I would say no. Or at least that I have not encountered a new abstraction of sufficiently strong stylistic coherence to proclaim it as such, and still less have I found works with which I manage to learn something new, something I did not know before seeing them. There are artists who explore aesthetic problems, even problems relating to beauty (Caldas himself, Magdalena Fernández, Marco Maggi, Daniel Joglar), who are relatively abstract, and who perhaps would not have been fully possible without the precedent of Latin American geometric abstraction, inasmuch as it was culturally internalized. But I do not think that abstraction served these artists consciously as a platform on which to speculate about how they might continue it. I think they formulated their own problems, and I find that very healthy.

Jesús Carrillo

1.

From a contemporary critical perspective, which eschews categorization by "styles" and the concatenated narrative of successive "isms," there is no doubt at all of the relationship between the "modernist" avant-gardes and the "conceptual" avant-gardes in Latin America. These connections can be located at different levels. First, at the scene of each place, where individuals, experiences, and knowledge are inextricably bound up with the local social and cultural atmosphere, beyond the strict definition of movements or schools. Next, in the specificity of debates on the modern project in Latin America in which the various agents took part, whose development in time allows us to trace the passage from the canvas/piece to the concept/action without resorting to the dialectical dynamics typical of the narrative of the neo-avant-gardes in the United States. And finally, in the diverse genealogies of the contemporary by means of which artists, critics, and historians today establish diagrammatic relations between different items from the history of the art of North and South, and of one side of the Atlantic and the other, on the basis of a radical questioning of the unidirectional nature of modernity.

2.

Detecting that danger is a good starting point in itself. Such tension is always provoked when a formally marginalized artistic movement is "discovered" by collectors, critics, and museums, normally in a dominant position. This is so, we should not forget, because the revelation in question implicitly entails a struggle for significance, in which institutions often find their claims contested by other organizations of the same order, and increasingly frequently by "minor" critical agents who impugn their legitimacy to own and interpret the works.

There are also frequent attempts to recognize a degree of authenticity and originality in the discovered object that was not to be found inscribed in the canonical narrative thus far, and to use those differential features for a cosmetic renewal of the narrative transmitted from the center. Honesty, intelligence, and commitment to the principles incarnated by these works are the best weapons in this sense. These attitudes are shown fundamentally in respect for the specificity in which artistic practices occur, dialogue with agents who vindicate their interpretation and activation from other non-hegemonic positions, and finally a determination that this passage from the margin to the center should help to decenter the discourse itself by means of curatorial strategies that make its crisis patently clear.

3.

Perhaps it is best not to define this circumstance in terms of influence. What may be going on is that in the general revision of the genealogies of modernity, there is a growing interest in other modernities and in those lines of force of the modern project that were obscured by the hegemony of the discourse of the neo-avant-gardes of the North. It is possible that in the aesthetic proposals of Latin American geometric abstraction, contemporary artists recognize some of the freshness of their original articulation and some trace of their utopian potency, which is discredited in the central narrative of modernism. It is also possible that certain "Southern" artists find a solid and recognizable substratum in their modernities upon which to situate a possible articulation at a time when the Babel of art makes it hard to tell differentiated voices apart. In any case, the ubiquity of references to these artists and movements in many curatorial projects at the world's most important museums has enabled their images to enter the common vocabulary of global art.

Sofía Hernández Chong Cuy

1.

The questions presuppose that there exists, or has existed, a strong bond within and between artistic communities in a specific geographical region, here called Latin America. I don't know if this was really possible; that is, if that bond truly existed or was felt in the mid-to-late twentieth century. Linking is a practice of historiography, curatorial to an extent, which was established much later and more recently. Every artistic community generates its own plastic problematics that it has to resolve, and with that it creates its own narratives, and with these their own limits. So I couldn't say whether its avant-garde depends on continuity or rupture, nor could I venture to assess how important it might be to identify the avant-garde as such.

For those of us who think about contemporary artistic production, the most pertinent questions have to do with how certain ideas were communicated or circulated—or not—at the time, and how and why they are disseminated and valued today. As to the question of whether there is a relationship—which is not necessarily a link or bond—between abstraction and conceptualism, it seems to me that what we have as a common denominator is the reconsideration of the position and, up to a point, of the responsibility of the art public, which is invited to construct an aesthetic experience by walking and looking, thereby completing the articulation of an image or message offered by the artwork.

2.

Is absorption into the market being viewed here as something negative? Isn't that just another supposition? It is important to reaffirm here that it is the ideas presented in the work, not only or exactly its authors, that have ceased to be marginal. This in itself is a gain, since the transition has broadened attention to several political contexts and philosophical starting points that had not previously been taken into consideration in art history. At root, I'm afraid absorption into the market as such is inevitable and that to fight against it would be a waste of time, causing disillusionment rather than generating energy. Many artists of our time exemplify countless ways of resisting all kinds of absorption, whether into art markets or markets of ideas. Rather than forms of revolution, it is policies of resistance that we historians and curators would do best to implement.

3.

It is a noteworthy fact that several curators and artists, from Sweden to Venezuela, are researching twentieth-century modernism, and that within that research there are certain artists or works constituting a production known as "geometric abstraction." But to go from there to saying that there is an influence on contemporary artistic production is, I think, to be answered with a definite no.

Some of the recent curatorial and artistic proposals that cast a contemporary eye over modernism in, say, Latin America conclude that modernism was a failed project, a tenacious and rootless functionalism, a project of the few for the many, and a measured—not to say geometric— aesthetic that at the time transformed idea into style.

All this might seem to imply that geometric abstraction was not greatly influential in Latin America, but that is not what I mean. Of course it has been influential, but only to a point, since it is not in fact a history that has been narrated, written, or studied regionally. Not, at least, as systematically as it has been by some Western institutions, specifically in the United States, England, and Spain. Art schools and history of art courses in Latin America largely continue to base their curricula on Western art, combining it in each country where it is taught with the nation's own art from the pre-Hispanic to the modern periods.

We should cease to suppose that what is called geometric abstraction was a movement that occurred and had repercussions in a region as large as Latin America, since

it did not actually happen that way all over the continent. A close examination of where and when it was put into practice reveals that the intentions and references that upheld interest in abstraction in the plastic arts were not the same. In fact, some proposals were sustained by a reconsideration of the pre-Hispanic, and others by a reassessment of the European.

Conclusion (albeit tentative, as I think one should be on these subjects): geometric abstraction is one of several narratives posited by those of us interested in cultural management—political, beyond a doubt—to make insertions in art history with sensible and convincing discourses on communities of thought, and on those agents—their ideas, and their work on authorships—who have contributed to an aesthetic thought and practice. In other words, the type of discourse that is consolidated to the extent of gaining in strength and weight follows the necessary strategy of the avant-gardes, and the work of the art historian or curator in Latin America will continue on this path until the region's artistic manifestations secure a more stable and appropriate position in the writing of art history. And it's about time.

Ana Longoni

1.

As formulated, the question contains certain implicit assumptions that I should like to dwell on and examine briefly. The first problem is the very idea that Latin American geometric abstraction can be conceived as a compact historic block with a duration of forty years. Even when the common denominator of abstraction is to be detected in the productions gathered under the heading, it is risky from my point of view to subsume under a single umbrella the artistic programs originated by (to give one example I know better than others) Movimiento de Arte Concreto-Invención, which arose in Buenos Aires in the mid-forties, and its more moderate and decorative derivates like the Grupo de los Cinco, active at the end of the next decade. A second problem is composing a narrative by means of an art history based on a succession of phases or moments (first abstraction, then Conceptual Art) when the relations, conflicts, and affinities between positions in the artistic field suggest a cartography that is much more complex and difficult to grasp, since it is often traversed by simultaneities, mistimings, and anachronisms. And so, finally to answer the question, unquestionable parallels are most certainly to be found between "abstract" and "conceptual" artistic productions, but the real issue is whether in pointing this out we are remarking on their formal affinities or if we are addressing questions like the magnitude of the rupture they implied for the artistic convention of their time, their overflowing of the boundaries of the hegemonic idea of art, their capacity to provoke an alteration in the perception or the eye of the period, their articulation with emancipatory political projects, etc.

2.

Without a doubt, this contemporary process, which marks the entry into the art market of the material remains of artistic practices that were not only marginal but also disruptive and confrontational, is also observable—inexorably and vertiginously in recent decades—with the so-called Latin American conceptualisms. It was because we were alerted to the growing deactivation of the critical power of many of the experiments that emerged in different parts of Latin America from the sixties onward, largely owing to their incorporation in the canon (and the market), that a group of researchers and artists, myself included, formed the Conceptualismos del Sur network in 2007. Since then, it has been a platform for collective thought, common action, and active positioning. The various experiments we have been conducting through this network, which relate to the constitution and socialization of archives and to research and dissemination through books and exhibitions, may turn out to be more or less unsuccessful or insignificant given the magnitude of the machinery set in motion by cognitive capitalism for the purpose of assimilating critical creativities. It is not a fair fight, and yet the struggle to understand the senses of these legacies and activate them in our present is not one we are prepared to relinquish. The strategies are at the same time sustained and variable. What is sustained is the long job of exhuming, rescuing from oblivion, and granting some legibility to silenced or unknown episodes. What varies is deciding which fissures and junctures to take advantage of, which alliances to establish, and which modes to employ in interpellating many others and helping to articulate a public debate able to intervene with efficacy, lucidity, and collective inventiveness in the current state of things.

3.

There are undoubtedly reverberations and dialogues that are both disturbing and promising. I shall mention one recent case: the intersections between sexed bodies and geometry proposed by the queer (or better yet, *cuir*) Argentine artists Adriana Minoliti and Mariela Scafati. Another is the affective return to the Russian avant-gardes that has been effected by another Argentine, the artist and musician Magdalena Jitrik, in her installations in old anarchist libraries, and there is also the Orquesta Roja and its performances set to silent films by Dziga Vertov. The legacy of abstraction (not only Latin American) is also a future that comes to us from the past.

Biographies

Txomin Badiola

Txomin Badiola received his BFA from the Universidad del País Vasco, where he taught from 1982 to 1988. He lived in London from 1988 to 1989 and in New York from 1990 to 1998. Alongside fellow artist Angel Bados, he conducted, between 1994 and 1998, several courses at Arteleku, San Sebastián, that were very influential for several generations of Basque artists. In 1988 he was curator of the retrospective exhibition *Oteiza. Propósito Experimental*, organized by La Caixa Foundation and held in Madrid, Bilbao, and Barcelona, and with Margit Rowell he curated the exhibition *Oteiza: Myth and Modernity* for the Guggenheim Museum in Bilbao (2004), New York (2005), and the Museo Nacional Centro de Arte Reina Sofía in Madrid (2005). He is also the author of the forthcoming *Catalogue Raisonné of Oteiza's Sculpture*. An artist in his own right, he has exhibited in numerous national and international galleries and institutions. The Museu d'Art Contemporani de Barcelona (MACBA), the Museo de Bellas Artes de Bilbao, and the Musée d'Art Moderne, Saint Etienne-Metropole, have presented retrospectives of his work. Badiola's work is influenced by the dialects of construction and deconstruction. He combines traces of "classic" constructivism with everyday, readymade, utilitarian objects in order to create forms that are abstract in their effect. Ultimately, these forms enter into a dialogue with the viewer by allowing him or her to associate a new cultural history with the objects that have become so familiar in our everyday lives. By this means Badiola sensitizes the latent self-reflective processes of modern art.

Luis Camnitzer

Luis Camnitzer is a Uruguayan artist born in Germany, 1937. He immigrated to Uruguay when he was one year old and has lived in the United States since 1964. He is a Professor Emeritus of Art at the State University of New York, College at Old Westbury. He graduated with a degree in sculpture from the Escuela de Bellas Artes, Universidad de la República, Uruguay, and studied architecture at the same university. He received a Guggenheim Fellowship for printmaking in 1961 and for visual arts in 1982. In 1965 he was declared Honorary Member of the Academy in Florence. In 1988 he represented Uruguay in the Venice Biennale. In 1998 he received the Latin American Art Critic of the Year award from the Argentine Association of Art Critics, in 2002 the Konex Mercosur Award in the visual arts for Uruguay, and in 2011 the Frank Jewitt Mather Award of the College Art Association and the Printer Emeritus Award of the SGCI. In 2012 he was awarded the Skowhegan Medal and the USA Ford Fellow award. He participated in the Liverpool Biennial in 1999 and 2003, in the Whitney Biennial of 2000, and Documenta 11 in 2003. His work is in the collections of over thirty museums, among them the Museum of Modern Art, Metropolitan Museum, and the Whitney Museum in New York; Museo de Bellas Artes, Caracas; Museo de Arte Contemporâneo, São Paulo; Museo de Arte Latinoamericano de Buenos Aires; and the Museo de Arte y Diseño Contemporáneo de Costa Rica. He is the author of *New Art of Cuba* (1994/2004), *Arte y Enseñanza: La ética del poder* (2000), *Didactics of Liberation: Conceptualist Art in Latin America* (2007), and *On Art, Artists, Latin America, and Other Utopias* (2010).

Jesús Carrillo Castillo

Jesús Mª Carrillo Castillo holds a BA in art history from the Universidad de Murcia, an MA in historical studies from the Warburg Institute, University of London, and a PhD in history from the University of Cambridge (King's College). He has been an invited research scholar at Brown University, Providence, and the Spanish National Research Council in Madrid, among others. Since 1997 he is a professor in the Department of Art History and Theory at the Universidad Autónoma de Madrid. He combines the critical reading of empire and its representations in the early Modern period with the analysis of contemporary culture and art. He has published numerous works, including: *Arte en la Red* (2004), *Naturaleza e Imperio* (2004), and *Tecnología e Imperio* (2003); and has edited, among others: *Modos de hacer. Arte crítico, esfera pública y acción directa* (2001), *Tendencias del Arte. Arte de Tendencias* (2003), *Desacuerdos. Sobre arte, políticas y esfera pública en el Estado español*, vols 1, 2, 3, and 4 (2004–07), *Douglas Crimp. Posiciones críticas* (2005), and *Martha Rosler. Imágenes Públicas* (2008). He is currently the head of the Department of Cultural Programs at the Museo Nacional Centro de Arte Reina Sofía.

José León Cerrillo

José León Cerrillo lives in Mexico City. He received his BFA from the School of Visual Arts, New York, and his MFA from Columbia University, New York. His work has been shown at MoMA PS1, New York; Tensta Konsthall, Spånga, Sweden; Museo Rufino Tamayo, Mexico City; Galeria Nara Roesler, São Paulo; Eastside Projects, Birmingham; Proyectos Monclova, Mexico City; Dispatch, New York; and Circuit, Lausanne, among other venues. Working through a variety of media, from print posters to sculptural installations, José León Cerrillo's practice focuses on interrogations of graphical ideologies and language systems, and reconsiders the legacies of the modernist program, particularly in the history of Latin America. Central to his practice is the problematic inherent in the act of communication and abstraction. Cerrillo assembles his work with an idea of fracture and dispersal as process: destabilizing the notion of the static image or neutral presentation, drawing out the ideological motivations a program or image might conceal, and investigating these systems of contemporary culture. Adopting familiar graphic elements that are then altered, obfuscated, or otherwise renegotiated, his objects might further be activated through ephemeral gestures.

Olga Fernández López

Olga Fernández López has taught undergraduate and graduates courses in contemporary art history in the Department of Art History and Theory at the Universidad Autónoma Madrid since 2009. In 2010, she became the vice-coordinator of the master's degree program in Contemporary Art History and Visual Culture at this university. She received her doctorate in art history from the Universidad Complutense Madrid in 2001. Between 2001 and 2006 she was head of the Research and Education Department and subsequently chief curator at the Museo Patio Herreriano in Valladolid, Spain. Since 2007, she has been a visiting lecturer at the Royal College of Art in London in the Curating Contemporary Art Department. Fernández López has recently organized the conference "Coloniality, Curating and Contemporary Art" at the Universidad Internacional de Andalucía (2012) in collaboration with the Centro Andaluz de Arte Contemporáneo (CAAC, Seville). Her essays have been published in numerous journals and exhibition catalogues. Her most recent publications include *Ángel Ferrant*, Fundación Mapfre (2008); "Conceptualism, a Historic Necessity for Latin American Art?," Center for Latin American Visual Studies, University of Texas (2010); "Just What is it That Makes 'Curating' so Different, so Appealing," *Oncurating.org*, no. 8 (2011); and "Travesía site-specific: Institucionalidad e imaginación," Matadero, Madrid (2011).

Andrea Giunta

Andrea Giunta is an art historian, curator, and professor of Latin American art at the University of Texas at Austin, where she holds the Chair in Latin American Art History and Criticism and is founder and director of the Center of Latin American Visual Studies. She received her PhD from the University of Buenos Aires, Argentina. She is the recipient of several awards, including a Guggenheim Fellowship. Dr. Giunta was founder and director of the Center for Documentation, Research and Publications at the Centro Cultural Recoleta, Buenos Aires. She was curator of the retrospective exhibition of Leon Ferrari, Centro Cultural Recoleta, Buenos Aires (2004) and Pinacoteca de São Paulo (2006). She also co-curated with Néstor García Canclini the exhibition *Extranjerías / Alienations*, Museo de Arte Contemporáneo de la Universidad Nacional Autónoma de México (2012). Her articles have appeared in more than a hundred journals and exhibition catalogues. She is the author of the books *Escribir las imágenes. Ensayos sobre arte argentino y latinoamericano* (2011), *Objetos mutantes. Sobre arte contemporáneo* (2010), *Post crisis. Arte argentino después del 2001*

(2009), and *Goeritz/Romero Brest. Correspondencias* (2000). She has also edited several volumes, such as *El Caso Ferrari. Debates y polémicas durante la Retrospectiva realizada en el Centro Cultural Recoleta* (2008) and *Cándido Portinari y el sentido social del arte* (2005). Her book *Avant-Garde, Internationalism, and Politics: Argentine Art in the Sixties* (2008) was praised by the Argentina Association of Art Critics as "the best book of the year."

Sofía Hernández Chong Cuy

Sofía Hernández Chong Cuy is a curator of contemporary art. Much of her curatorial work has consisted in working closely with visual artists in conceptualizing meeting points—whether these are in the form and space of exhibitions, events, or printed matter—for audiences to experience art in unconventional ways. Sofía writes regularly for exhibition catalogues, magazines, and in the blog she started, *Sideshows.org*. In 2009, she initiated the editorial project Murmur. Since 2011, Sofía is the curator of contemporary art for the Colección Patricia Phelps de Cisneros, and was recently appointed chief curator of the 9th Mercosul Biennial, opening in 2013 in Porto Alegre, Brazil. She is also an agent for Documenta 13, and is part of the team of research advisors to the upcoming 55th Venice Biennale. Throughout the past decade, Sofía has been the director of the Museo Tamayo in Mexico City and has held curatorial positions at Art in General and the Americas Society in New York. She has curated exhibitions for the Kadist Art Foundation in Paris, MALBA in Buenos Aires, the Center for Contemporary Art in Vilnius, and MUSAC in Leon.

Reinaldo Laddaga

Reinaldo Laddaga (Rosario, Argentina, 1963) is an author and associate professor of romance languages and Hispanic studies at the University of Pennsylvania, where he specializes in contemporary Latin American literature and critical theory. Laddaga has published numerous books including *Un prólogo a los libros de mi padre* (2011), *Estética de laboratorio* (2010), *Tres vidas secretas: John D. Rockefeller, Walt Disney, Osama bin Laden* (2008), and *Espectáculos de realidad* (2007). In his book *Estética de la emergencia* (2006), Laddaga analyzes the current reorientation of the arts in terms of its production and deployment in experimental communities. His upcoming publications include a collaboration with fourteen musicians and composers in a reimagining of a Borges and Bioy Casares' anthology of short stories, and (together with Jorge Carrión and a large number of writers and artists), a collective rewriting of the first edition of Robert Ripley's *Believe it or Not*. Through his website, Laddaga continues to explore innovative forms of writing and audio performance.

Ana Longoni

Ana Longoni is a professor at the University of Buenos Aires as well as a researcher for CONICET, a playwright, political essayist, and one of the most recognized art historians of avant-garde and contemporary Latin American art. In 2011, she curated a retrospective of Roberto Jacoby, *El deseo nace del derrumbe*, and, as part of the Conceptualismos del Sur network, organized a monumental panorama on art and social activism in Latin American during the 1980s, both for the Museo Nacional Centro de Arte Reina Sofía. Longoni received a BA in literature and a PhD in arts from the University of Buenos Aires. Longoni also teaches in the Independent Studies Programme of the MACBA, Barcelona. She has published numerous books that include *De los poetas malditos al video clip* (1998), *Revolución en el arte* (2004), *Del Di Tella a Tucumán Arde* (2008), *El Siluetazo* (2008), and *Traiciones* (2007). Her theatrical work *La Chira* premiered in 2004 and was directed by Ana Alvarado. Longoni is a part of the editorial board for the magazines *ramona*, *Ojos Crueles*, and *Des-bordes*. She is the director of the investigation group "¿La cultura como resistencia?: lecturas desde la transición de producciones culturales y artísticas durante la ultima dictadura argentina."

Jorge Pedro Núñez

Born in Caracas, Venezuela, Jorge Pedro Núñez graduated from the École Nationale Supérieure d'Arts de Paris, Cergy in 2006. He has presented numerous solo exhibitions, including *Concetto Spaziale* at KaBe Contemporary, Miami (2011); *Inevitable y Obvio*, Periférico Caracas / Arte Contemporáneo, Caracas (2011); *Imágenes Souvenirs* at Galeria Ignacio Liprandi, Buenos Aires (2012); and a solo show at FIAC Paris, Galería Crévecoeur (2012). In 2011, Nuñez took part in the 12th Istanbul Biennial. In 2010 he was an artist in residence at Le Pavillon, Palais de Tokyo, Paris and participated in the exhibition *Dynasty* (2010) at the Museé d'art moderne de la Ville de Paris.

Gabriel Pérez-Barreiro

Gabriel Pérez-Barreiro has been director of the Colección Patricia Phelps de Cisneros, New York and Caracas, since 2007. From 2002 to 2007 he was curator of Latin American art at the Blanton Museum of Art, the University of Texas at Austin. Prior to that he was director of visual arts at the Americas Society, New York, exhibitions and projects coordinator at the Casa de América, Madrid, and founding curator of the University of Essex Collection of Latin American Art in Colchester, England. He holds a PhD in art history and theory from the University of Essex, and an MA in Latin American studies and art history from the University of Aberdeen. In 2007 he was chief curator of the 6th Mercosul Biennial in Porto Alegre, Brazil. His 2007 exhibition *The Geometry of Hope* was awarded Best Thematic Museum Show Nationally by the US chapter of the International Association of Art Critics. Dr. Pérez-Barreiro has published extensively on modern and contemporary art from Latin America, including *María Freire* (2001); "The Accidental Tourist: American Collections of Latin American Art," in Bruce Altshuler, ed., *Collecting the New: Museums and Contemporary Art* (2005); editor and contributor, *The Geometry of Hope: Latin American Abstract Art from the Patricia Phelps de Cisneros Collection* (2007); and co-editor with Ursula Davila-Villa and GinaTarver, *The New York Graphic Workshop, 1964–1970* (2009).

Steve Roden

Steve Roden received his MFA from the Art Center College of Design in Pasadena, California in 1989, and his BFA from Otis Parsons in Los Angeles in 1986. Since the mid-1980s, his work has been exhibited in museums and art spaces worldwide, including the Menil Collection, Houston; UCLA Hammer Museum, Los Angeles; La Casa Encendida, Madrid; Museum of Contemporary Art, Athens; San Diego Museum of Contemporary Art, and others. Performances include San Francisco Museum of Modern Art; Walker Art Center, Minneapolis; Hamburger Banhof, Berlin; Institute of Contemporary Arts, London; and others. His writing has appeared in numerous journals, and his book *i listen to the wind that obliterates my traces* was published in 2011 by Dust to Digital. Roden's work includes painting, drawing, sculpture, film/video, sound installation, text, and performance. His working process uses pre-existing forms (texts, music, objects) towards the creation of self-invented systems that generate scores, which influence the process of making a painting, drawing, sculpture, text, or composition. The scores generally contain a fixed set of parameters and rules, although there is always room for intuitive decisions, failures, and unpredictable turns.

List of Exhibited Works

All the works listed below belong to the Colección Patricia Phelps de Cisneros unless otherwise stated.

Josef Albers (Bottrop, Germany, 1888 – New Haven, US, 1976)
Hommage au carré
[Homage to the Square], 1972
Oil on board, 61 x 61 cm
1998.41
p. 39

Geraldo de Barros
(Chavantes, Brazil, 1923 – São Paulo, Brazil, 1998)
Função diagonal
[Diagonal Function], 1952
Lacquer on plywood,
62.9 x 62.9 x 1.3 cm
1995.16
p. 65

Max Bill (Winthertur, Switzerland, 1908 – Berlin, Germany, 1994)
1–8 in vier Gruppen
[1–8 in Four Groups], 1955–63
Oil on canvas, 80.3 x 80.3 cm
1998.18
p. 38

Pol Bury (Haine-Saint-Pierre, Belgium, 1922 – Paris, France, 2005)
Septante-deux boules, grosses, petites et moyennes [Seventy-Two Balls, Big, Small, and Average], 1964
Stained wood, wire, and electric motor, 87.5 x 62.2 x 28 cm
1992.35

Lygia Clark (Belo Horizonte, Brazil, 1920 – Rio de Janeiro, Brazil, 1988)
Composição n.º 5
[Composition No. 5], 1954
Oil on canvas and wood,
106.5 x 91 x 2 cm
1997.54

Lygia Clark
Composição [Composition], 1953
Oil on canvas, 117 x 81 x 2 cm
1997.73
p. 33

Lygia Clark
Máquina-Md
[Machine-Md], 1962
Aluminum with gold patina, variable dimensions, approx. 48.2 x 66.1 x 61 cm
1998.68
p. 99

Lygia Clark
Monumento a todas as situações [Monument to All Situations], 1962
Aluminum, variable dimensions, approx. 41 x 66 x 54 cm
1992.38
p. 86

Lygia Clark
Relógio de sol [Sundial], 1960
Aluminum with gold patina, variable dimensions,
approx. 52.8 x 58.4 x 45.8 cm
The Museum of Modern Art, New York. Gift of Patricia Phelps de Cisneros in honor of Rafael Romero, 2004
312.2004
p. 87

Lygia Clark
Abrigo poético [Poetic Shelter], 1960
Painted metal, 14 x 63 x 51 cm
The Museum of Modern Art, New York. Gift of Patricia Phelps de Cisneros in honor of Milan Hughston, 2004
313.2004
p. 96

Lygia Clark
O dentro é o fora
[The Inside Is the Outside], 1963
Stainless steel,
40.6 x 44.5 x 37.5 cm
The Museum of Modern Art, New York. Gift of Patricia Phelps de Cisneros through the Latin American and Caribbean Fund in honor of Adriana Cisneros de Griffin, 2011
1117.2011
p. 97

Lygia Clark
Estudo para Obra mole
[Study for Soft Work], 1964
Rubber, 49.5 cm (diameter)
1998.67
p. 98

Lygia Clark
Casulo n.º 2 [Cocoon No. 2], 1959
Enamel on aluminum,
30 x 30 x 11 cm
1999.65
p. 100

Lygia Clark
Radar-Pq., 1960. Executed in 1984
Aluminum, variable dimensions, approx. 12.7 x 45.7 x 33 cm
2000.11
p. 101

Lygia Clark
Planos em superfície modulada n.º 4 [Planes in Modulated Surface No. 4], 1957
Formica and industrial paint on wood, 99.7 x 99.7 x 1.2 cm
The Museum of Modern Art, New York. Gift of Patricia Phelps de Cisneros through the Latin American and Caribbean Fund in honor of Kathy Fuld, 2008
205.2008
p. 69

Lygia Clark
Contra-relevo n.º 1
[Counter Relief No. 1], 1958
Industrial paint on plywood,
141 x 141 x 3.3 cm
1997.112

Waldemar Cordeiro (Rome, Italy, 1925 – São Paulo, Brazil, 1973)
Idéia visível [Visible Idea], 1956
Acrylic on plywood,
59.9 x 60 cm
1996.190
p. 31

Carlos Cruz-Diez
(Caracas, Venezuela, 1923)
Physichromie No. 500, 1970
Casein on PVC, and acrylic strips on plywood, 183 x 484 x 8 cm
1988.18
pp. 120–21

Carlos Cruz-Diez
Proyecto para un muro exterior [Maquette for an Exterior Wall], 1954–65
Acrylic on plywood,
40 x 55.2 x 6.4 cm
1997.144

Carlos Cruz-Diez
Physichromie No. 21, 1960
Casein and cardboard on plywood, 103.4 x 106.4 x 6.5 cm
1997.145
p. 131

Willys de Castro (Uberlandia, Minas Gerais, Brazil, 1926 – Belo Horizonte, Minas Gerais, Brazil, 1988)
Objeto ativo [Active Object], 1961
Oil on canvas mounted on wood,
100 x 4.1 x 4.1 cm
1992.39

Willys de Castro
Objeto ativo [Active Object], 1959
Gouache on paper mounted
on wood, 32.5 x 5.5 x 1 cm
1996.63
p. 46

Willys de Castro
Objeto ativo [Active Object], 1961
Oil on canvas mounted on wood,
150 x 4 x 4 cm
The Museum of Modern Art,
New York. Promised gift of
Patricia Phelps de Cisneros
through the Latin American and
Caribbean Fund in honor of Kathy
Halbreich

Willys de Castro
Composição modulada
[Modulated Composition], 1954
Lacquer on board, 40.3 x 40 cm
1997.21

Willys de Castro
Objeto ativo (amarelo) [Active
Object (Yellow)], 1959–60
Oil on canvas on board,
35 x 70 x 0.5 cm
1997.56

Willys de Castro
*Objeto ativo (cubo vermelho/
branco)* [Active Object
(Red/White Cube)], 1962
Oil on canvas mounted on
plywood, 25 x 25 x 25 cm
1997.127

Willys de Castro
Objeto ativo [Active Object], 1961
Oil on canvas mounted on wood,
92.1 x 2.2 x 11.1 cm
The Museum of Modern Art,
New York. Gift of Patricia Phelps
de Cisneros through
the Latin American and Caribbean
Fund in honor of Estrellita
Brodsky, 2007
2.2007

Hermelindo Fiaminghi
(São Paulo, Brazil, 1920–2004)
Seccionado n.º 1 [Sectional No. 1],
1958
Enamel on wood, 60 x 60 x 6 cm
1997.26
p. 70

Hermelindo Fiaminghi
Alternado 2 [Alternated 2], 1957
Lacquer on board, 61 x 61 cm
1997.62
p. 71

Héctor Fuenmayor
(Caracas, Venezuela, 1949)
Citrus 6906 (originalmente
Amarillo Sol K7YV68)
[Citrus 6906 (originally Sun
Yellow K7YV68)], 1973/2013
Installation. Vinyl-acrylic paint
on wall, variable dimensions
pp. 169–74

Gego [Gertrud Goldschmidt]
(Hamburg, Germany, 1912 –
Caracas, Venezuela, 1994)
Ocho cuadrados [Eight Squares],
1961
Painted iron, 170 x 64 x 40 cm
2000.99
p. 77

Gego
Esfera [Sphere], 1976
Stainless steel,
99.1 x 91.4 x 88.9 cm
1977.5
p. 138 and cover

Gego
Dibujo sin papel 86/13
[Drawing Without Paper 86/13],
1986
Iron, aluminum, plastic,
and string, 97.8 x 64.8 x 7.6 cm
1988.20

Gego
Reticulárea cuadrada 71/6
[Square *Reticulárea* 71/6], 1971–76
Stainless steel and copper,
70 x 100 x 130 cm
1988.23

Gego
Tronco decagonal n.º 4
[Decagonal Trunk No. 4], 1976
Stainless steel and lead,
215 x 56 x 58 cm
1988.25

Gego
Tejedura 90/41
[Weaving 90/41], 1990
Collage of latticed paper strips,
32.4 x 25.4 cm
1990.90

Gego
Tejedura 90/42
[Weaving 90/42], 1990
Collage of latticed paper strips,
32.8 x 24.8 cm
1990.91

Gego
Dibujo sin papel 85/16
[Drawing Without Paper 85/16],
1985
Stainless steel and iron,
55.9 x 53.3 x 12.7 cm
1998.48

Gego
Cornisa II, n.º 88/37
[Cornice II, No. 88/37], 1988
Steel, lead, and plastic,
200 x 40 x 40 cm
1999.94

Gego
Dibujo sin papel
[Drawing Without Paper], 1984
Stainless steel and copper,
25 x 25 x 20 cm
2000.29

Gego
Chorro n.º 7 [Flow No. 7], 1971
Iron and aluminum,
218.5 x 40.7 x 40.7 cm
2000.42

Gego
Haare [Hair], 1985
Cardboard, wire, beads,
and metal, 51 x 34 x 8.5 cm
2004.8

Gego
Reticulárea cuadrada 71/6
[Square *Reticulárea* 71/6], 1971
Stainless steel and copper,
205 x 140 x 55 cm
2005.47

Gego
Reticulárea, 1973–76
Stainless steel, nylon, and lead,
86 x 56 x 53 cm
sf.65

Alfredo Hlito (Buenos Aires,
Argentina, 1923–1993)
Ritmos cromáticos III
[Chromatic Rhythms III], 1949
Oil on canvas, 100 x 100 cm
1997.67
p. 32

Gyula Kosice
(Košice, Czechoslovakia, 1924)
Escultura móvil articulada
[Mobile Articulated Sculpture],
1948
Brass, variable dimensions,
approx. 165.1 x 30.5 x 1.3 cm
The Museum of Modern Art,
New York. Gift of Patricia
Phelps de Cisneros in honor
of Jay Levenson, 2004
321.2004
p. 103

Judith Lauand
(Pontal, Brazil, 1922)
Concreto 61 [Concrete 61],
1957
Synthetic paint on board,
60 x 60 cm
1996.37
p. 64

Raúl Lozza (Alberti, Buenos
Aires Province, Argentina,
1911 – Buenos Aires, Argentina,
2008)
Invención n.º 150
[Invention No. 150], 1948
Oil on plywood, 94 x 111.2 x 5 cm
1998.4
p. 36

Raúl Lozza
Relieve n.º 30 [Relief No. 30],
1946
Oil on plywood and painted
metal, 41.9 x 53.7 x 2.7 cm
1998.52
p. 41

Tomás Maldonado
(Buenos Aires, Argentina, 1922)
Composición 208
[Composition 208], 1951
Oil on canvas, 50.2 x 50.2 cm
1998.9

Mateo Manaure (Uracoa,
Monagas, Venezuela, 1926)
El negro es un color
[Black Is a Color], 1954
Synthetic paint on board,
76.5 x 51 x 4.1 cm
1996.29

Cildo Meireles
(Rio de Janeiro, Brazil, 1948)
Fio [Thread], 1990–95
48 bales of hay, 18-carat gold
needle, 100 meters of gold thread,
variable dimensions,
approx. 215.9 x 185.5 x 182.9 cm

The Museum of Modern Art,
New York. Gift of Patricia Phelps
de Cisneros, 2001
1175.2001.a-c
p. 148

Cildo Meireles
Malhas da liberdade
[Points of Freedom], 1973
Iron and glass,
120 x 122.6 x 3.8 cm
1998.55

Juan Melé (Buenos Aires,
Argentina, 1923–2012)
Marco recortado n.º 2
[Irregular Frame No. 2], 1946
Oil on board, 71.1 x 50.2 x 2.5 cm
1997.102
p. 35

Juan Alberto Molenberg
(Buenos Aires, Argentina, 1921)
Composición [Composition],
1946
Oil on board mounted on acrylic,
99.5 x 70 x 3 cm
1998.82
p. 45

Piet Mondrian (Amersfoort,
Netherlands, 1872 – New York,
US, 1944)
*Composition No. II with Yellow
and Blue*, 1931
Oil on canvas, 50.8 x 50.8 cm
2000.115
p. 20

Hélio Oiticica (Rio de Janeiro,
Brazil, 1937–1980)
Untitled, from the series *Relevos
espaciais* [Spatial Reliefs],
1959. Reconstructed in 1991
Acrylic on plywood,
143 x 143 x 10.5 cm
1996.77
p. 89

Hélio Oiticica
Box bolide 12, 'archeologic',
1964–65
Synthetic polymer paint with
earth on wood structure, nylon
net, corrugated cardboard,
mirror, glass, rocks, earth,
and fluorescent lamp,
36.8 x 131.1 x 52.1 cm
The Museum of Modern Art,
New York. Gift of Patricia Phelps
de Cisneros in honor of Paulo
Herkenhoff, 2004
326.2004.a-d
p. 90

Hélio Oiticica
Monocromático vermelho
[Red Monochrome], c. 1959
Oil on board,
29.8 x 29.8 x 2.9 cm
2000.10

Hélio Oiticica
Pintura 9 [Painting 9], 1959
Oil on canvas, 115.9 x 88.9 cm
1996.44
p. 67

Hélio Oiticica
Metaesquema
[Metascheme], 1957
Gouache on cardboard,
41.9 x 49 cm
1996.123

Hélio Oiticica
Metaesquema
[Metascheme], 1959
Oil on board,
37.5 x 33.3 x 2.5 cm
1997.80

Hélio Oiticica
Sin título (*Grupo Frente*)
[Untitled (*Frente* Group)], 1957
Oil on board,
40.6 x 40.6 x 4.1 cm
1997.82

Hélio Oiticica
Metaesquema
[Metascheme], 1957
Gouache on cardboard,
44.5 x 54 cm
1998.105

Hélio Oiticica
Metaesquema
[Metascheme], 1958
Gouache and ink on cardboard,
50 x 61 cm
1998.106
p. 76

Alejandro Otero (El Manteco,
Bolivar State, Venezuela,
1921 – Caracas, Venezuela,
1990)
Tablón 23 [Board 23],
November 1974
Lacquer on wood,
200 x 55 x 2.5 cm
1988.28

Alejandro Otero
Coloritmo 38
[Colorhythm 38], 1958
Lacquer on wood,
197.5 x 57.5 x 3 cm
1989.26

Alejandro Otero
Coloritmo 62
[Colorhythm 62], 1960
Lacquer on wood,
200 x 54.6 x 2.7 cm
1989.27

Alejandro Otero
Tablón de Pampatar
[Pampatar Board], 1954
Lacquer on wood,
320 x 65.1 x 2.7 cm
1990.58

Alejandro Otero
Coloritmo 39
[Colorhythm 39], 1959
Lacquer on wood,
200 x 53.5 x 3 cm
1990.59

Alejandro Otero
Estudio 4 [Study 4], 1952
Gouache, ink, and graphite
on paper, 19.5 x 25 cm
1990.92

Alejandro Otero
Estudio 1 [Study 1], 1952
Gouache, ink, and graphite
on paper, 19.7 x 24.8 cm
1990.94

Alejandro Otero
Estudio 2 [Study 2], 1952
Gouache, ink, and graphite
on paper, 19.5 x 24.8 cm
1990.95

Alejandro Otero
Estudio 3 [Study 3], 1952
Gouache, ink, and graphite
on paper, 19.4 x 24.8 cm
1990.96

Alejandro Otero
Tablón 1 [Board 1], 1976
Lacquer on wood,
198.4 x 54.8 x 2.6 cm
1991.58

Alejandro Otero
Ortogonal (Collage) 1, 1951
Cut-and-pasted colored paper
mounted on paper, 32 x 32 cm
The Museum of Modern Art,
New York. Gift of Patricia
Phelps de Cisneros in honor
of Marie-Josée Kravis, 2007
185.2007.1

Alejandro Otero
Ortogonal (Collage) 2, 1951
Cut-and-pasted colored paper
mounted on paper, 32 x 32 cm
The Museum of Modern Art,
New York. Gift of Patricia
Phelps de Cisneros in honor
of Marie-Josée Kravis, 2007
185.2007.2

Alejandro Otero
Ortogonal (Collage) 3, 1951
Cut-and-pasted colored paper
on paper, 31.5 x 32.7 cm
The Museum of Modern Art,
New York. Gift of Patricia
Phelps de Cisneros in honor
of Marie-Josée Kravis, 2007
185.2007.3

Alejandro Otero
Ortogonal (Collage) 4, 1951
Cut-and-pasted colored paper
on paper, 32.4 x 32.4 cm
The Museum of Modern Art,
New York. Gift of Patricia
Phelps de Cisneros in honor
of Marie-Josée Kravis, 2007
185.2007.4

Alejandro Otero
Ortogonal (Collage) 5, 1951
Cut-and-pasted colored paper
on paper, 32.4 x 32.4 cm
The Museum of Modern Art,
New York. Gift of Patricia
Phelps de Cisneros in honor
of Marie-Josée Kravis, 2007
185.2007.5

Alejandro Otero
Ortogonal (Collage) 6, 1951
Cut-and-pasted colored paper
on paper, 32 x 32 cm
The Museum of Modern Art,
New York. Gift of Patricia
Phelps de Cisneros in honor
of Marie-Josée Kravis, 2007
185.2007.6

Alejandro Otero
Ortogonal (Collage) 7, 1951
Cut-and-pasted colored paper
on paper, 32.4 x 32.4 cm
The Museum of Modern Art,
New York. Gift of Patricia Phelps
de Cisneros in honor
of Marie-Josée Kravis, 2007
185.2007.7

Alejandro Otero
Ortogonal (Collage) 8, 1952
Cut-and-pasted colored paper
on colored paper, 32.4 x 32.4 cm
The Museum of Modern Art,
New York. Gift of Patricia Phelps
de Cisneros in honor
of Marie-Josée Kravis, 2007
185.2007.8

Alejandro Otero
Ortogonal (Collage) 9, 1952
Cut-and-pasted colored paper
on colored paper, 32 x 32 cm
The Museum of Modern Art,
New York. Gift of Patricia Phelps
de Cisneros in honor
of Marie-Josée Kravis, 2007
185.2007.9

Alejandro Otero
Ortogonal (Collage) 10, 1952
Cut-and-pasted colored
paper on colored paper,
32.4 x 32.4 cm
The Museum of Modern Art,
New York. Gift of Patricia Phelps
de Cisneros in honor
of Marie-Josée Kravis, 2007
185.2007.10

Lygia Pape (Nova Friburgo,
Rio de Janeiro, Brazil, 1927 –
Rio de Janeiro, Brazil, 2004)
Livro da criação
[Book of Creation], 1959–60
Gouache on cardboard, 16 pieces,
each: 30.5 x 30.5 cm

The Museum of Modern Art,
New York. Gift of Patricia Phelps
de Cisneros, 2001
1349.2001.a-r
pp. 92–95

César Paternosto
(La Plata, Argentina, 1931)
The Hidden Order, 1972
Acrylic on canvas,
106.7 x 106.7 x 7 cm
1996.23

Rhod Rothfuss (Montevideo,
Uruguay, 1920–1969)
Cuadrilongo amarillo
[Yellow *Cuadrilongo*], 1955
Paint on wood,
37 x 33 cm
2010.69
p. 44

Luiz Sacilotto (Santo André,
São Paulo State, Brazil, 1924
– São Bernardo do Campo,
São Paulo State, Brazil, 2003)
Concreção 58 [Concretion 58],
1958
Enamel on metal and acrylic
on plywood, 20 x 60 x 30.5 cm
1997.131
p. 73

Mira Schendel (Zurich,
Switzerland, 1919 – São Paulo,
Brazil, 1988)
Sin título, de la serie Droguinhas
[Untitled, from the series
Droguinhas (Little Nothings)],
1966
Japanese paper, variable
dimensions, approx. 66.6 cm
(extended)
1997.163
p. 163

Mira Schendel
Untitled, c. 1960
Oil transfer drawing on
Japanese paper, 47 x 23 cm
1998.90

Mira Schendel
Untitled, c. 1960
Oil transfer drawing on
Japanese paper, 47 x 23 cm
1998.91

Mira Schendel
Untitled, c. 1964
Oil transfer drawing on
Japanese paper, 47 x 23 cm
1998.94

Mira Schendel
Untitled, 1965
Oil transfer drawing on
Japanese paper, 47 x 23 cm
1998.99

Mira Schendel
Untitled, c. 1965
Oil transfer drawing on
Japanese paper, 47 x 23 cm
1998.101
p. 165

Mira Schendel
Untitled, c. 1964
Oil transfer drawing on
Japanese paper, 47 x 23 cm
1998.102
p. 164

Mira Schendel
Sin título, de la serie *Objetos
gráficos* [Untitled, from the series
Objetos gráficos (Graphic
Objects)], 1967
Graphite, transfer type, and oil
on Japanese paper between
acrylic sheets with transfer type,
99.8 x 99.8 x 1 cm
2001.95
p. 167

Jesús Soto
(Ciudad Bolivar, Venezuela,
1923 – Paris, France, 2005)
Doble transparencia
[Double Transparency],
1956
Oil on acrylic and wood,
55 x 55 x 32 cm
1989.35
p. 123

Jesús Soto
Cubo de nylon
[Nylon Cube], 1990
Painted nylon,
276.5 x 120.5 x 120.5 cm
1990.63

Jesús Soto
Untitled (Maquette for a mural
at Universidad Central de
Venezuela), 1952–53
Gouache on board,
27.6 x 48.3 x 3.5 cm
2003.2
p. 43

Jesús Soto
Vibración metálica
[Metallic Vibration], 1962
Wire and synthetic paint on wood,
110 x 78 x 9.5 cm
1990.61
p. 125

Jesús Soto
Baguettes rouges et noires
[Red and Black Rods], 1964
Acrylic on board, painted steel,
and nylon, 57.8 x 172.4 x 16.2 cm
1991.62
p. 57

Jesús Soto
Vibration, 1960
Oil and wire on wood,
99.7 x 99.7 x 2.5 cm
The Museum of Modern Art,

New York. Gift of Patricia Phelps
de Cisneros in honor of Luis
Enrique Pérez Oramas, 2004
330.2004
p. 127

Jesús Soto
Vibración [Vibration], 1960
Wire and synthetic paint on wood,
99.7 x 99.7 x 4.2 cm
1994.41
p. 128

Jesús Soto
Hommage à Yves Klein
[Homage to Yves Klein], 1961
Wire, metal sheet, and synthetic
paint on board, 55 x 95.6 x 4 cm
1995.21
p. 129

Jesús Soto
Pre-penetrable, 1957
Painted iron,
165.5 x 126 x 85 cm
1997.118
p. 130

Jesús Soto
Untitled, 1962
Iron and brass wire and synthetic
paint on canvas on board,
57.2 x 60.3 x 13 cm
1997.126

Joaquín Torres-García
(Montevideo, Uruguay,
1874–1949)
Construcción en blanco y negro
[Construction in White and Black],
1938
Oil on paper mounted on wood,
80.7 x 102 cm
The Museum of Modern Art,
New York. Gift of Patricia Phelps
de Cisneros in honor
of David Rockefeller, 2004
331.2004
p. 161

Joaquín Torres-García
Gare [Station], 1932
Oil on canvas, 65 x 54 cm
1982.2
p. 156

Joaquín Torres-García
Constructivo doble línea
[Constructive with Double Line],
1932
Oil on canvas, 61 x 49 cm
1986.3
p. 159

Joaquín Torres-García
Peinture constructive
[Constructive Painting], 1931
Oil on canvas, 74.9 x 54.9 cm
1997.32
p. 158

Franz Weissmann (Knittelfeld,
Austria, 1911 – Rio de Janeiro,
Brazil, 2005)
Coluna neoconcreta
[Neoconcrete Column], 1957
Painted iron, 197.6 x 77.4 x 47 cm
1997.132
p. 74

Franz Weissmann
Composição com semicírculos
[Composition with Semicircles],
1953
Aluminum, 81 x 64.7 x 56.1 cm
1997.134
p. 75

Franz Weissmann
Sin título (*Escultura neoconcreta*)
[Untitled (Neoconcrete
Sculpture)], 1958–84
Painted iron, 30.2 x 20 x 20 cm
1996.66

Works Not Exhibited

Lygia Clark
Estudo para plano em superfície modulada [Planes on Modulated Surface (Study)], 1957
Collage, 30.5 x 26 cm
1996.101
p. 66

Milton Dacosta (Niterói, Rio de Janeiro State, Brazil, 1915 – Rio de Janeiro, Brazil, 1988)
Em branco [In White], 1958–59
Oil on canvas, 81 x 100 cm
1997.47
p. 30

Mathias Goeritz
(Danzig, Germany [actually Gdańsk, Poland], 1915 – Mexico City, Mexico, 1990)
Untitled, 1960
Brass, 80 x 80 cm
2004.32
p. 104

Alfredo Hlito
Desarrollo de un tema [Development of a Theme], 1952
Oil on canvas, 60.6 x 70.5 cm
1997.100
p. 34

Alfredo Hlito
Ritmos cromáticos II [Chromatic Rhythms II], 1947

Oil on canvas, 69.9 x 70.2 cm
1998.39
p. 40

Tomás Maldonado
Desarrollo de un triángulo [Development of a Triangle], 1949
Oil on canvas, 80.6 x 60.3 cm
1998.6
p. 37

Hélio Oiticica
Untitled, from the series *Relevos espaciais* [Spatial Reliefs], 1959. Reconstructed in 1991
Acrylic on plywood, 104 x 118 x 12.7 cm
1996.76
p. 88

Hélio Oiticica
P 16 Parangolé capa 12 "Da adversidade vivemos" [P 16 *Parangolé* Cape 12: "We Live from Adversity"], 1965. Reconstructed in 1992
Jute, fabric, wood shavings and plastic materials, 114 x 27 x 22 cm
1996.208
p. 91

Hélio Oiticica
Metaesquema [Metascheme], 1957
Gouache on cardboard,

45.5 x 52.5 cm
1996.122
p. 52

Hélio Oiticica
Sin título (*Grupo Frente*) [Untitled (*Frente* Group)], 1955
Gouache on cardboard, 37 x 36 cm
1997.81
p. 72

Lygia Pape
Sin título. *Tecelar* [Untitled. Weaving], 1959
Woodcut on paper, 30.5 x 32.4 cm
1996.206
p. 68

Mira Schendel
Sin título, de la serie *Objetos gráficos* [Untitled, from the series *Objetos gráficos* (Graphic Objects)], 1973
Transfer type on Japanese paper between acrylic sheets with transfer type, 55.9 x 55.9 x 1 cm
1999.34
p. 166

Mira Schendel
Perfurados I [Perforated I], n.d.
Perforated paper, 31.8 x 31.8 cm
2004.10
p. 147

Jesús Soto
Desplazamiento de un elemento luminoso [Displacement of a Luminous Element], 1954
Vinyl dots on acrylic, tempera on board and wood, 50 x 80 x 3.3 cm
1989.36
p. 16

Jesús Soto
Vibración III [Vibration III], 1960–61
Synthetic paint, fabric and wire on board, 150.1 x 60.6 x 19 cm
1993.40
p. 124

Joaquín Torres-García
Locomotora con casa constructiva [Locomotive with Constructive House], 1934
Oil on canvas, 71.3 x 59 cm
1980.1
p. 155

Joaquín Torres-García
Constructivo con madera superpuesta [Constructive with Superimposed Wood], 1932
Oil on wood, 44.5 x 26 x 3.8 cm
1996.88
p. 157

CATALOGUE

Edited by the MNCARS Publications
Department and TURNER

Head of Department
Maria Luisa Blanco

Editorial Coordination
Mafalda Rodríguez

General Coordination
Turner
Magda Anglès

Design
gráfica futura

Translations
From Spanish into English: Philip Sutton

Copyediting and proofreading
Jonathan Fox

Plates
Lucam

Printing
Artes Gráficas Palermo

Binding
Ramos

The citations that accompany each of
the catalogue's sections may be in found
in the following publications:

Raúl Lozza, "Ante la decadencia y espíritu
negativo" in *Raúl Lozza. Primera exposición
de pintura perceptista*, exh. cat. Van Riel
Galería de Arte, Buenos Aires, 1949;
translated on the artist's website.

"Neoconcrete Manifesto," reproduced in
*Ferreira Gullar in Conversation with Ariel
Jiménez*, New York and Caracas: Fundación
Cisneros, 2012.

"Madí Manifesto," originally published in
Arte Madí Universal, No. 0–1, Buenos Aires,
1947; translated in Dawn Ades, ed., *Art in Latin
America: The Modern Era, 1820–1980*, exh.
cat. South Bank Centre, London, New Haven:
Yale University Press, 1993, 322.

Jesús Soto in Conversation with Ariel Jiménez,
New York and Caracas: Fundación Cisneros,
2011.

Joaquín Torres-García, "La Escuela del Sur,"
Uruguay, February 1935, in Mari Carmen
Ramírez, ed., *El Taller Torres-García: The
School of the South and Its Legacy*, exh. cat.
Archer M. Huntington Art Gallery, Austin:
University of Texas, 1992.

Page 118: A copy of the letter was sent by fax
from Lía Bermúdez to Ariel Jiménez in 2000.

ISBN: 978-84-15427-97-1
NIPO: 036-13-010-1
Depósito legal: M-1179-2013

General catalogue of Official Publications
http://www.060.es

Distributed in the United States by:
DAP
orders@dapinc.com
www.artbook.com

Distributed in Europe by:
IDEA BOOKS
webform@ideabooks.nl
www.ideabooks.nl

Distributed in United Kingdom by:
ART DATA
orders@artdata.co.uk
www.artdata.co.uk

SPANISH EDITION AVAILABLE
Distributed in Spain by:
Machado Grupo de Distribución
machadolibros@machadolibros.com
and
Les Punxes Distribuidora
punxes@punxes.es
www.punxes.es

Distributed in Latin America by:
Océano
info@oceano.com
www.oceano.com

Artists's Credits
All reasonable efforts have been made to state
copyright holders of material used in this
book; any oversight will be corrected in future
editions, provided the Publishers have been
duly informed.

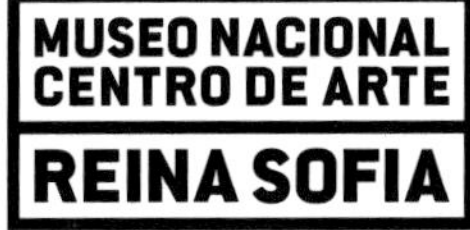
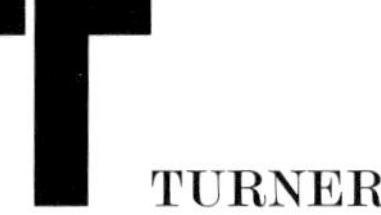

TURNER

ACKNOWLEDGMENTS

The Museo Nacional Centro de Arte Reina Sofía wishes first and foremost to express its most sincere gratitude to the Colección Patricia Phelps de Cisneros, particularly Patricia Phelps de Cisneros and Gabriel Pérez-Barreiro, as well as Sara Meadows, Skye A. Monson, and John Thomas Robinette, for their enthusiastic support for this exhibition, and for having made available to us the full breadth of their collection.

We would also like to thank the Museum of Modern Art in New York, and in particular its director, Glenn D. Lowry, as well as Luis Pérez-Oramas, Cora Rosevear, Kathleen S. Curry, Lily Goldberg, Carla Caputo, and Eliza Frecon, for their unconditional cooperation on this project.

Finally, our most profound gratitude goes out to all the artists taking part in the exhibition, and to all those who have helped to make this possible.

We also thank the collaboration of Michelle Sommer and Madeline Turner.

HIGH HEELS

FRANK RISPOLI

CIRCA

ON PEDESTALS

Frank Rispoli has spent a lifetime using his camera to capture aspects of city life that most of us never notice, let alone consider worthy of such expressive documentation. He is, however, far more than a mere recorder of striking images. He is a composer of unexpected serendipity, crafting tableaux that transmute urban grit and squalor into visions of casual elegance. Rispoli's images reverberate with decadence.

Peering through the cracked surfaces of the battered cityscape, he harnesses the inherent power of women's fashion and its effect on the world around it. He is not only a composer; he is also a conductor, channelling the electricity that courses through the streets of New York City, his camera the exposed wire, shooting sparks and snatching pure moments from thin air.

Rispoli was a diffident child who found it difficult to look women in the eye. His tendency to cast his eyes downwards gradually developed into a fixation with women's shoes, legs and feet. It is said that women dress for other women, but Rispoli noticed too. Their feet were destined to dominate his work. A schism between his conservative Catholic upbringing and his emerging desires was inevitable. And thus, compulsive childhood behaviour and ecstatic art merged into something extraordinary.

In the late 1970s, inspired by Guy Bourdin's groundbreaking photography of Charles Jourdan's shoes, Rispoli began pounding the sidewalks of New York City, looking for likely subjects. He sought the sultry and the surreal in the shadows, intent on outlining the contours of those who lived on the margins of polite society. Provided, of course, that they strutted around town in a pair of killer heels.

Rispoli was then working full-time as an environmental designer, and while his day job paid the rent, it wasn't until the sun went down, and he was behind the lens, that his creative impulse truly found expression. Downtown haunts such as CBGB, Max's Kansas City and Danceteria were a living, thriving theatre, tailor-made for Rispoli's lens. In this realm, fashion doubled as art and he exploited the milieu to the full. 'The epicentre of everything was Danceteria', recalls

Rispoli of the club where Madonna made her debut, LL Cool J worked the elevators and Sade tended bar. Rispoli explored the clubs, 'six-and-a-half nights a week', fine-tuning his aesthetic. And as he and his images became better known, he no longer had to search for subjects – they began to find their way to him.

One of his signature innovations is that he attaches more importance to the pedestal of the heel than the person who rests atop it. Heels find themselves tangled in spiral phone cords, kept just out of reach by electrical wires on tenement roofs, or framed by taxi door jambs. A washbasin presents a pair of stilettos and mismatched socks as if it were an exquisite dish at an uptown restaurant. In Rispoli's photographs, there is always a sense of the forbidden at play. Bathrooms serve as ready-made sets, encompassing a particular mix of glamour, decadence, desperation and raw sexuality. The satisfaction comes from framing these obscure objects of desire as if they are works of art in themselves.

Until the French Revolution (just imagine Rispoli's take on all that red!), high heels were worn by both sexes, but when they came back in vogue during the late-nineteenth century, they were the sole preserve of women. After the Second World War, designers such as Roger Vivier and Salvatore Ferragamo took the heel to the pinnacle of decadence – the stiletto, the enduring symbol of the dominatrix and the femme fatale.

In a certain sense, Rispoli's entire photographic output has been a paean to the enduring attraction of the high heel. After a decade when they faded from fashion, stilettos made a roaring comeback in the 1970s. As women sought to subvert the cliché of the femme fatale, the stiletto was a key weapon in their arsenal. At the same time LGBTQ+ activists, among them the Queens Liberation Front, hosted drag balls where the stiletto was not simply a shoe, but a symbol of defiance. This is where Rispoli enters the picture, in the rarefied atmosphere of Manhattan's fashion and art demi-mondes.

As a native son, he has been able to make sense of the non-stop kaleidoscope of New York City. In his mind's eye, the erotic is always at play with the thrilling chaos of urban living. Harsh backdrops and crumbling infrastructure are transformed into a glorious canvas that has the appeal of modern myth. And what makes the myth plausible is the women. For they are the true stars of Rispoli's photographs. These portraits reveal just enough about the characters that populate them to ignite the imagination and prompt us to speculate about the hidden elements of each story.

There is a kind of magic imprinted on Rispoli's trusty Kodachrome film. The high contrast, saturated colour and crystal clarity of Kodachrome 25 yields incredible images. Taken at night with a Vivitar flash, the pictures radiate light. The shots come alive, uncanny in their ability to draw the viewer into the scene. This is no easy feat. Through trial and error, Rispoli mastered the art of bracketing until he found the formula that allowed him to frame his portraits just so.

Tiny details accumulate and assume significance – a crumpled cigarette pack, a dented dustbin, a bouquet of synthetic flowers. Deprived of the distraction of faces, texture assumes dominance. Leather, lace, mini skirts, fishnets, retro socks, vintage dresses – all are rich material for Rispoli's lens. Although inspired by advertising, you would never confuse these pictures with the banal offerings on display in the magazine era. They at once comment upon, and wilfully disregard, the ubiquitous glossiness of consumer culture.

While the photographer acknowledges the agency of his subjects, he does not hide his own gaze. He zeroes in on street-level moments of grace that consist of sharp lines, faceless models and bursts of colour that illuminate a sense of blink-and-you-miss-it glamour. Revelling in an unerring sense of now, Rispoli stretches small gestures into an infinite scroll of beauty that teeters on the edge of obsession. He combines contradictory approaches into a seamless whole of refined yet abstract compositions that teem with questions of identity, belonging and thwarted desire. The high-low duality of Rispoli's photographs functions as a bridge between aesthetic imperatives that are often at odds with one another: two women meet in the middle of the street, or pose amid the rubble of an abandoned building, and of course, they look fabulous.

To see these pictures is to tap into an undercurrent of mutual respect between photographer and model. Even at their most risqué, Rispoli's portraits venerate their subjects, elevating them to a level that borders on the religious. He presents the women who wear these shoes in their natural habitat, gliding about the city on their pedestals, hovering just above the rest of us.

Erick Bradshaw Hughes

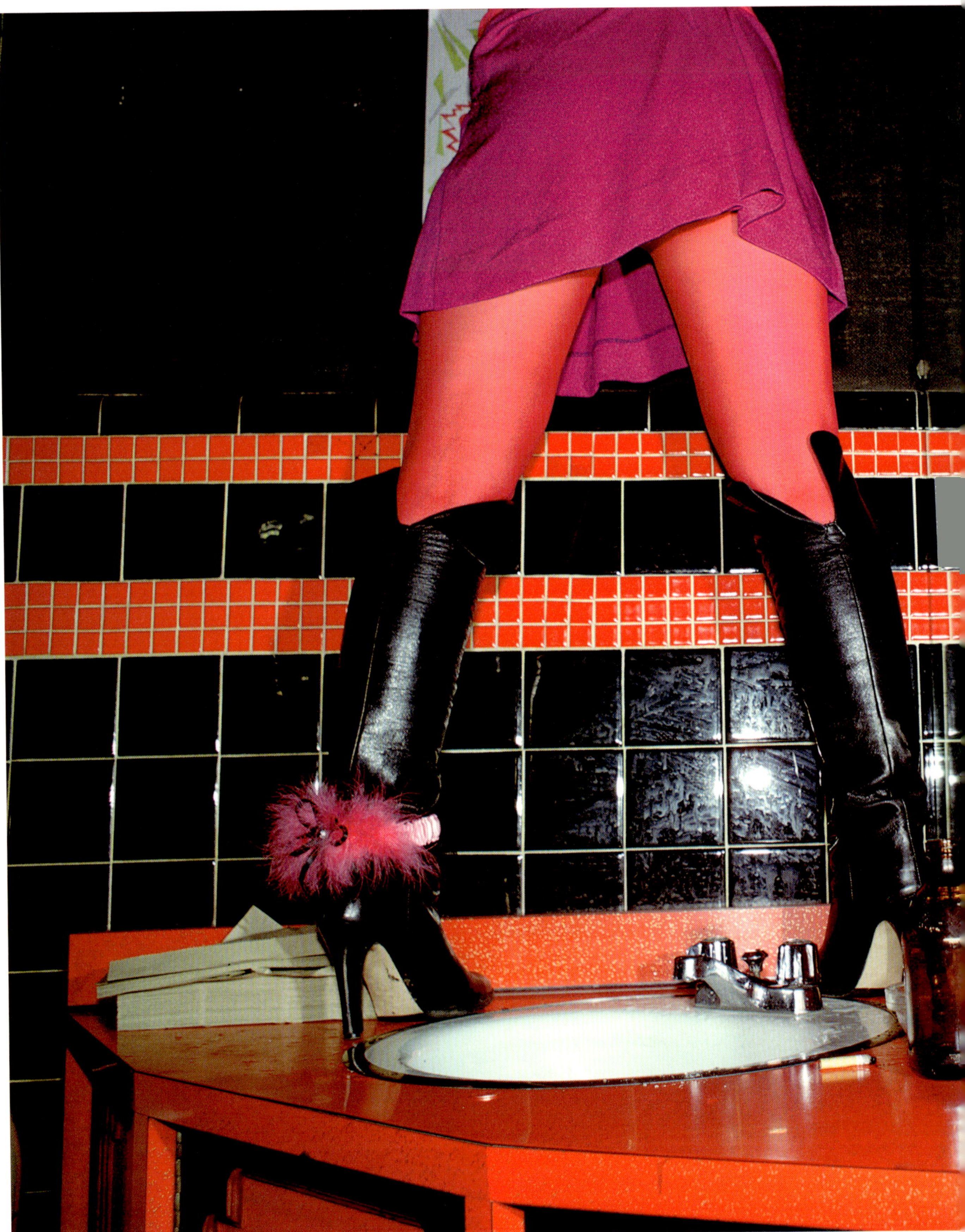

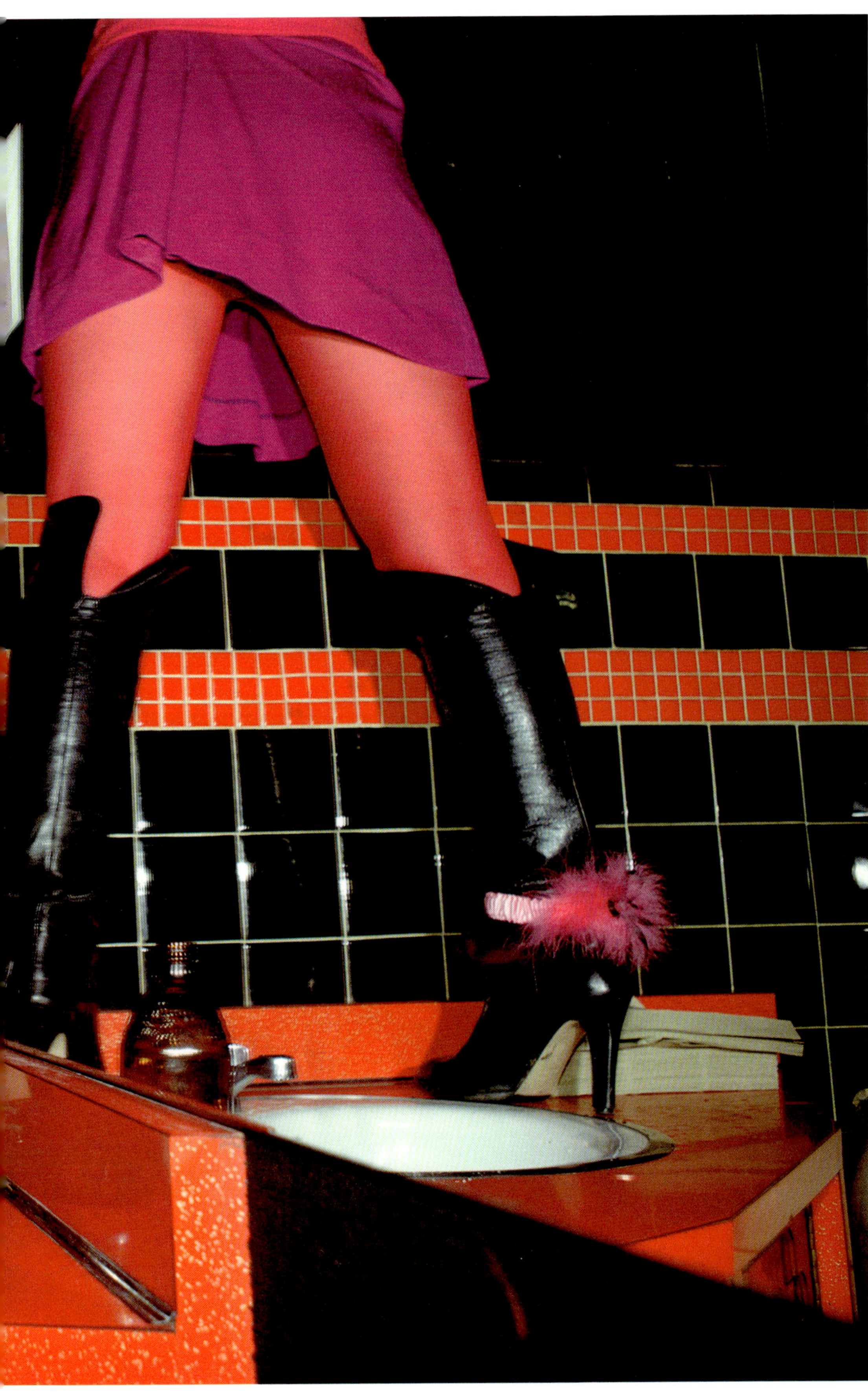

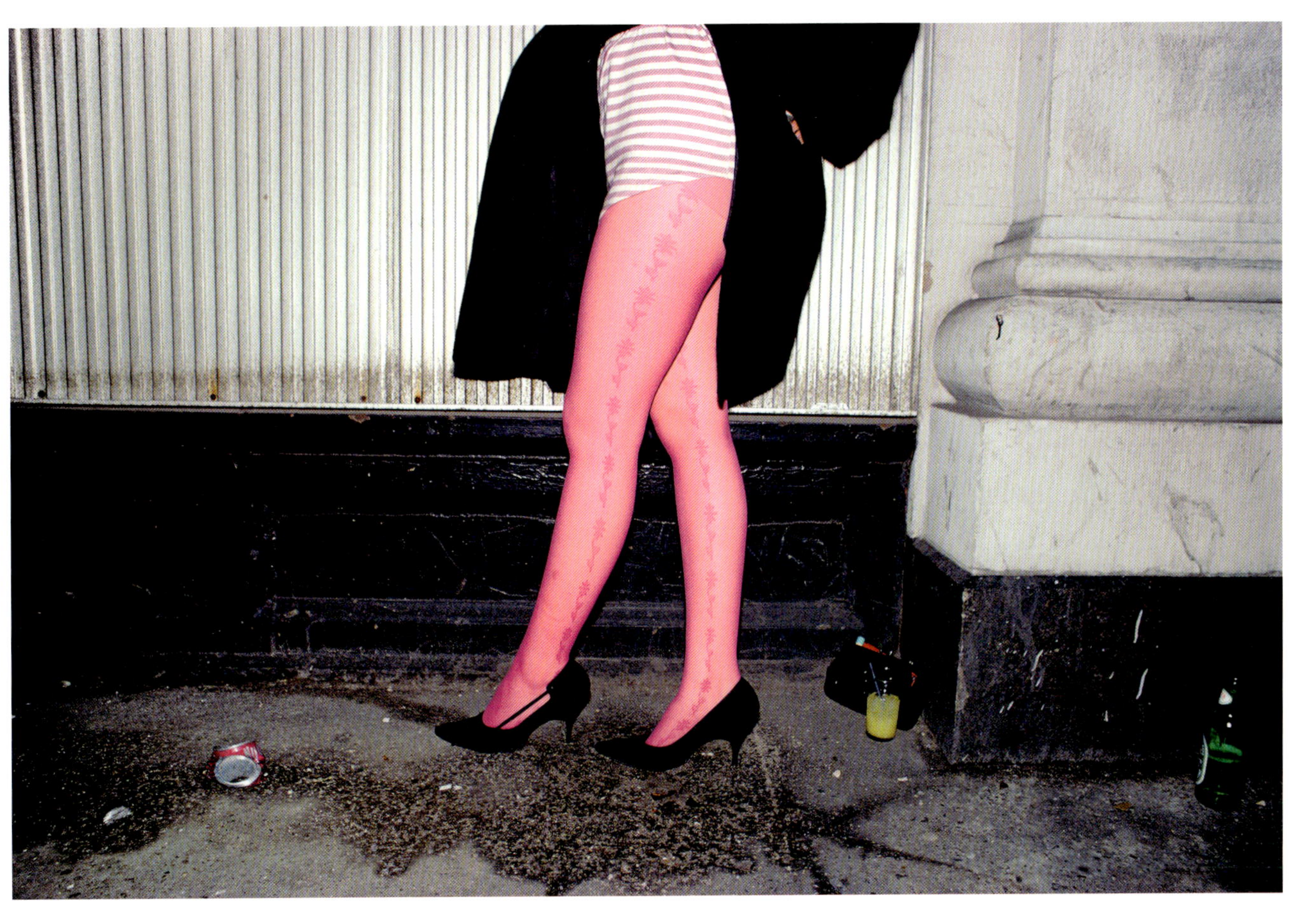

Outside Mudd Club, Tribeca, early 1980s

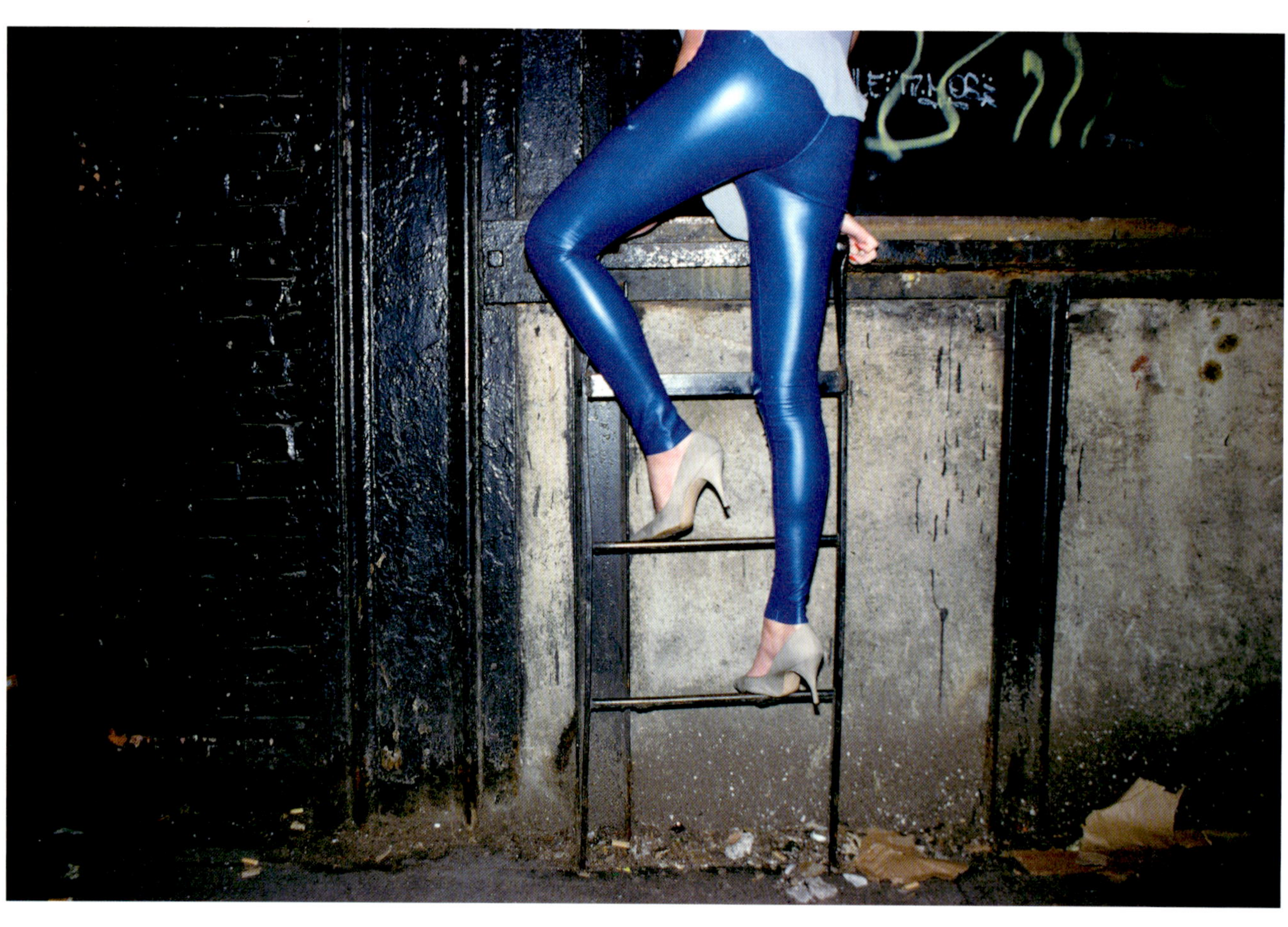

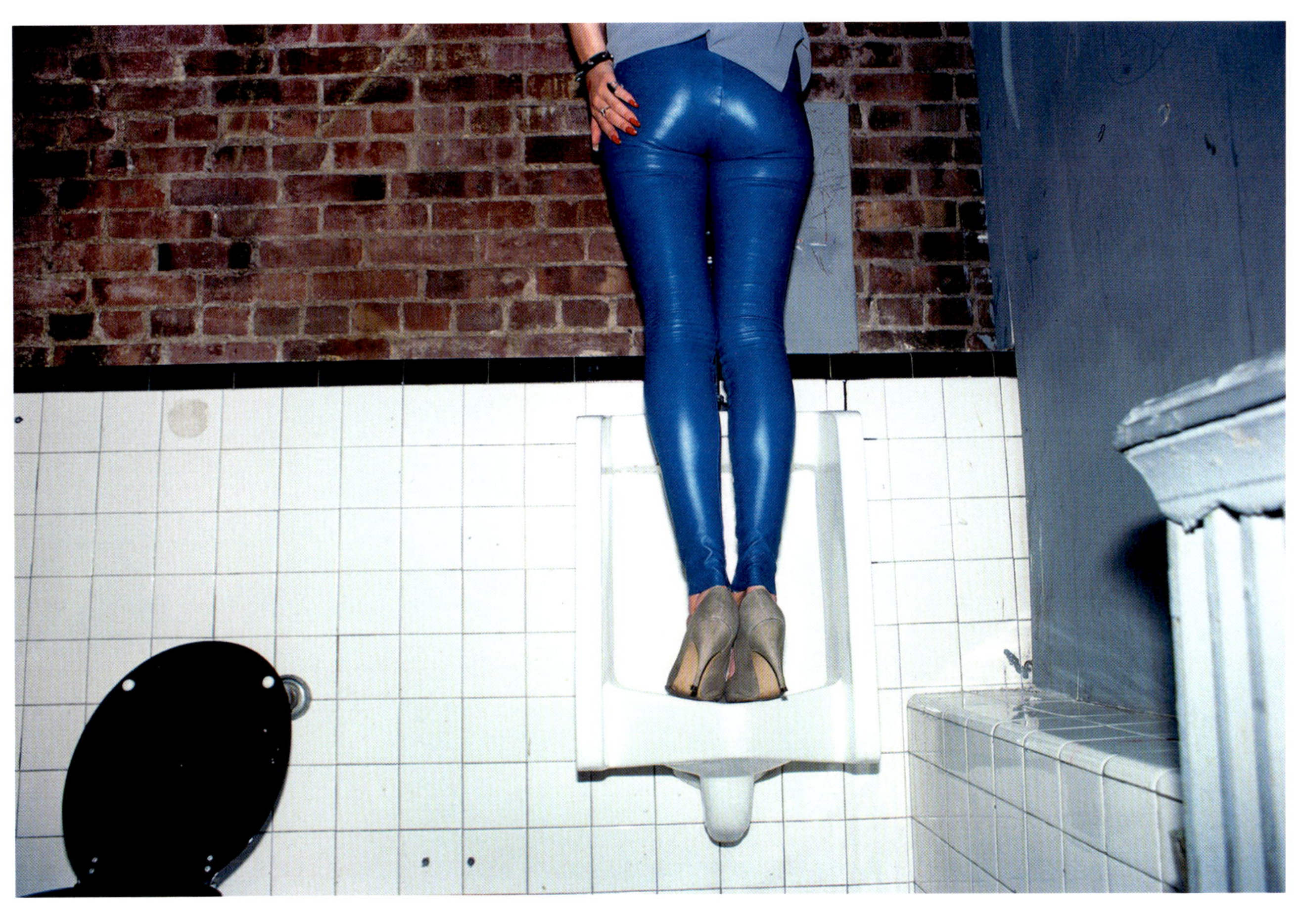

Mudd Club, Tribeca, early 1980s

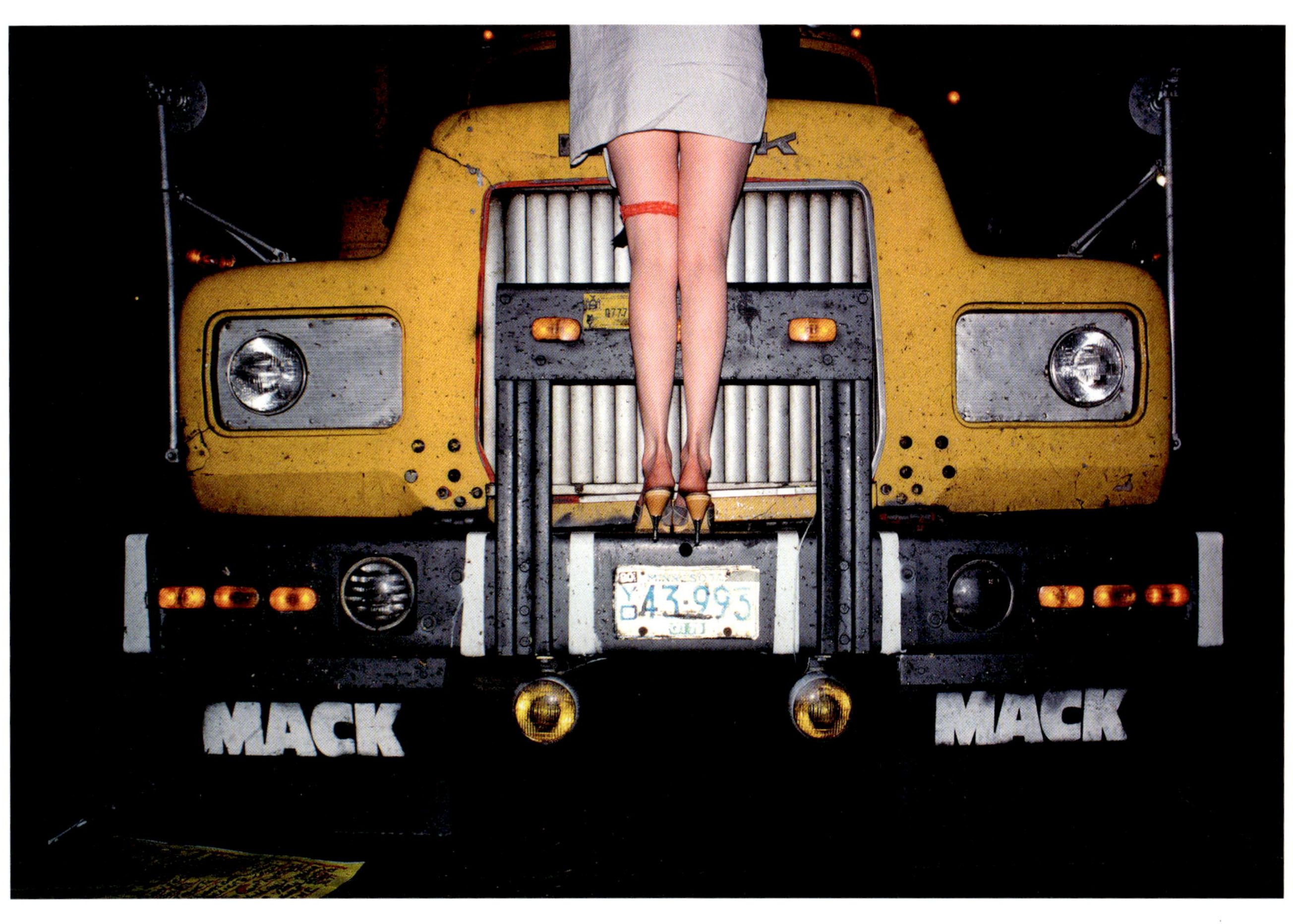

Outside CBGB, The Bowery, late 1970s

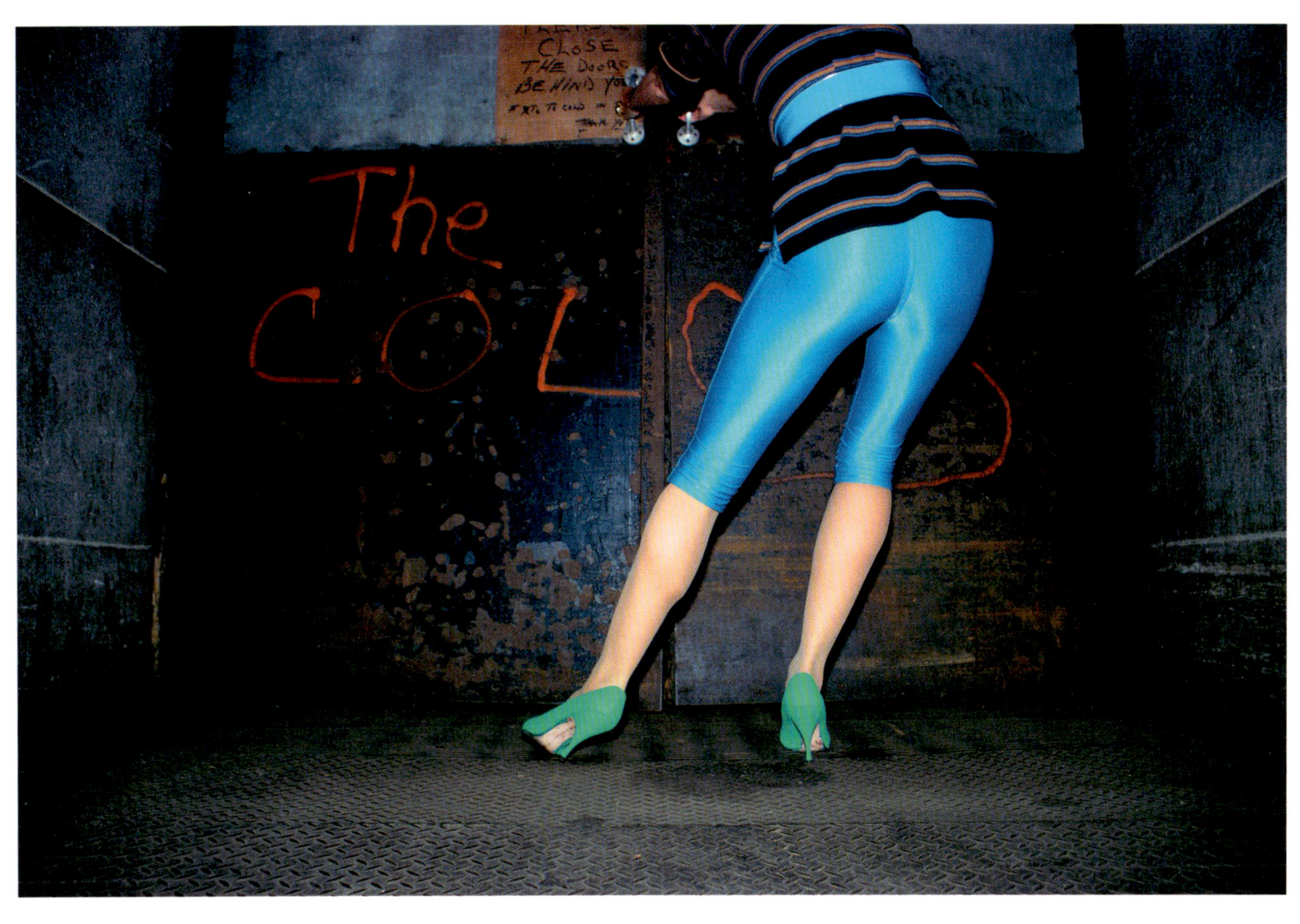

TR3 club, Tribeca, late 1970s

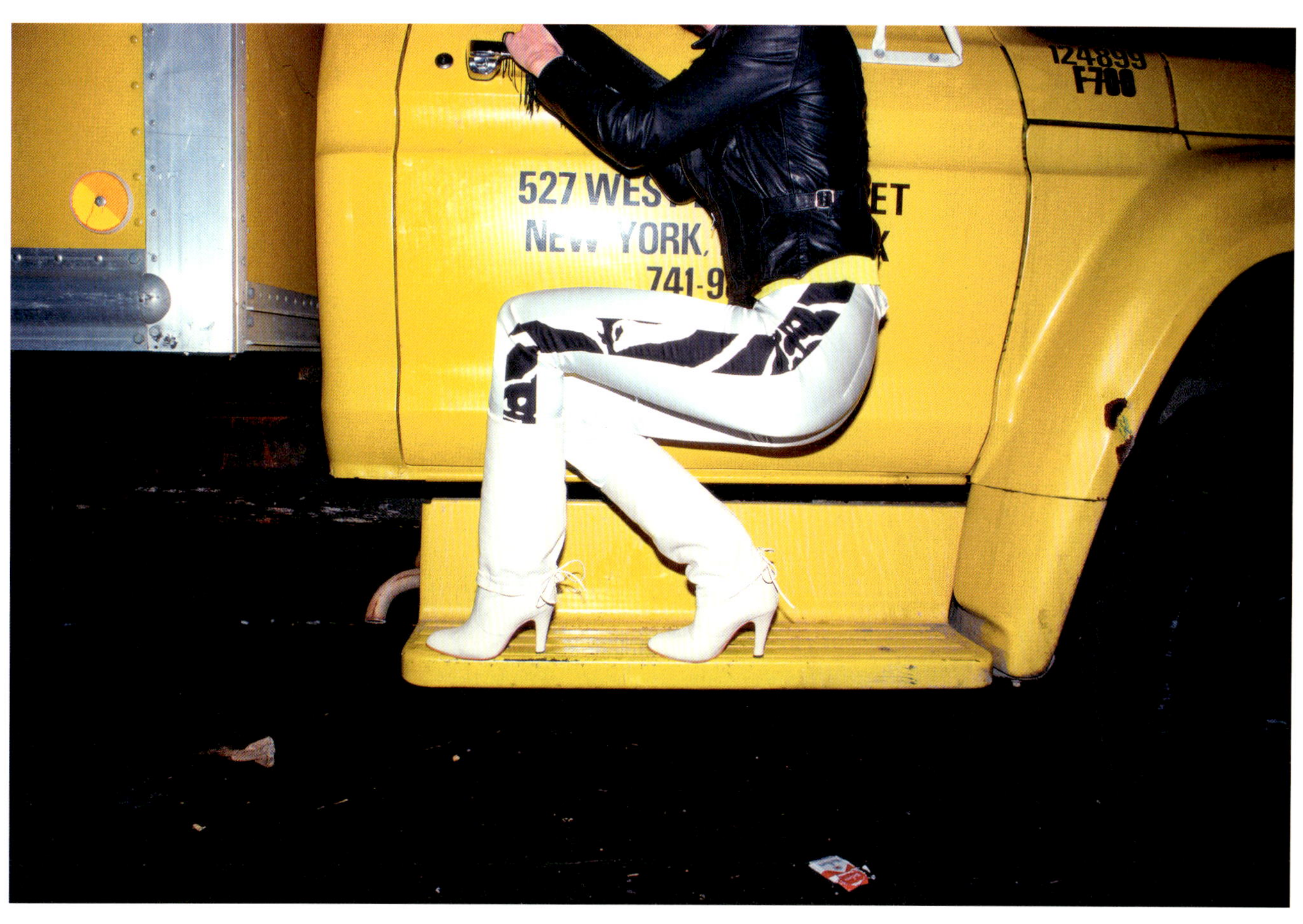

Outside CBGB, The Bowery, late 1970s

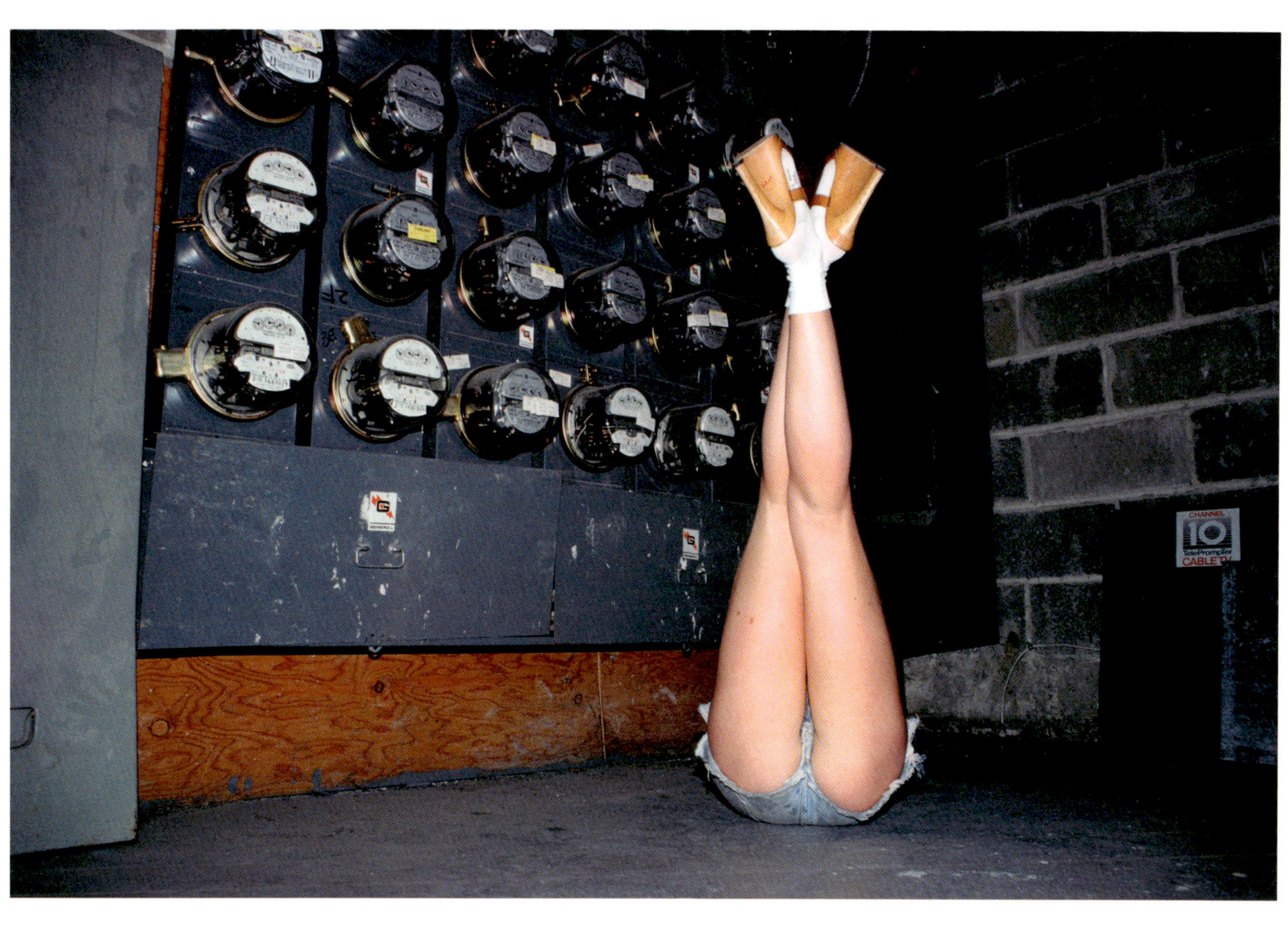

Upper East Side, Manhattan, late 1970s

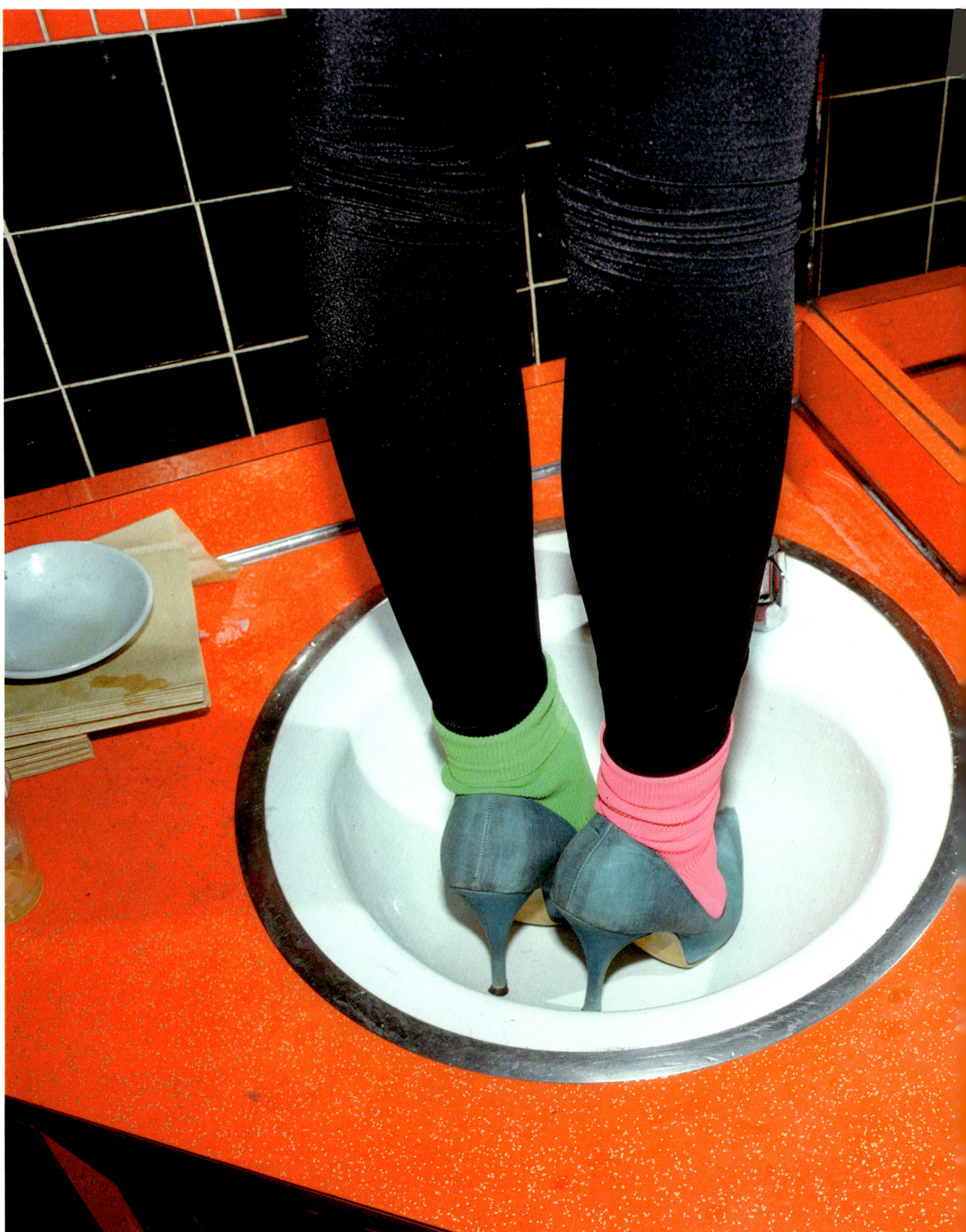

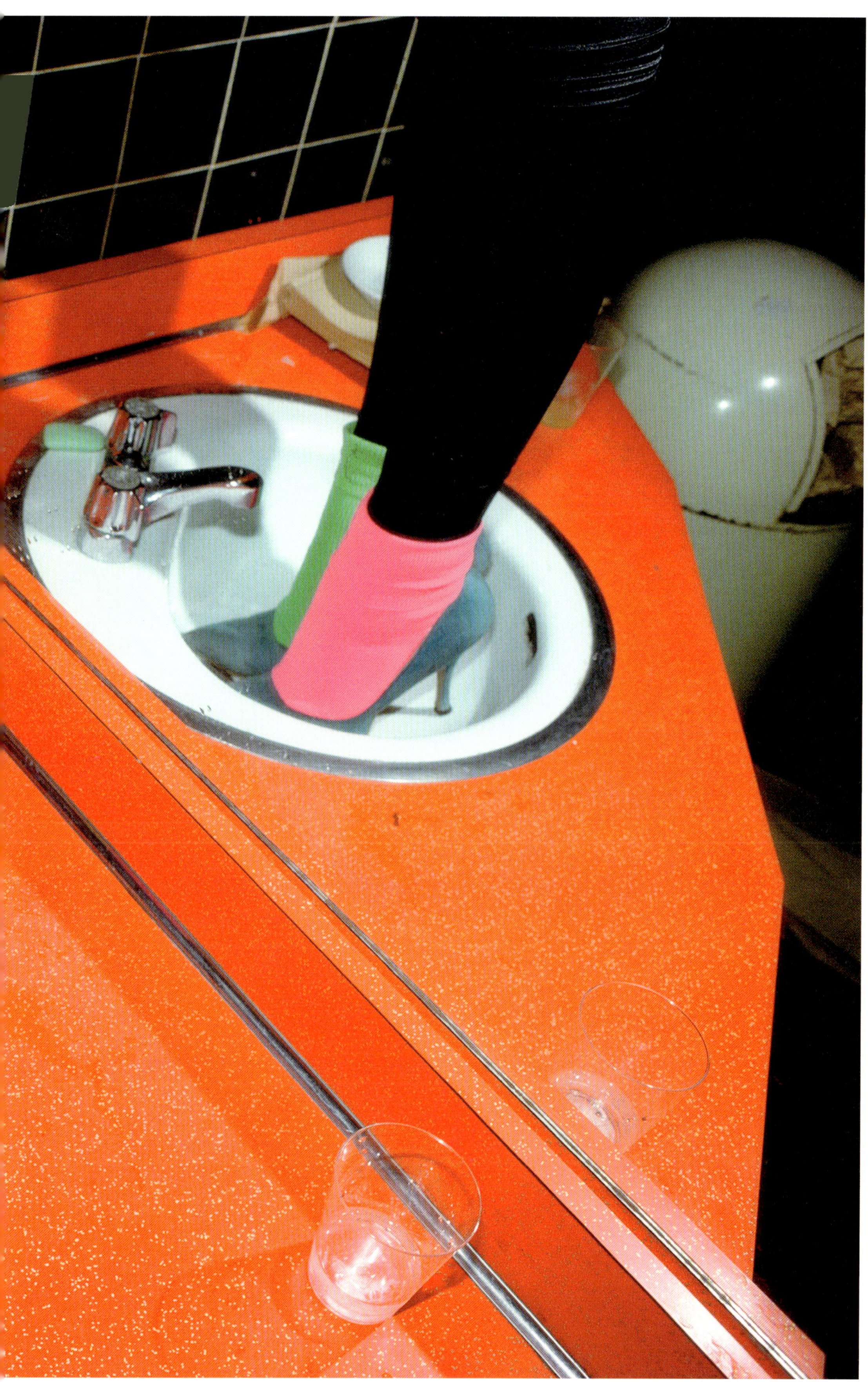

Previous pages: TR3 club, Tribeca, late 1970s

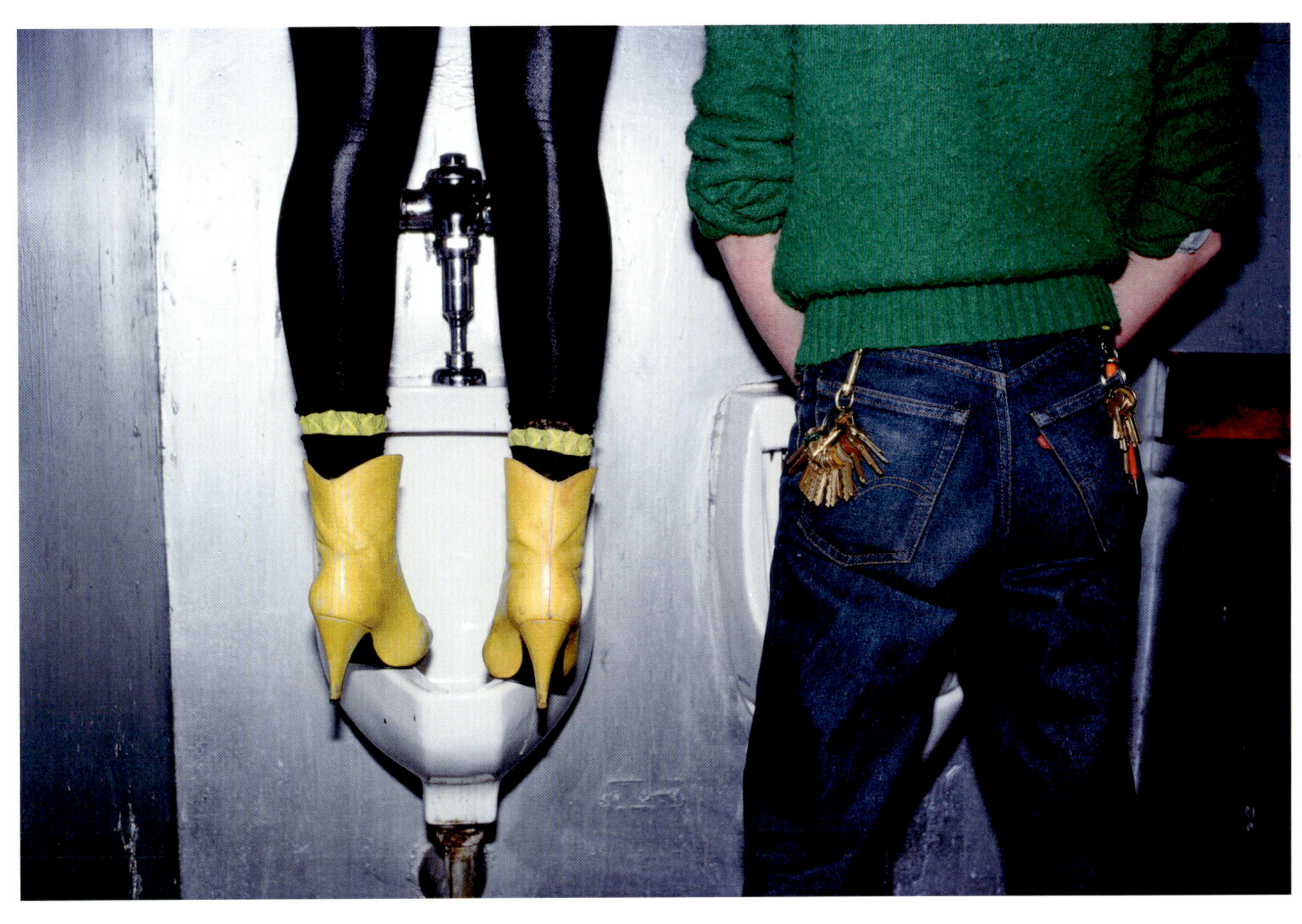

Irving Plaza, Chelsea, early 1980s

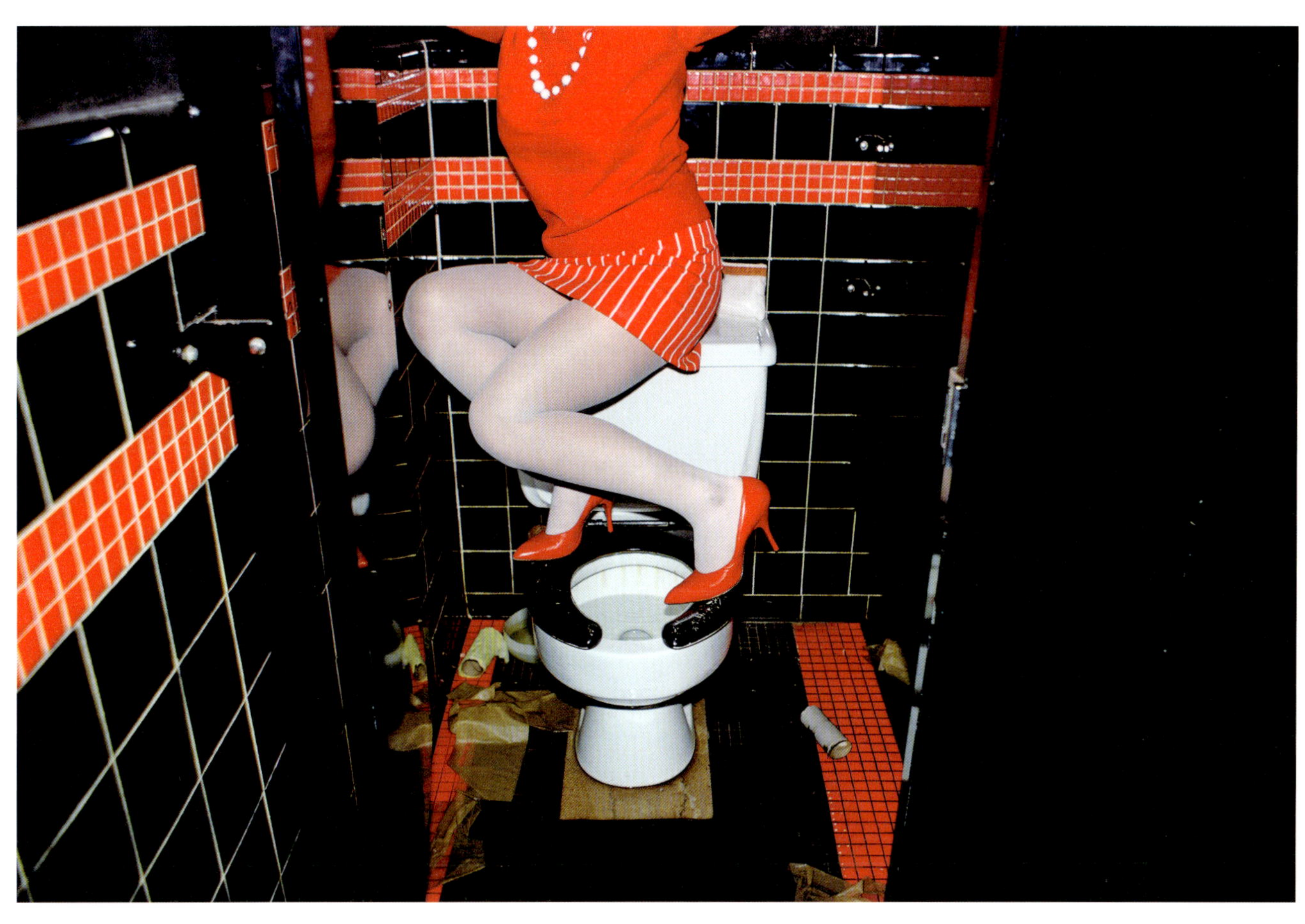

TR3 club, Tribeca, late 1970s

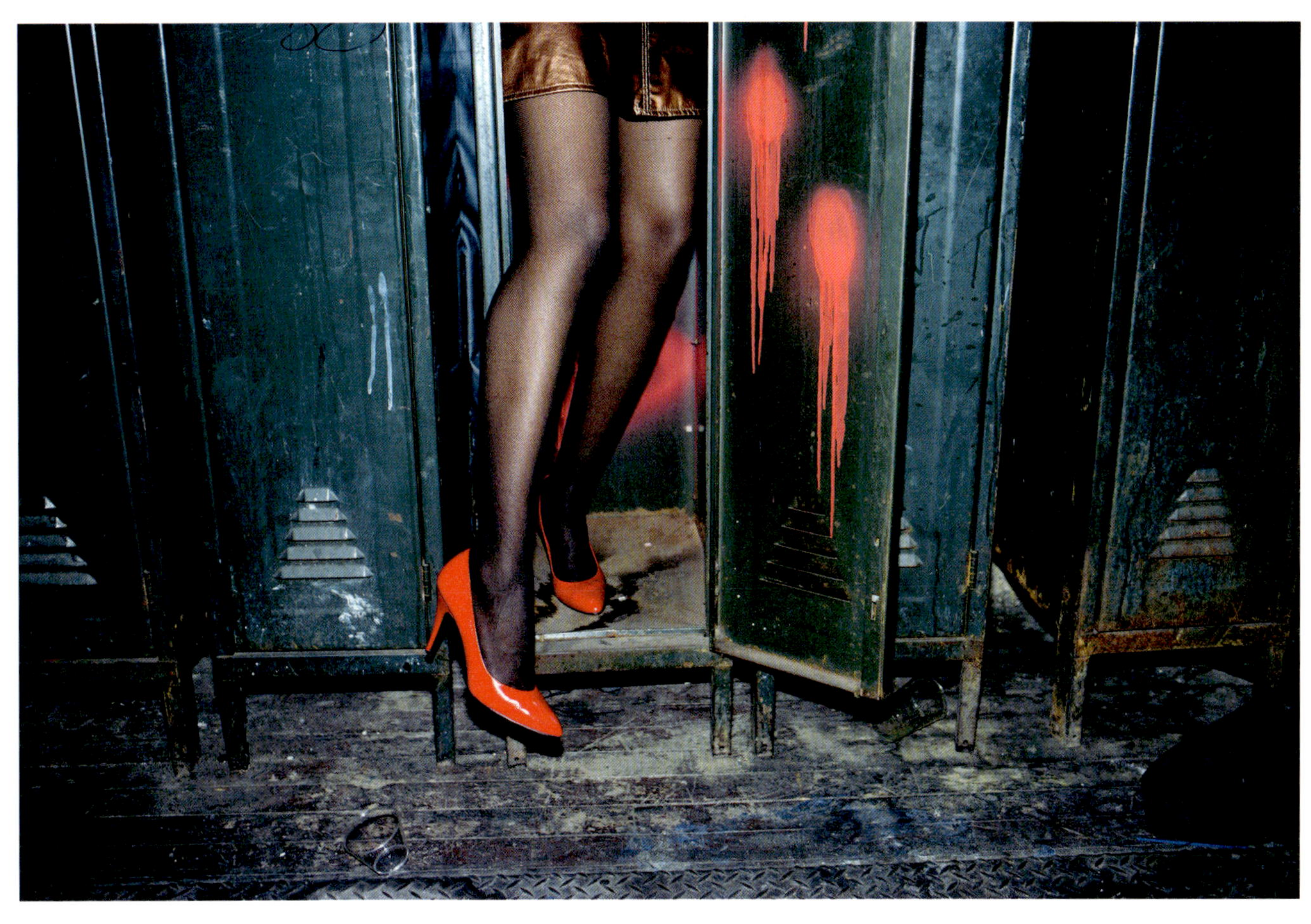

Danceteria, Chelsea, early 1980s

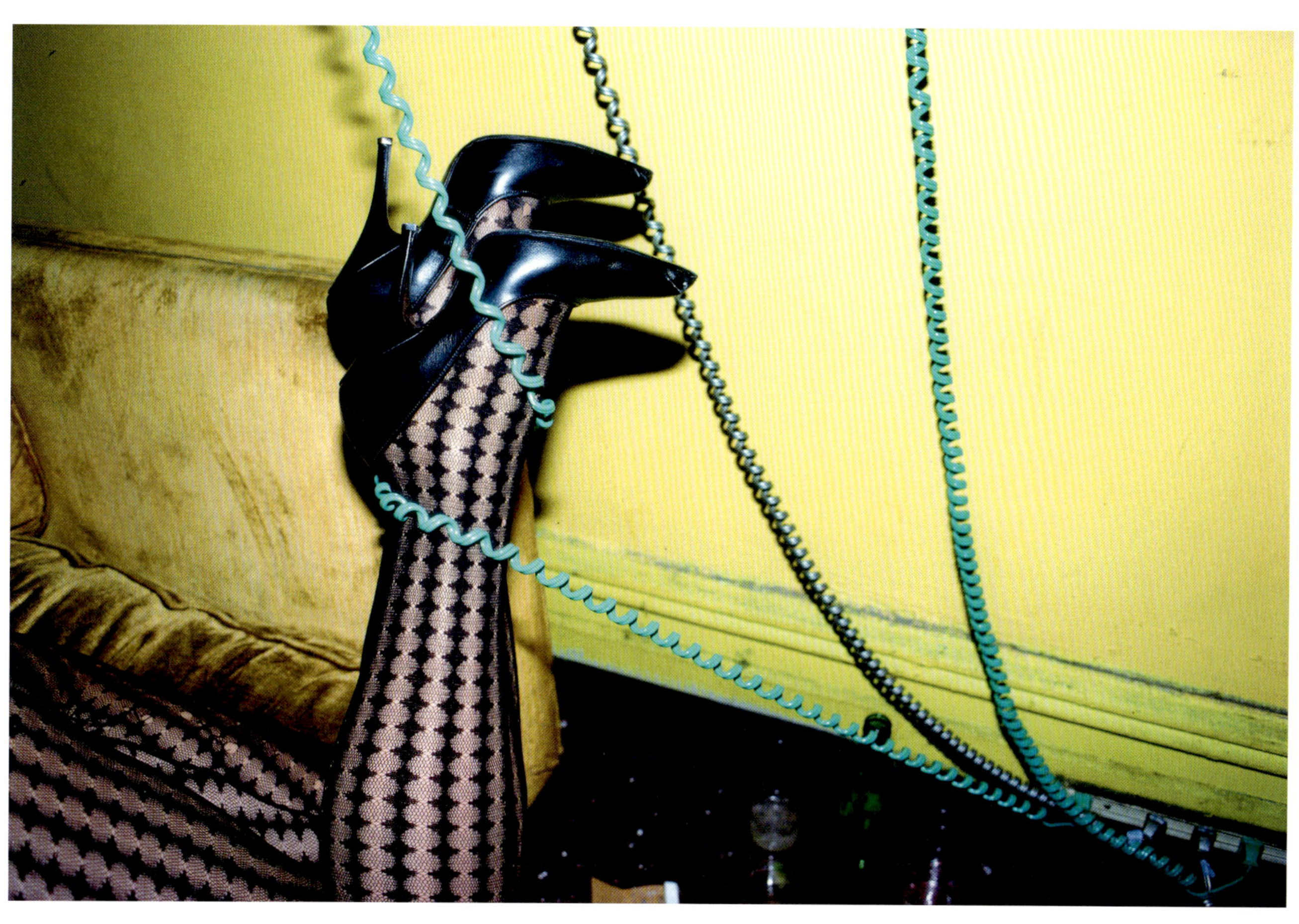

Danceteria, Chelsea, early 1980s

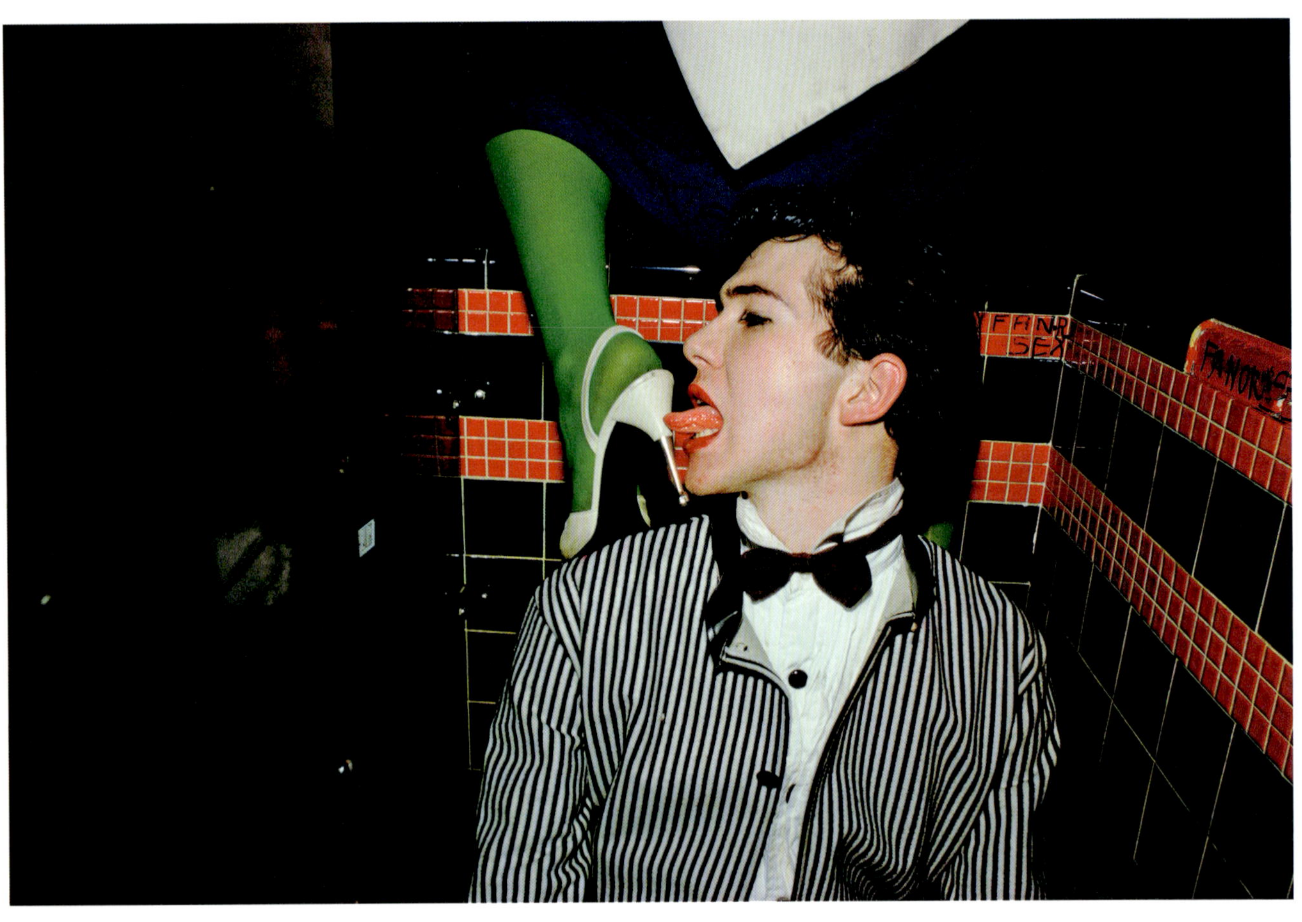

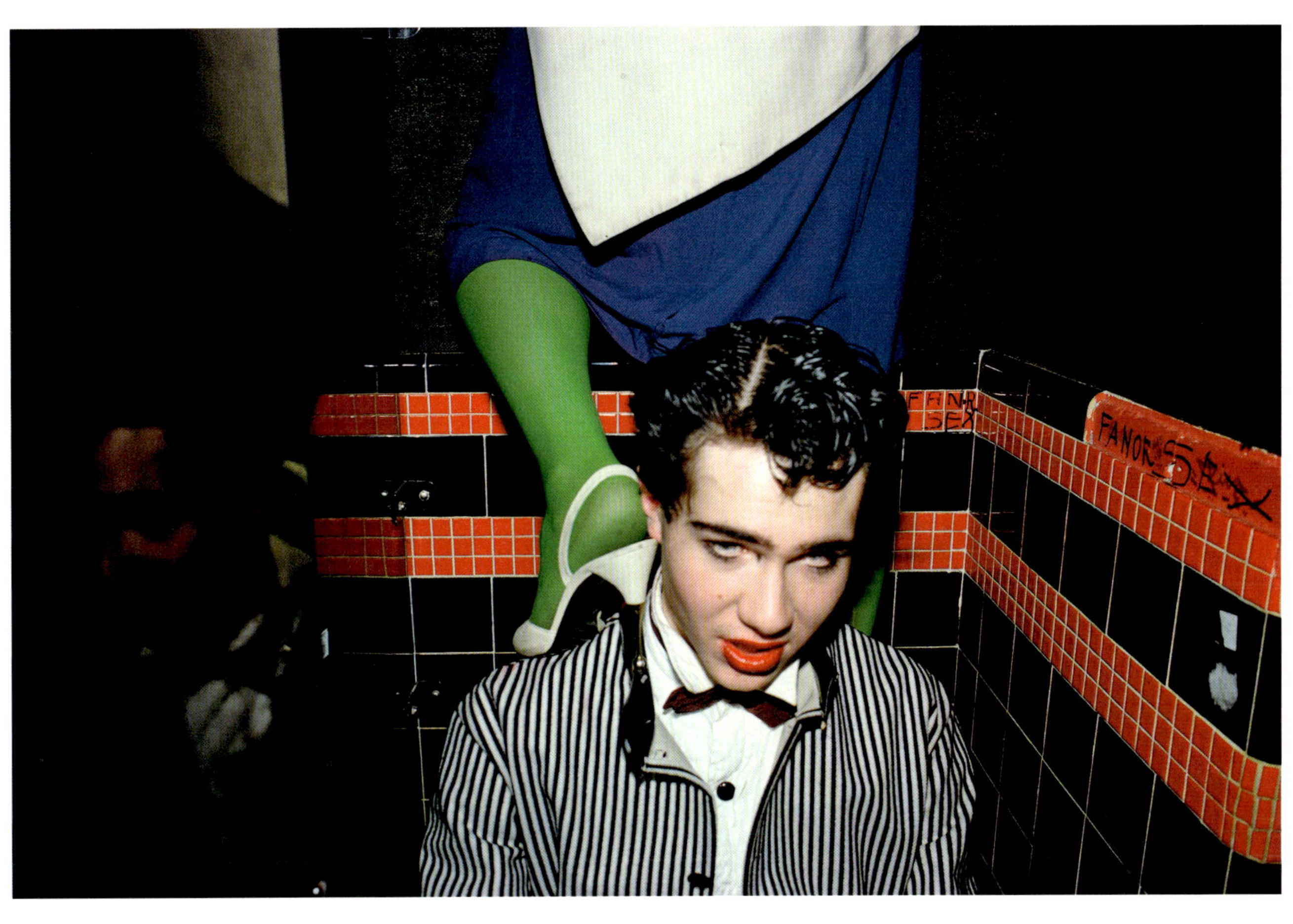

TR3 club, Tribeca, early 1980s

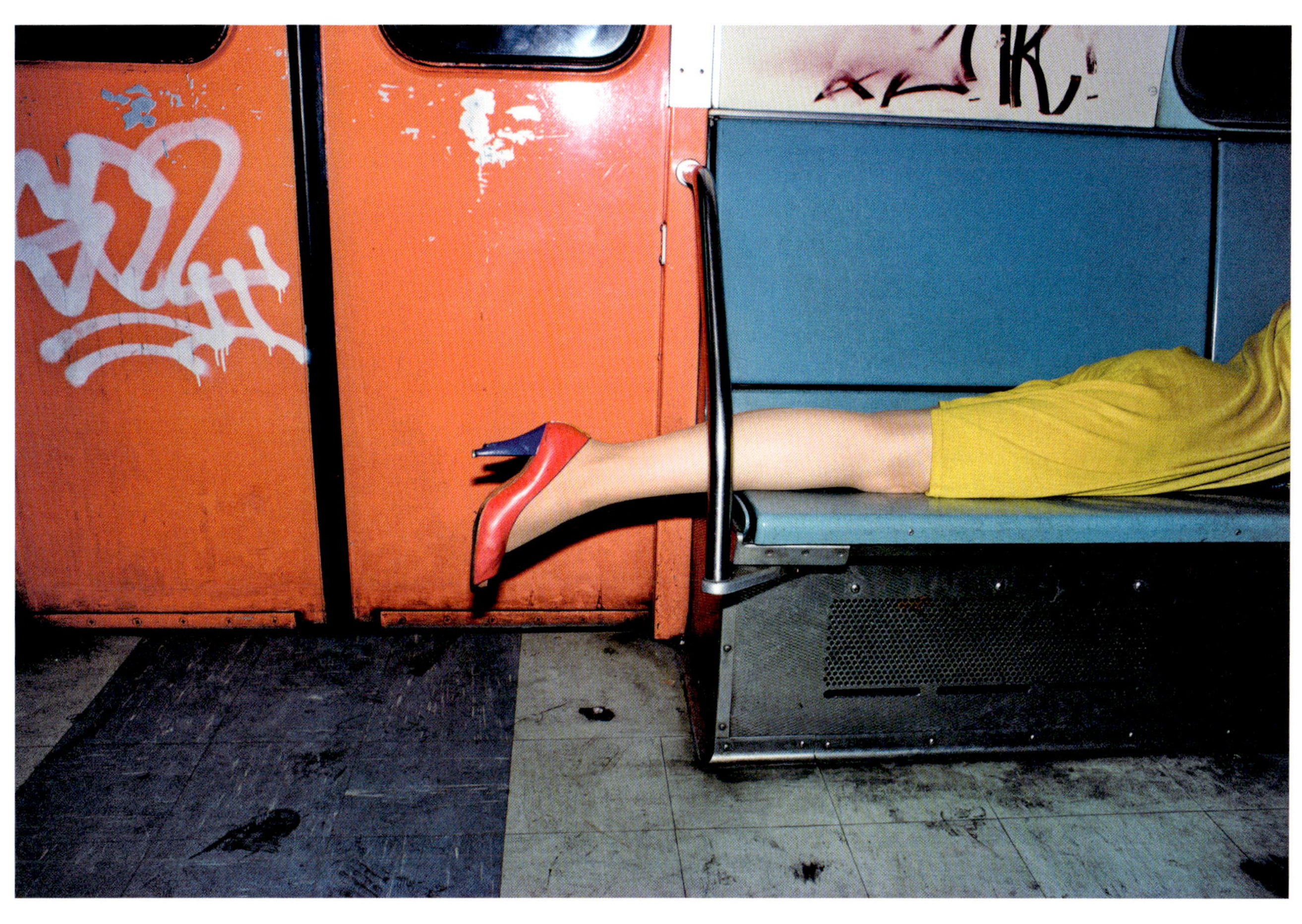

New York City Subway, late 1970s

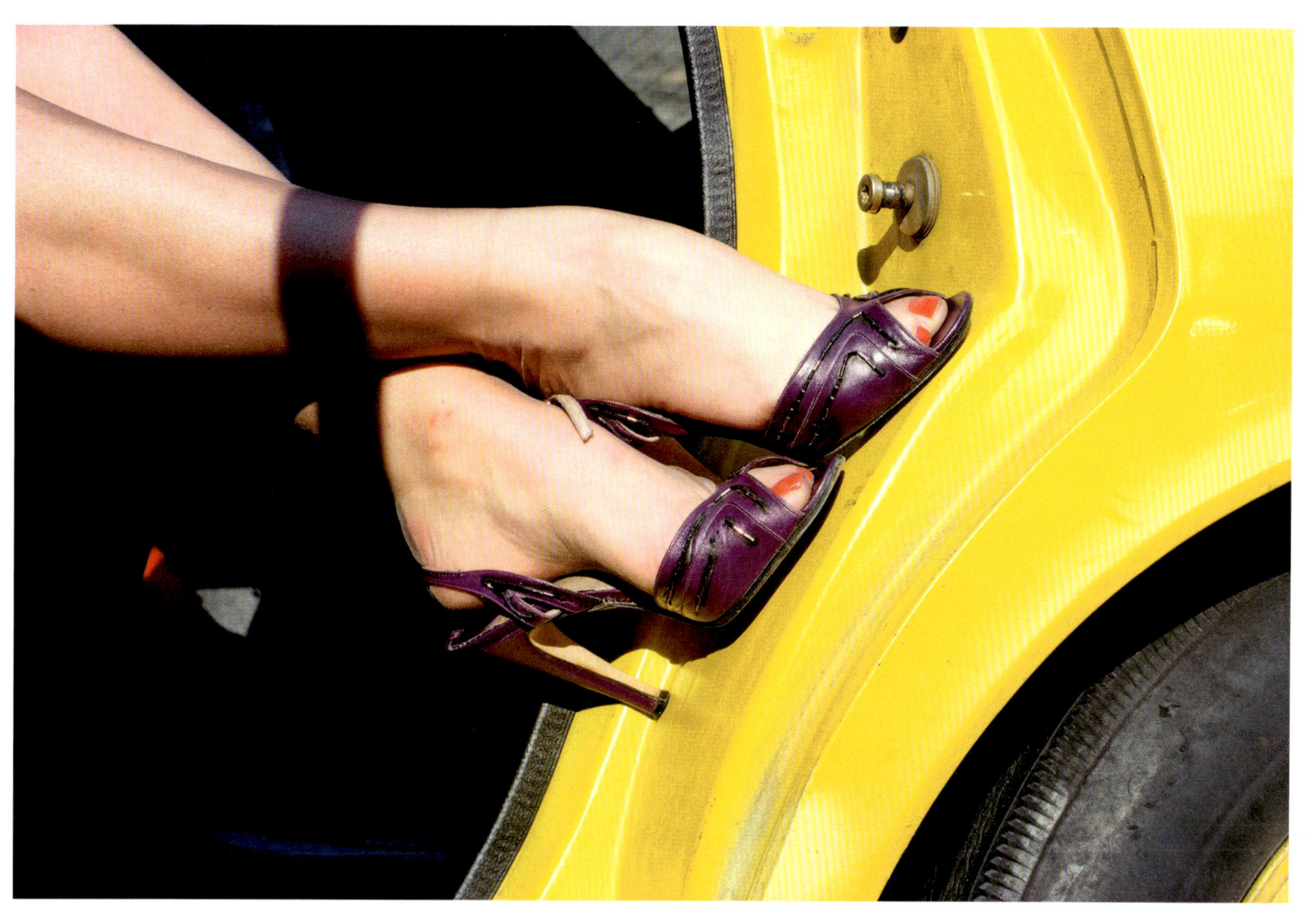

SoHo, Manhattan, early 1980s

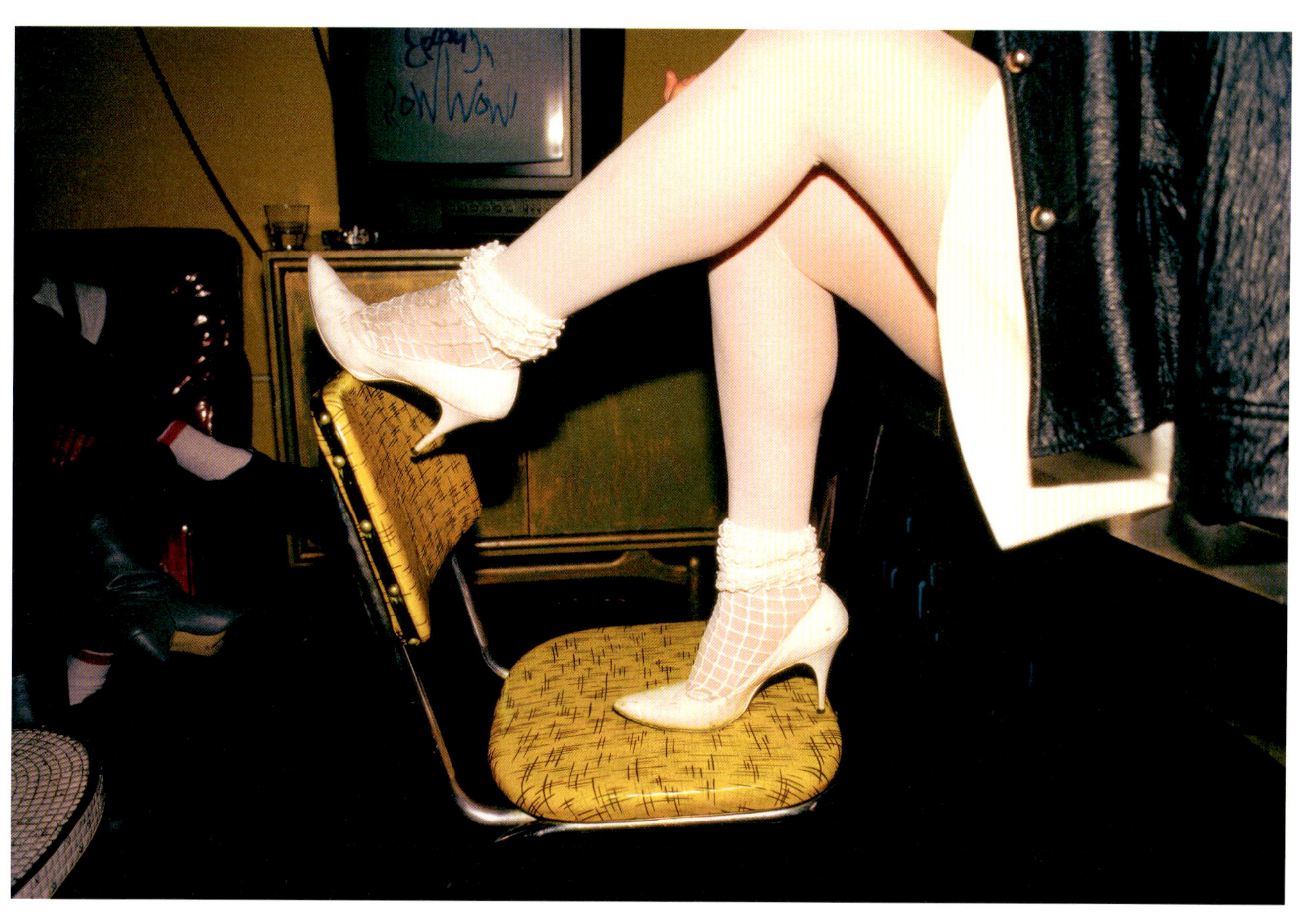

Danceteria, Chelsea, early 1980s

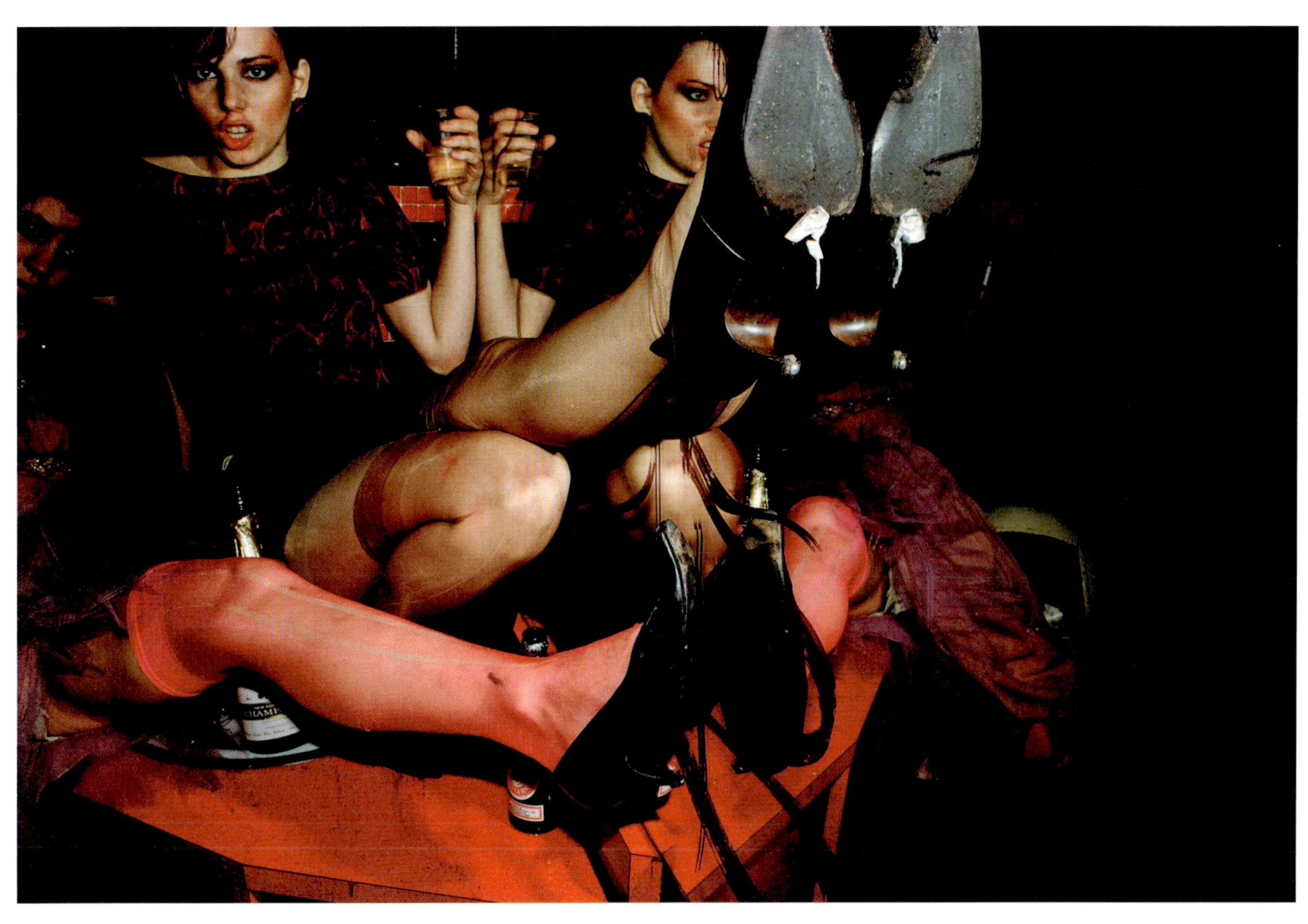

TR3 club, Tribeca, early 1980s

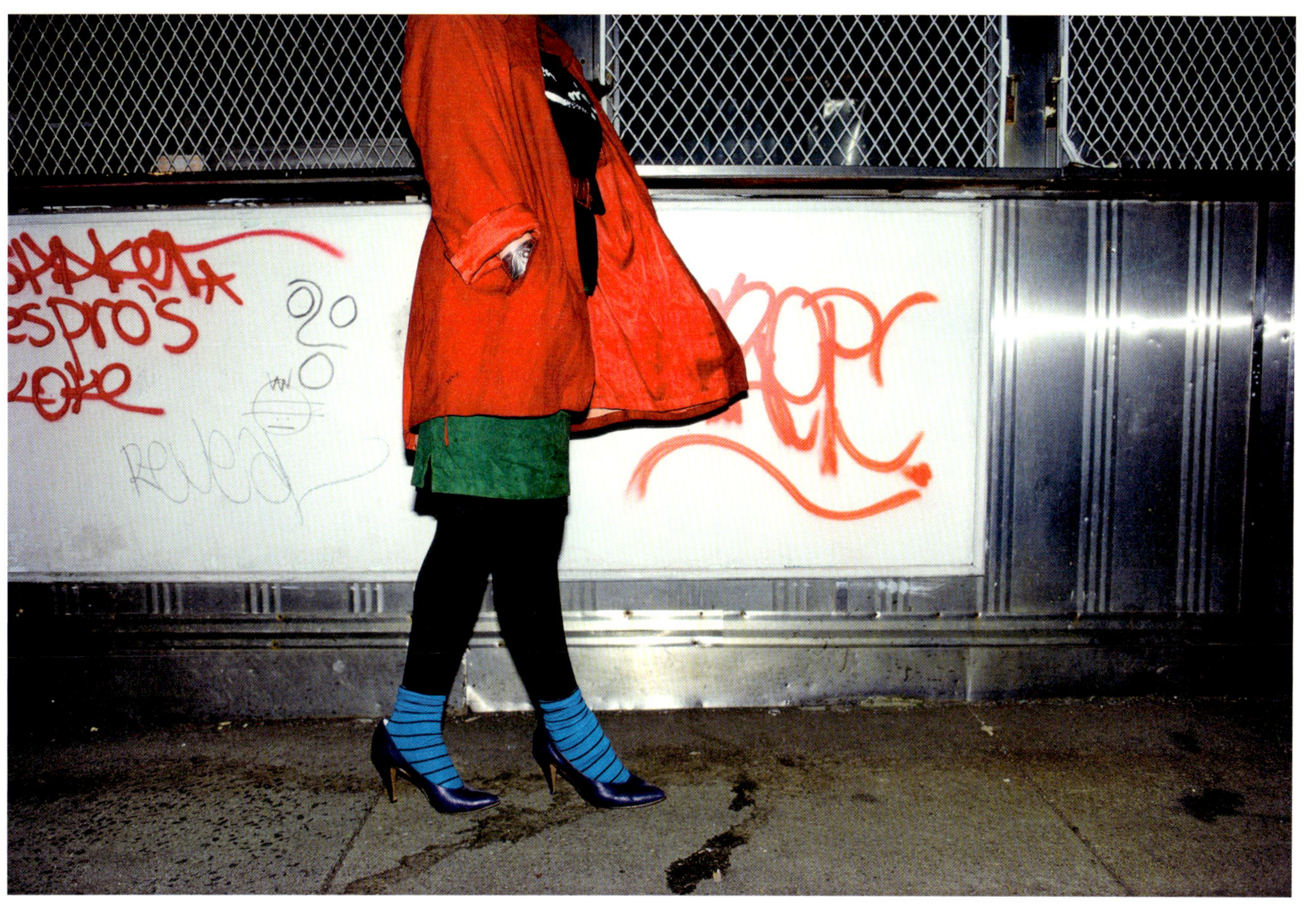

Outside Mudd Club, Tribeca, early 1980s

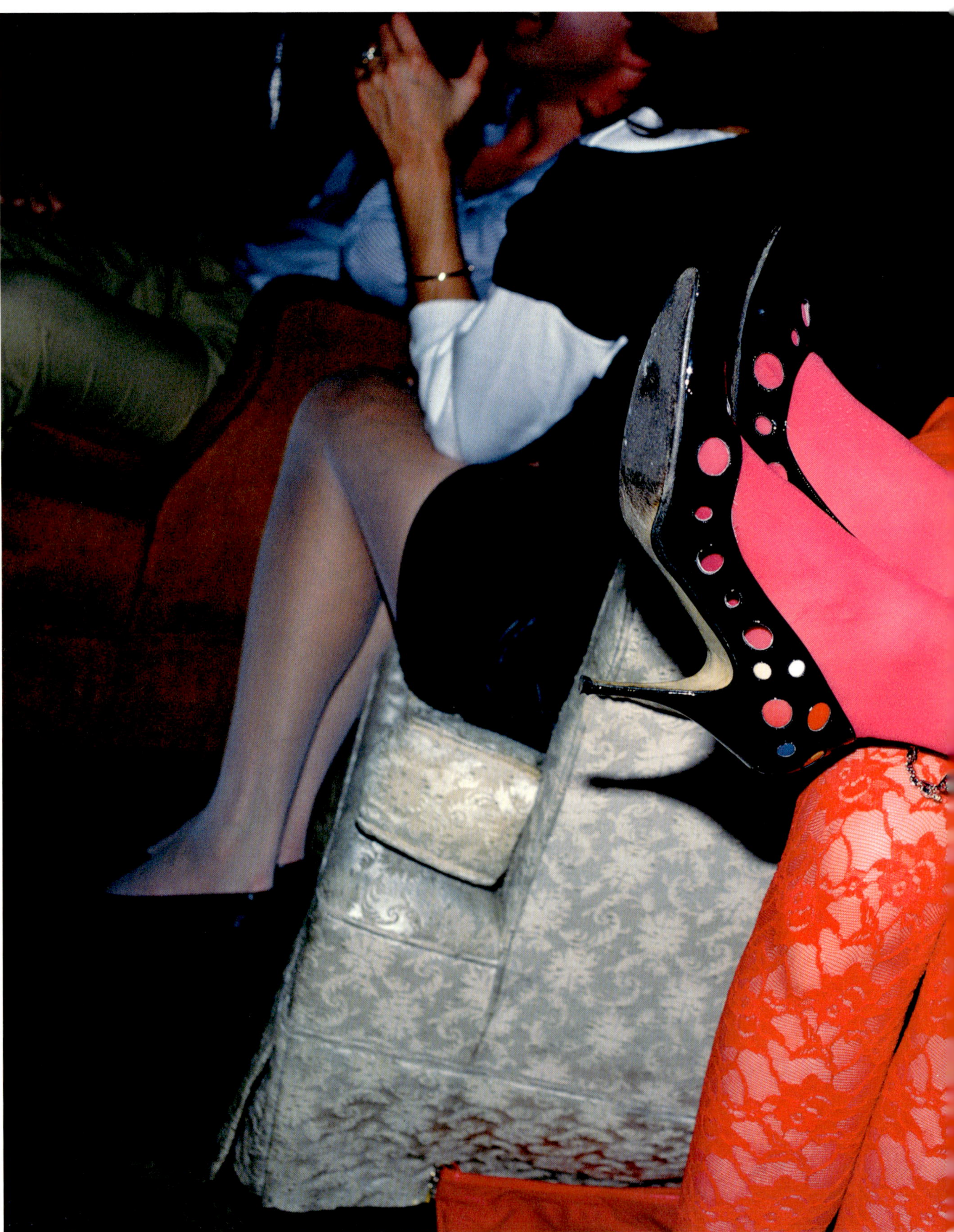

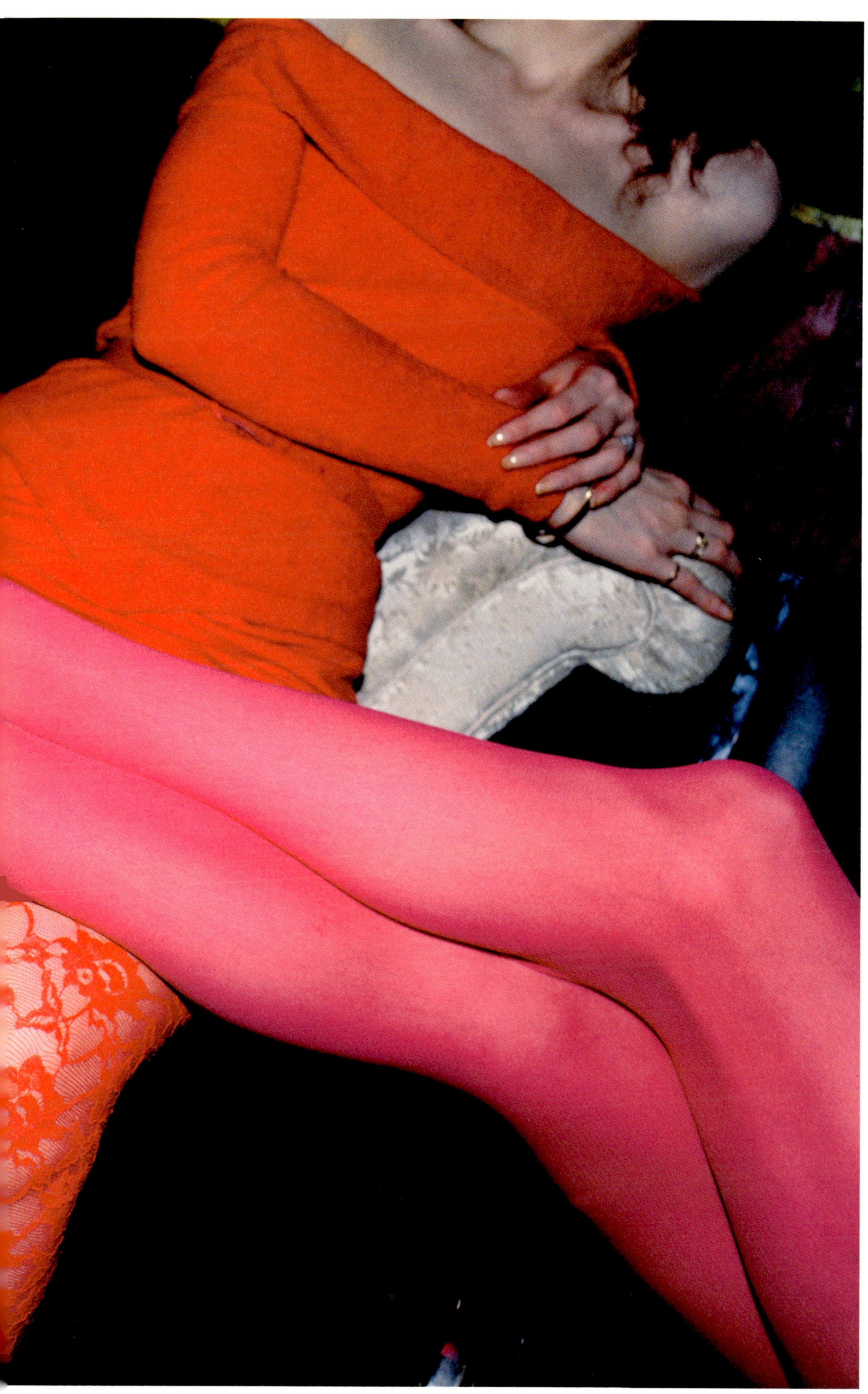

Previous pages: Danceteria, Chelsea, early 1980s

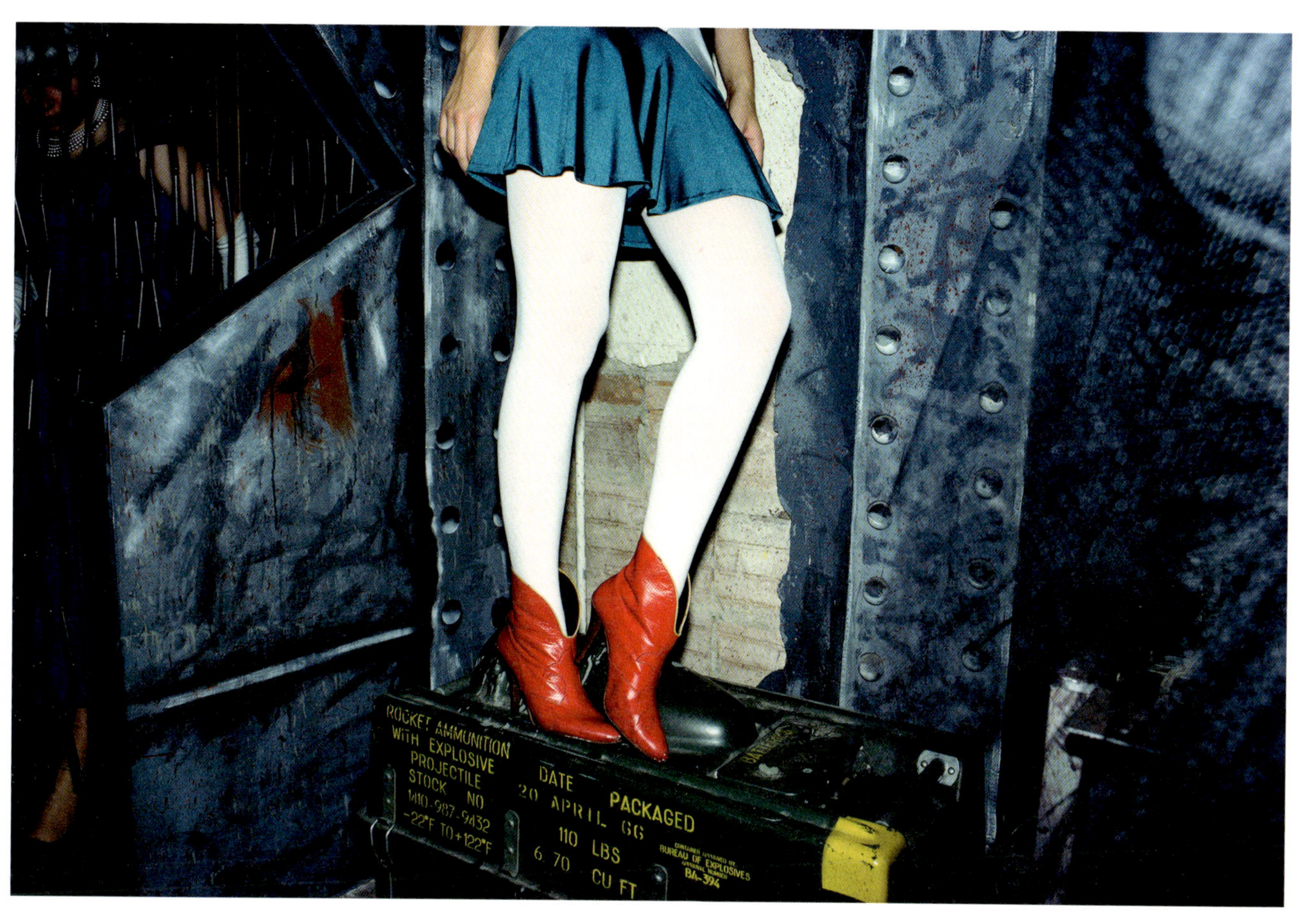

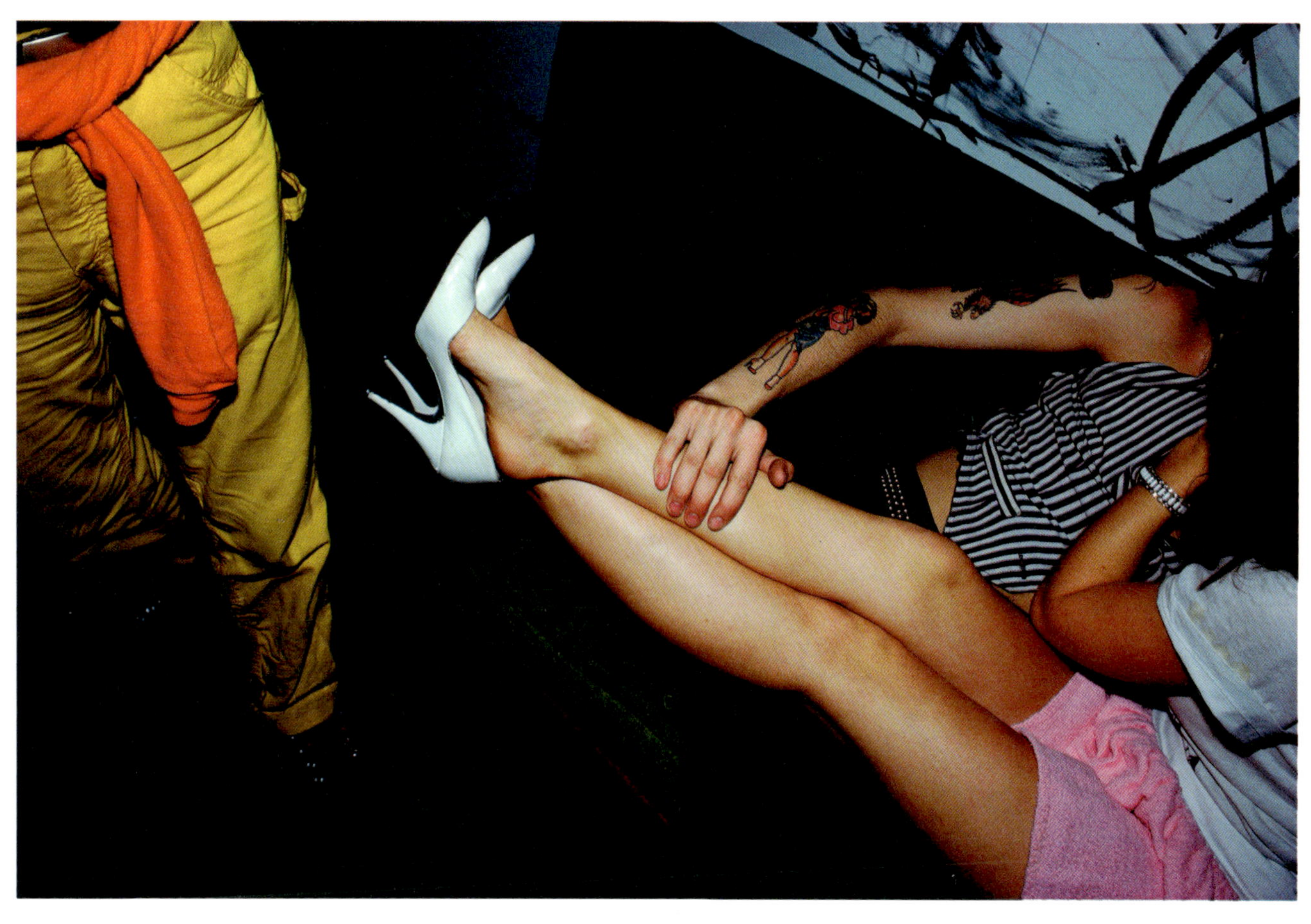

Danceteria, Chelsea, early 1980s

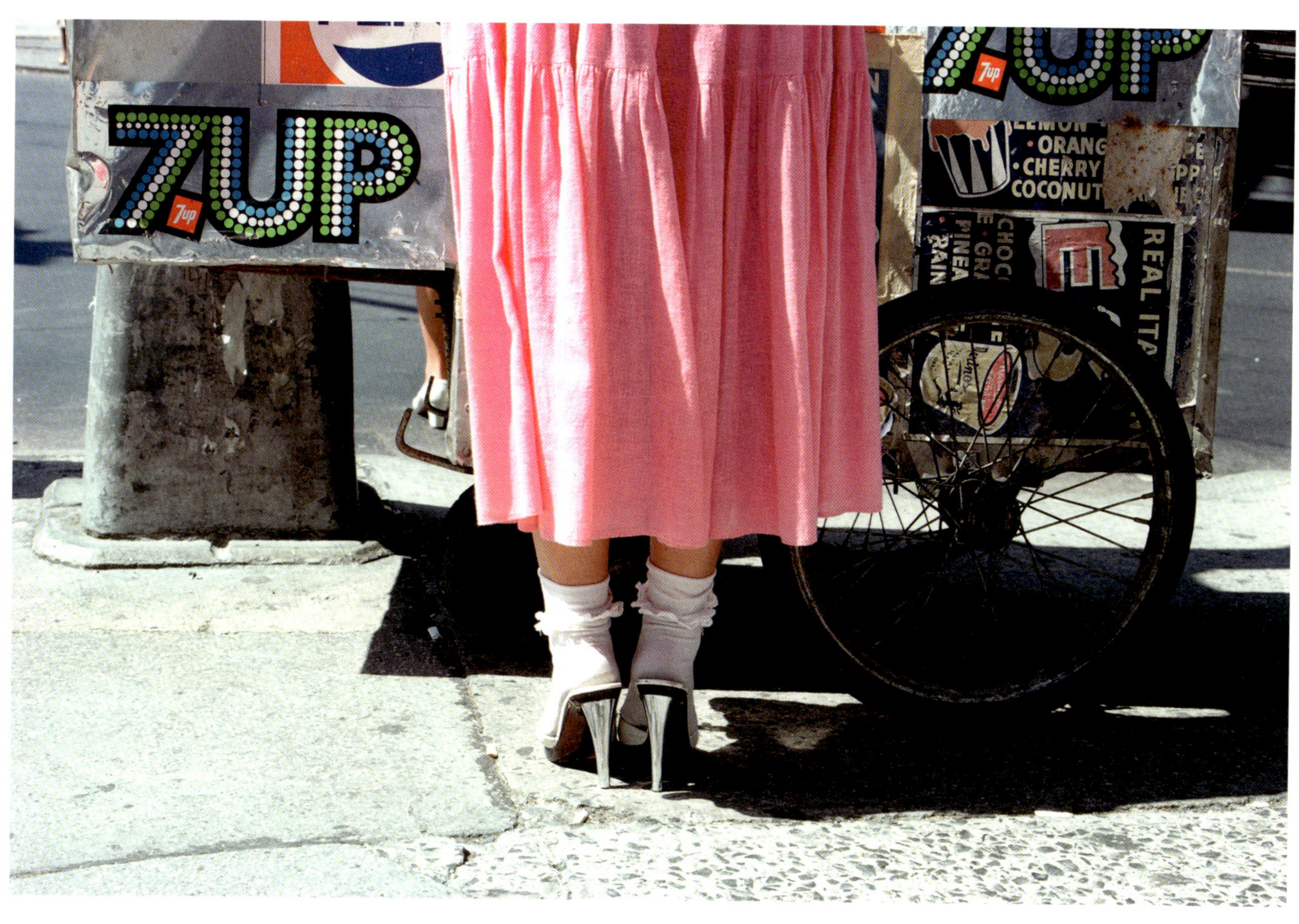

Delancey Street, Lower East Side, late 1970s

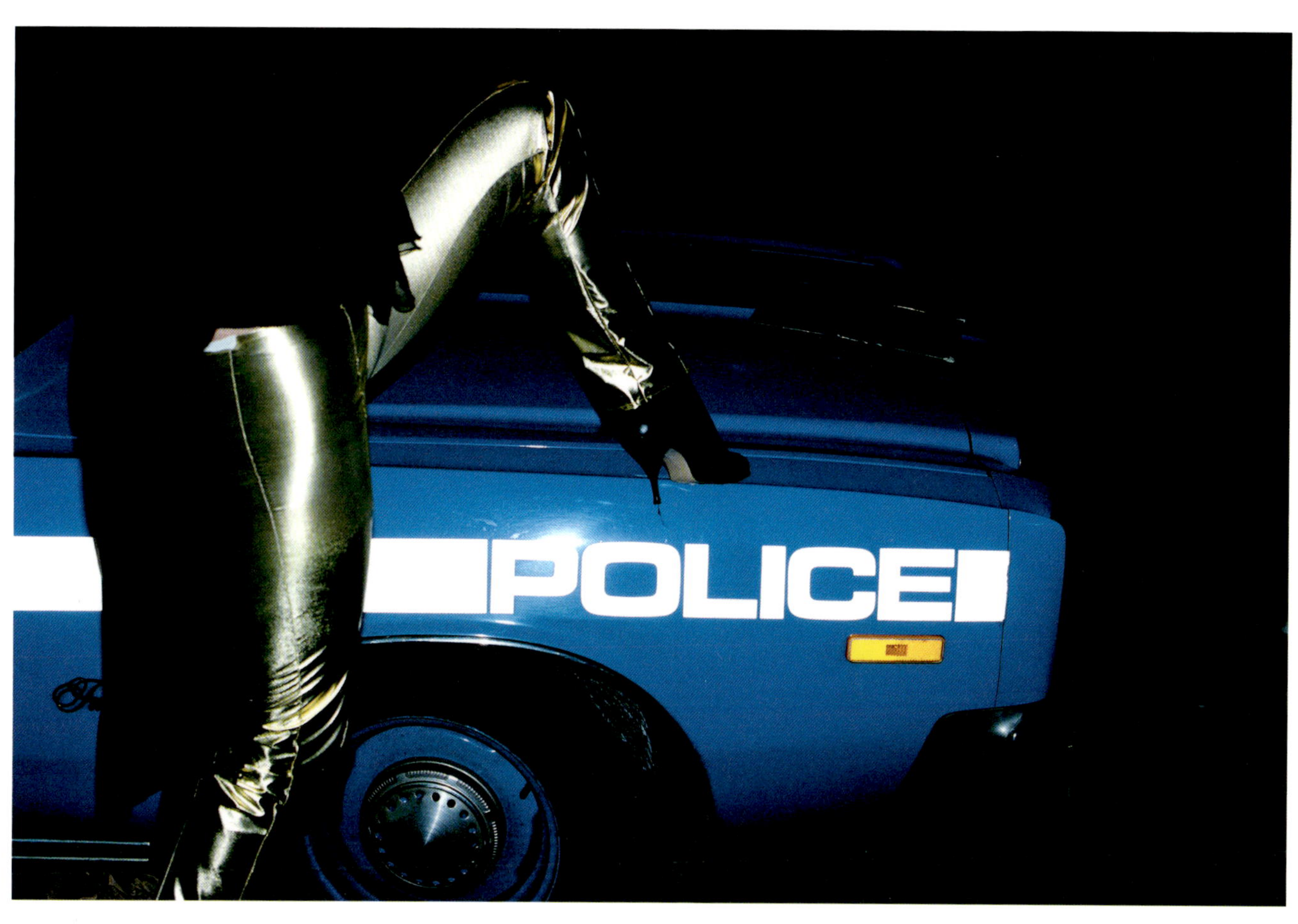

Outside CBGB, The Bowery, late 1970s

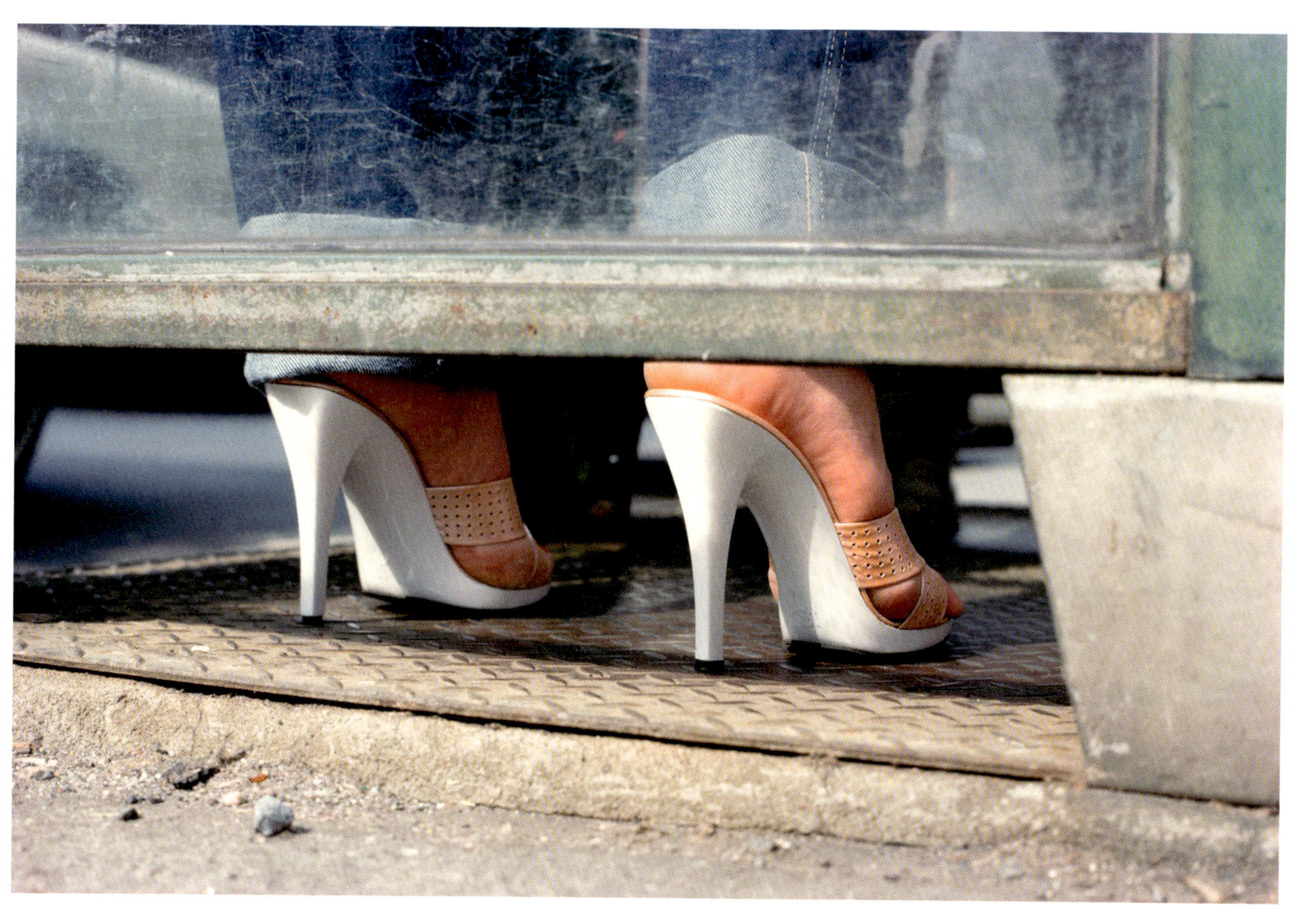

Outside Bloomingdale's, Midtown, late 1970s

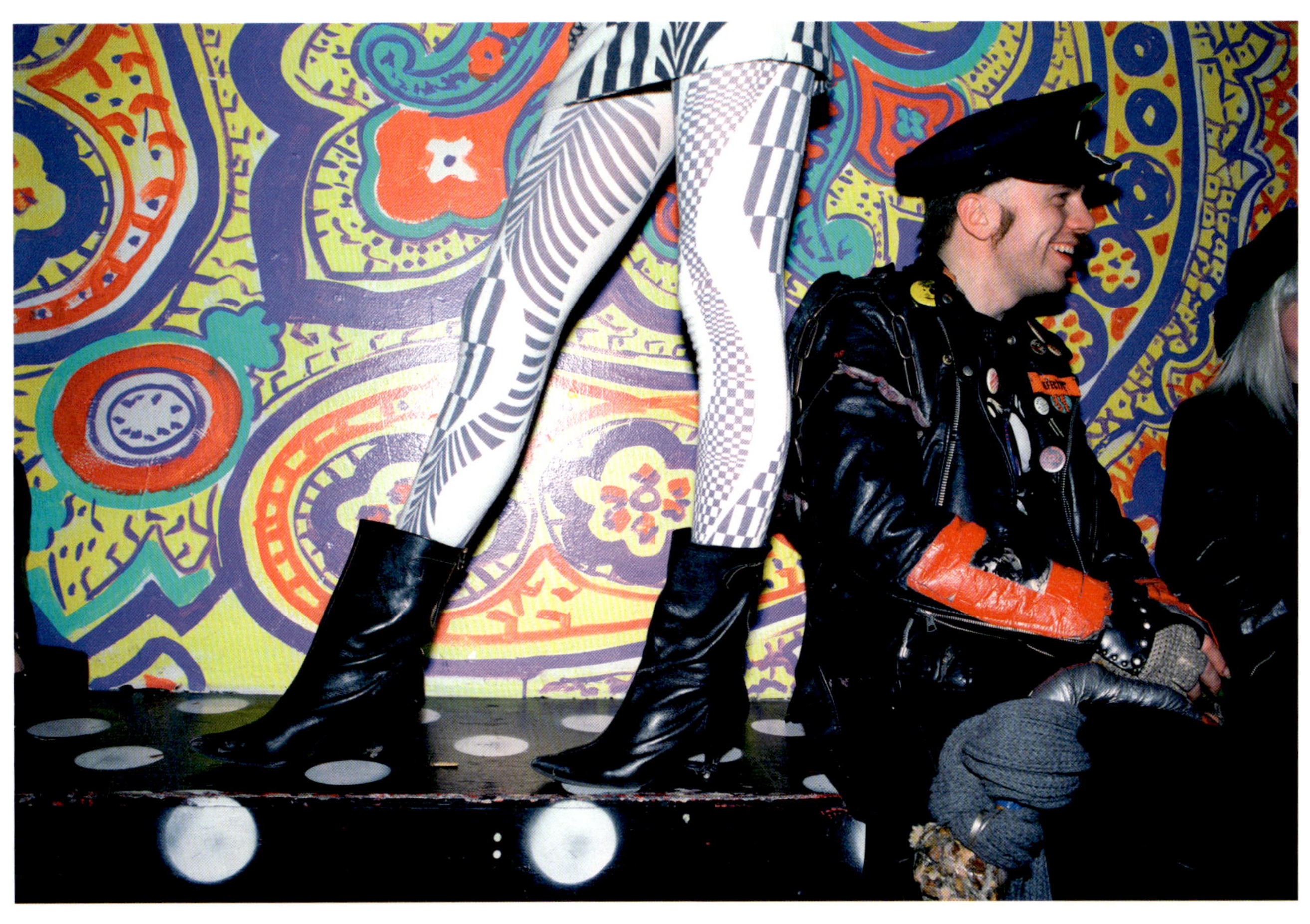

Danceteria, Chelsea, early 1980s

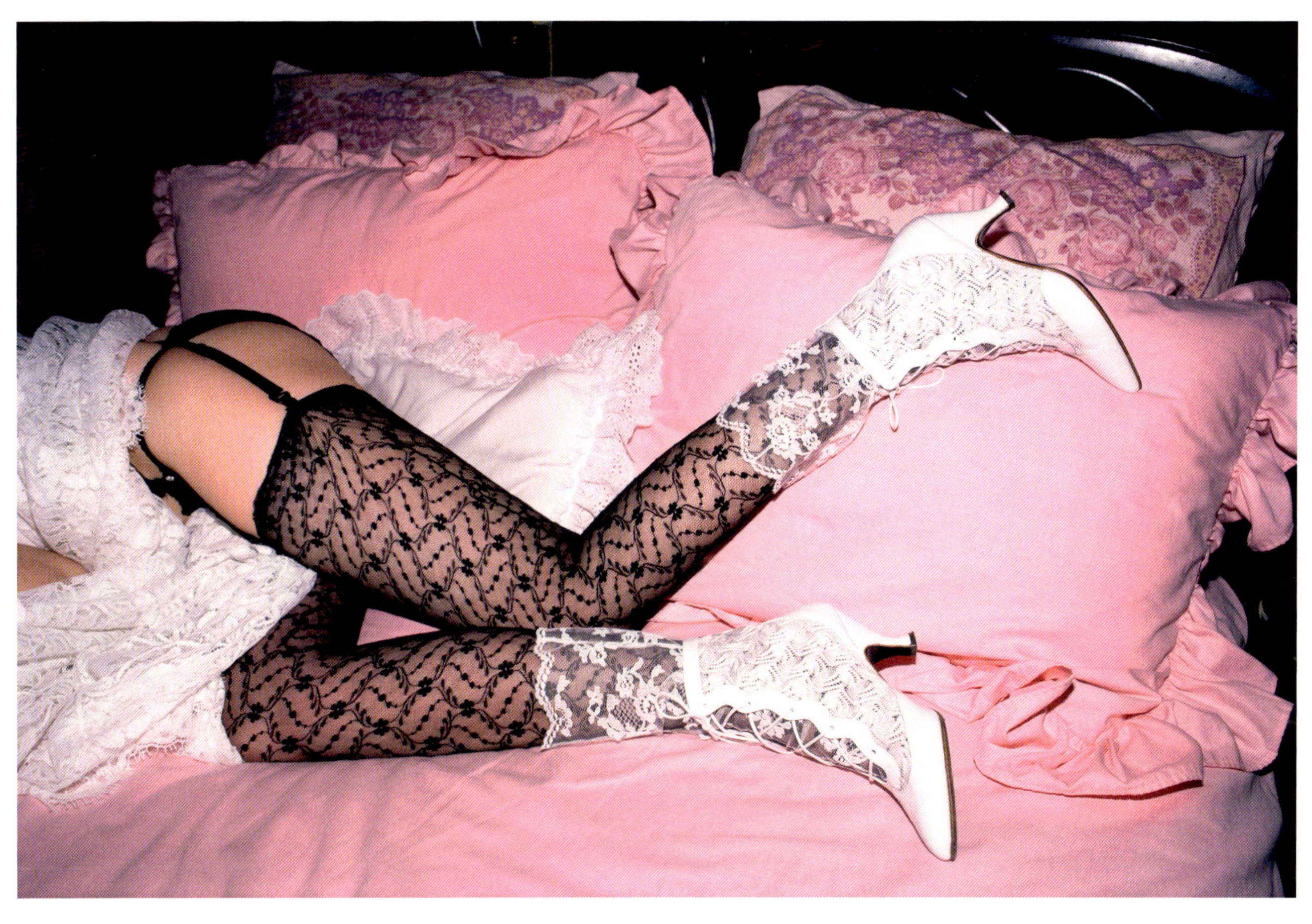

SoHo, Broadway, mid 1980s

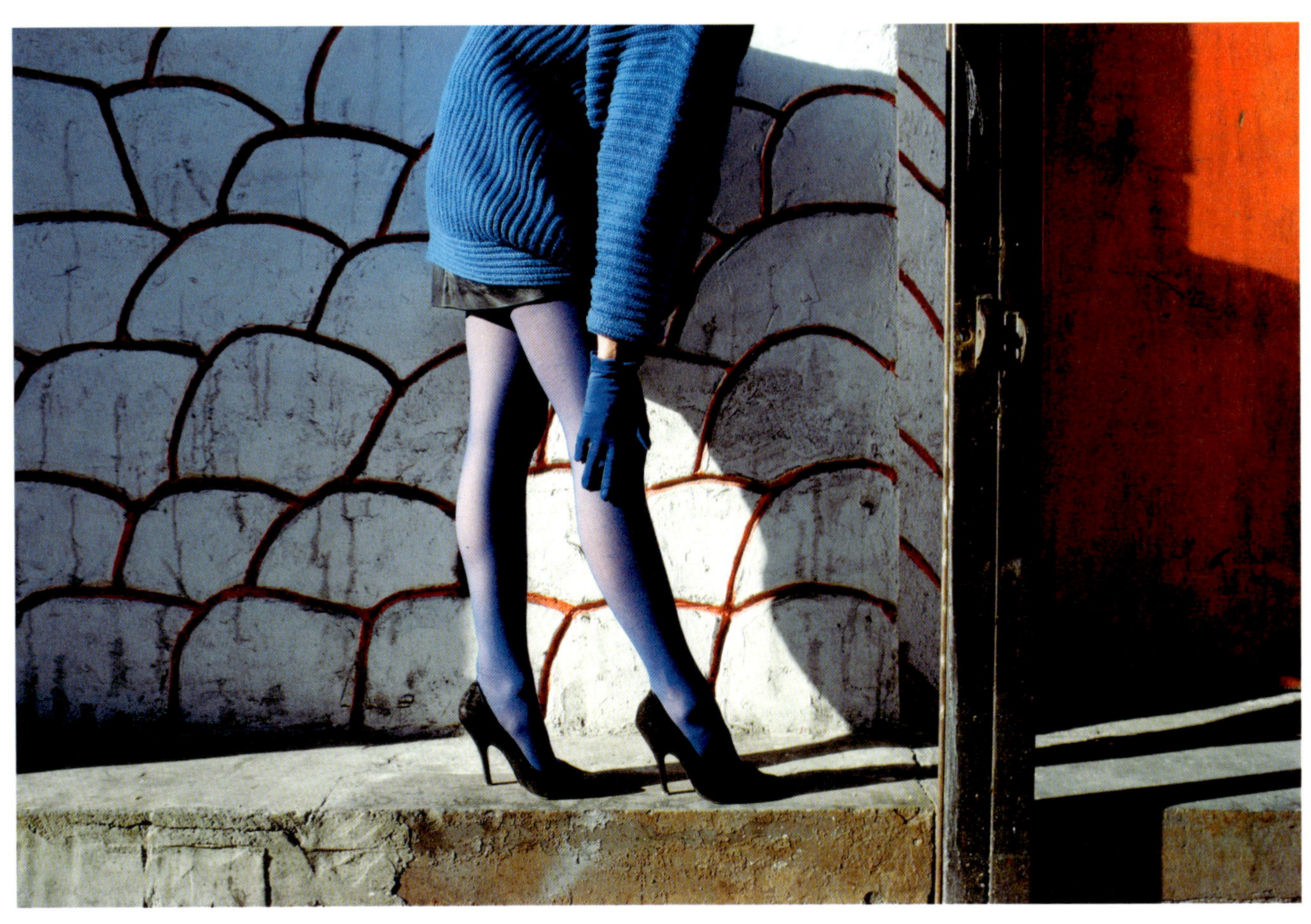

West Side, Manhattan, early 1980s

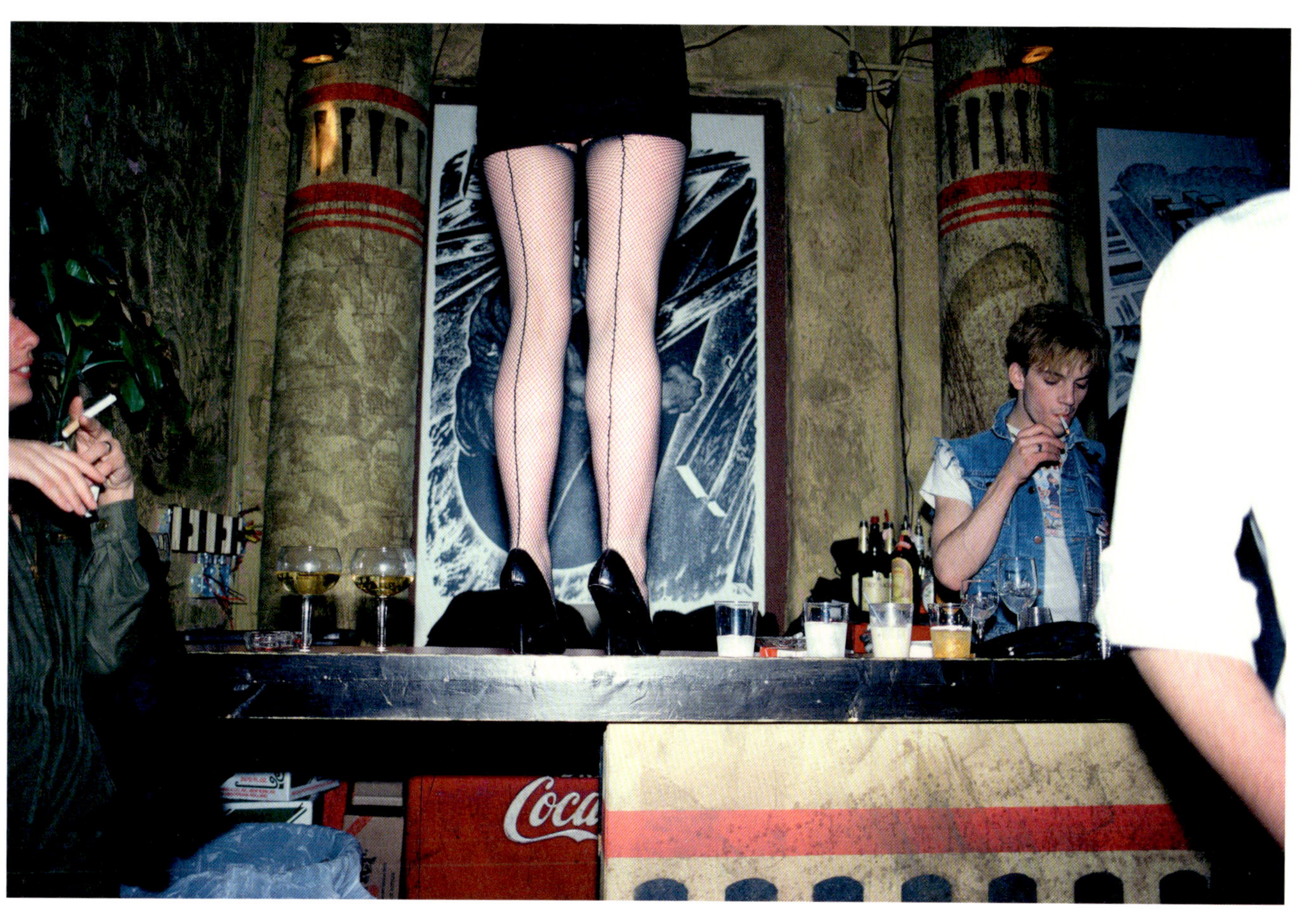

Danceteria, Chelsea, early 1980s

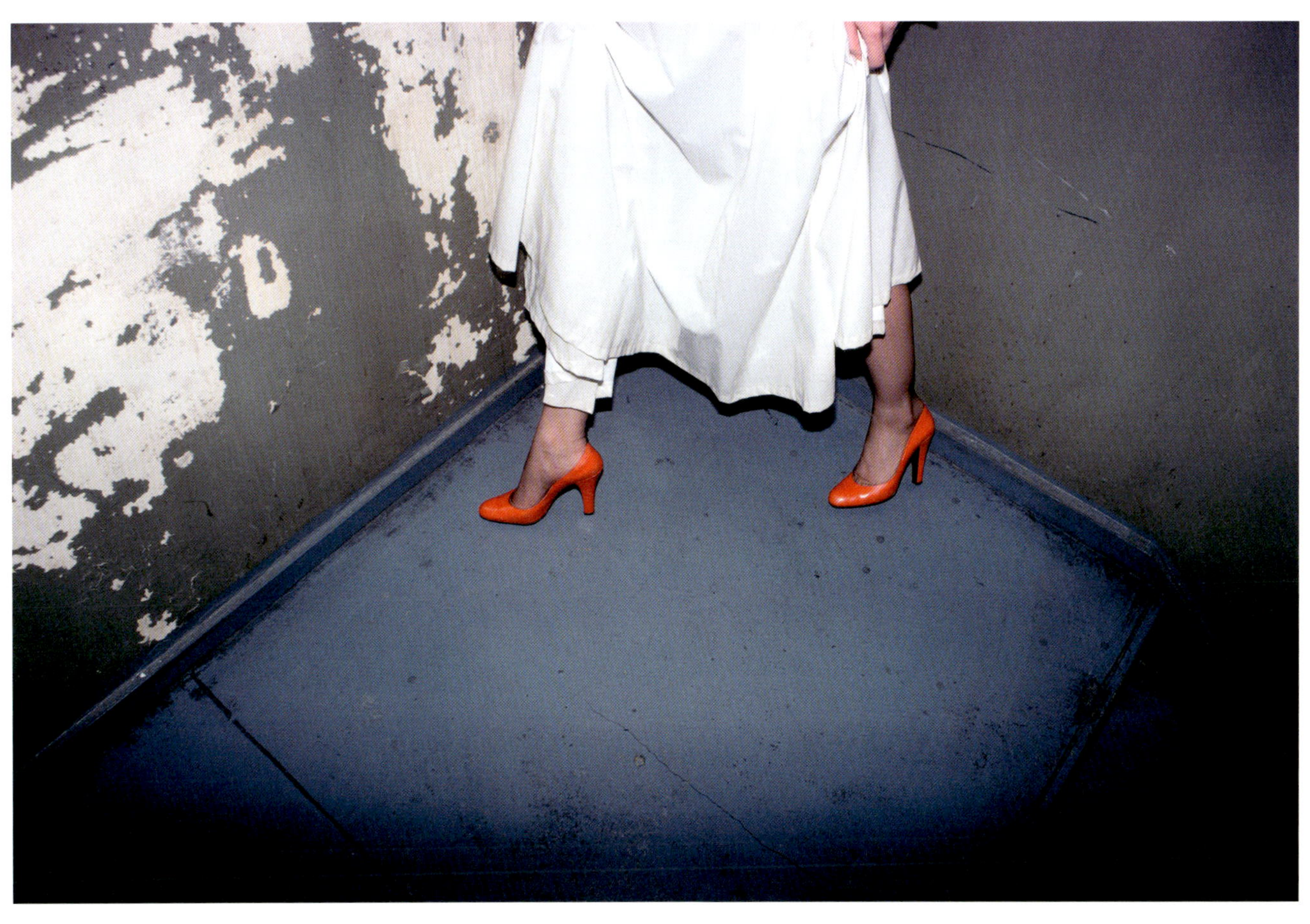

SoHo, West Broadway, late 1970s

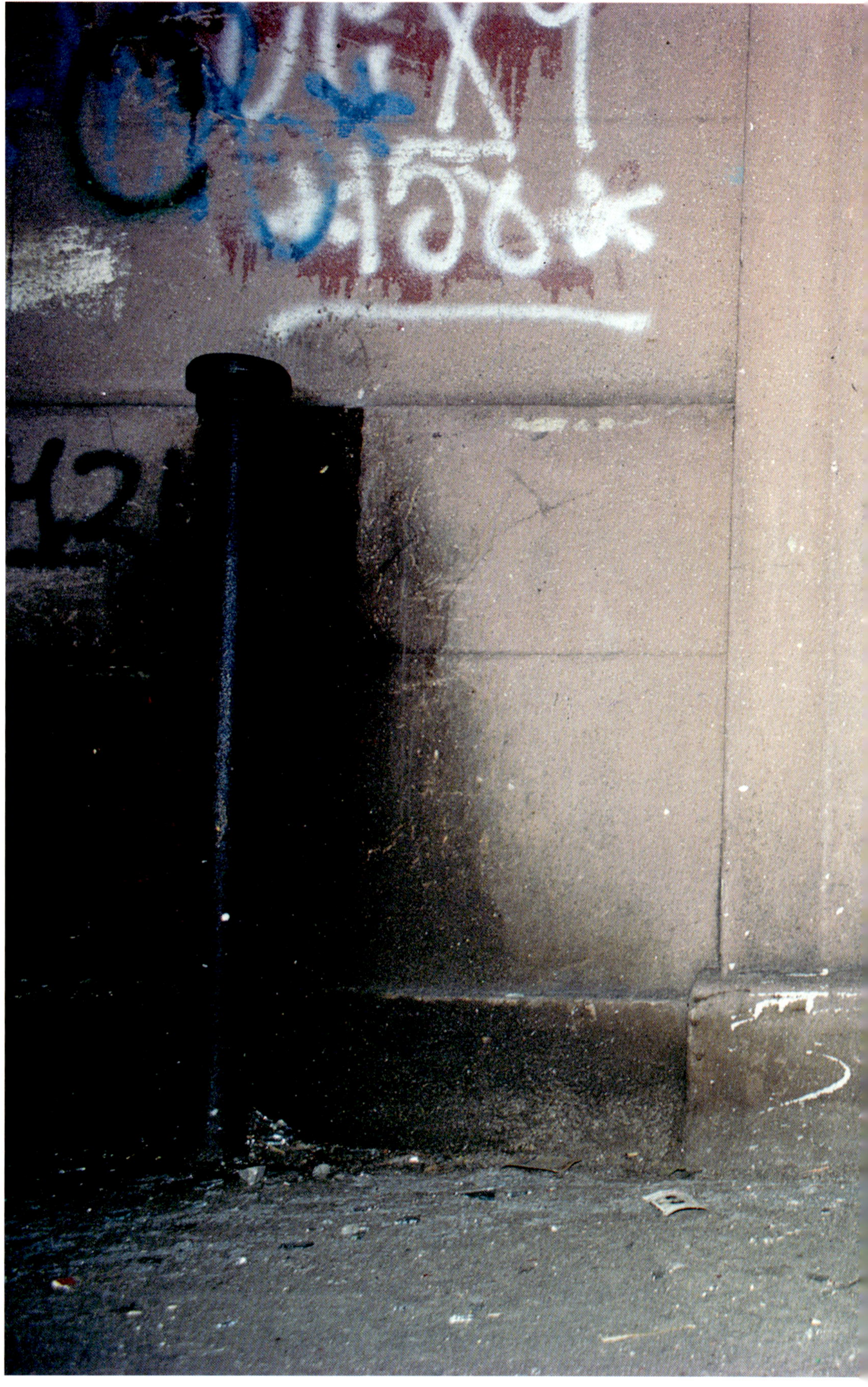

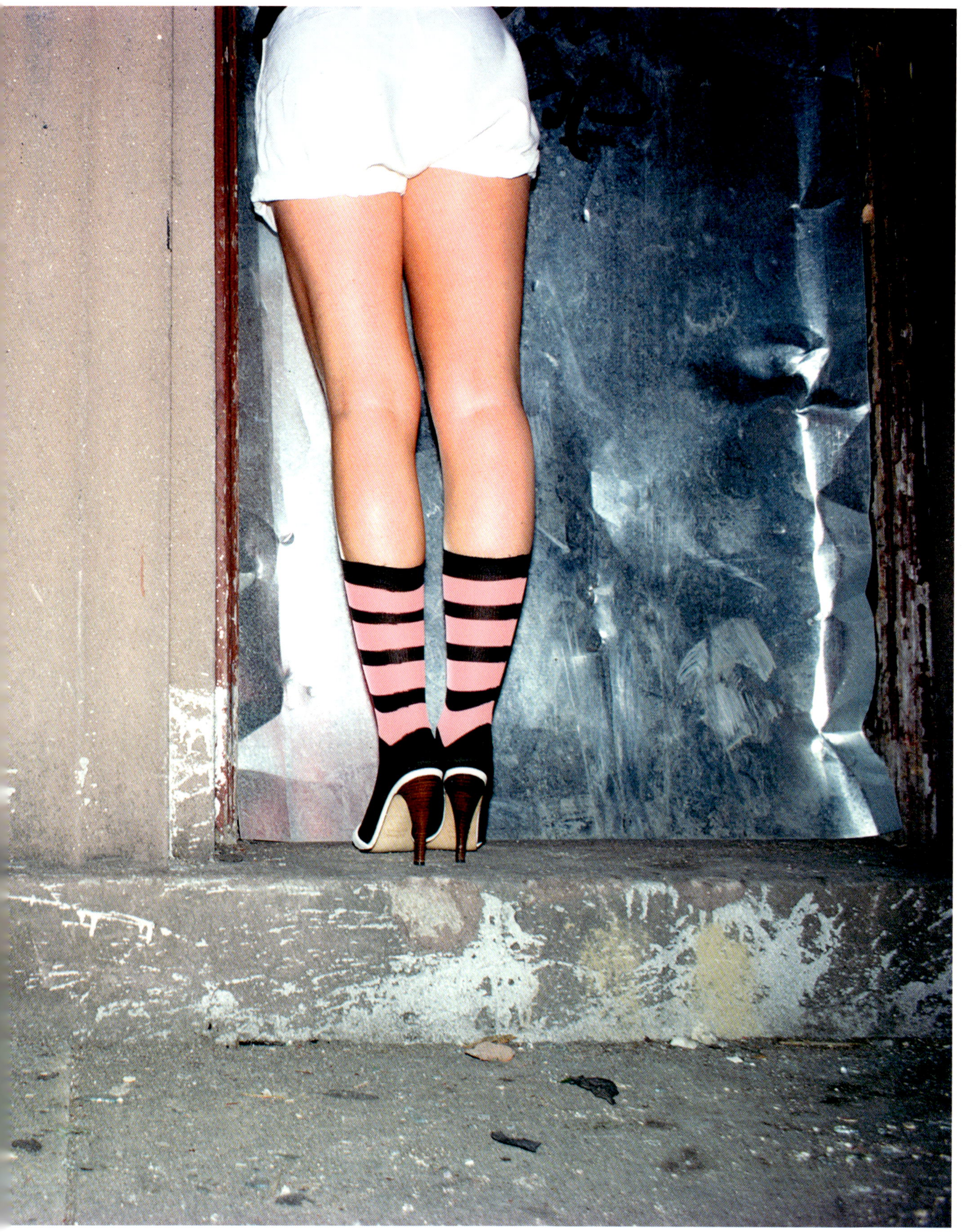

Previous pages: Upper East Side, Manhattan, late 1970s

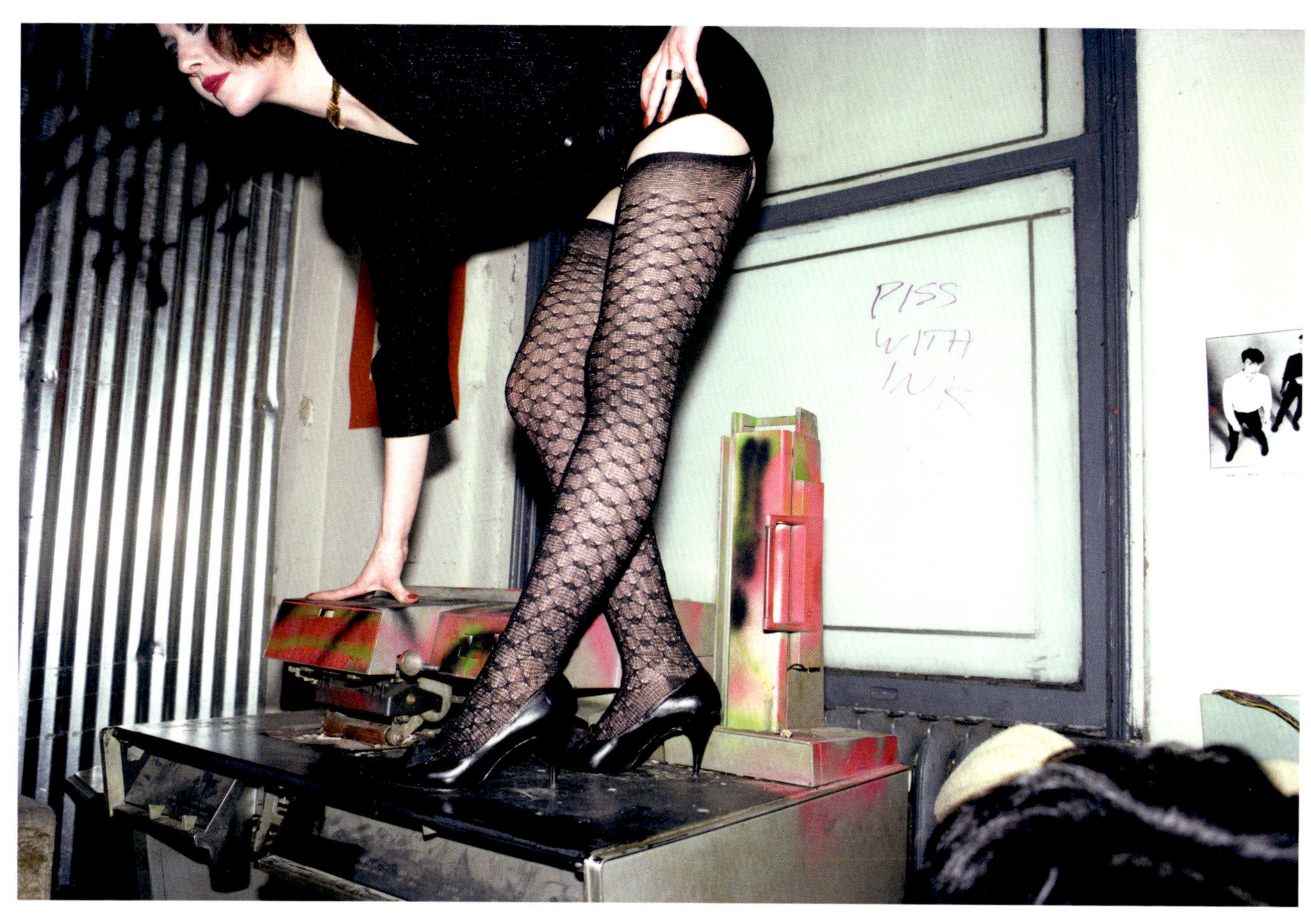

Danceteria, Chelsea, early 1980s

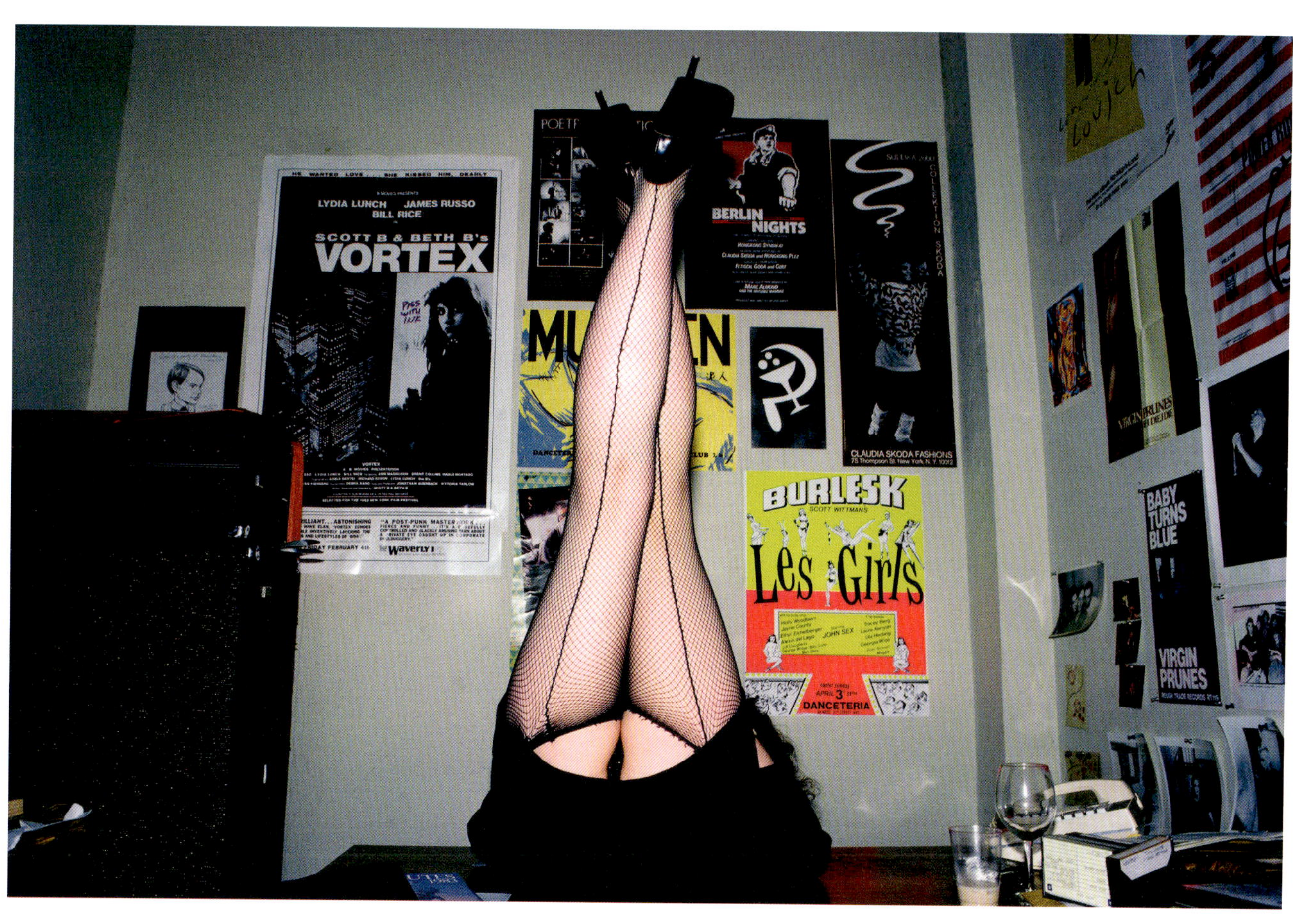

Danceteria, Chelsea, early 1980s

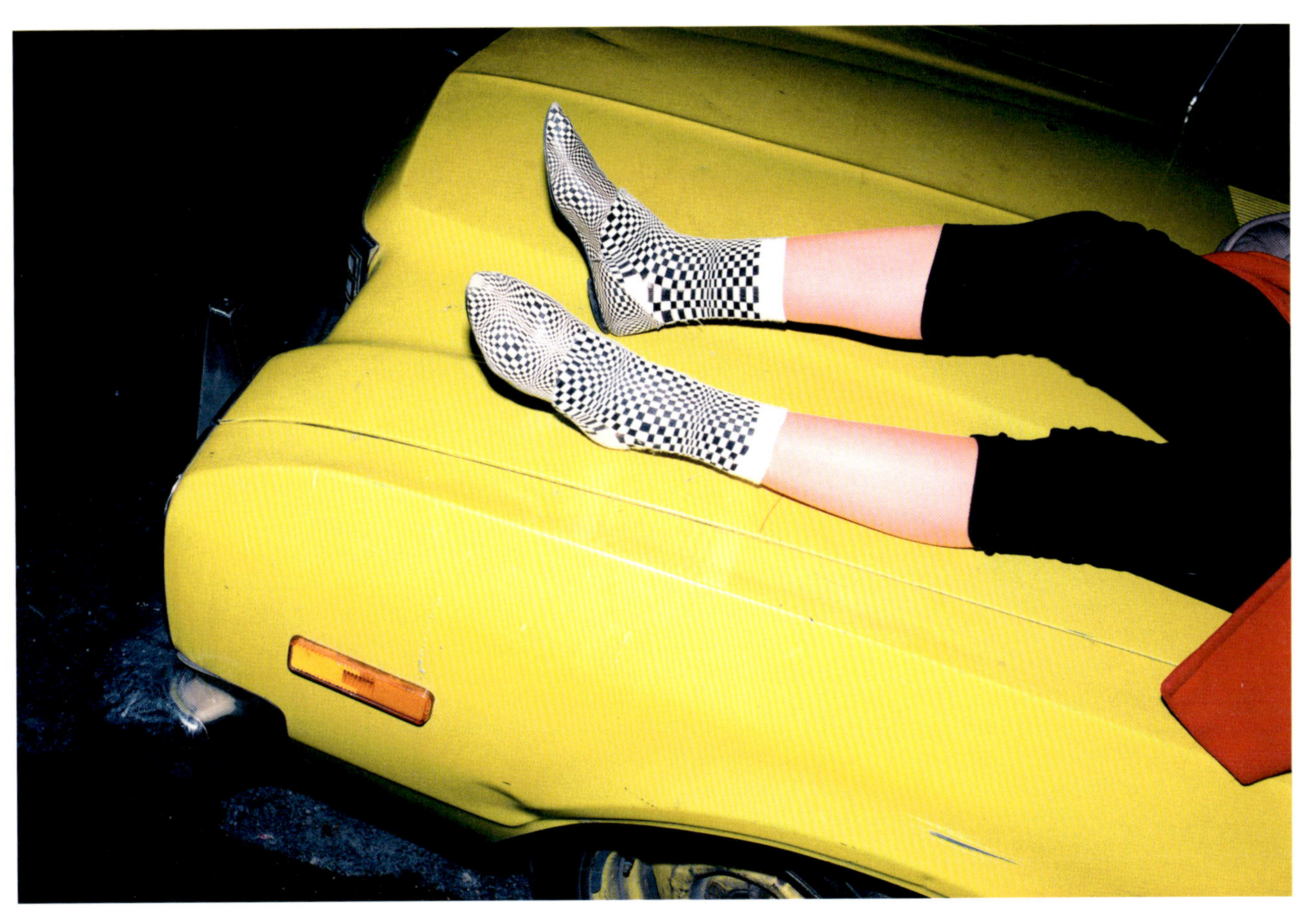

East Village, Manhattan, late 1970s

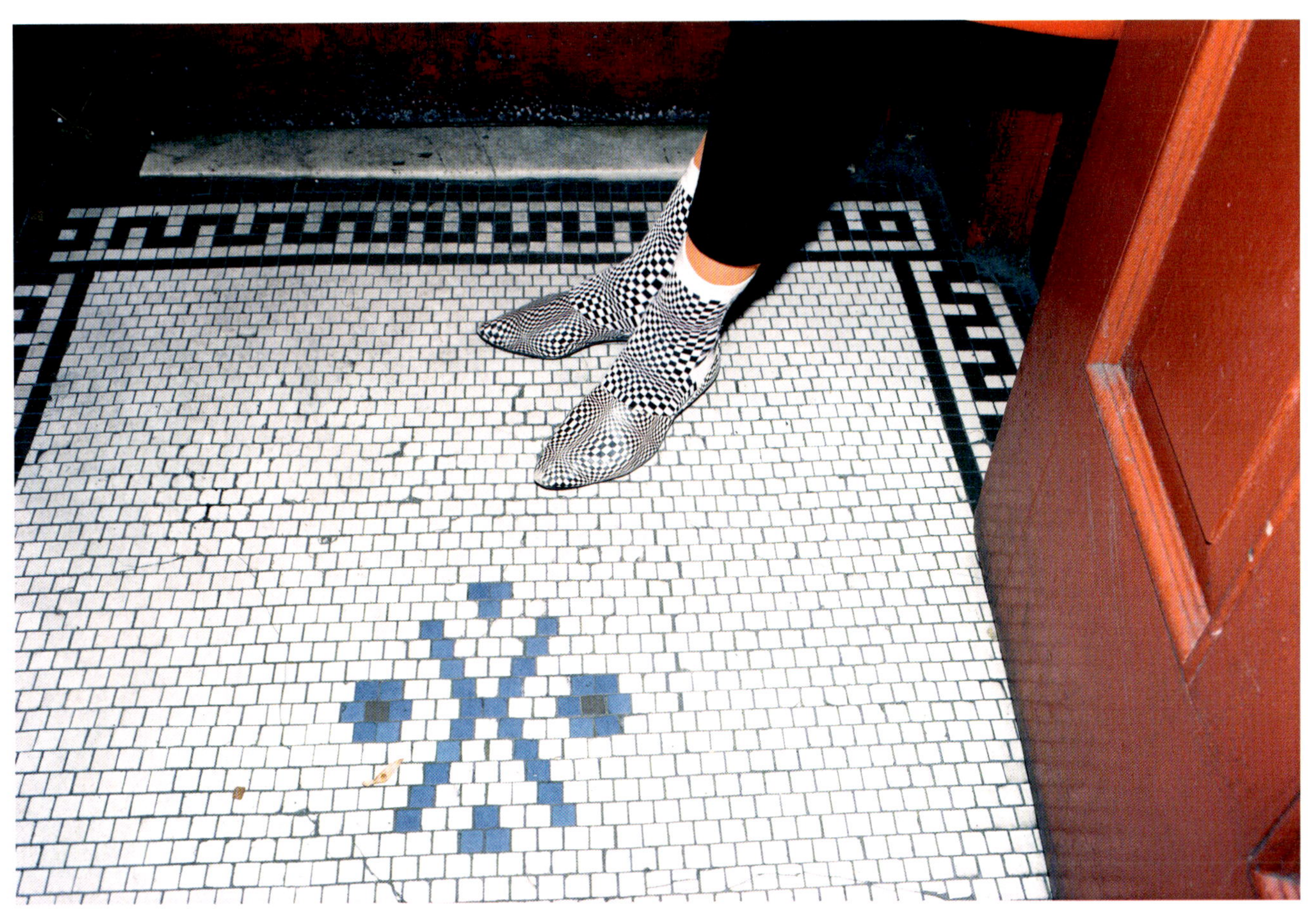

East Village, Manhattan, late 1970s

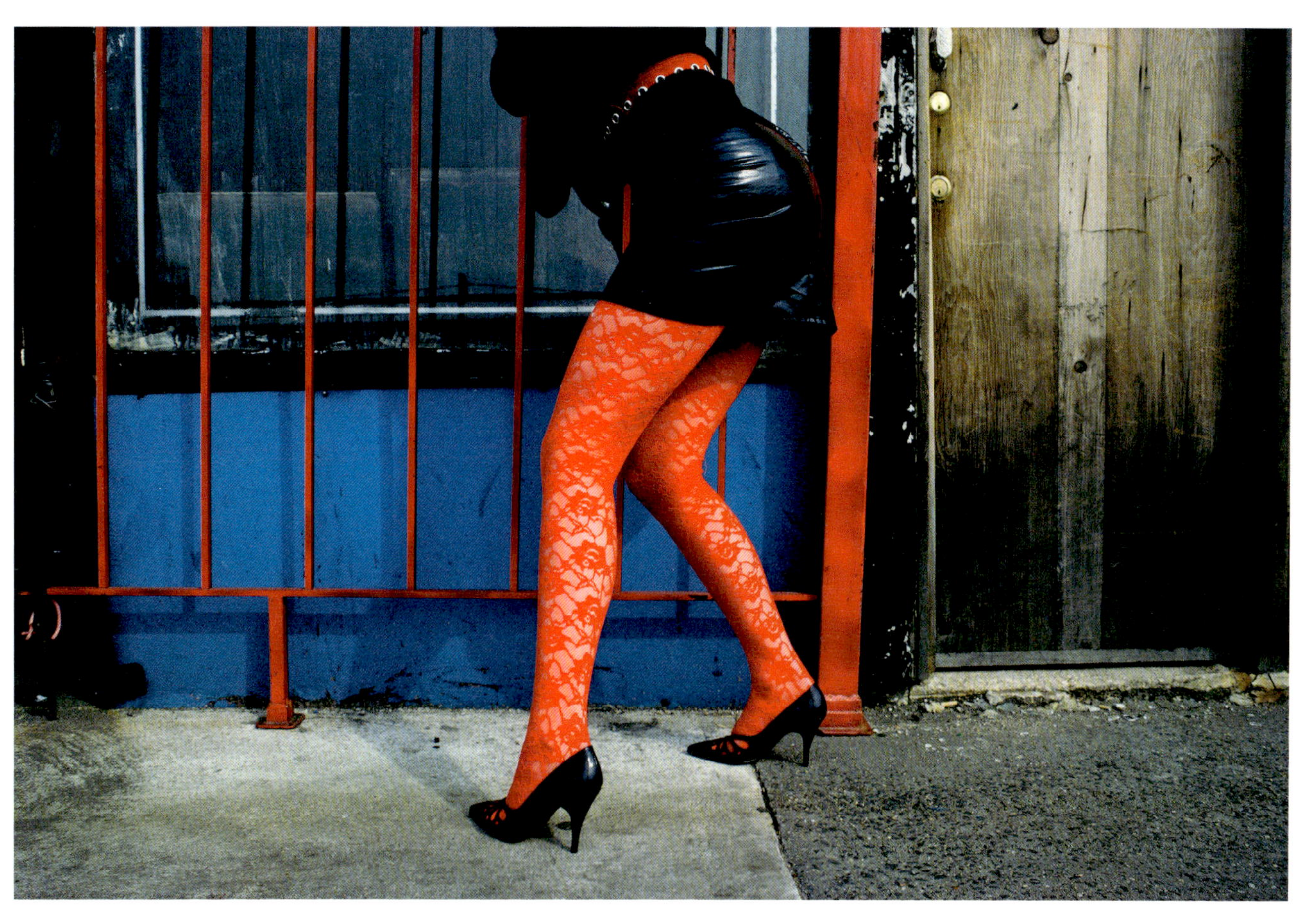

West Side, Manhattan, early 1980s

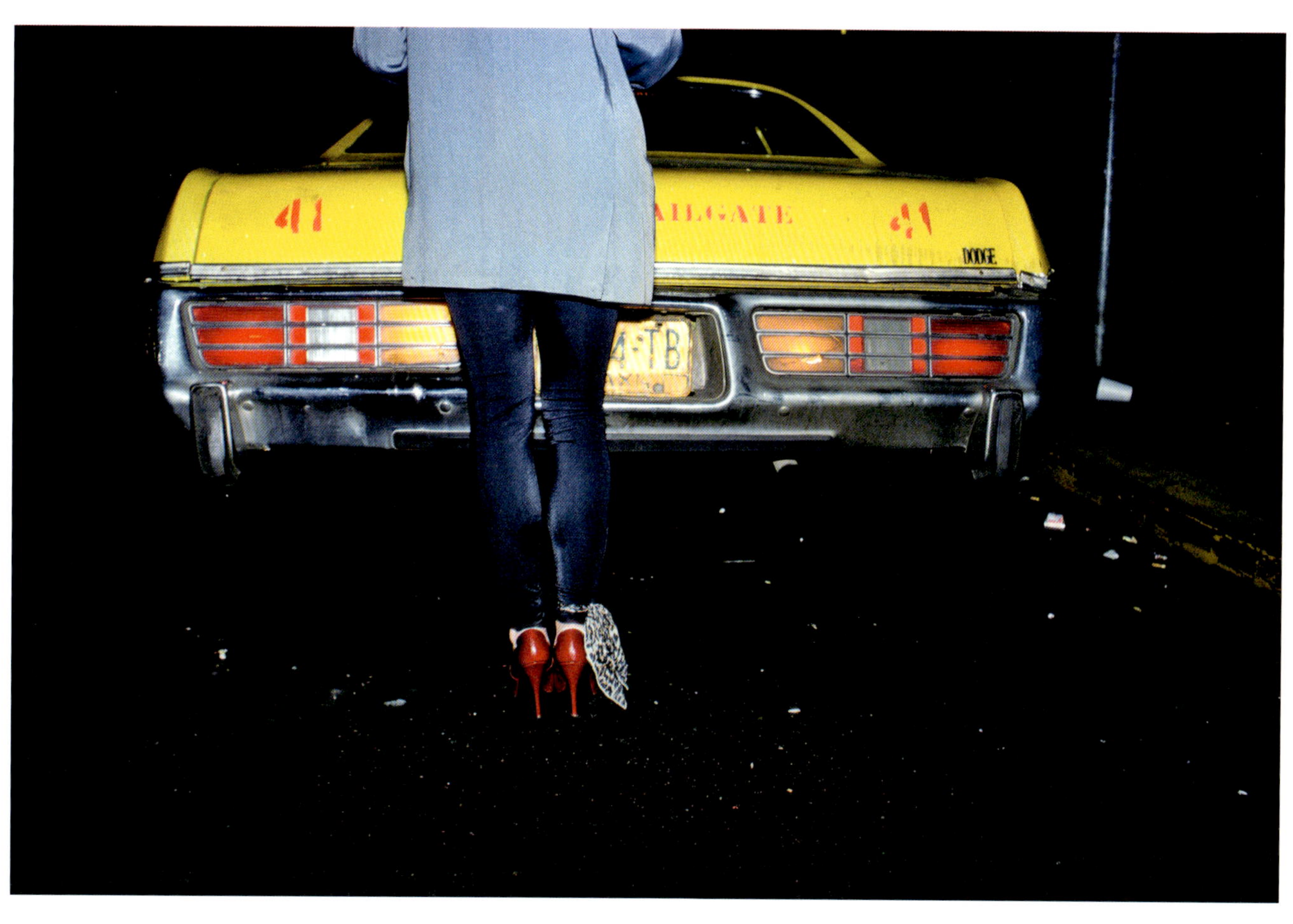

East Village, Manhattan, late 1970s

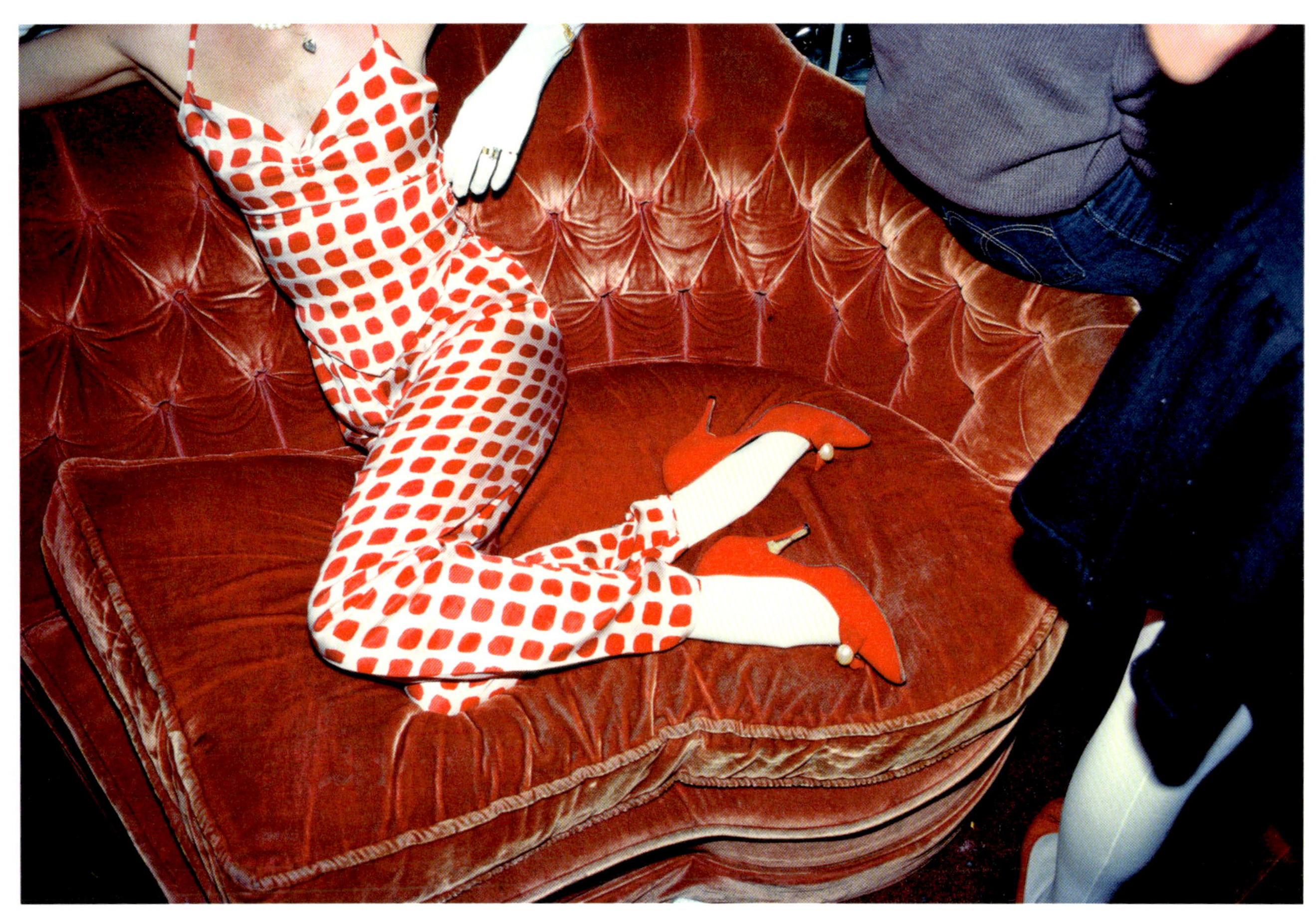

Danceteria, Chelsea, early 1980s

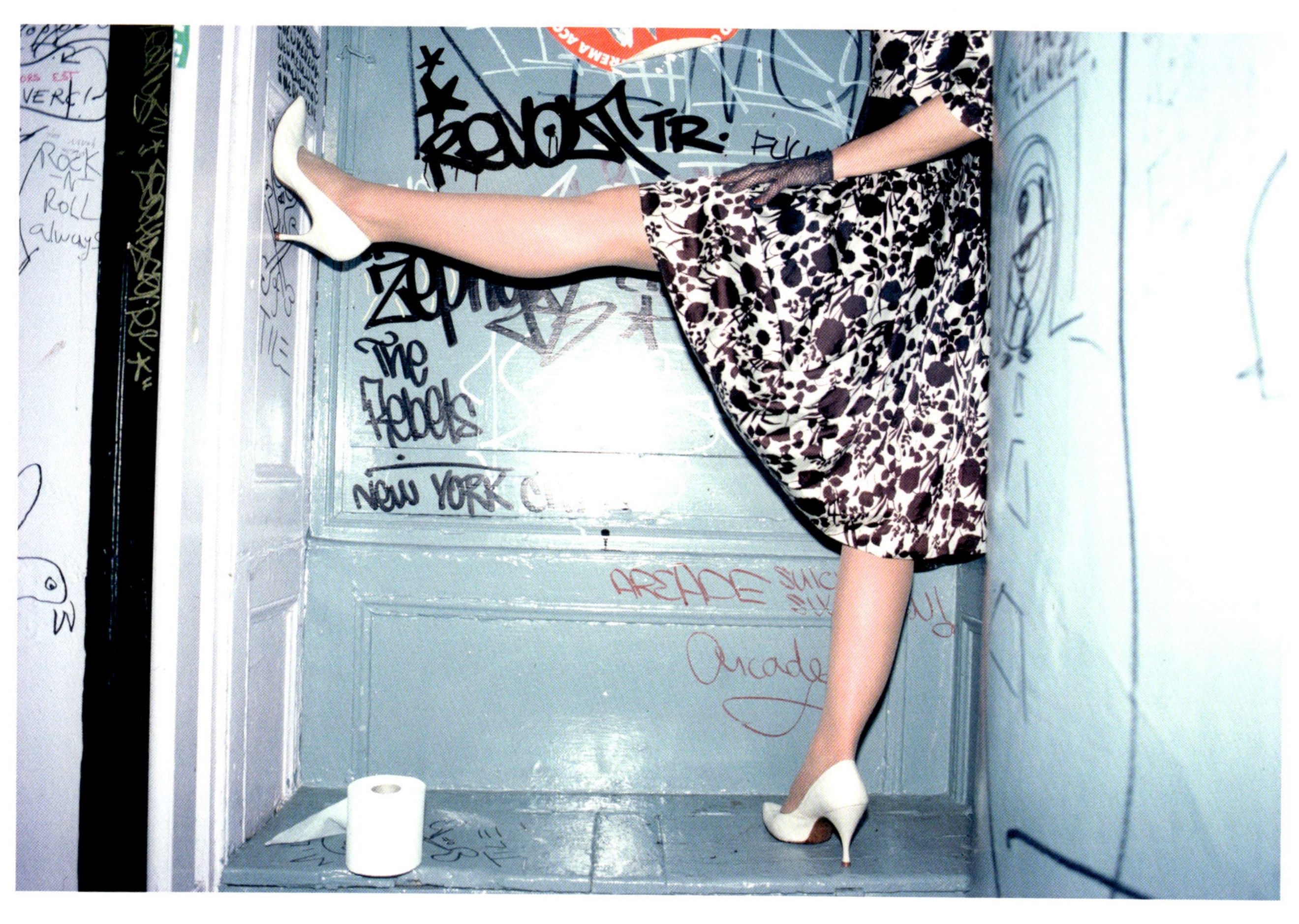

Club 57, East Village, late 1970s

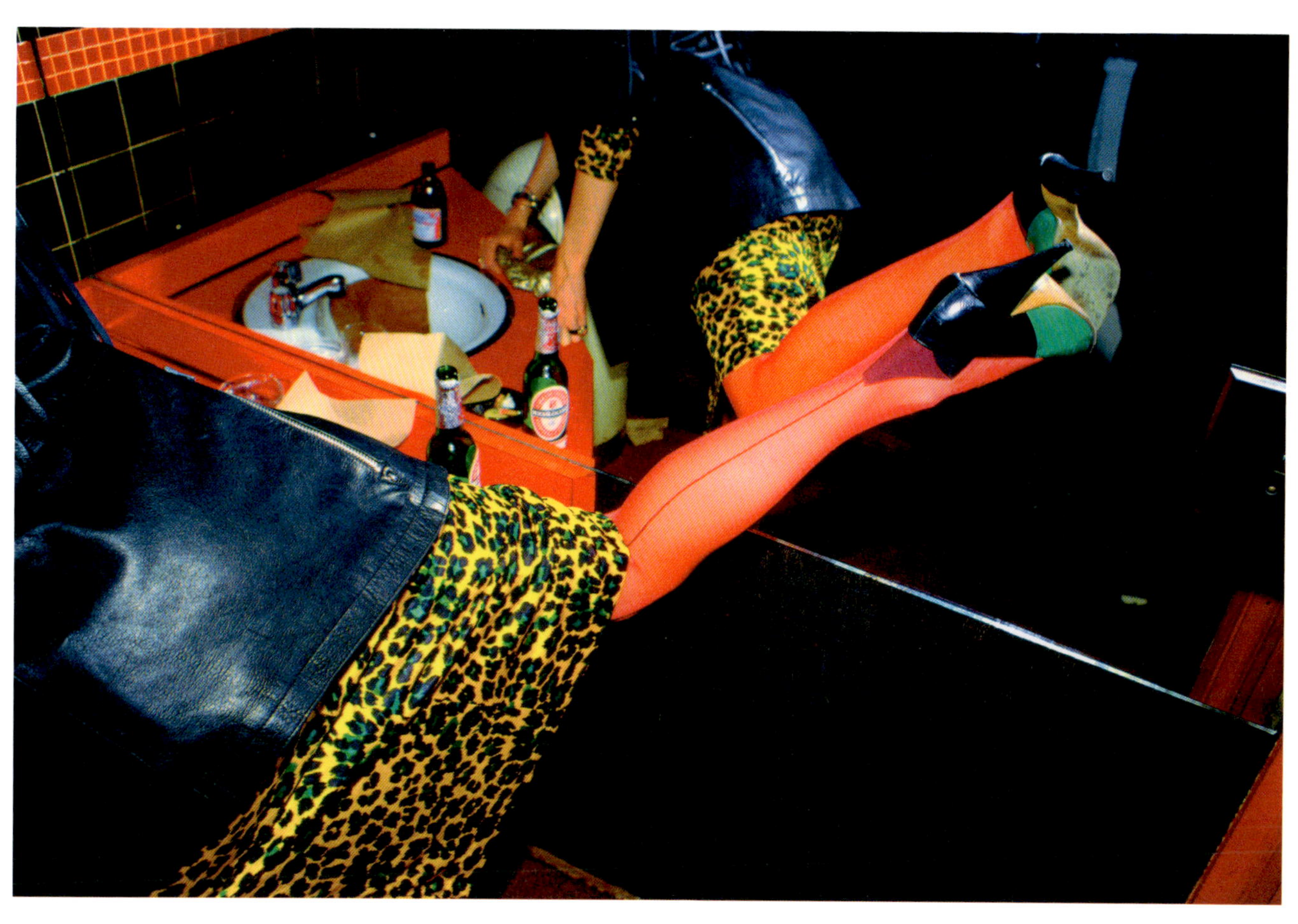

TR3 club, Tribeca, early 1980s

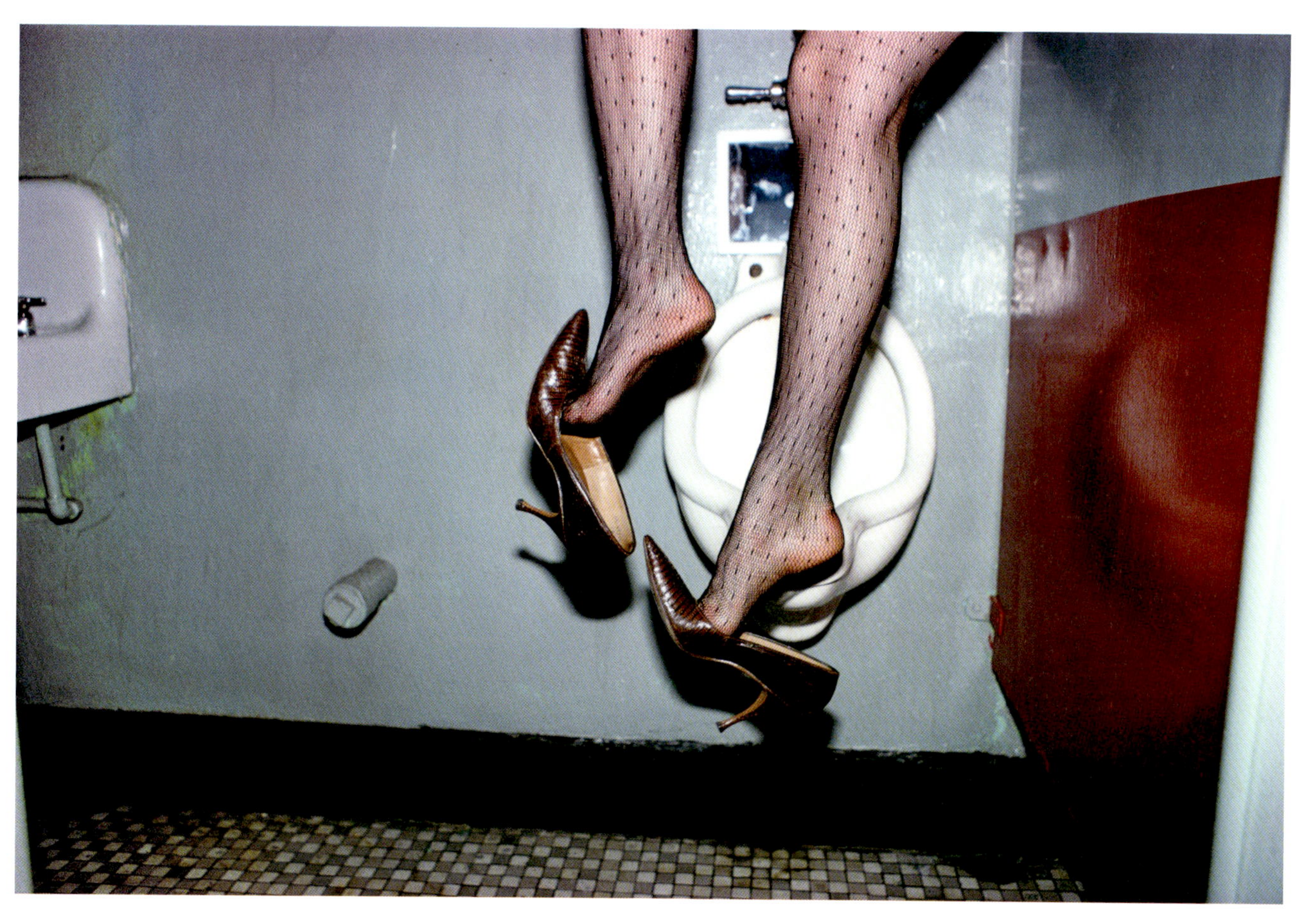

Club 57, East Village, late 1970s

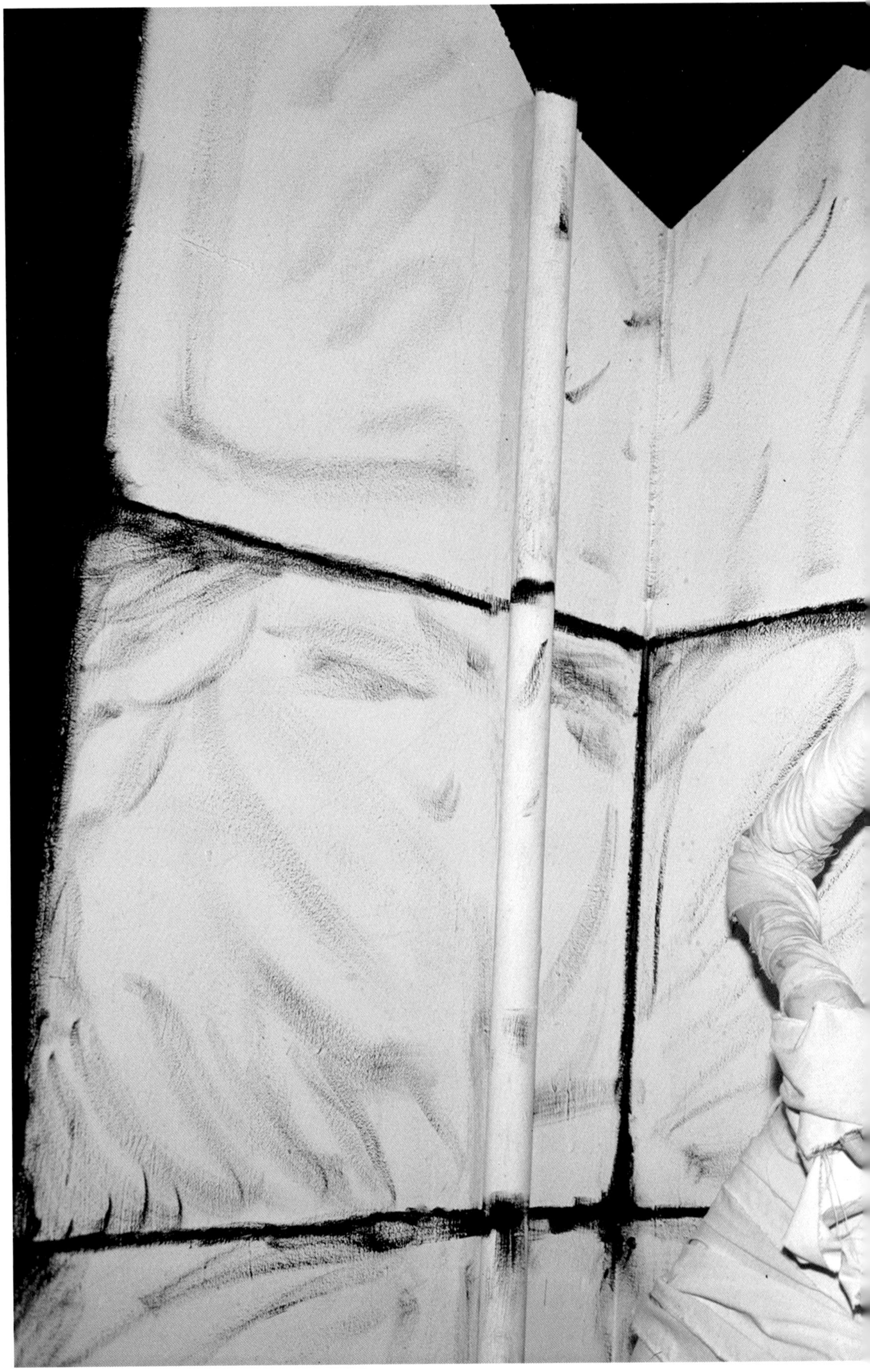

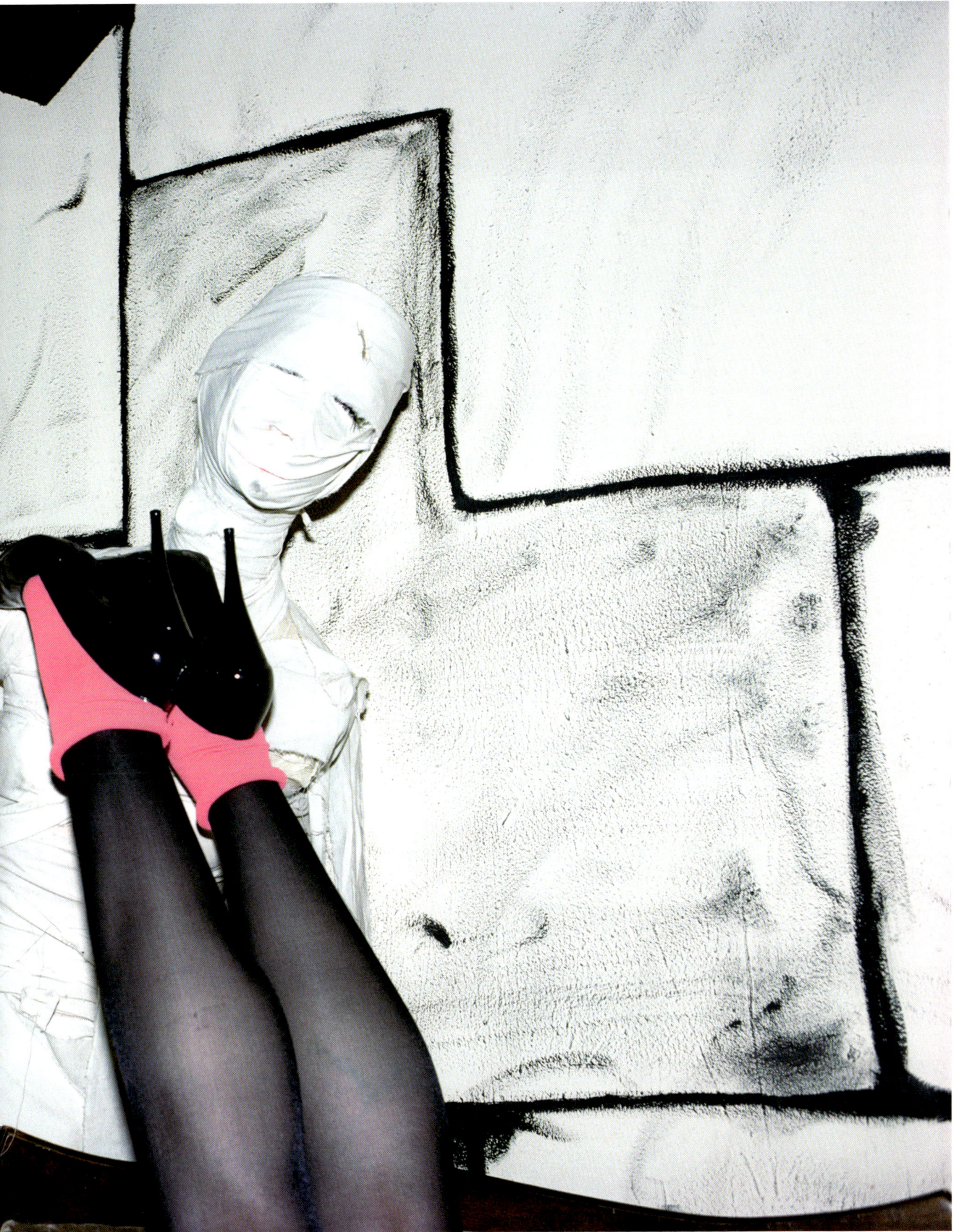

Previous pages: East Village, Manhattan, early 1980s

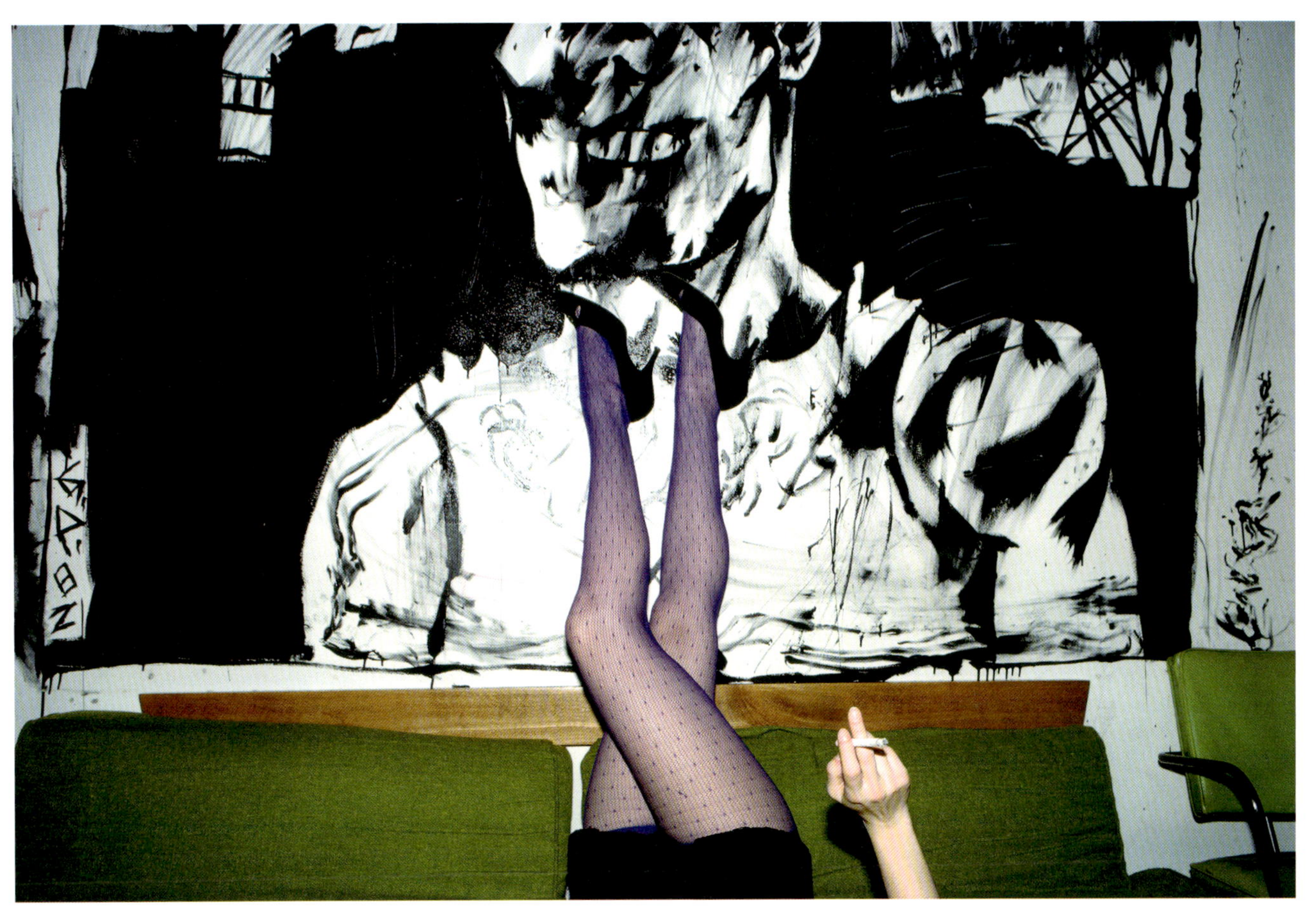

Danceteria, Chelsea, early 1980s

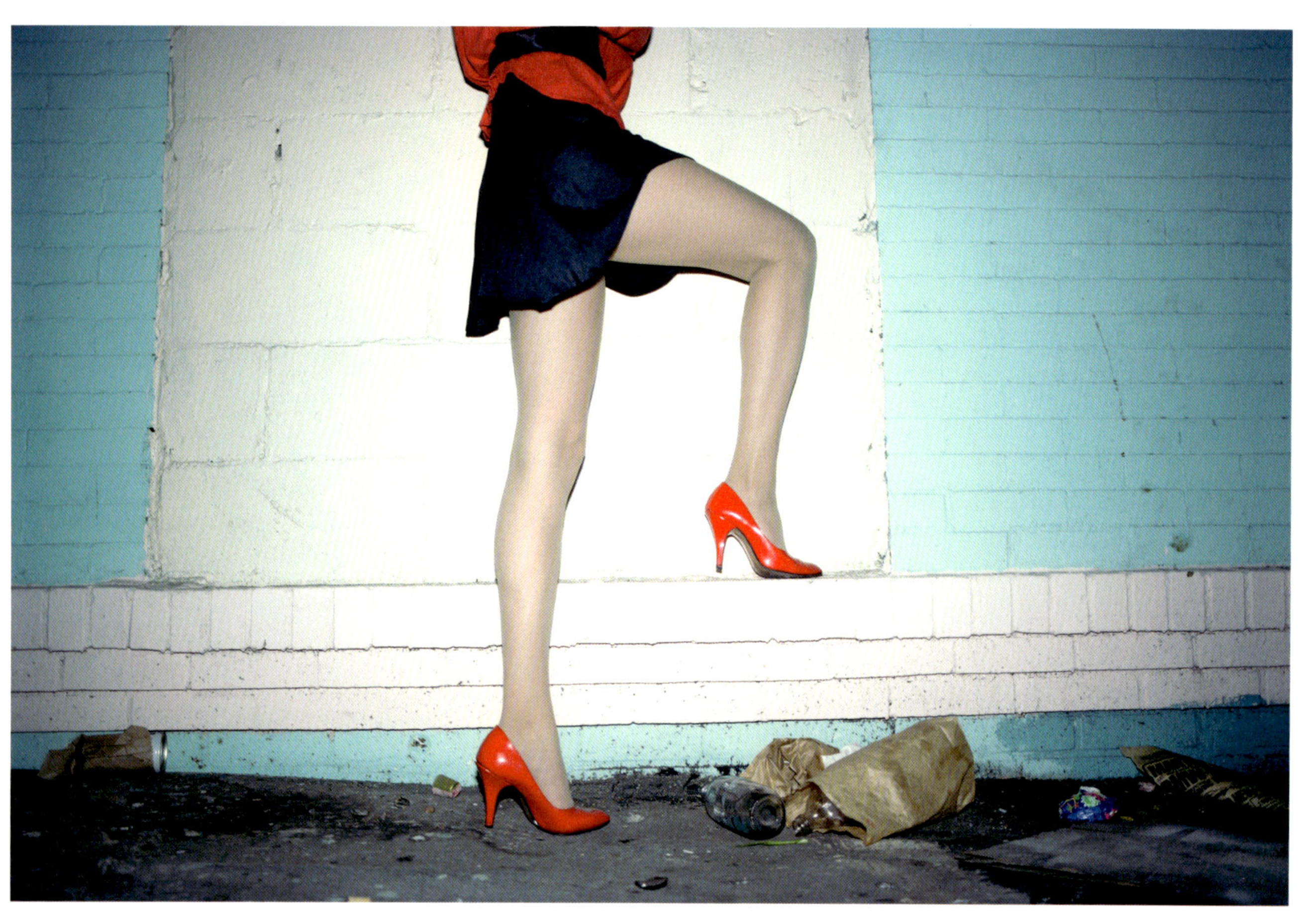

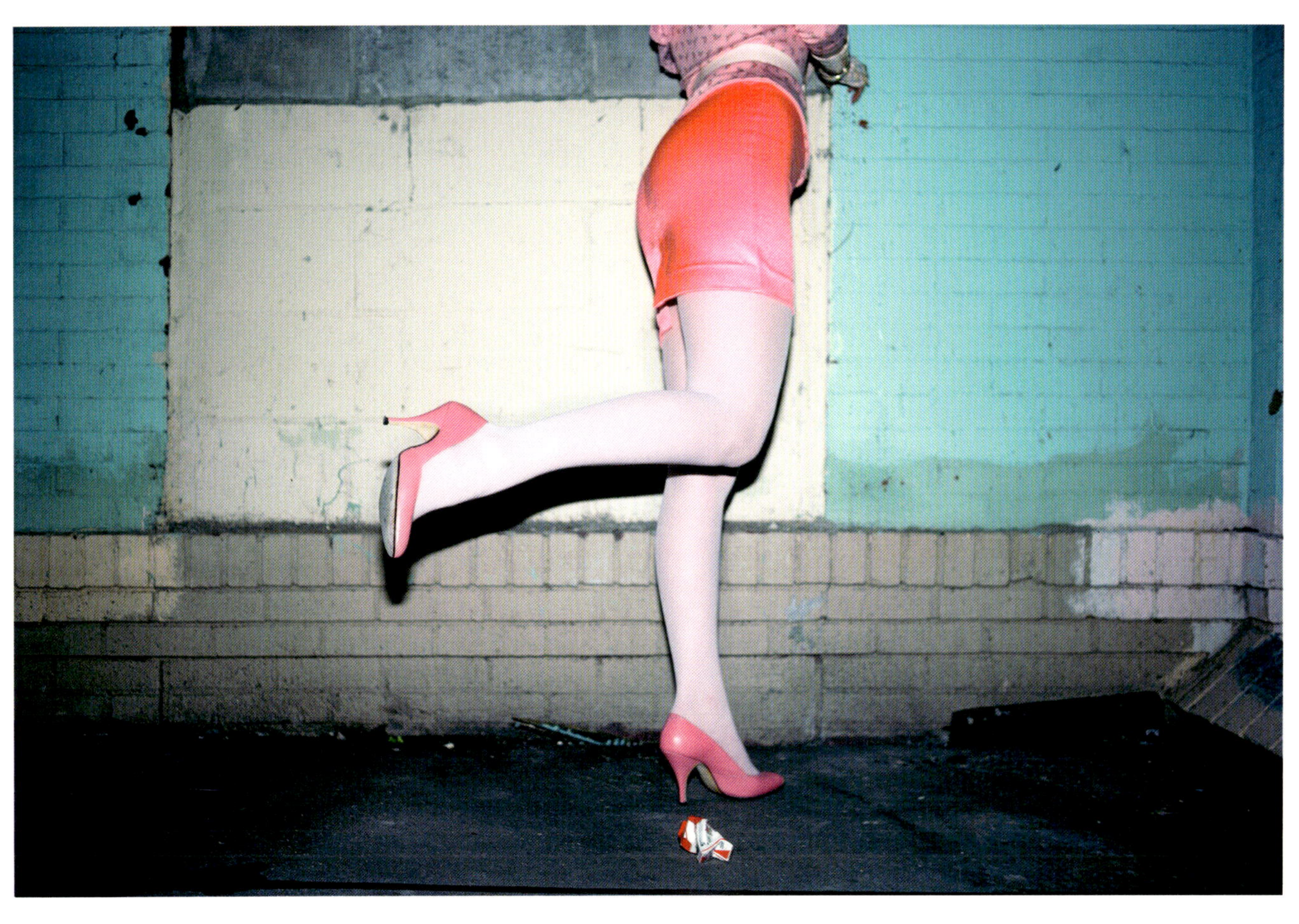

West Side, Manhattan, early 1980s

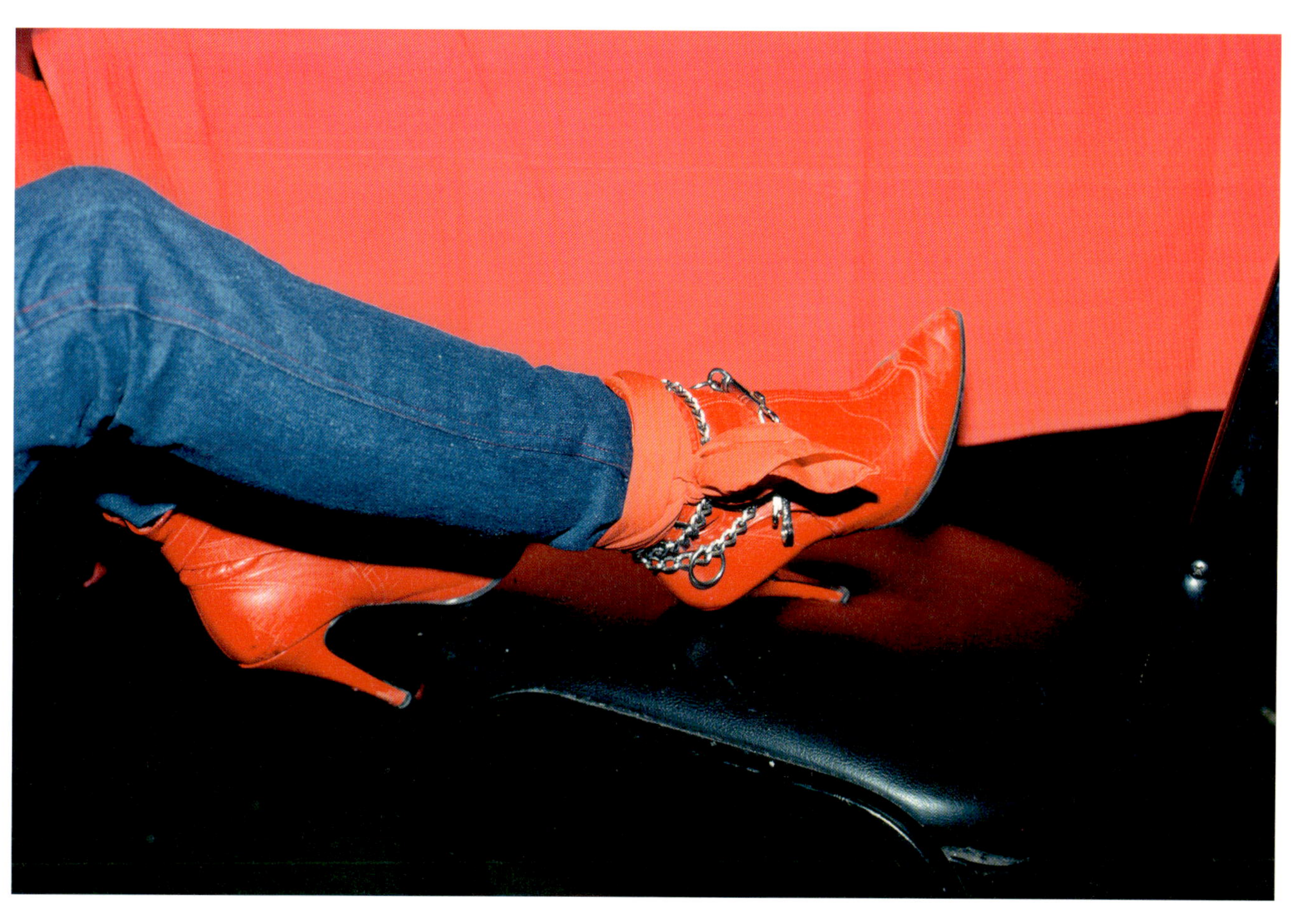

Max's Kansas City, Chelsea, late 1970s

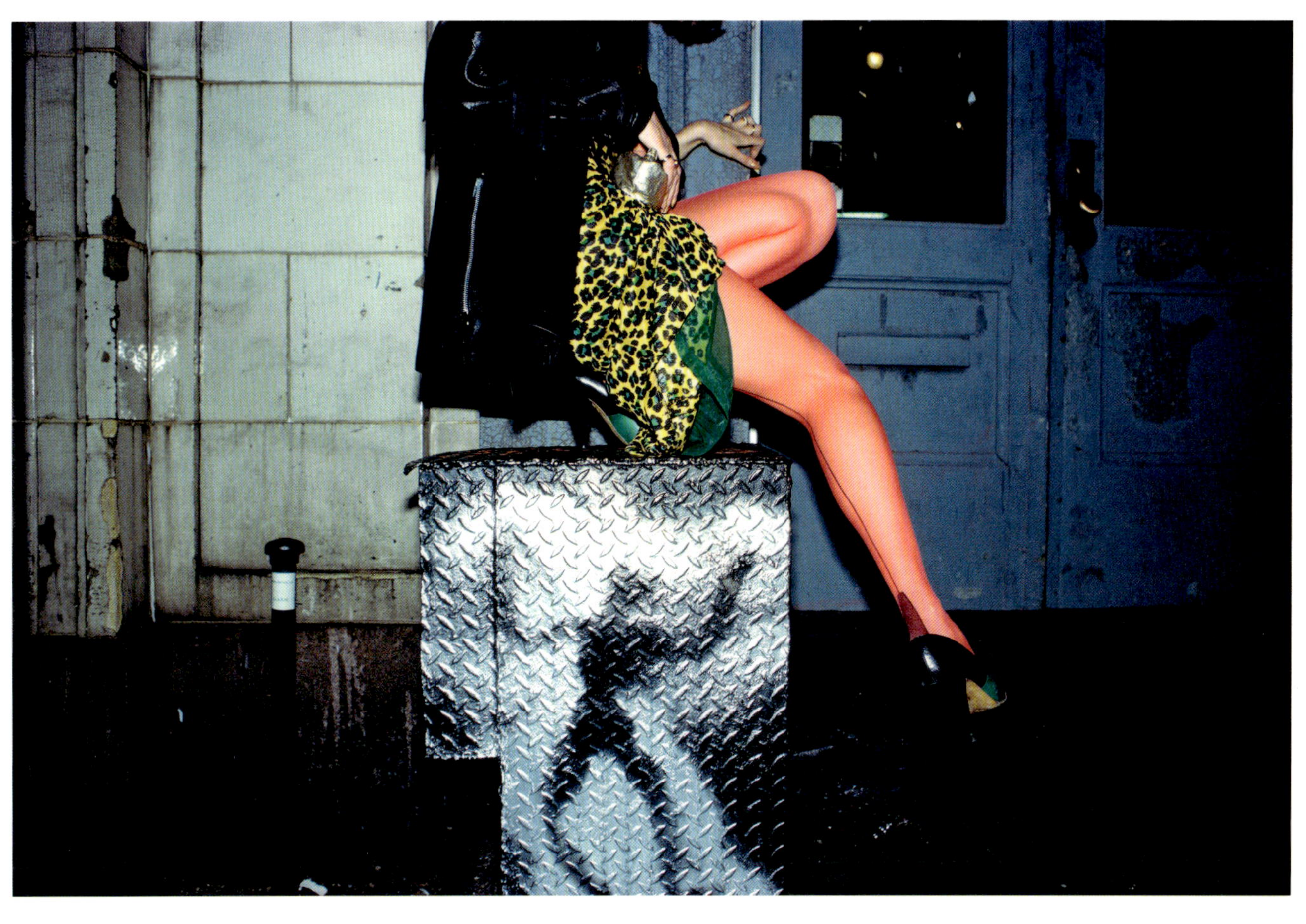

Outside TR3 club, Tribeca, early 1980s

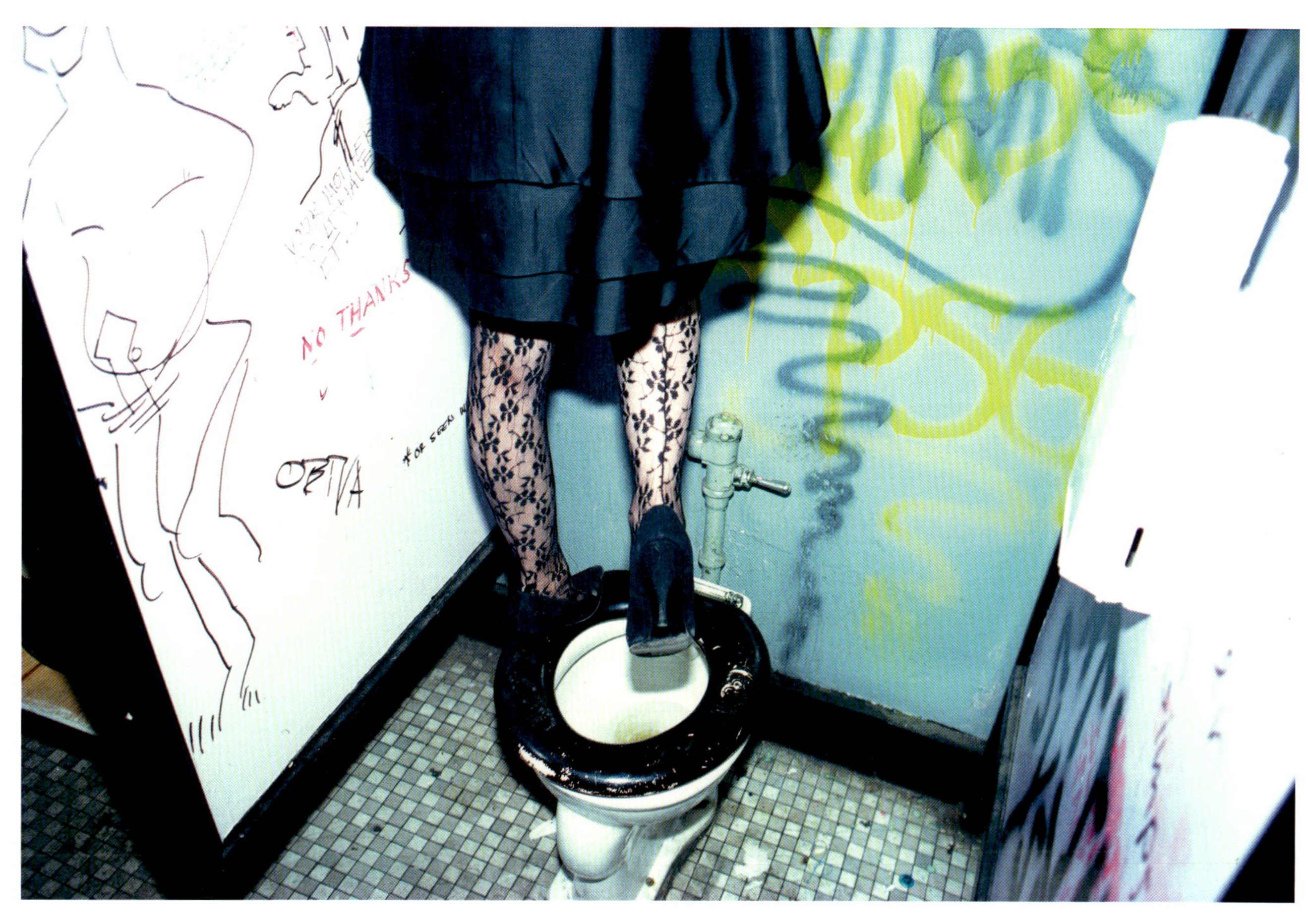

Danceteria, Chelsea, early 1980s

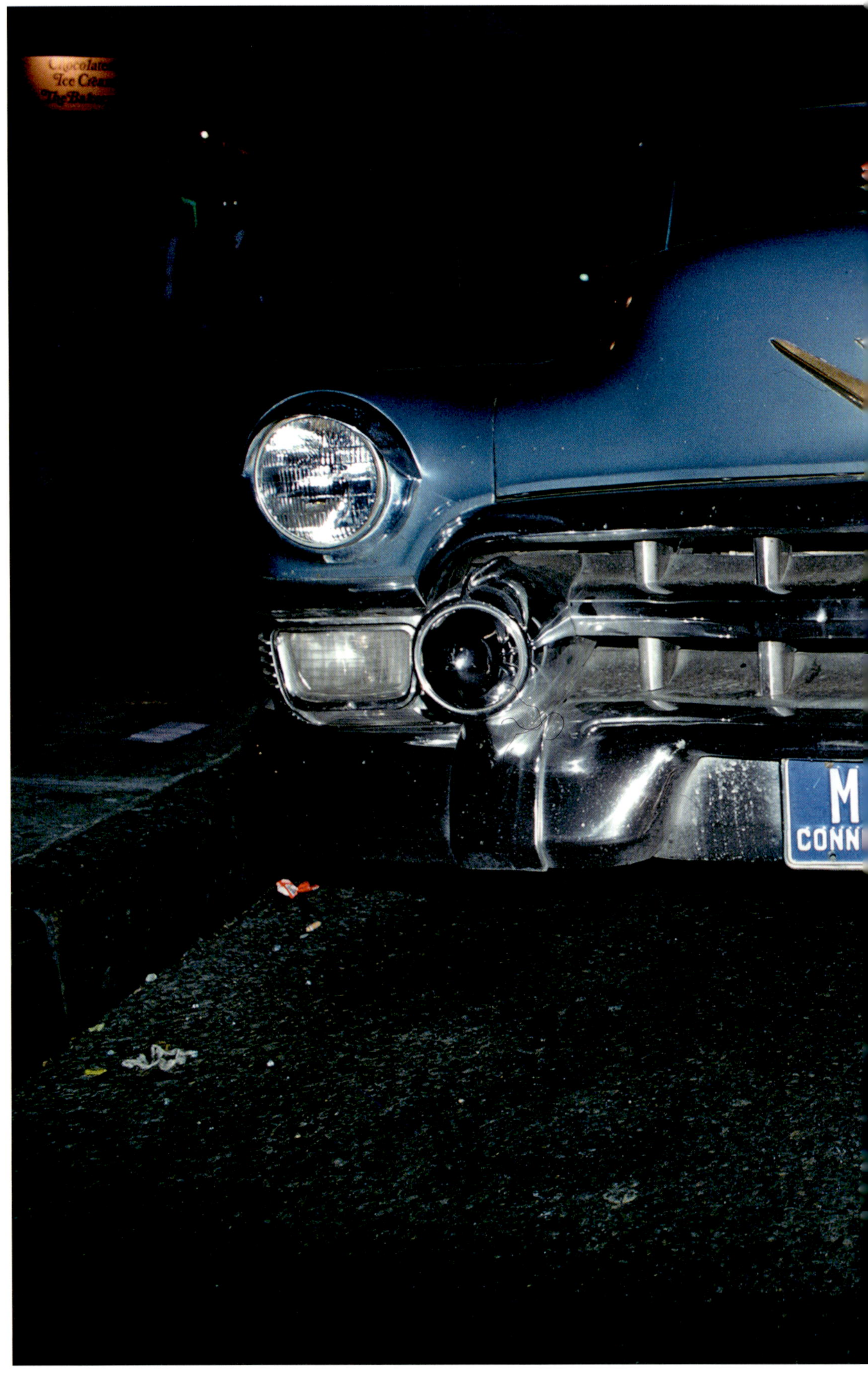
M
CONN

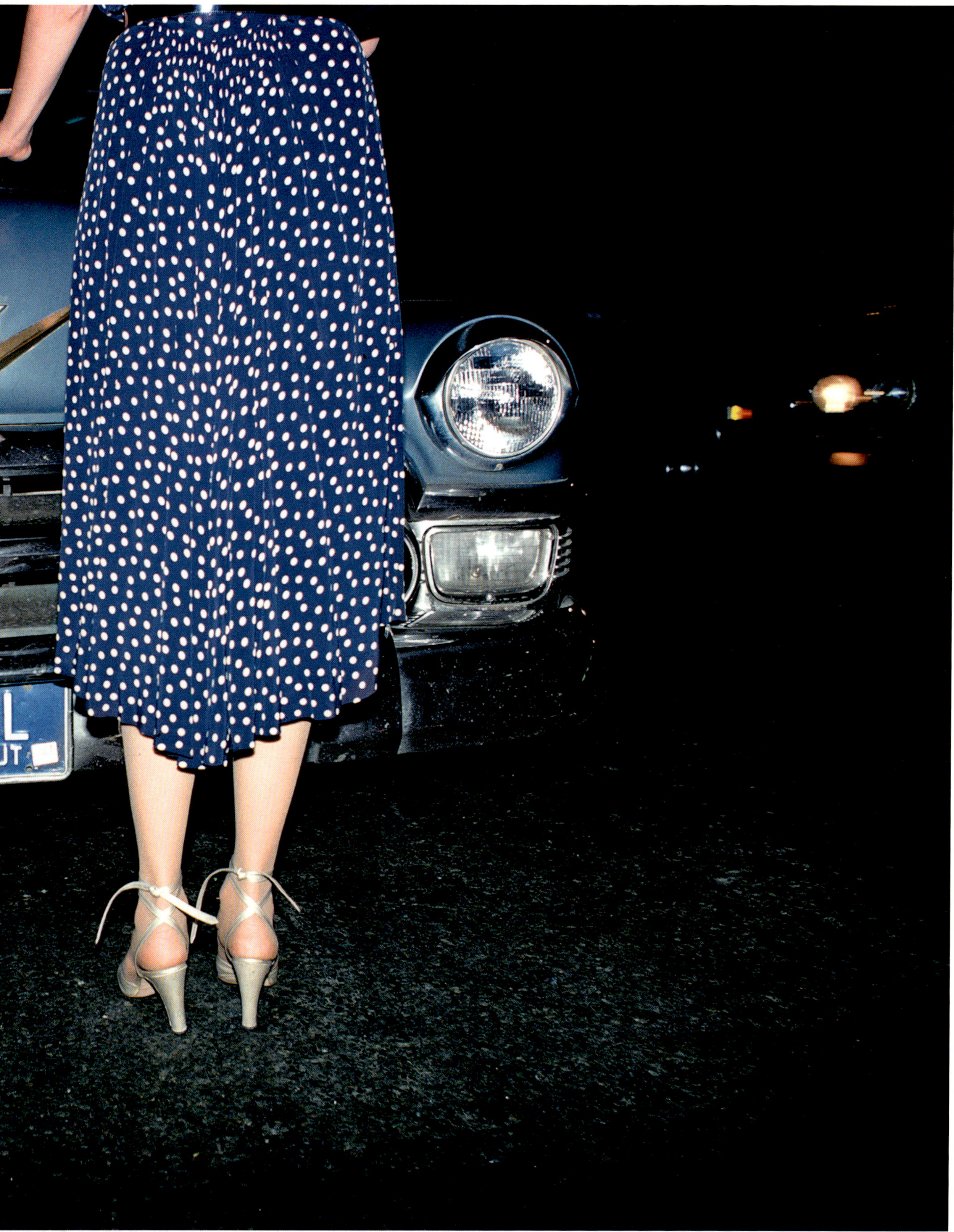

Previous pages: outside Max's Kansas City, Chelsea, late 1970s

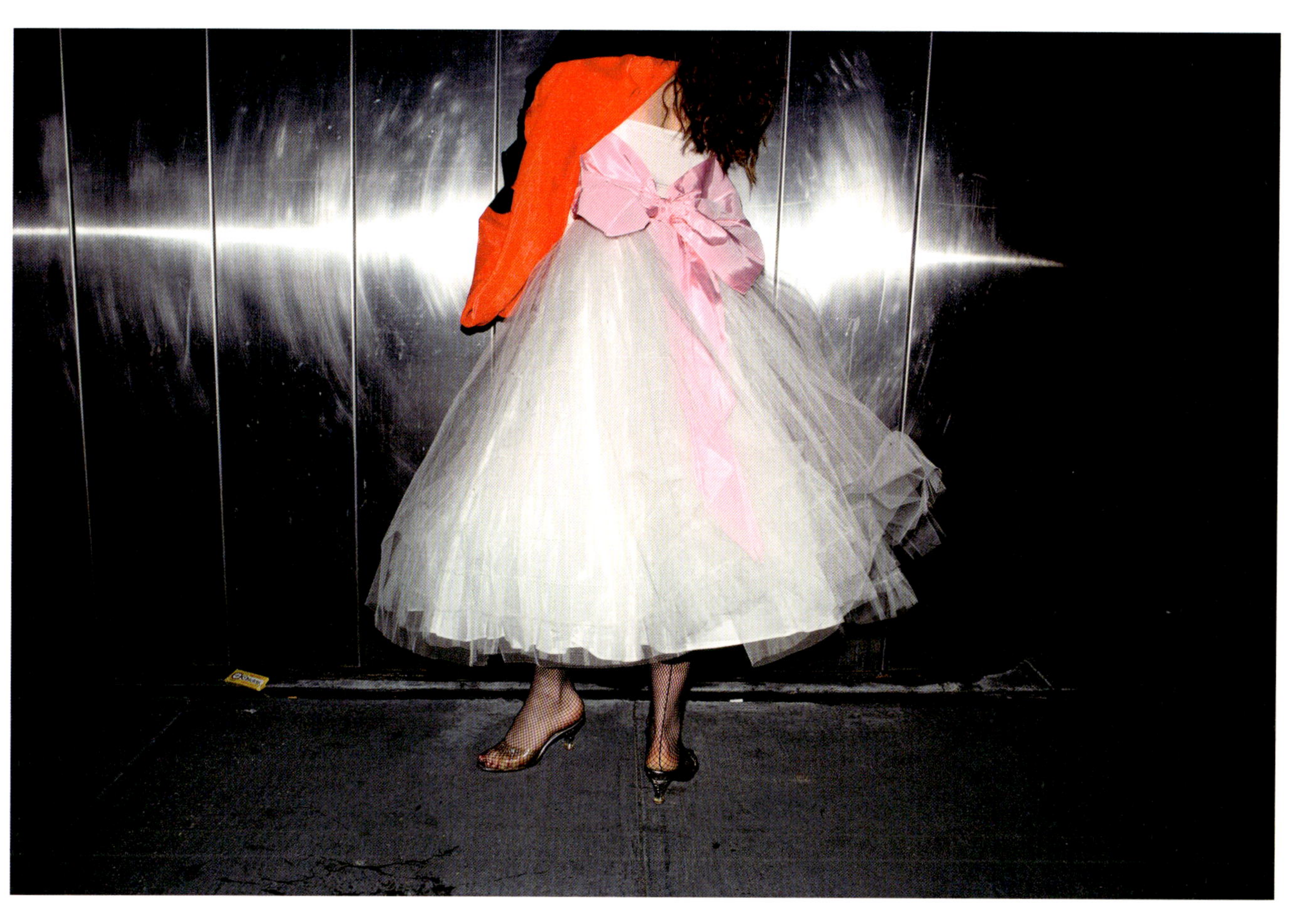

East Village, Manhattan, early 1980s

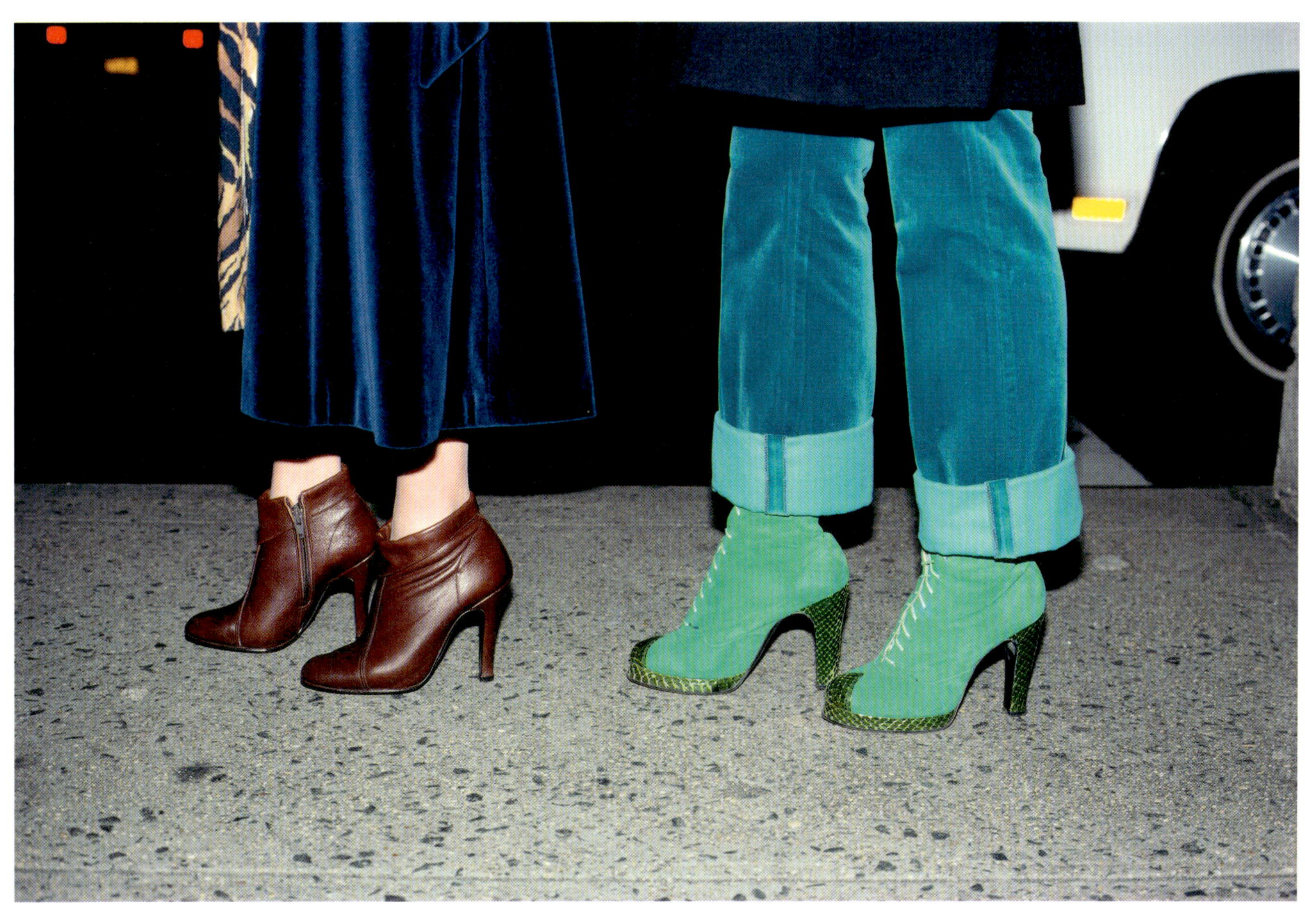

Outside Max's Kansas City, Chelsea, late 1970s

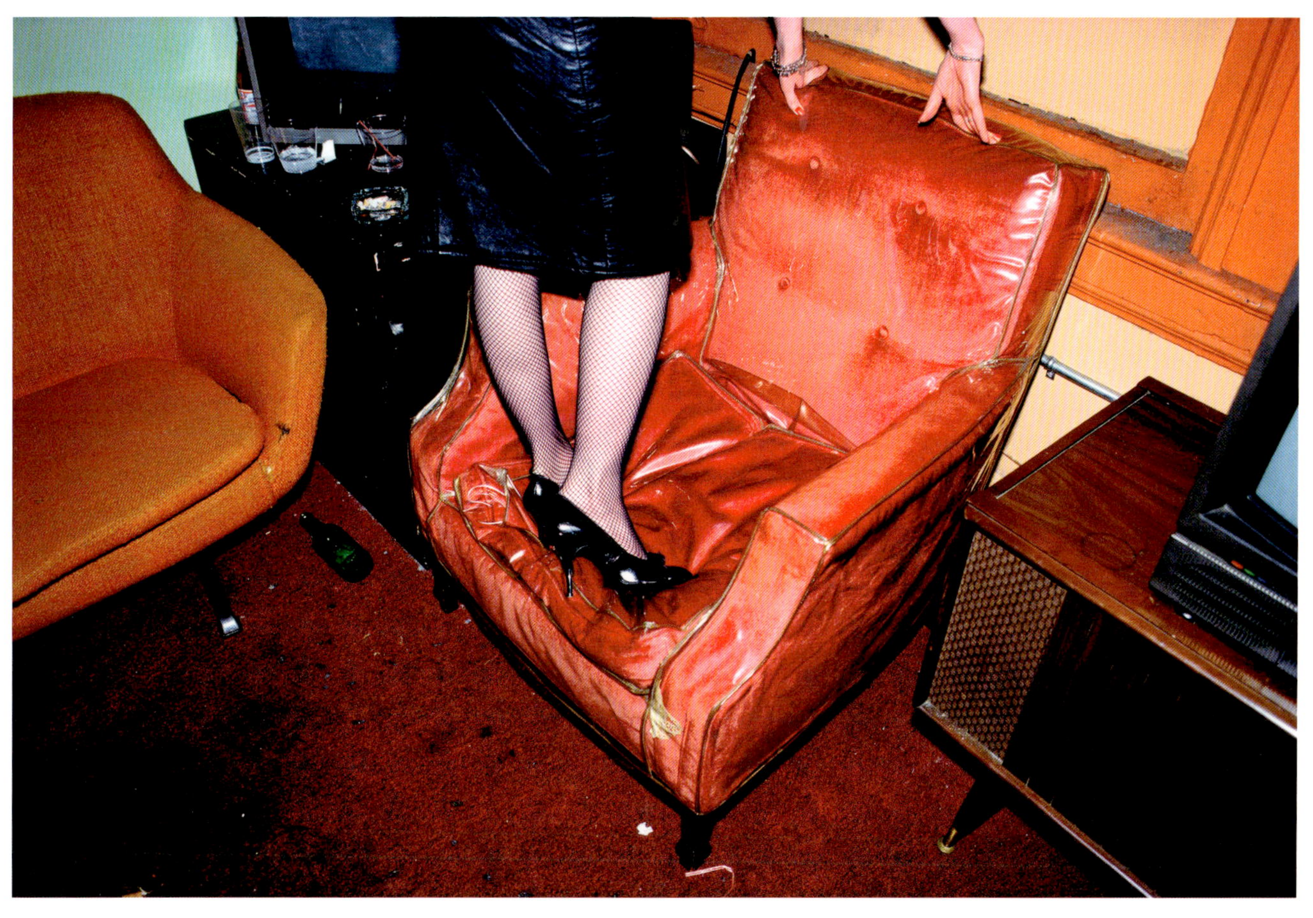

Danceteria, Chelsea, early 1980s

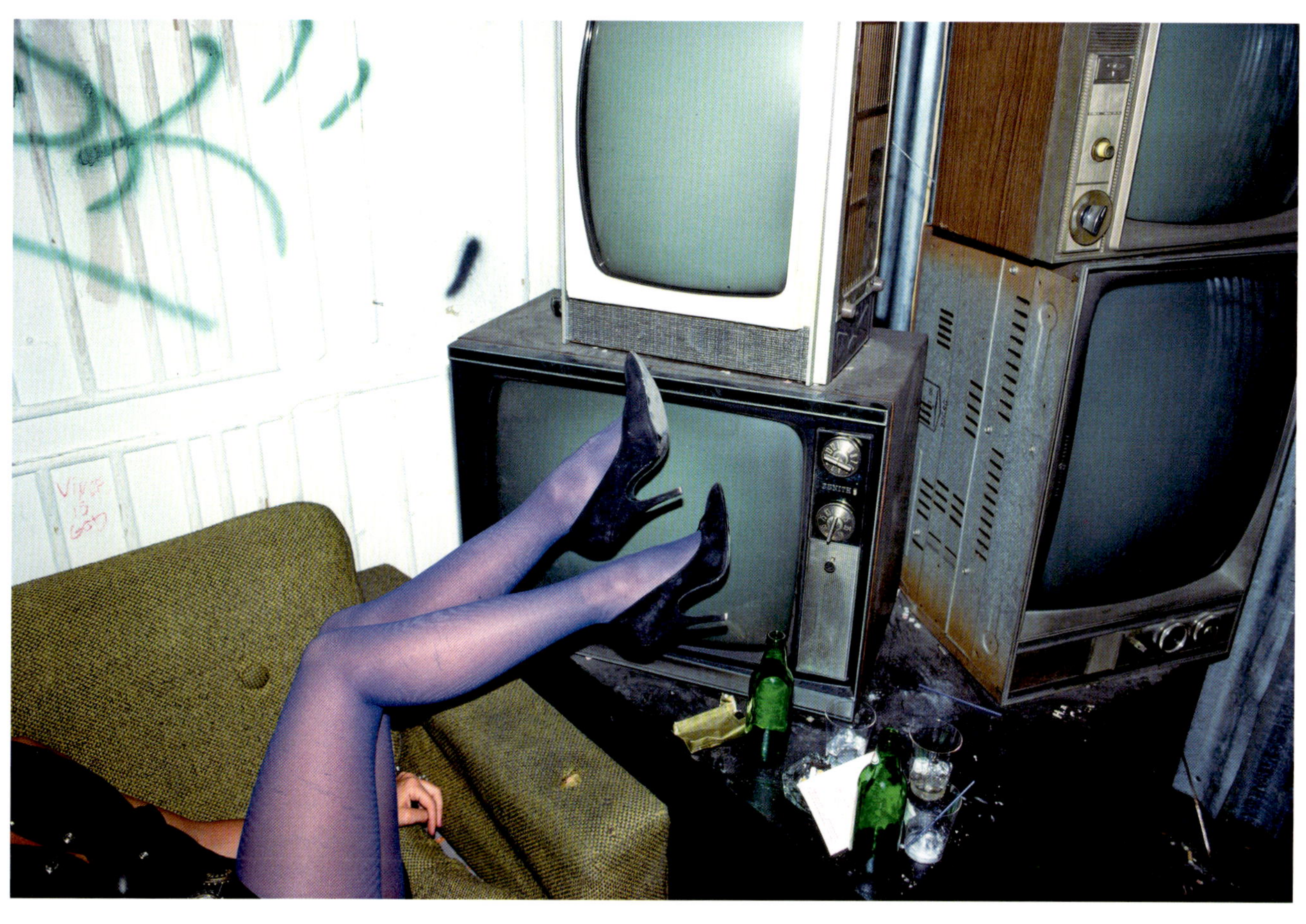

Danceteria, Chelsea, early 1980s

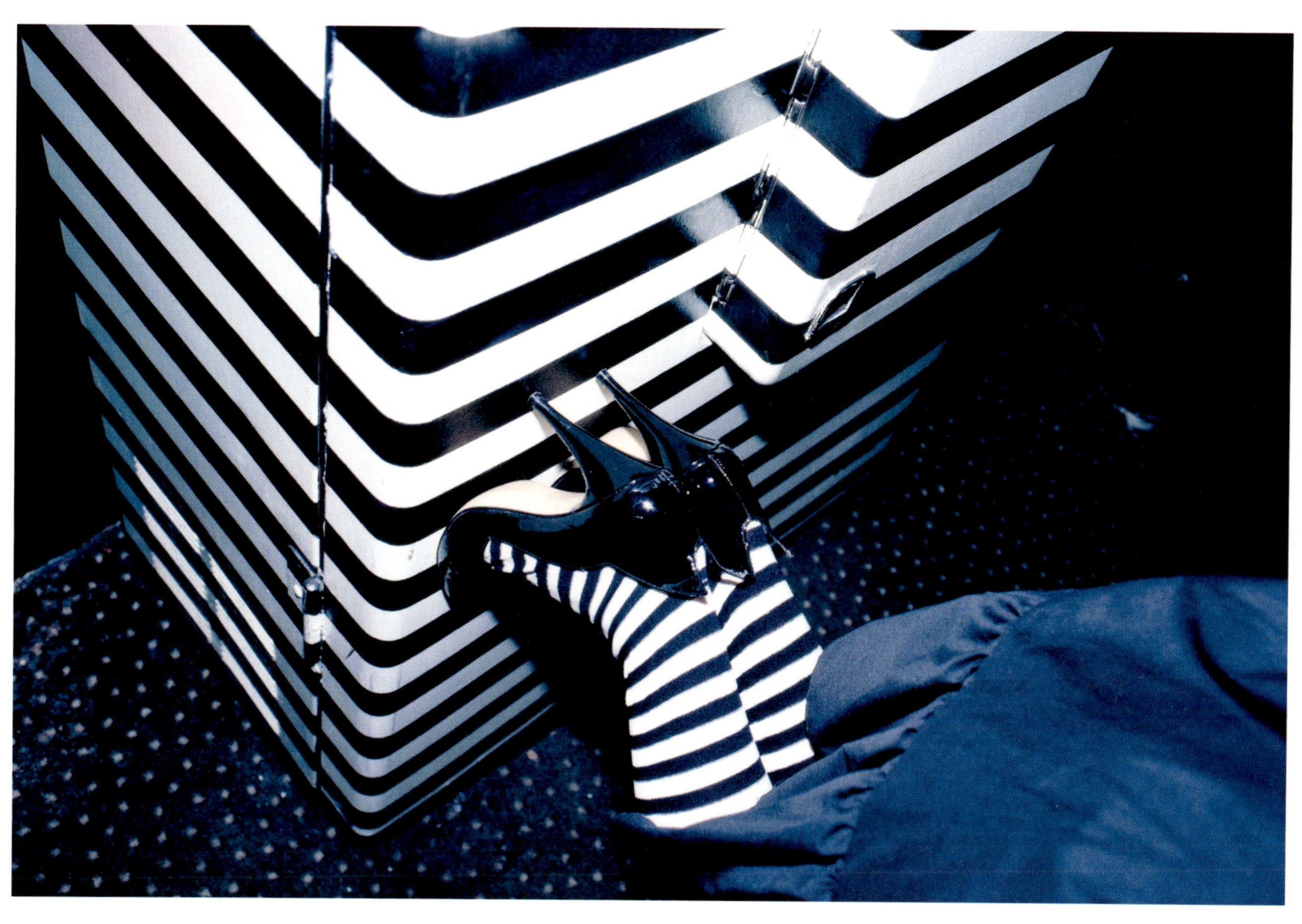

Hellfire Club, The Meat Market, Manhattan, late 1970s

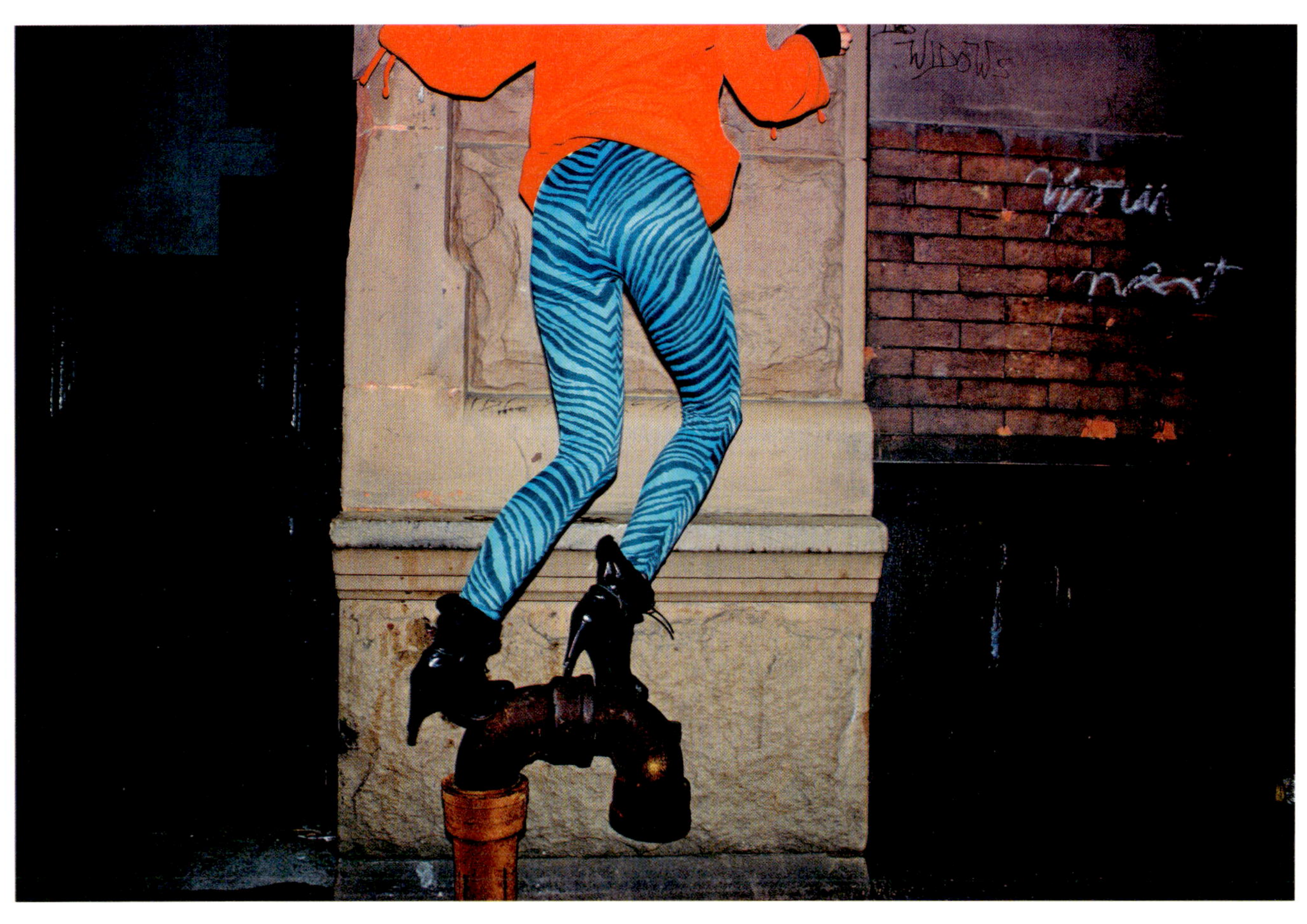

Outside Max's Kansas City, Chelsea, late 1970s

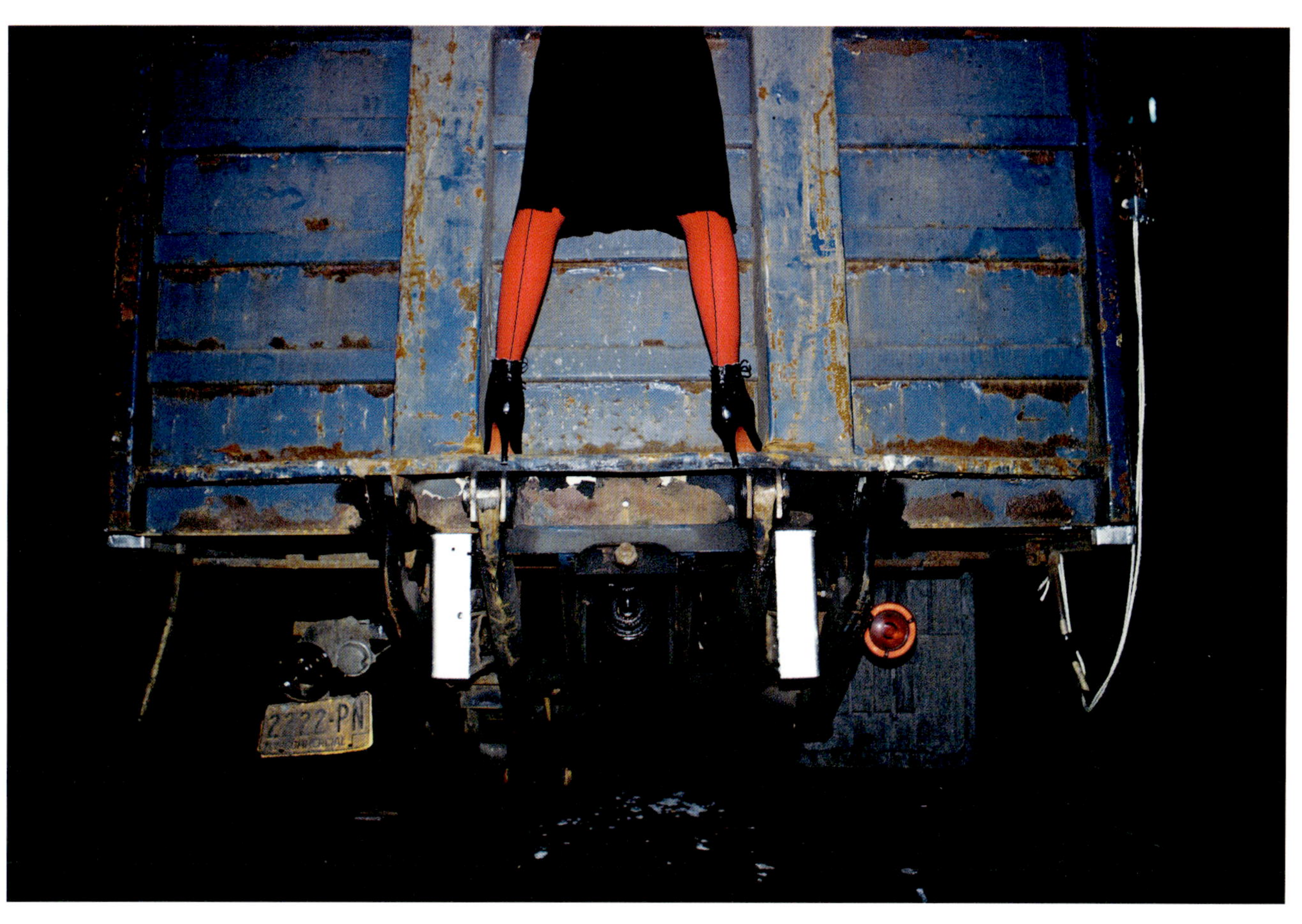

Outside CBGB, The Bowery, late 1970s

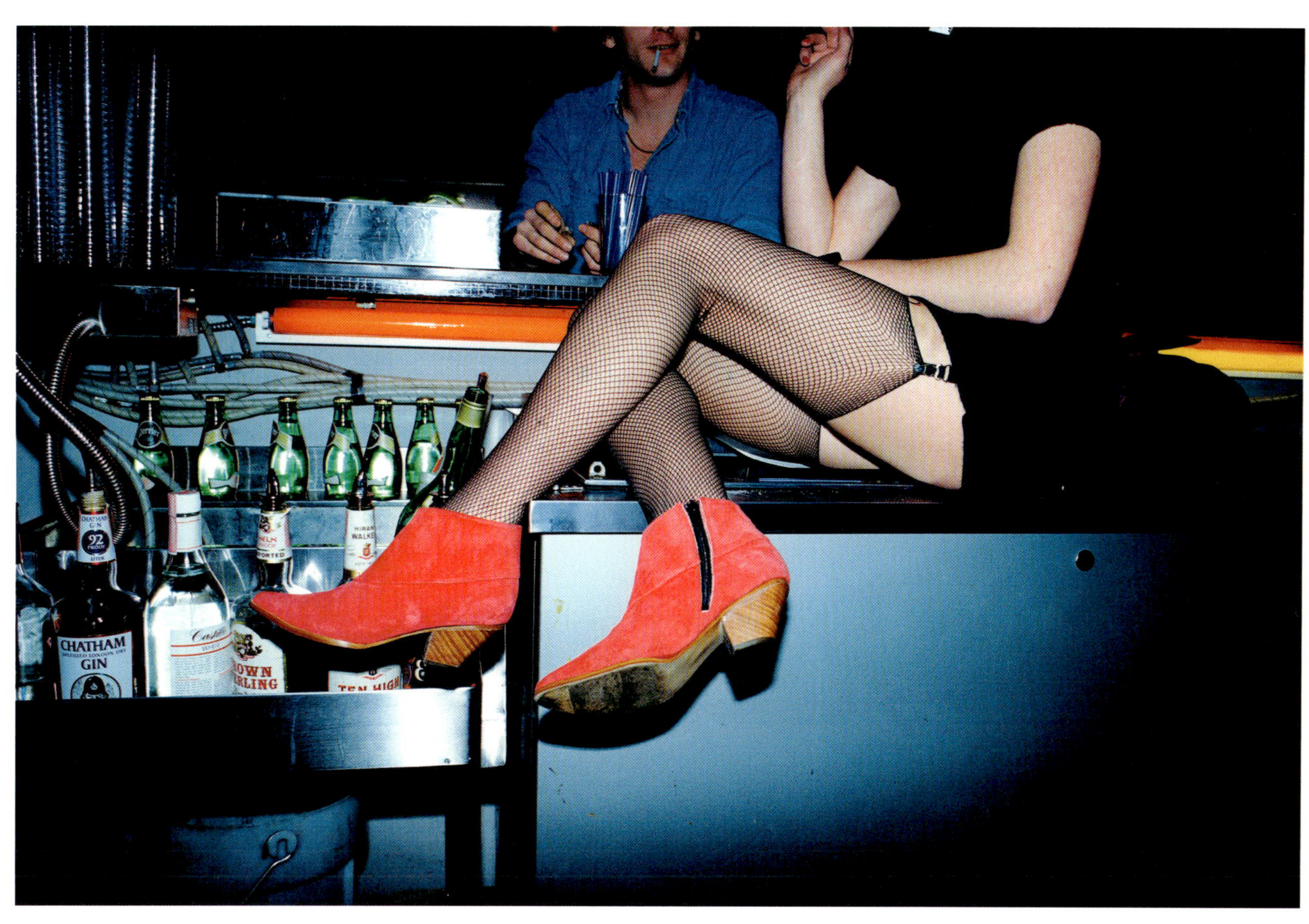

Danceteria, Chelsea, early 1980s

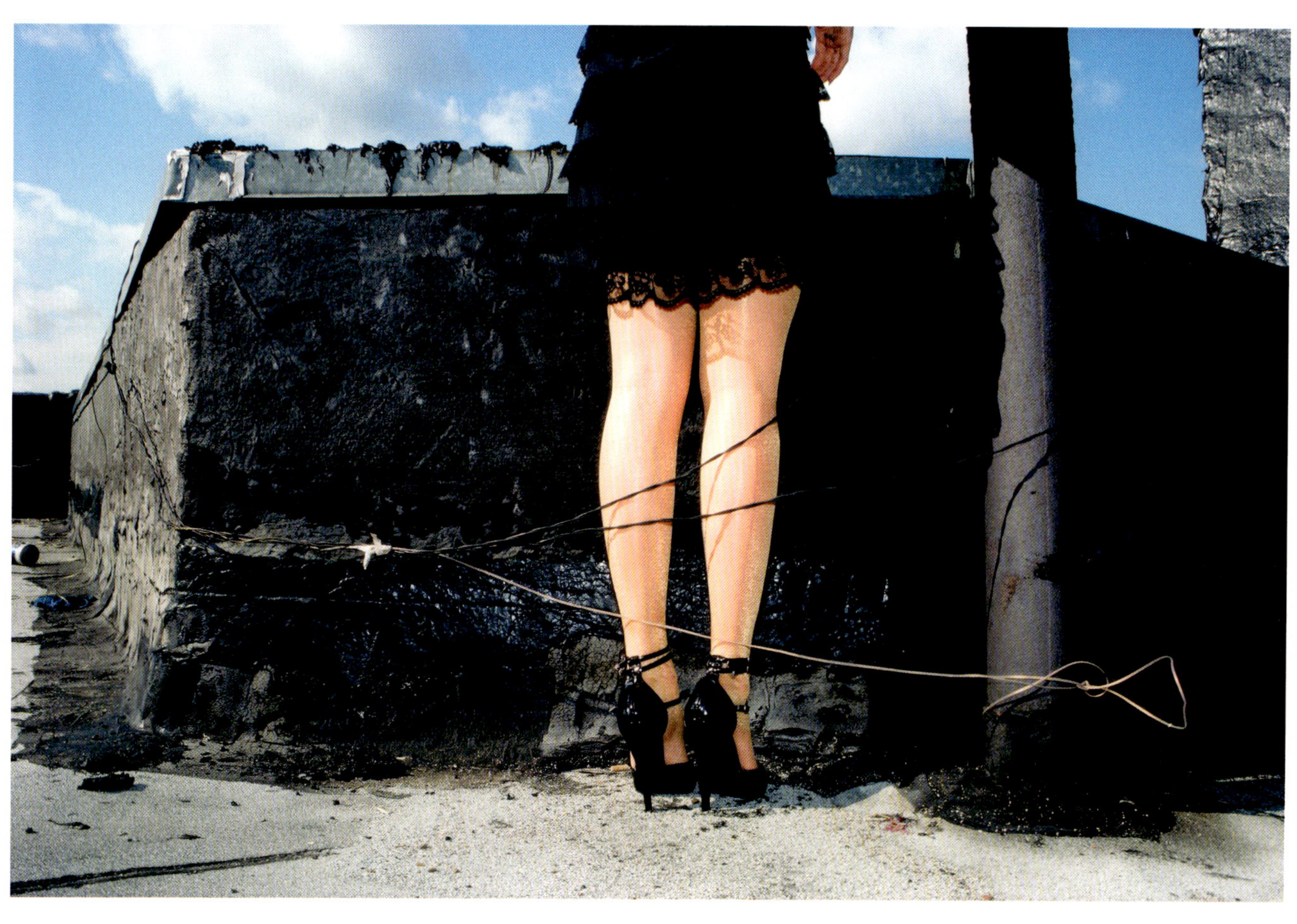

East Village rooftop, Manhattan, early 1980s

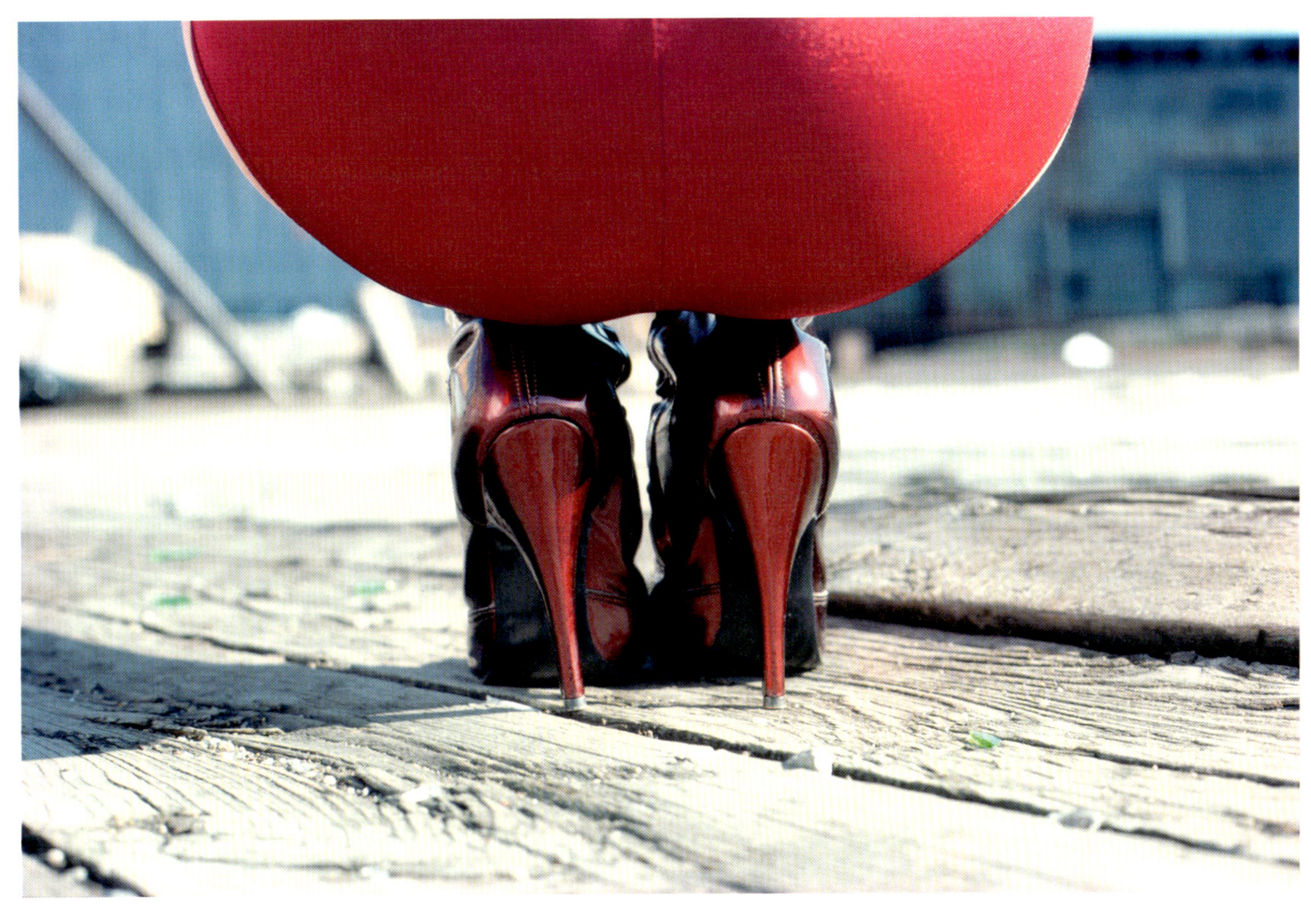

West Side Piers, Manhattan, late 1970s

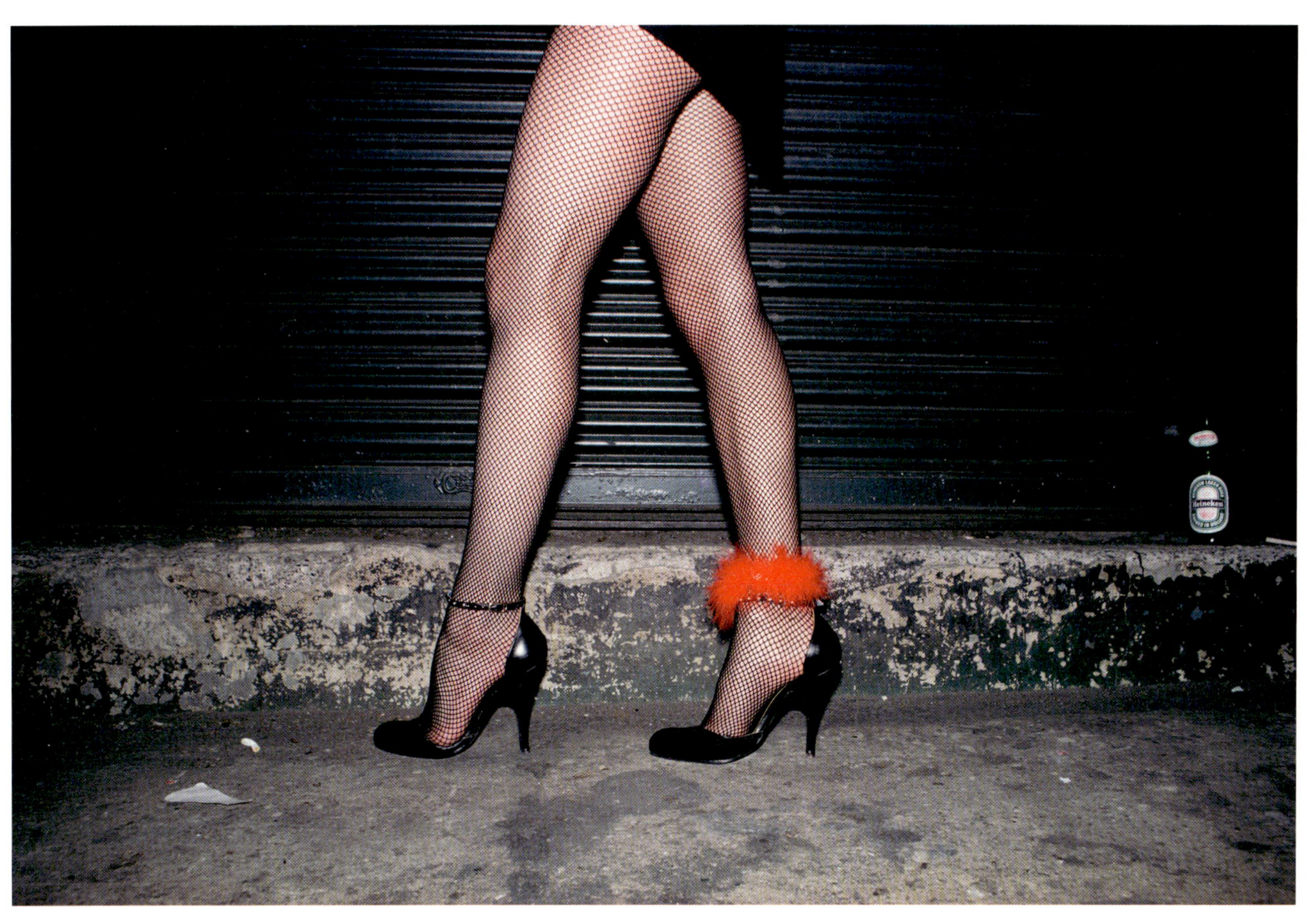

Outside Mudd Club, Tribeca, early 1980s

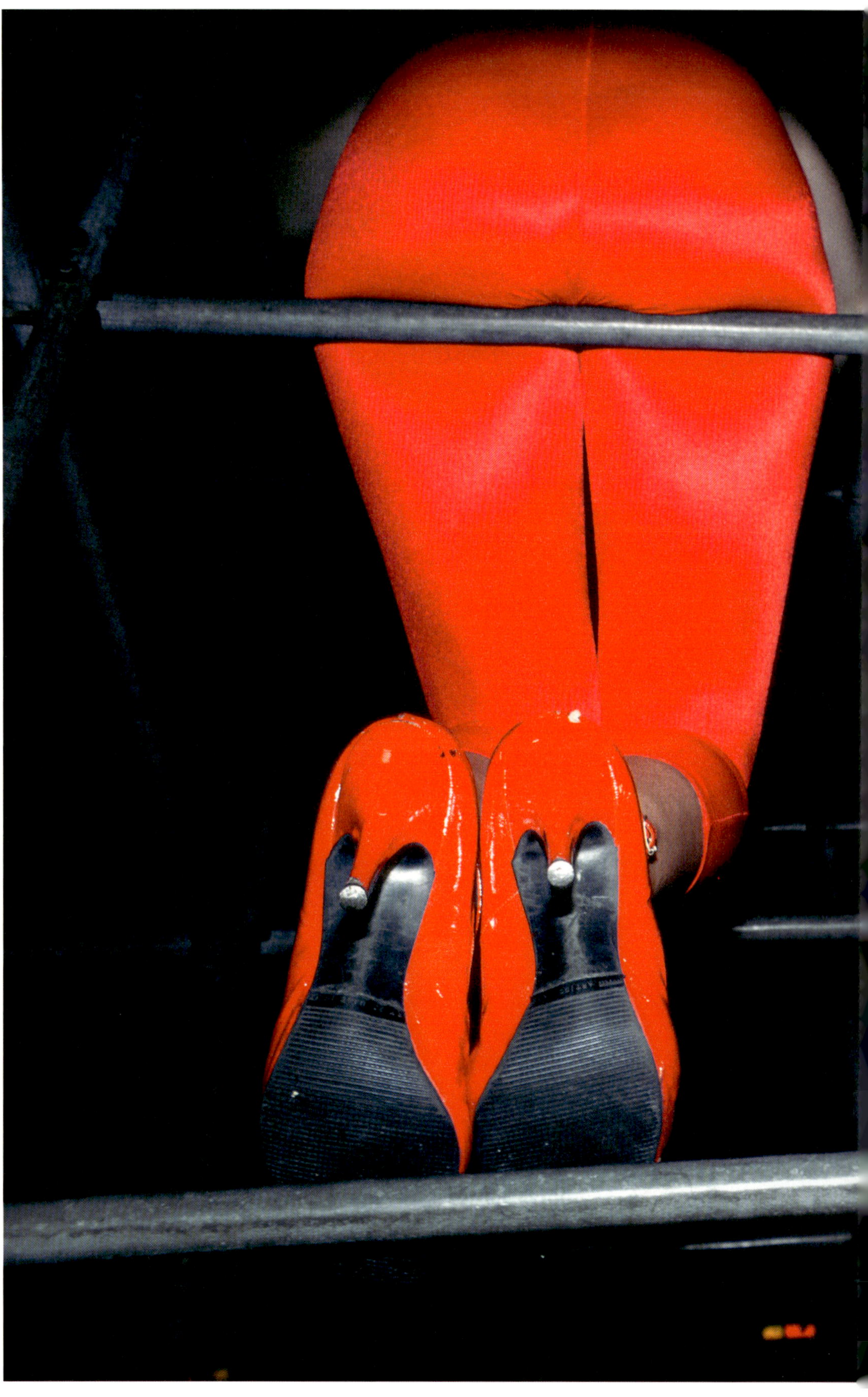

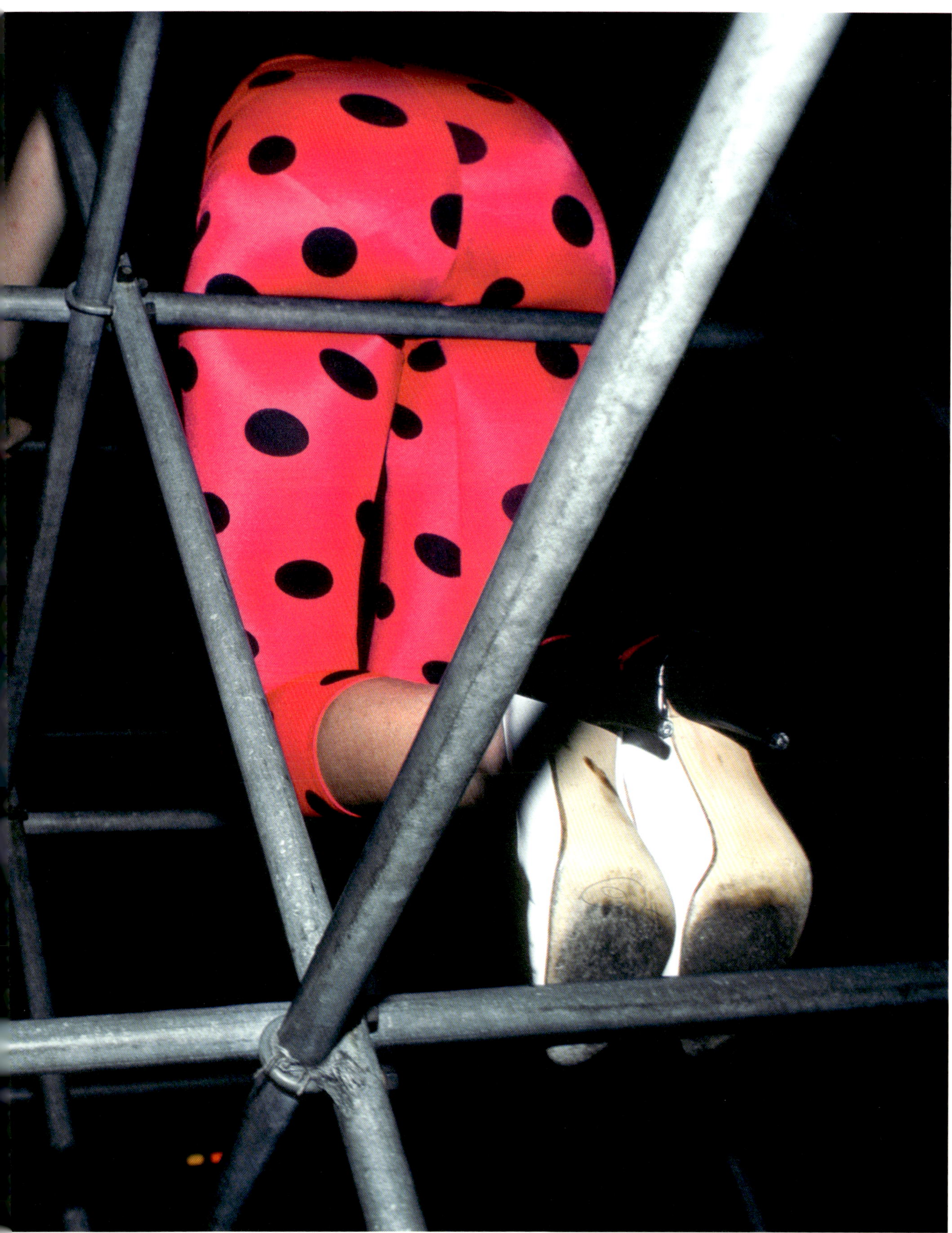

FRANK RISPOLI is a multi-media artist living and working in Brooklyn, New York. Raised in a repressive Catholic household, he found his sanctuary in the NYC Public School system where teachers recognized his artistic abilities. He attended the High School of Art and Design and then studied at FIT and the Pratt Institute, graduating with a BFA in Environmental and Interior Design in 1972. He received his MFA in Sculpture and Photography from the Pratt in 2000.

Rispoli has over thirty years of professional experience as an environmental designer and has taught undergraduate and graduate levels at the Fashion Institute of Technology, the Pratt, and the Laboratory Institute of Merchandising. His photographs have been exhibited at the Brooklyn Academy of Music, the Museum of Contemporary Crafts, and BLAM Projects. His work has been reviewed in i-D magazine, Dazed, and Mao Mag, and his photographs are a promised gift to the Downtown Collection of the Fales Library at New York University.

ERICK BRADSHAW HUGHES is a writer and musician living in New York City. He hosts Spin Age Blasters on WFMU.

Previous pages: monkey bars, Chelsea Park, early 1980s

ACKNOWLEDGEMENTS I miss the New York City I knew in the '70s and '80s. It was so much grittier and seedier. I hardly recognize anything in the East Village of Manhattan any more. It's become so antiseptic, especially The Bowery. No more individual characters or interesting situations.

These High Heel images were created while I was listening to bands at the various venues that I frequented such as CBGB's, Max's Kansas City, TR3 and Danceteria. There were many more, but these were by far my favourites. It was such an exciting time for music, and a visually exotic era as well. The Punk music phenomenon, followed by the New Wave movement, each had their own individual fashion styles. But to my delight and excitement, both embraced women's high heel shoes as important accessories.

Starting early in my adult life, I recognized my passion for high heels. Fortunately, I was able to combine my pursuit of live rock and roll music with making images of high heels as worn by the women who frequented the clubs. That also included making images on the streets of NYC. Not formally trained as a photographer, my aesthetic was formed by my multi-disciplined design background, my passions, and the incredible qualities of Kodak's Kodachrome 25 film.

I would like to thank the following people for helping to make this book happen: first, my amazingly focused, generous and determined wife Deborah, who twenty-five years ago agreed to marry me. And, of course, our Coney Island rescue cats Gus and Marie. Richard Steinbach at Borough Photo, in Brooklyn, whose contribution to my efforts was invaluable. Richard is a consummate professional and one of the most talented artists I've ever met. This book would not have been possible without his assistance. I cannot thank him enough. Erick Bradshaw Hughes for his ability to paint with words. Karissa Johnson, Bushwick artist, whose collaboration with me produced amazing new high heel images by contributing her time and fantastic fashion sense. Combining these attributes with the street art in Bushwick, Brooklyn, we formed 'rissy + frankie', our own brand of visual creativity that is a carnival for the eyes. Meaghan Cleary, for sincere enthusiasm and limitless energy, which are greatly appreciated. Torpedo Squadron 8, of the USS Hornet, and others who made the ultimate sacrifice at the Battle of Midway in 1942. And especially to the United States Marine Corps and United States Navy for their tenacity and determination at Guadalcanal, Tarawa, Saipan, Kwajalein, Eniwetok, Leyte Gulf, Iwo Jima and Okinawa. Their selfless dedication to freedom has allowed me to be the creative person I am, and I thank you.

Rock and Roll Music, especially The Who, Jefferson Airplane and Suicide.

First published in 2021 by Circa Press
©2021 Circa Press Limited and Frank Rispoli

Circa Press
50 Great Portland Street
London W1W 7ND
www.circa.press

ISBN 978-1-911422-30-3

Printed and bound in Italy

Design: Jean-Michel Dentand
Production: Dexter Premedia